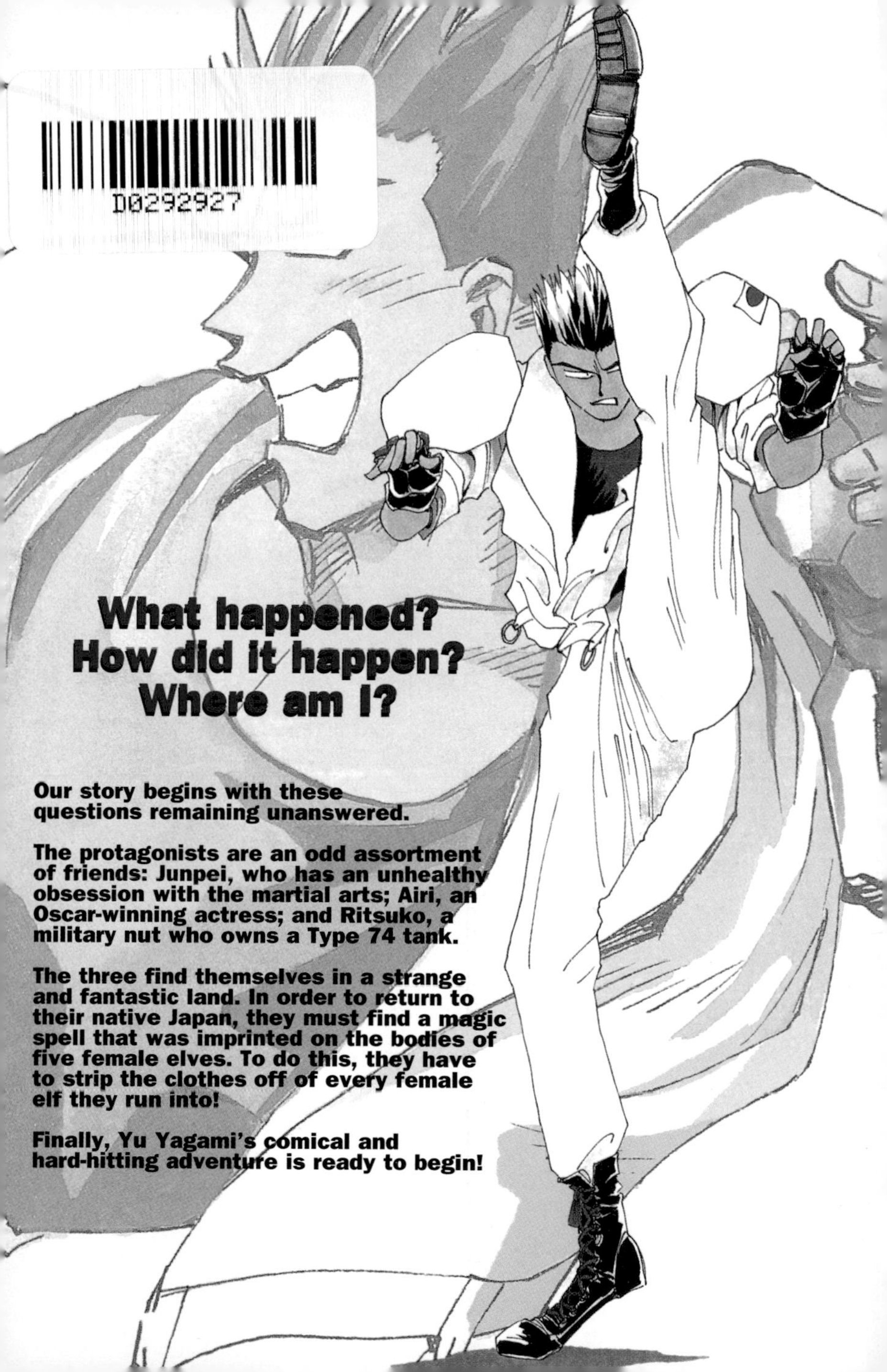

What happened?
How did it happen?
Where am I?

Our story begins with these questions remaining unanswered.

The protagonists are an odd assortment of friends: Junpei, who has an unhealthy obsession with the martial arts; Airi, an Oscar-winning actress; and Ritsuko, a military nut who owns a Type 74 tank.

The three find themselves in a strange and fantastic land. In order to return to their native Japan, they must find a magic spell that was imprinted on the bodies of five female elves. To do this, they have to strip the clothes off of every female elf they run into!

Finally, Yu Yagami's comical and hard-hitting adventure is ready to begin!

CONTENTS

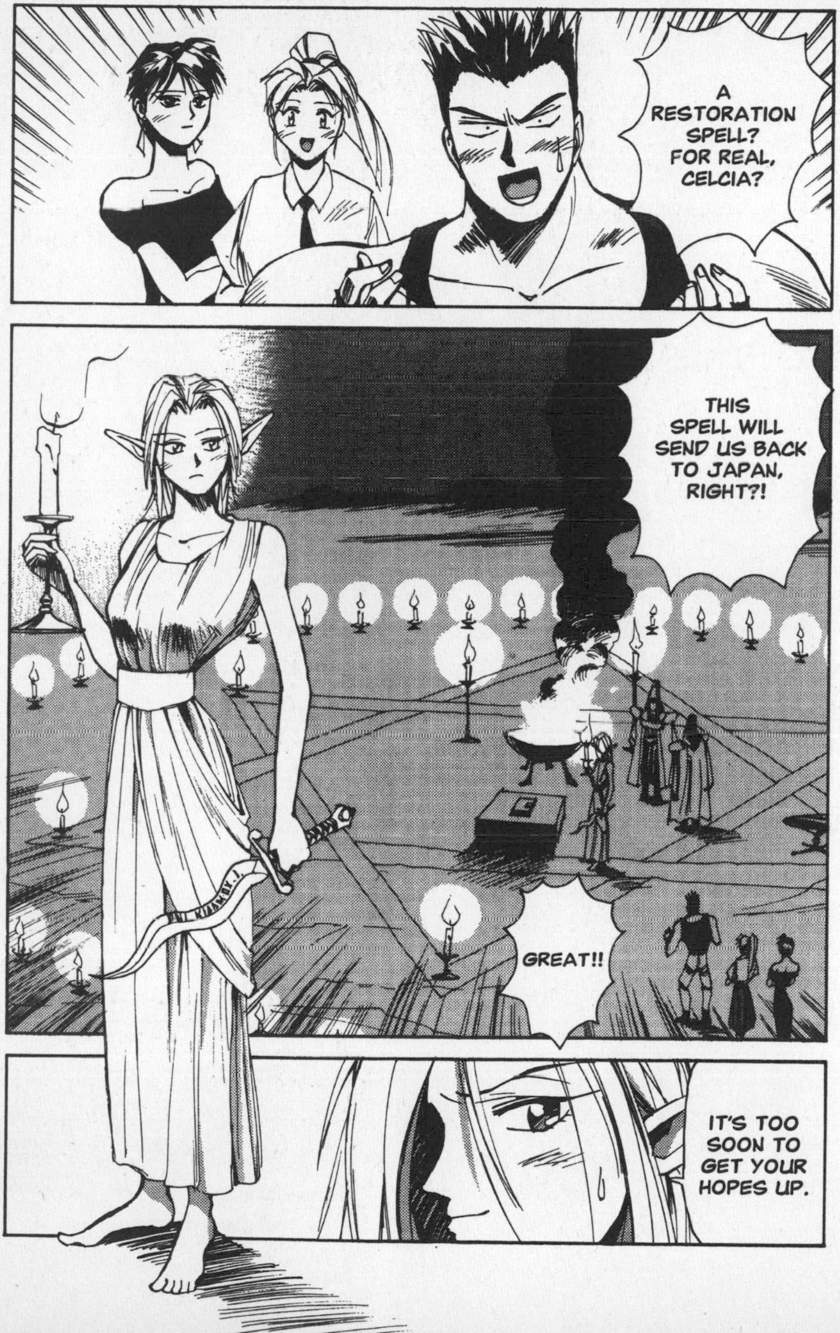
A RESTORATION SPELL? FOR REAL, CELCIA?
THIS SPELL WILL SEND US BACK TO JAPAN, RIGHT?!
GREAT!!
IT'S TOO SOON TO GET YOUR HOPES UP.

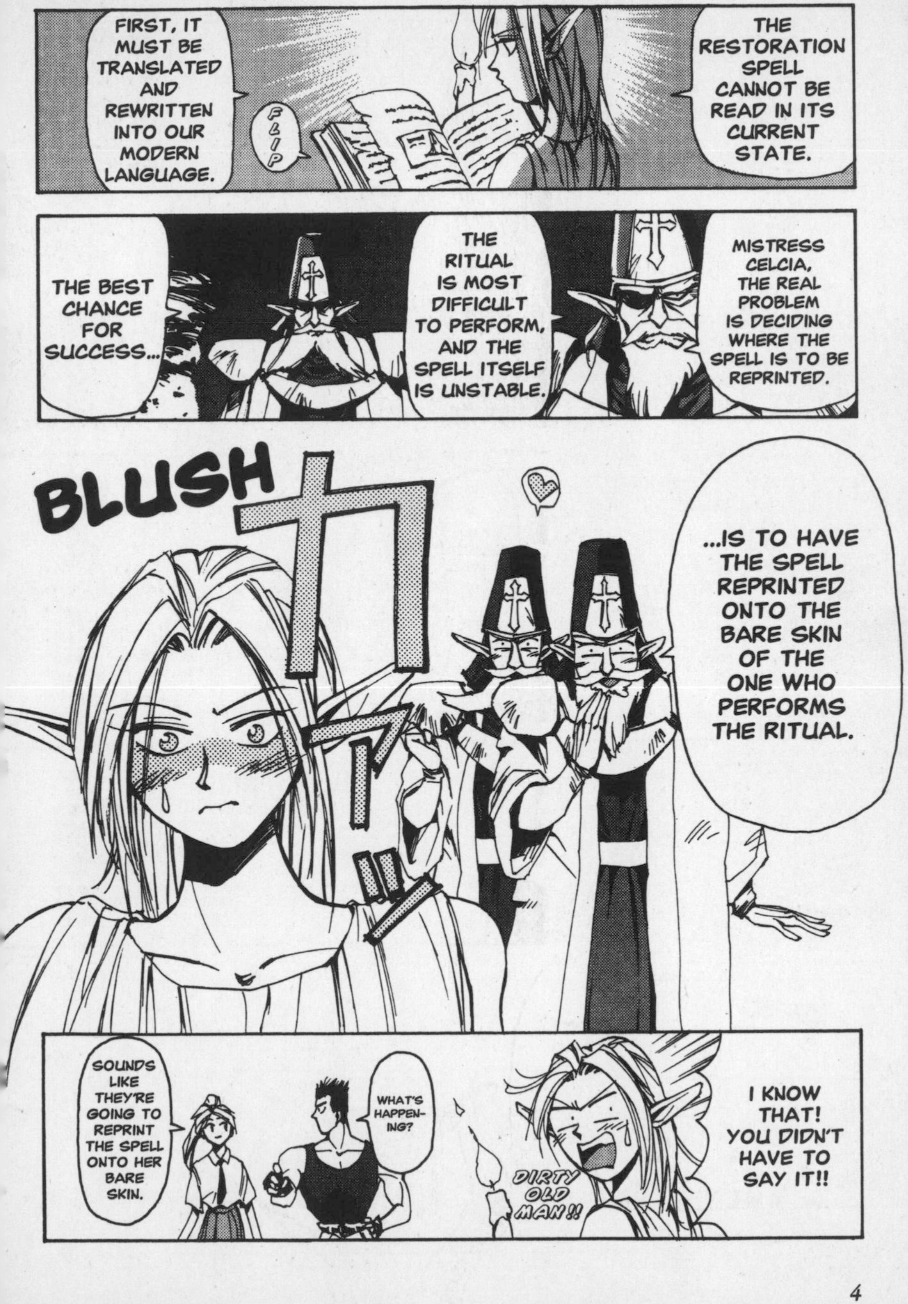
THE RESTORATION SPELL CANNOT BE READ IN ITS CURRENT STATE.
FLIP
FIRST, IT MUST BE TRANSLATED AND REWRITTEN INTO OUR MODERN LANGUAGE.
MISTRESS CELCIA, THE REAL PROBLEM IS DECIDING WHERE THE SPELL IS TO BE REPRINTED.
THE RITUAL IS MOST DIFFICULT TO PERFORM, AND THE SPELL ITSELF IS UNSTABLE.
THE BEST CHANCE FOR SUCCESS...
...IS TO HAVE THE SPELL REPRINTED ONTO THE BARE SKIN OF THE ONE WHO PERFORMS THE RITUAL.
BLUSH
WHAT'S HAPPEN-ING?
SOUNDS LIKE THEY'RE GOING TO REPRINT THE SPELL ONTO HER BARE SKIN.
I KNOW THAT! YOU DIDN'T HAVE TO SAY IT!!
DIRTY OLD MAN!!

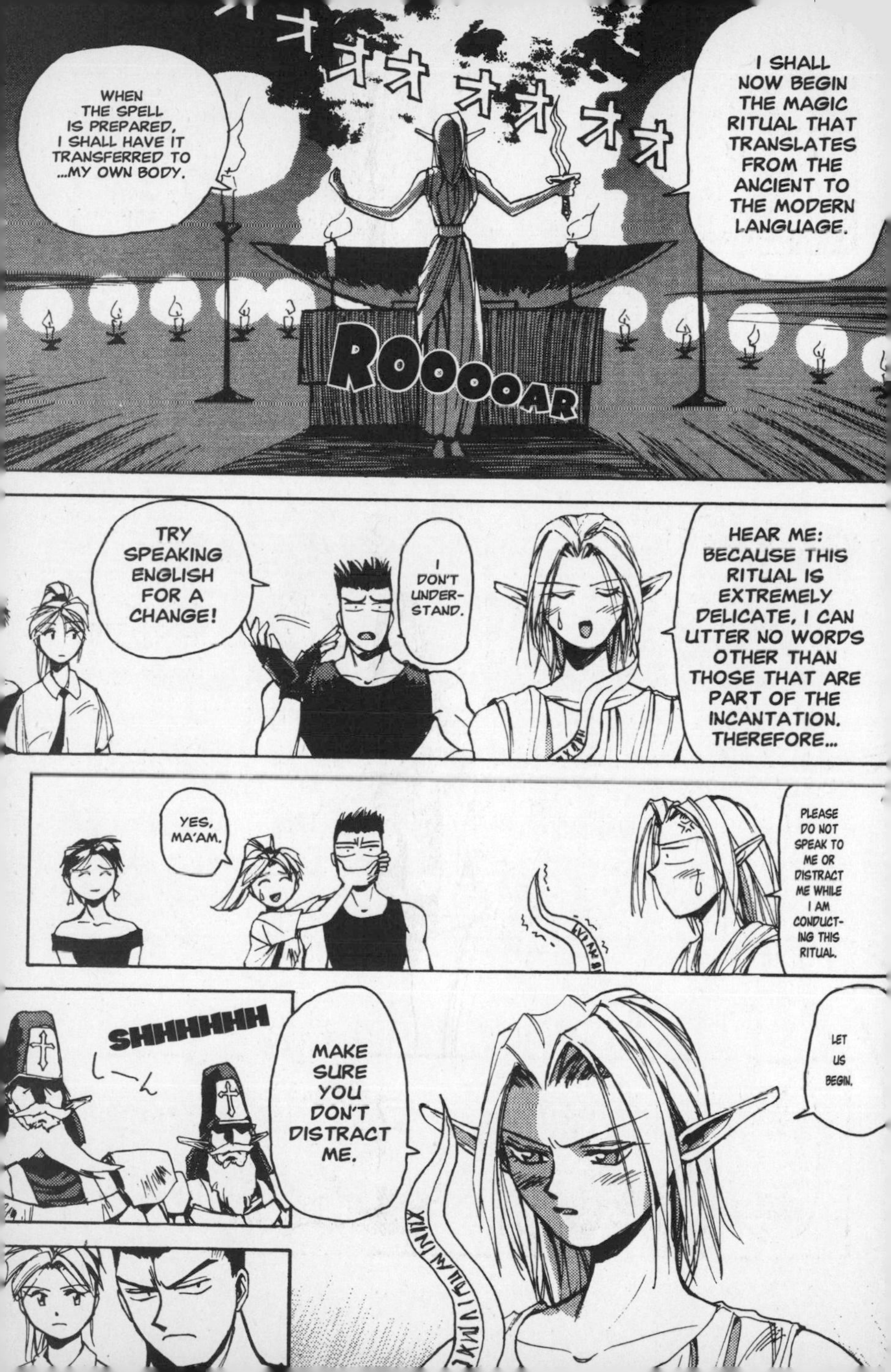
オオオオオオ
I SHALL NOW BEGIN THE MAGIC RITUAL THAT TRANSLATES FROM THE ANCIENT TO THE MODERN LANGUAGE.
WHEN THE SPELL IS PREPARED, I SHALL HAVE IT TRANSFERRED TO ...MY OWN BODY.
ROOOOOAR
HEAR ME: BECAUSE THIS RITUAL IS EXTREMELY DELICATE, I CAN UTTER NO WORDS OTHER THAN THOSE THAT ARE PART OF THE INCANTATION. THEREFORE...
I DON'T UNDER-STAND.
TRY SPEAKING ENGLISH FOR A CHANGE!
PLEASE DO NOT SPEAK TO ME OR DISTRACT ME WHILE I AM CONDUCT-ING THIS RITUAL.
YES, MA'AM.
LET US BEGIN.
MAKE SURE YOU DON'T DISTRACT ME.
SHHHHHH
しーん

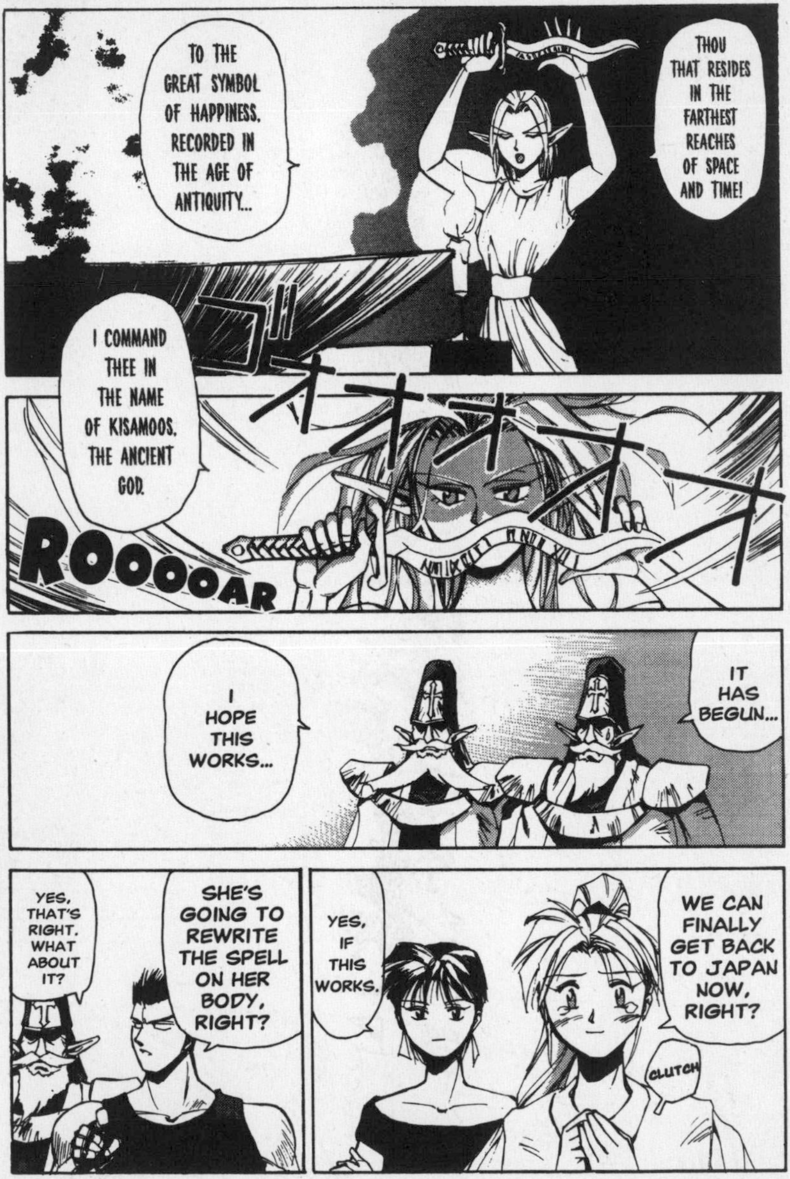

THOU THAT RESIDES IN THE FARTHEST REACHES OF SPACE AND TIME!
TO THE GREAT SYMBOL OF HAPPINESS, RECORDED IN THE AGE OF ANTIQUITY...
I COMMAND THEE IN THE NAME OF KISAMOOS, THE ANCIENT GOD.
ROOOOAR
IT HAS BEGUN...
I HOPE THIS WORKS...
WE CAN FINALLY GET BACK TO JAPAN NOW, RIGHT?
CLUTCH
YES, IF THIS WORKS.
SHE'S GOING TO REWRITE THE SPELL ON HER BODY, RIGHT?
YES, THAT'S RIGHT. WHAT ABOUT IT?

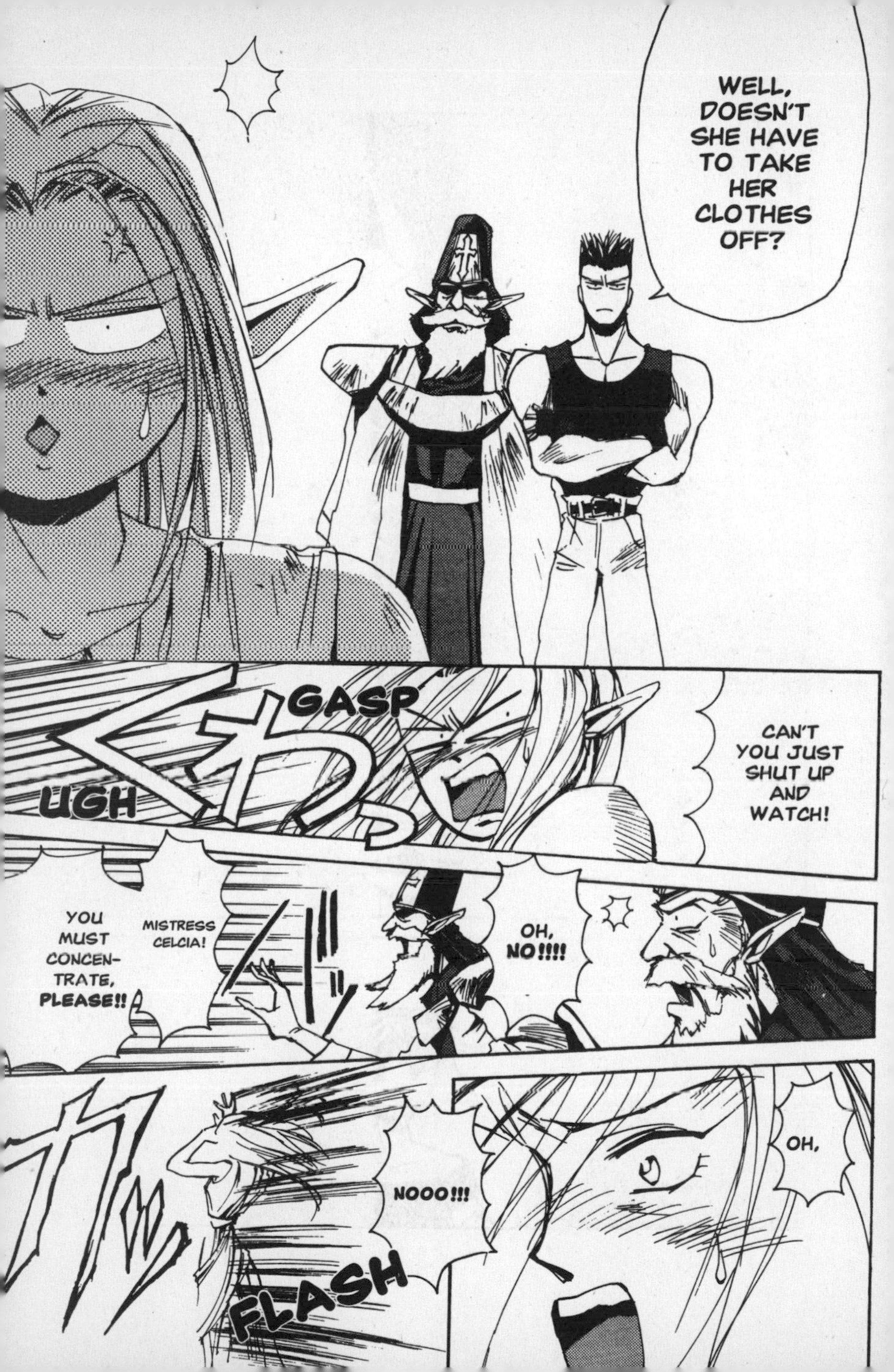
WELL, DOESN'T SHE HAVE TO TAKE HER CLOTHES OFF?
CAN'T YOU JUST SHUT UP AND WATCH!
GASP
UGH
OH, NO!!!!
MISTRESS CELCIA!
YOU MUST CONCENTRATE, PLEASE!!
OH,
NOOO!!!
FLASH

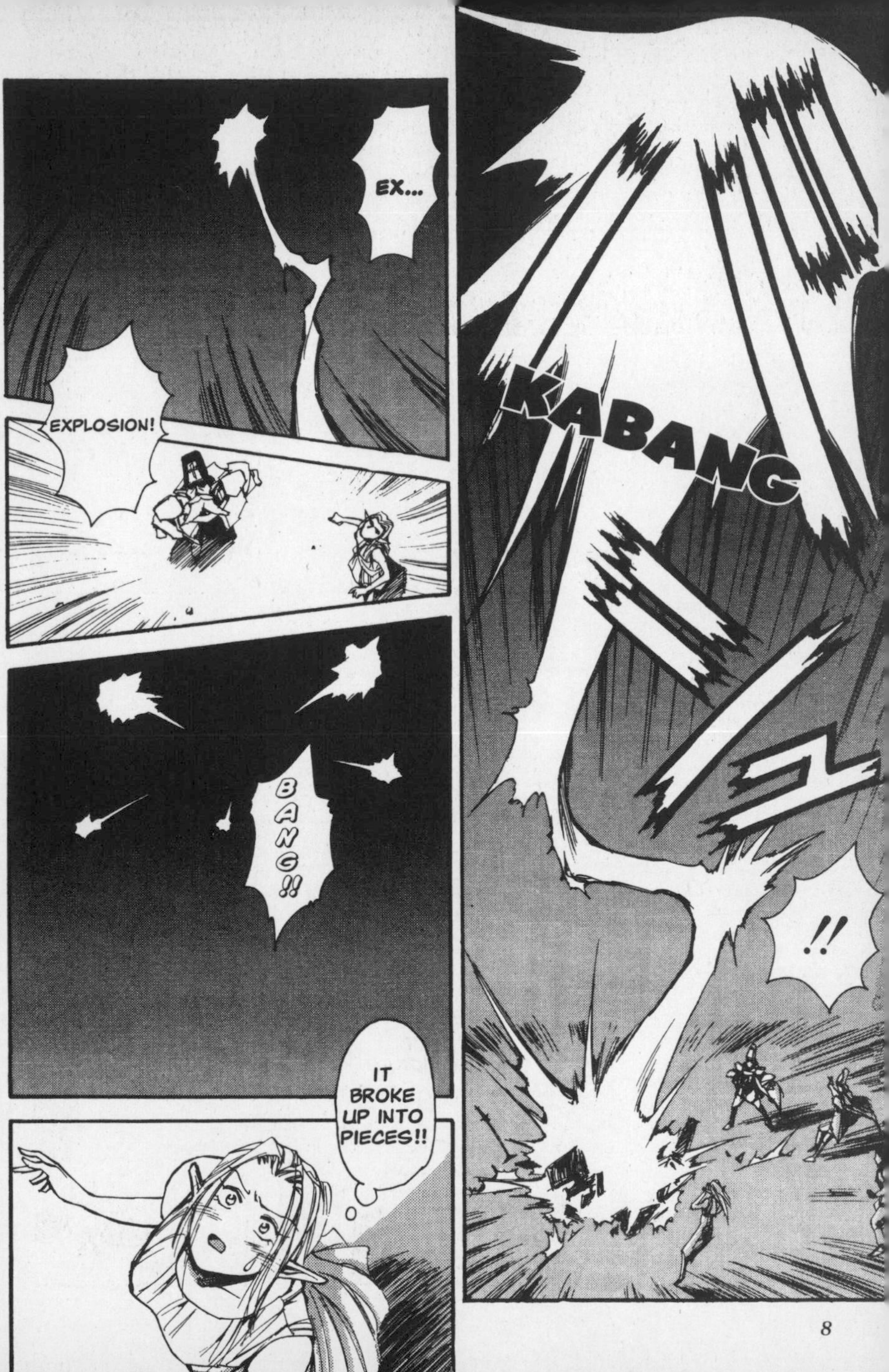
EX...
EXPLOSION!
KABANG
!!
BANG!!
IT BROKE UP INTO PIECES!!

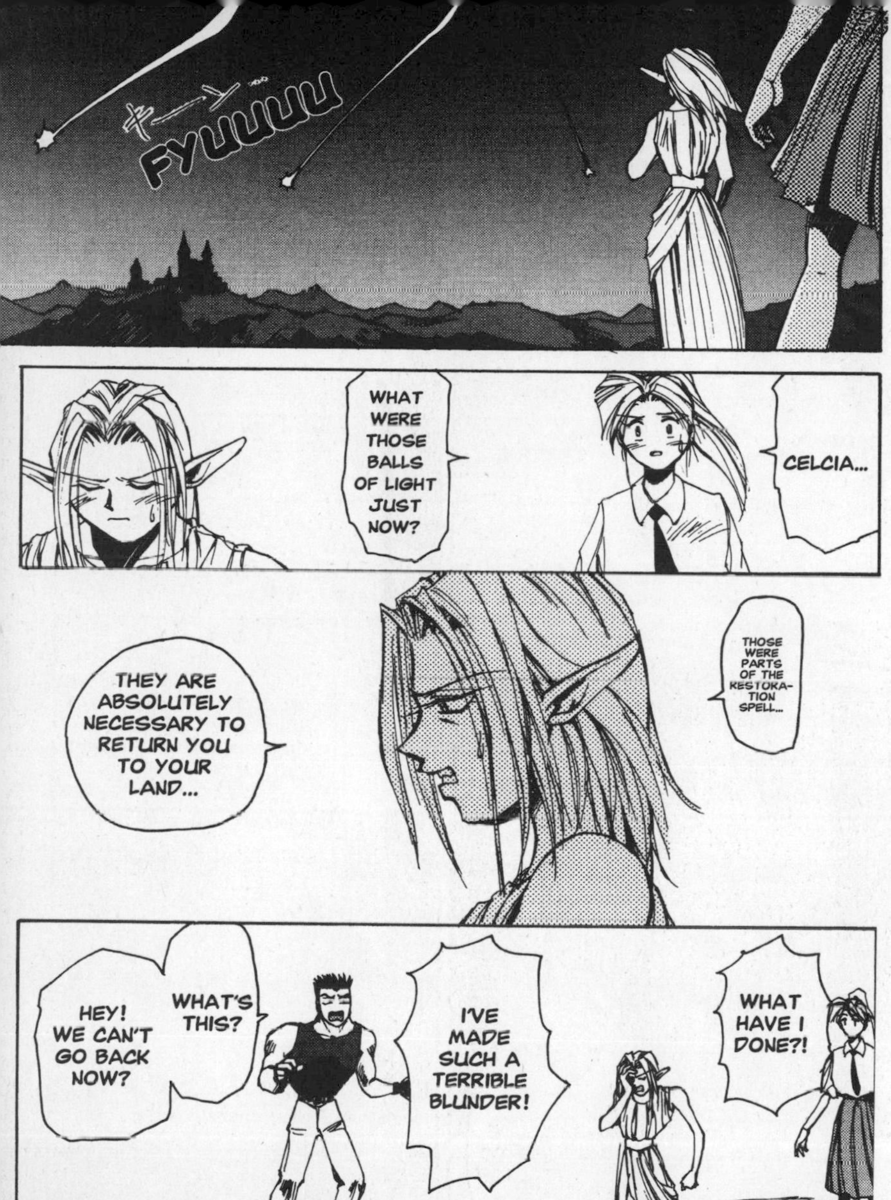
FYUUUU
CELCIA...
WHAT WERE THOSE BALLS OF LIGHT JUST NOW?
THOSE WERE PARTS OF THE RESTORATION SPELL...
THEY ARE ABSOLUTELY NECESSARY TO RETURN YOU TO YOUR LAND...
WHAT HAVE I DONE?!
I'VE MADE SUCH A TERRIBLE BLUNDER!
WHAT'S THIS?
HEY! WE CAN'T GO BACK NOW?

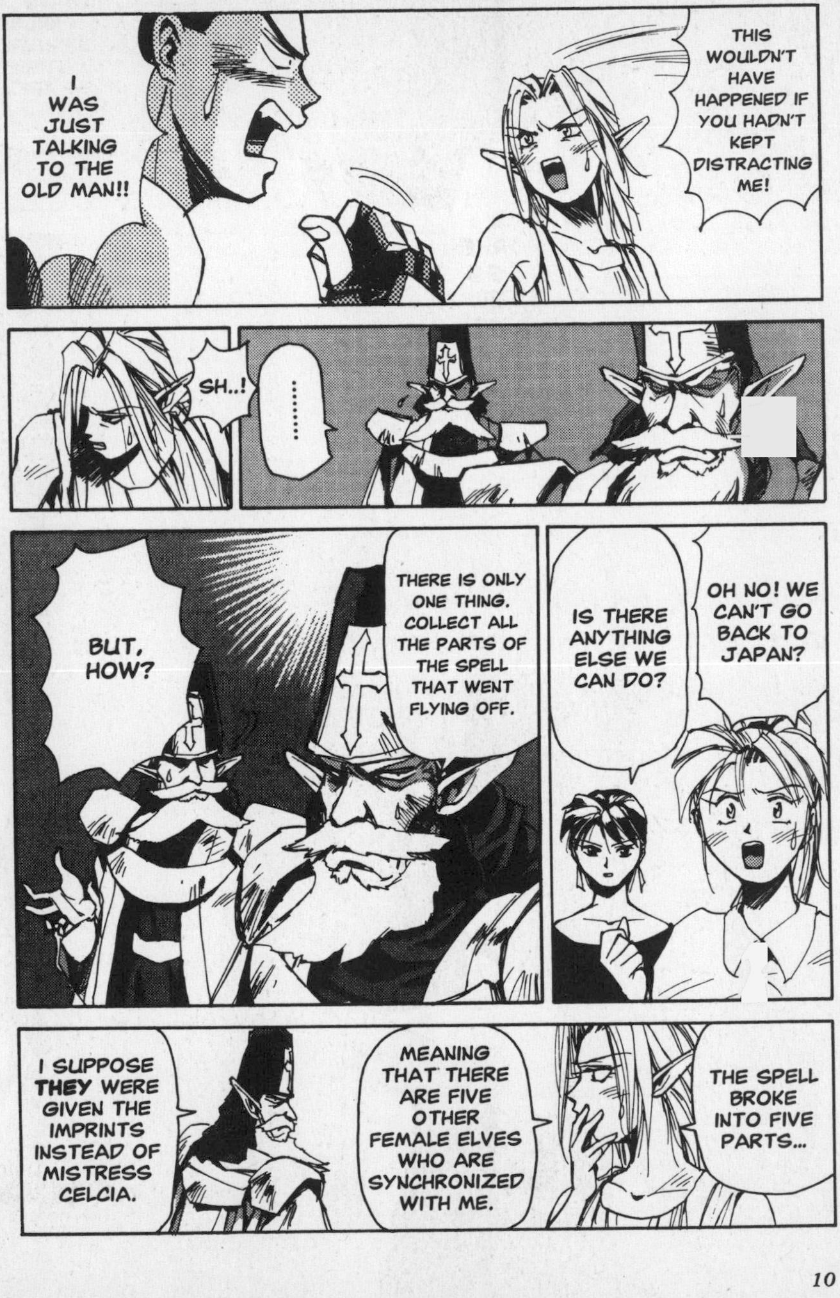
THIS WOULDN'T HAVE HAPPENED IF YOU HADN'T KEPT DISTRACTING ME!
I WAS JUST TALKING TO THE OLD MAN!!
....
SH..!
OH NO! WE CAN'T GO BACK TO JAPAN?
IS THERE ANYTHING ELSE WE CAN DO?
THERE IS ONLY ONE THING. COLLECT ALL THE PARTS OF THE SPELL THAT WENT FLYING OFF.
BUT, HOW?
THE SPELL BROKE INTO FIVE PARTS...
MEANING THAT THERE ARE FIVE OTHER FEMALE ELVES WHO ARE SYNCHRONIZED WITH ME.
I SUPPOSE **THEY** WERE GIVEN THE IMPRINTS INSTEAD OF MISTRESS CELCIA.

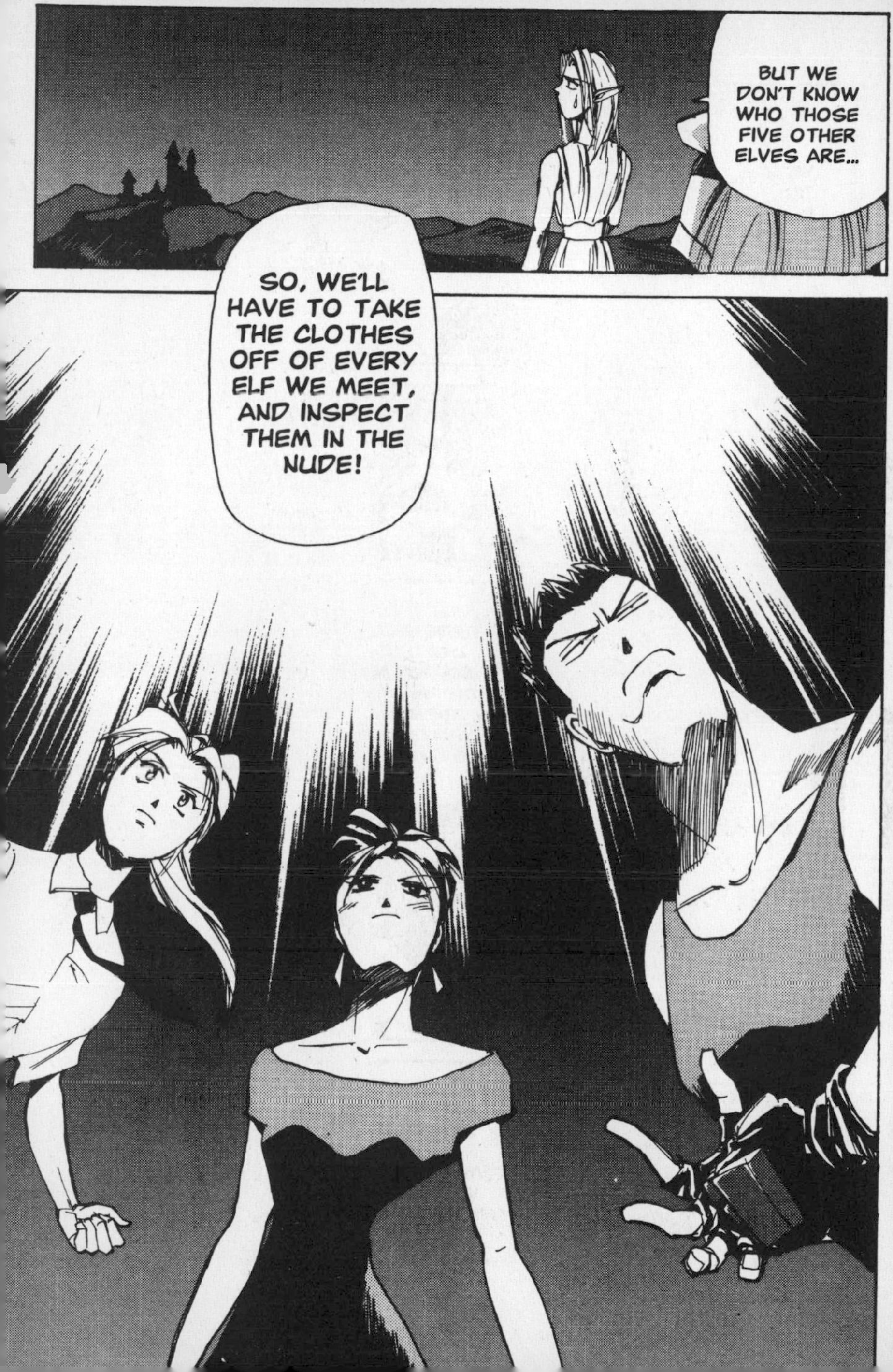
BUT WE DON'T KNOW WHO THOSE FIVE OTHER ELVES ARE...
SO, WE'LL HAVE TO TAKE THE CLOTHES OFF OF EVERY ELF WE MEET, AND INSPECT THEM IN THE NUDE!

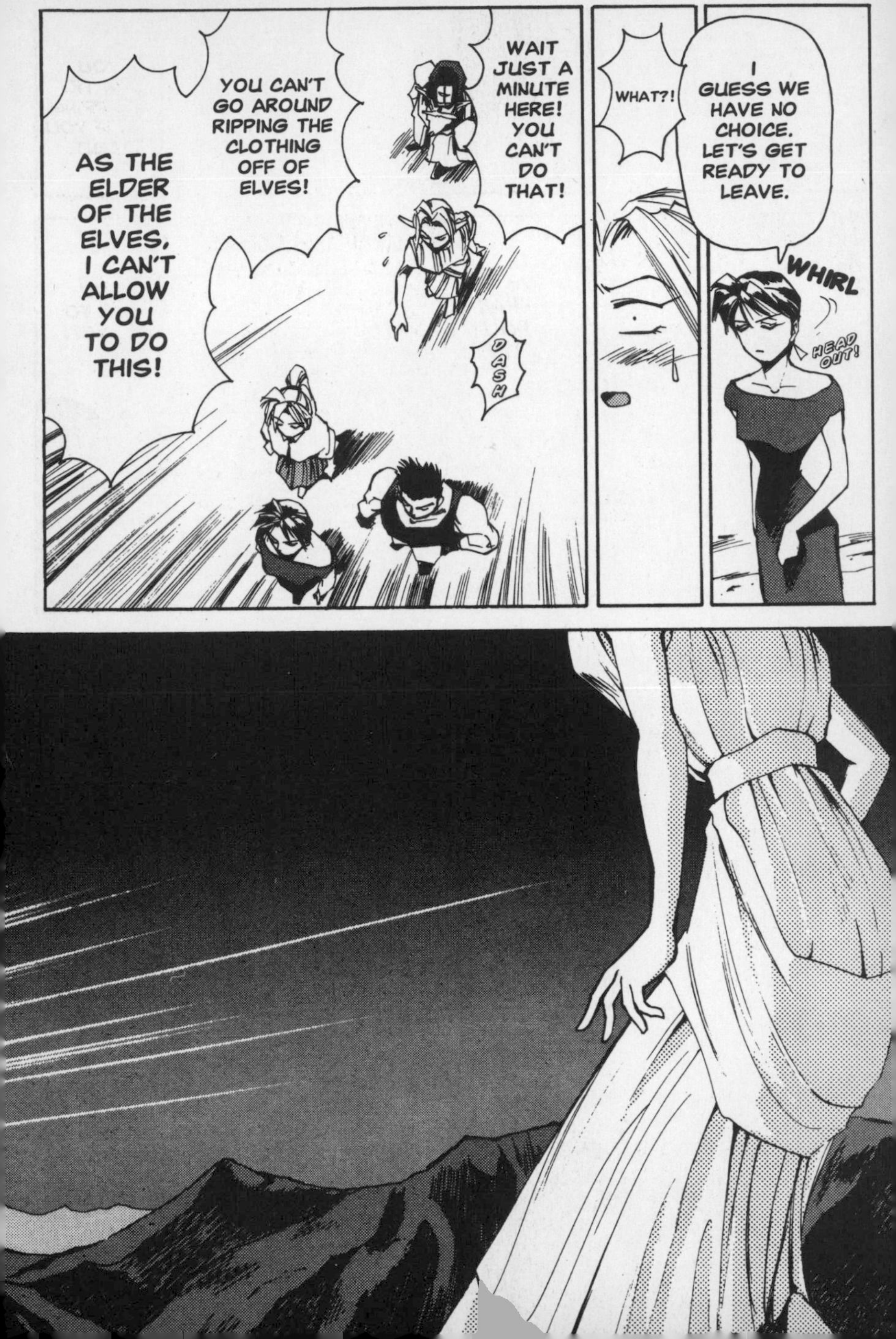
I GUESS WE HAVE NO CHOICE. LET'S GET READY TO LEAVE.
WHIRL
HEAD OUT!
WHAT?!
WAIT JUST A MINUTE HERE! YOU CAN'T DO THAT!
YOU CAN'T GO AROUND RIPPING THE CLOTHING OFF OF ELVES!
DASH
AS THE ELDER OF THE ELVES, I CAN'T ALLOW YOU TO DO THIS!

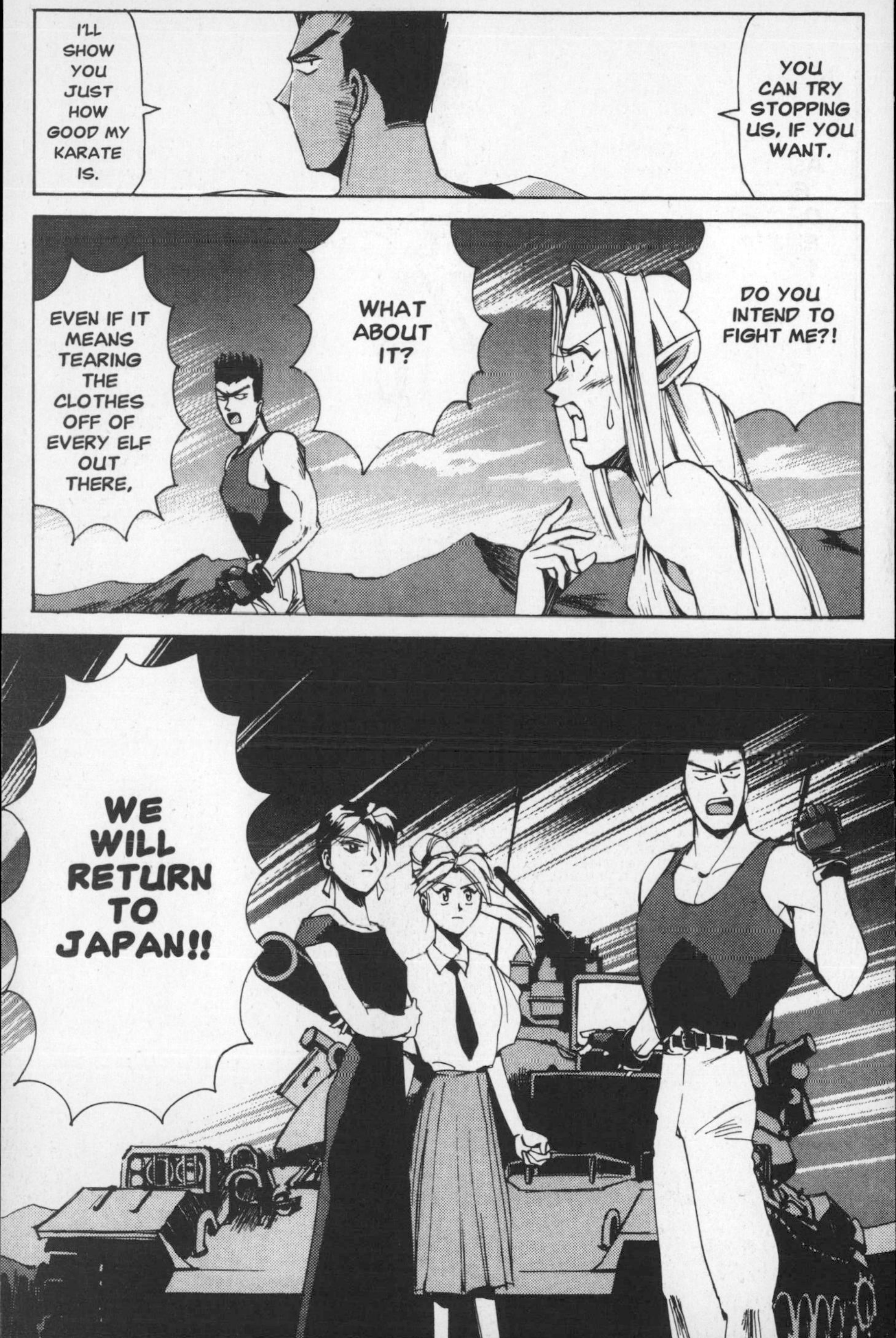
YOU CAN TRY STOPPING US, IF YOU WANT.
I'LL SHOW YOU JUST HOW GOOD MY KARATE IS.
DO YOU INTEND TO FIGHT ME?!
WHAT ABOUT IT?
EVEN IF IT MEANS TEARING THE CLOTHES OFF OF EVERY ELF OUT THERE,
WE WILL RETURN TO JAPAN!!

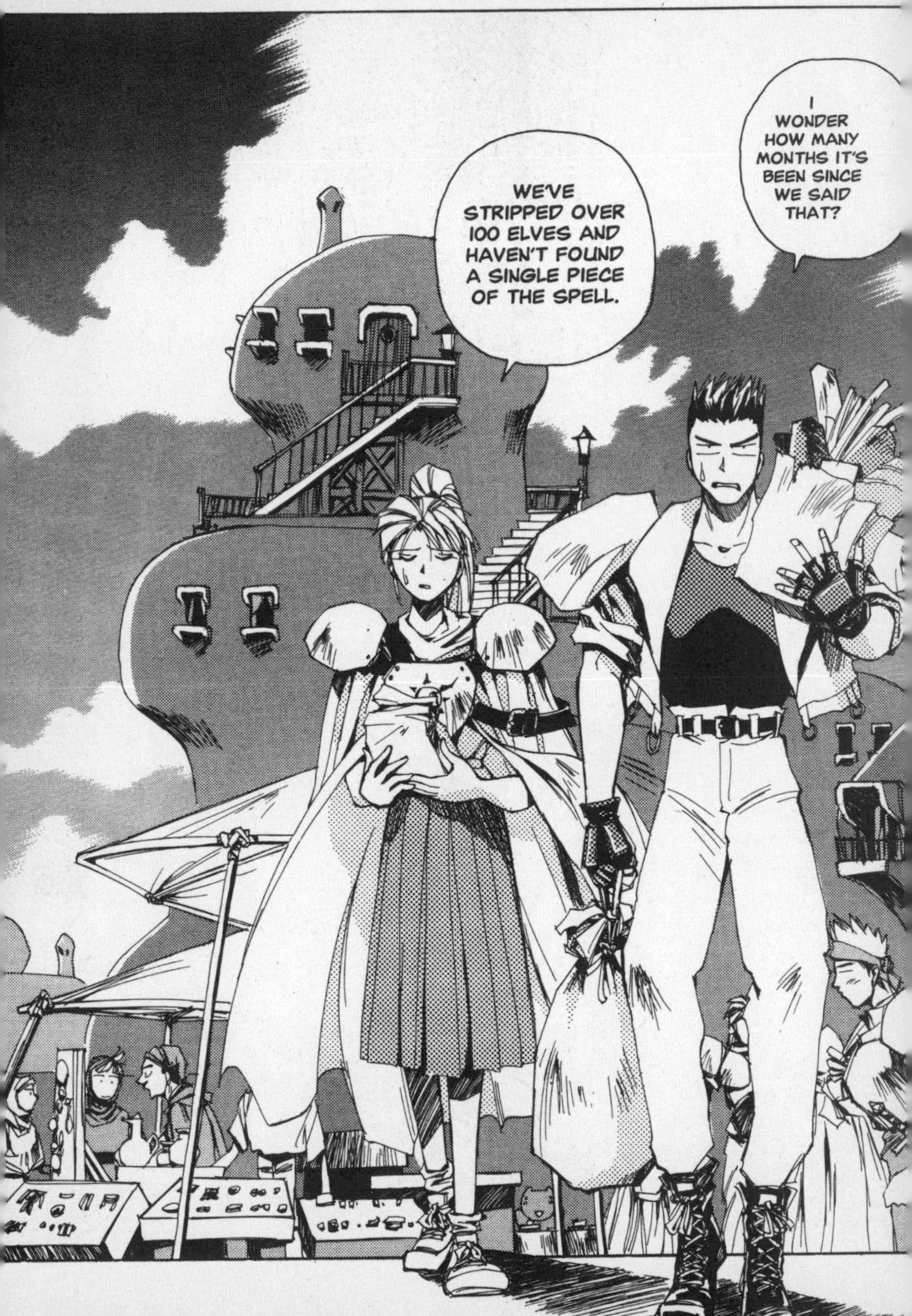
I WONDER HOW MANY MONTHS IT'S BEEN SINCE WE SAID THAT?
WE'VE STRIPPED OVER 100 ELVES AND HAVEN'T FOUND A SINGLE PIECE OF THE SPELL.

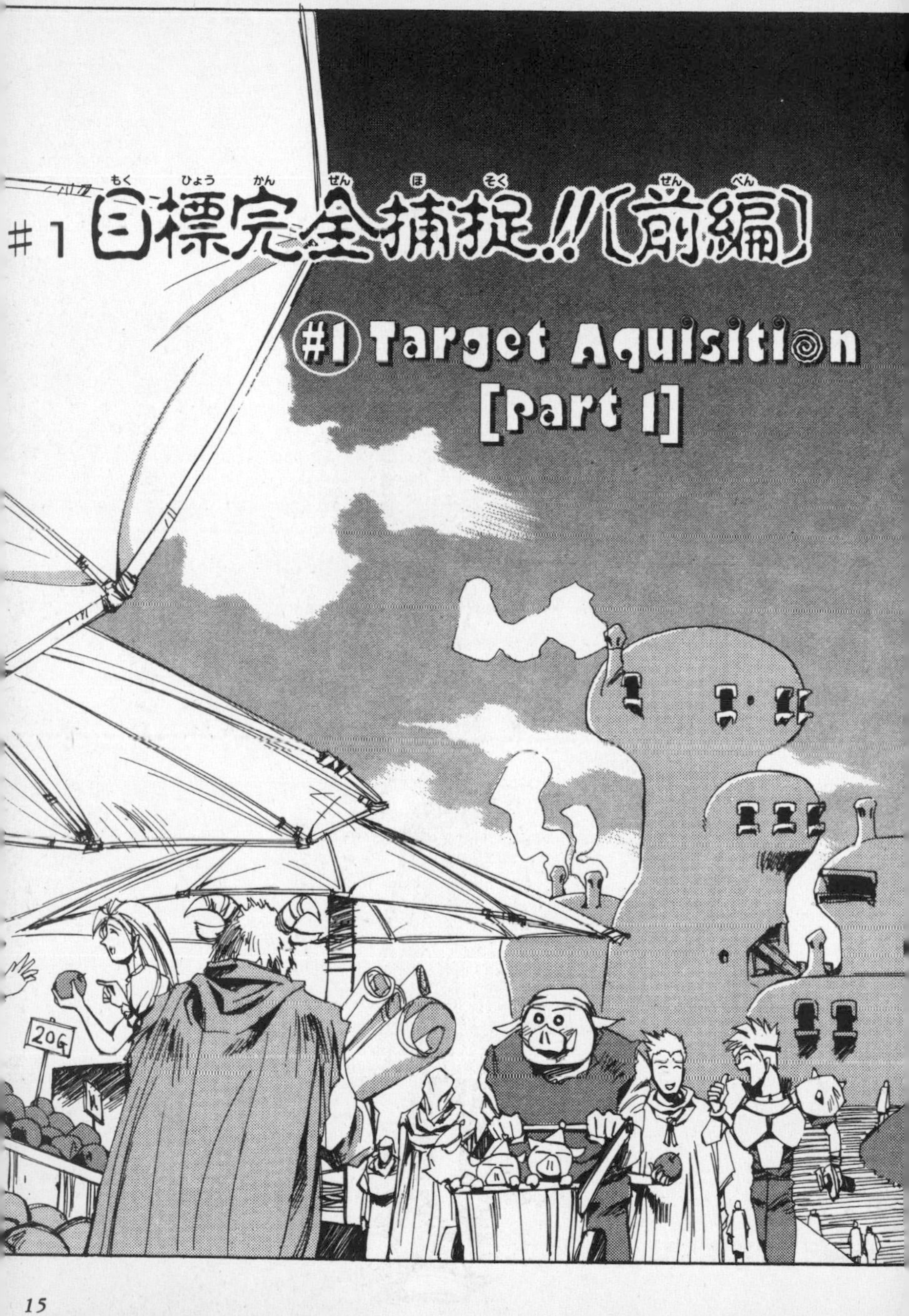
#1 目標完全捕捉!!〔前編〕
#1 Target Aquisition
[Part 1]

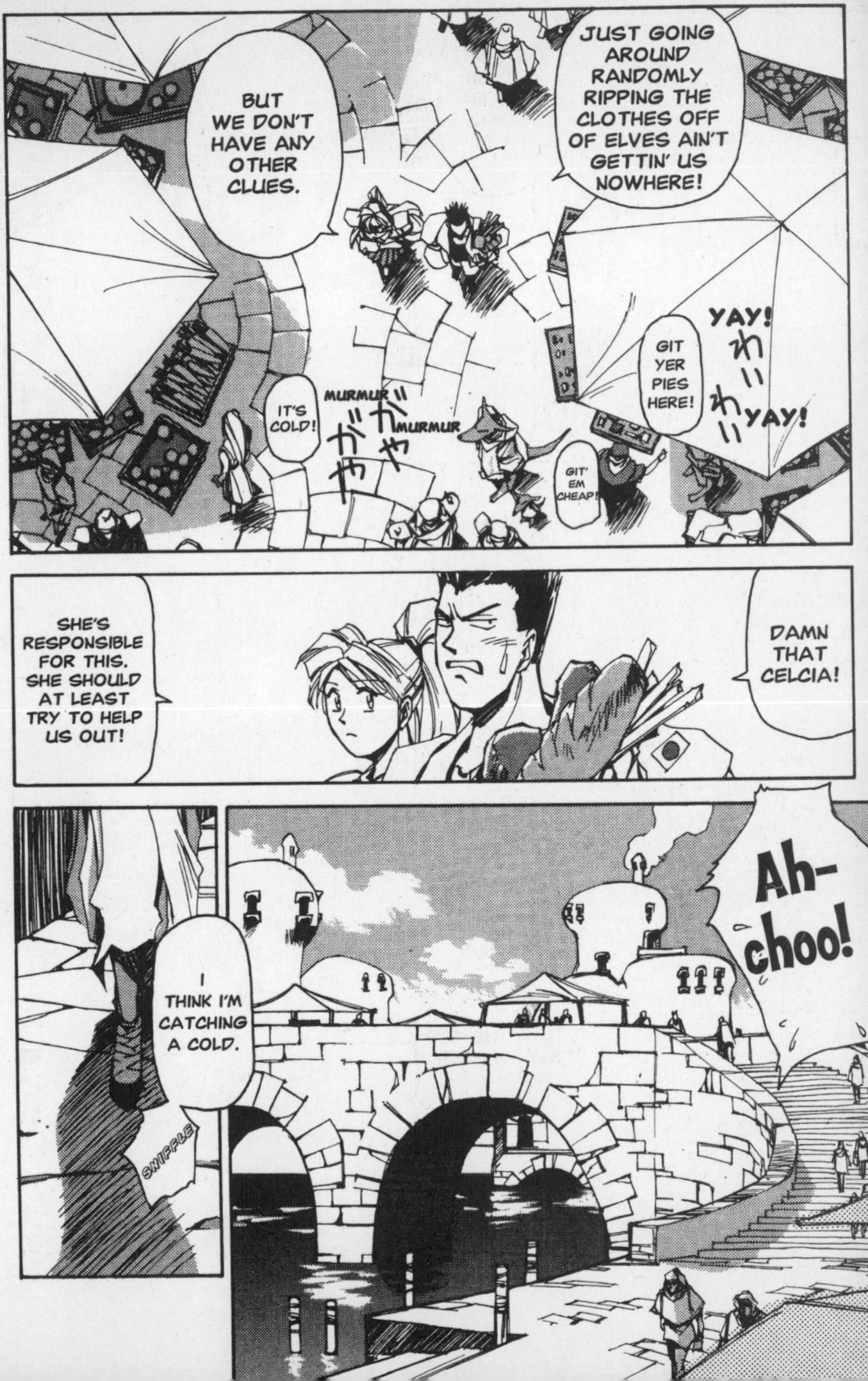
JUST GOING AROUND RANDOMLY RIPPING THE CLOTHES OFF OF ELVES AIN'T GETTIN' US NOWHERE!
BUT WE DON'T HAVE ANY OTHER CLUES.
YAY! わい
わい YAY!
GIT YER PIES HERE!
GIT' EM CHEAP!
MURMUR がや
がや MURMUR
IT'S COLD!
DAMN THAT CELCIA!
SHE'S RESPONSIBLE FOR THIS. SHE SHOULD AT LEAST TRY TO HELP US OUT!
Ah-choo!
I THINK I'M CATCHING A COLD.
SNIFFLE

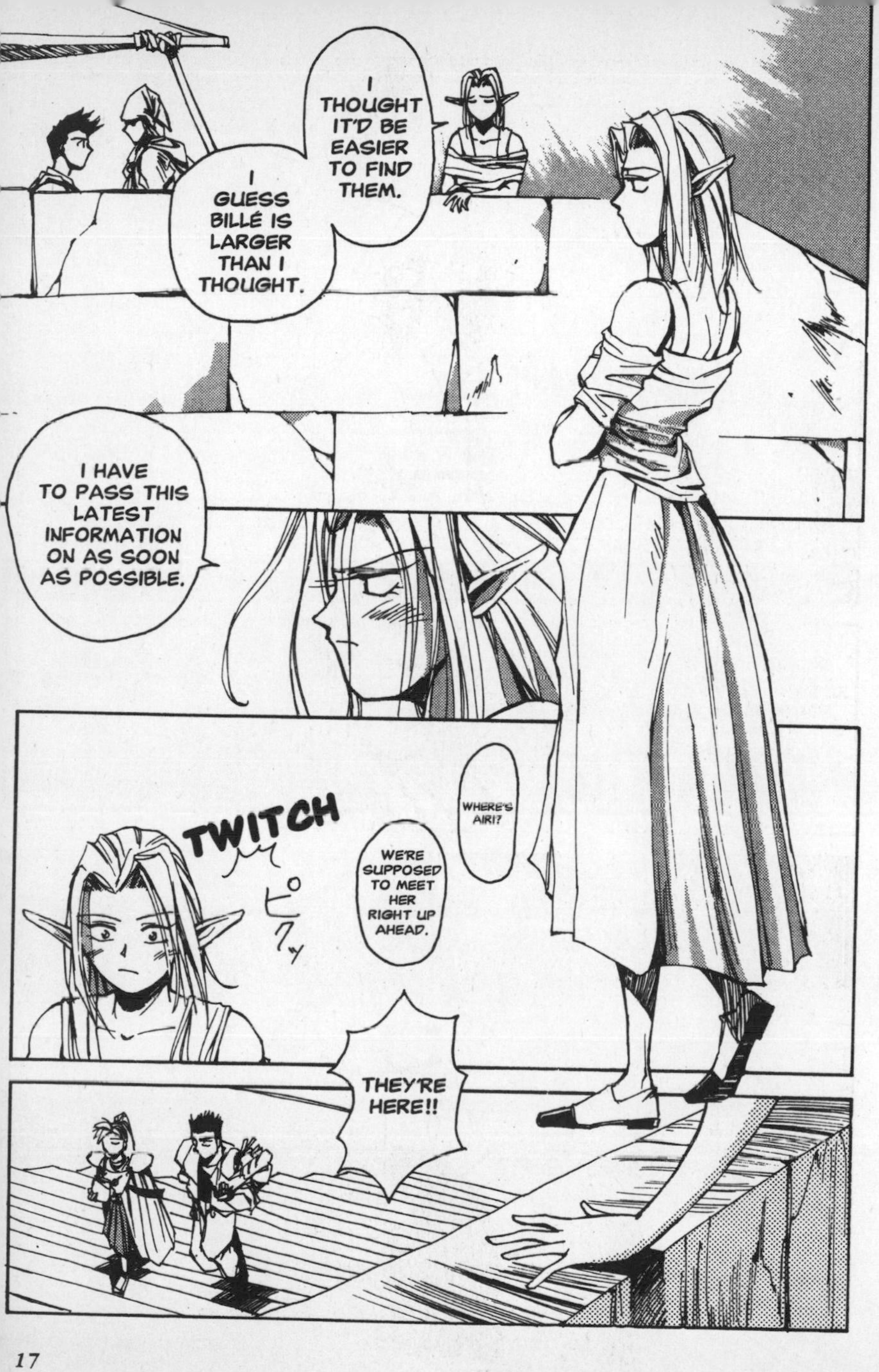
I THOUGHT IT'D BE EASIER TO FIND THEM.
I GUESS BILLÉ IS LARGER THAN I THOUGHT.
I HAVE TO PASS THIS LATEST INFORMATION ON AS SOON AS POSSIBLE.
WHERE'S AIRI?
WE'RE SUPPOSED TO MEET HER RIGHT UP AHEAD.
TWITCH
THEY'RE HERE!!

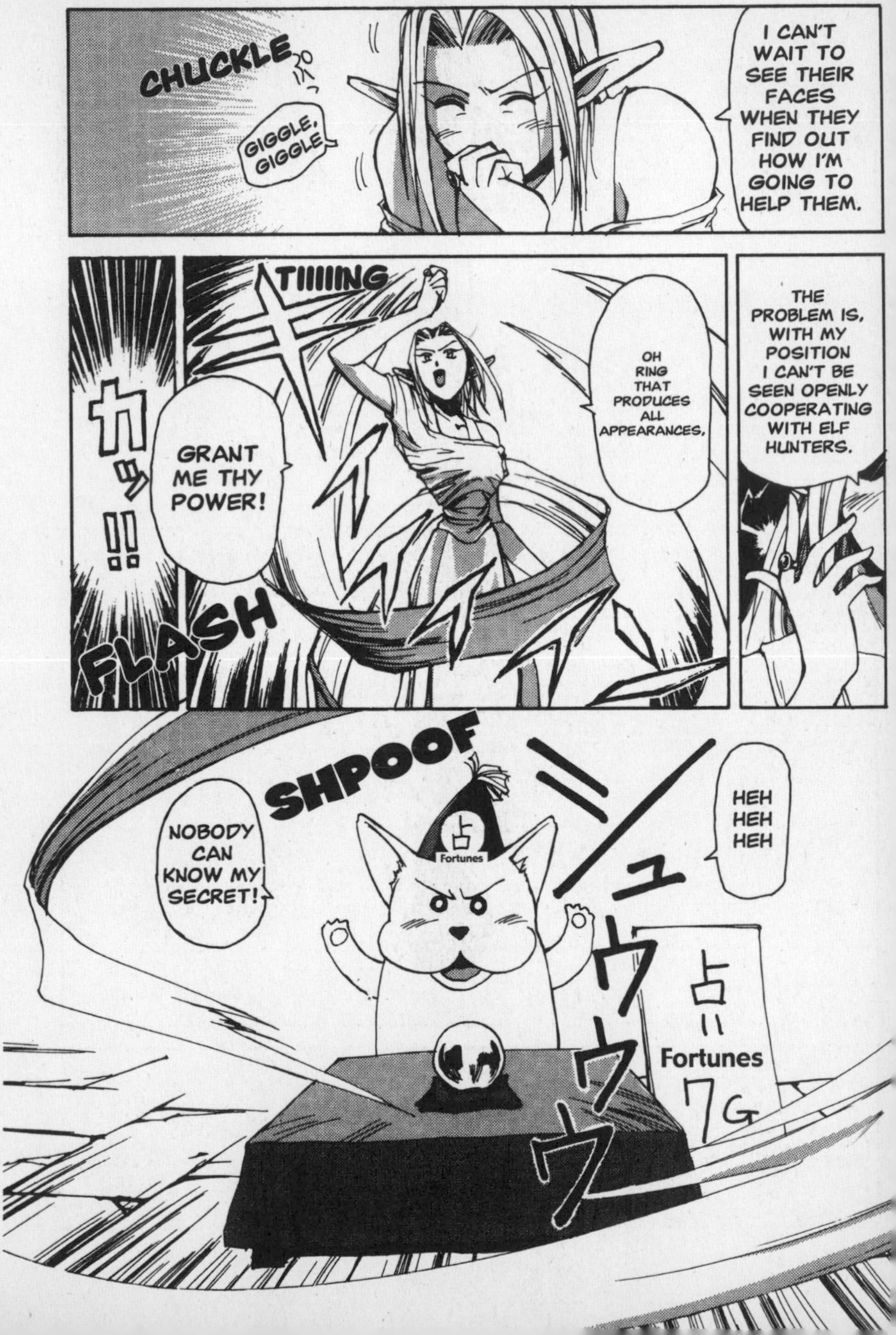
I CAN'T WAIT TO SEE THEIR FACES WHEN THEY FIND OUT HOW I'M GOING TO HELP THEM.
GIGGLE, GIGGLE
CHUCKLE
THE PROBLEM IS, WITH MY POSITION I CAN'T BE SEEN OPENLY COOPERATING WITH ELF HUNTERS.
TIIIIING
OH RING THAT PRODUCES ALL APPEARANCES,
GRANT ME THY POWER!
カッ!!
FLASH
HEH HEH HEH
SHPOOF
シュウウウ
NOBODY CAN KNOW MY SECRET!
占 Fortunes
占い Fortunes 7G

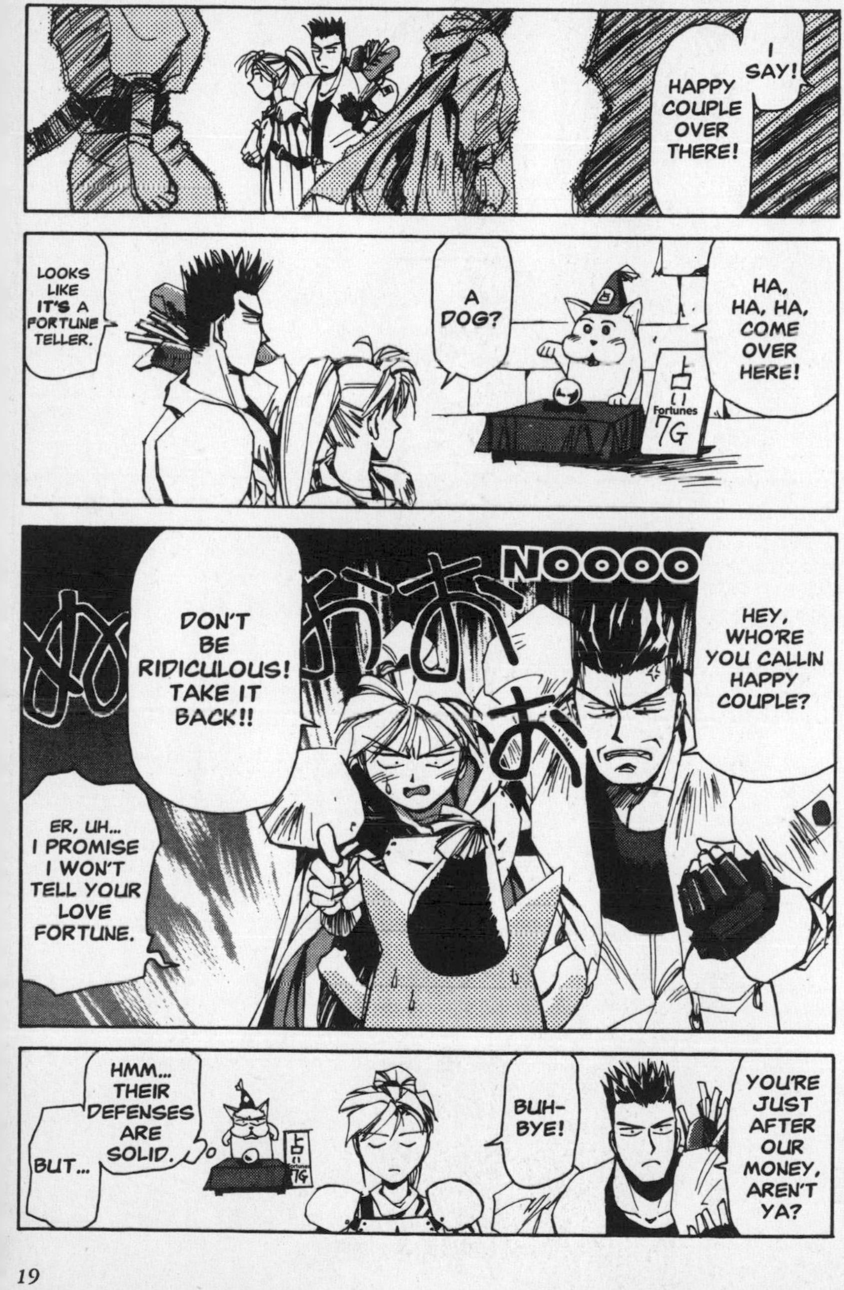
I SAY!
HAPPY COUPLE OVER THERE!
HA, HA, HA, COME OVER HERE!
Fortunes 7G
A DOG?
LOOKS LIKE IT'S A FORTUNE TELLER.
NOOOO
HEY, WHO'RE YOU CALLIN HAPPY COUPLE?
DON'T BE RIDICULOUS! TAKE IT BACK!!
ER, UH... I PROMISE I WON'T TELL YOUR LOVE FORTUNE.
YOU'RE JUST AFTER OUR MONEY, AREN'T YA?
BUH-BYE!
HMM... THEIR DEFENSES ARE SOLID.
BUT...

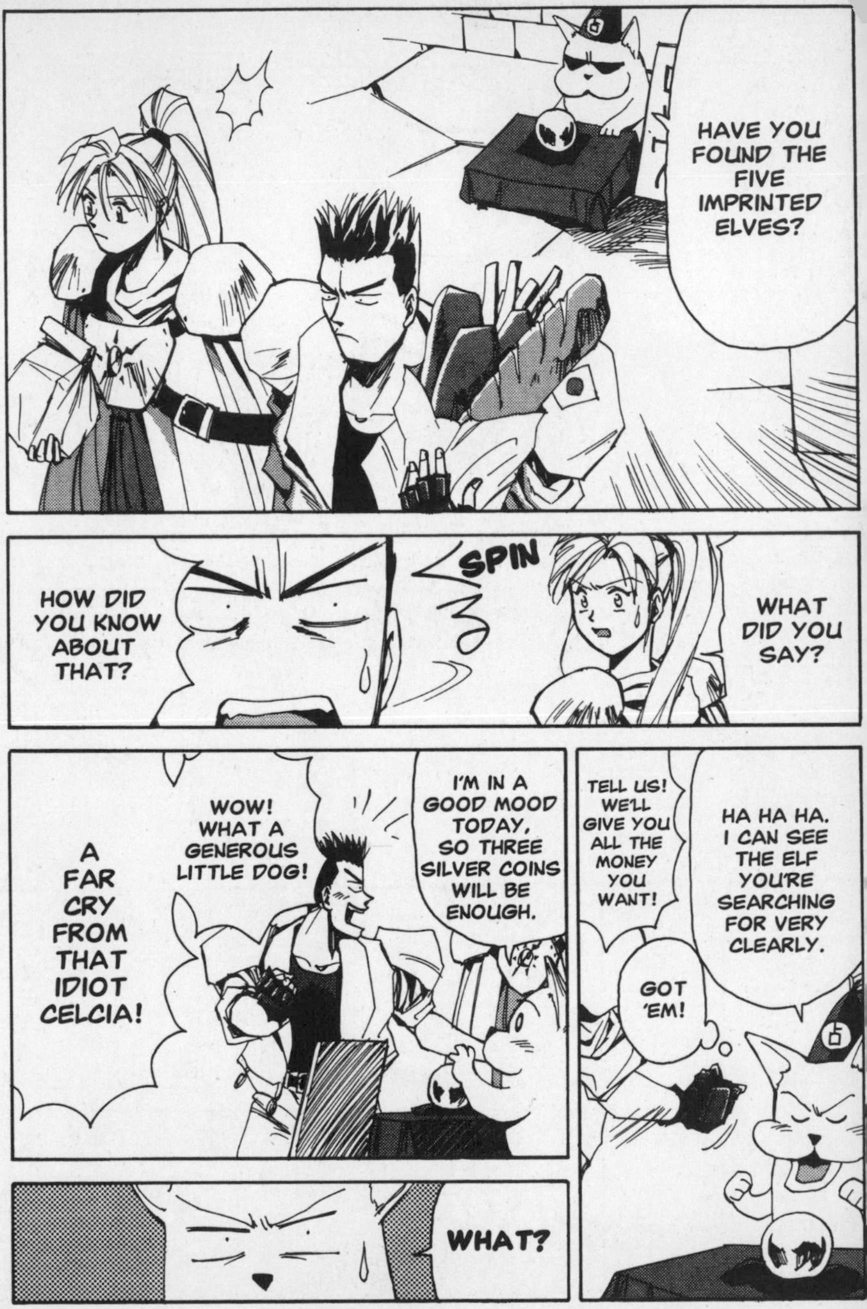
HAVE YOU FOUND THE FIVE IMPRINTED ELVES?
WHAT DID YOU SAY?
SPIN
HOW DID YOU KNOW ABOUT THAT?
HA HA HA. I CAN SEE THE ELF YOU'RE SEARCHING FOR VERY CLEARLY.
TELL US! WE'LL GIVE YOU ALL THE MONEY YOU WANT!
GOT 'EM!
I'M IN A GOOD MOOD TODAY, SO THREE SILVER COINS WILL BE ENOUGH.
WOW! WHAT A GENEROUS LITTLE DOG!
A FAR CRY FROM THAT IDIOT CELCIA!
WHAT?

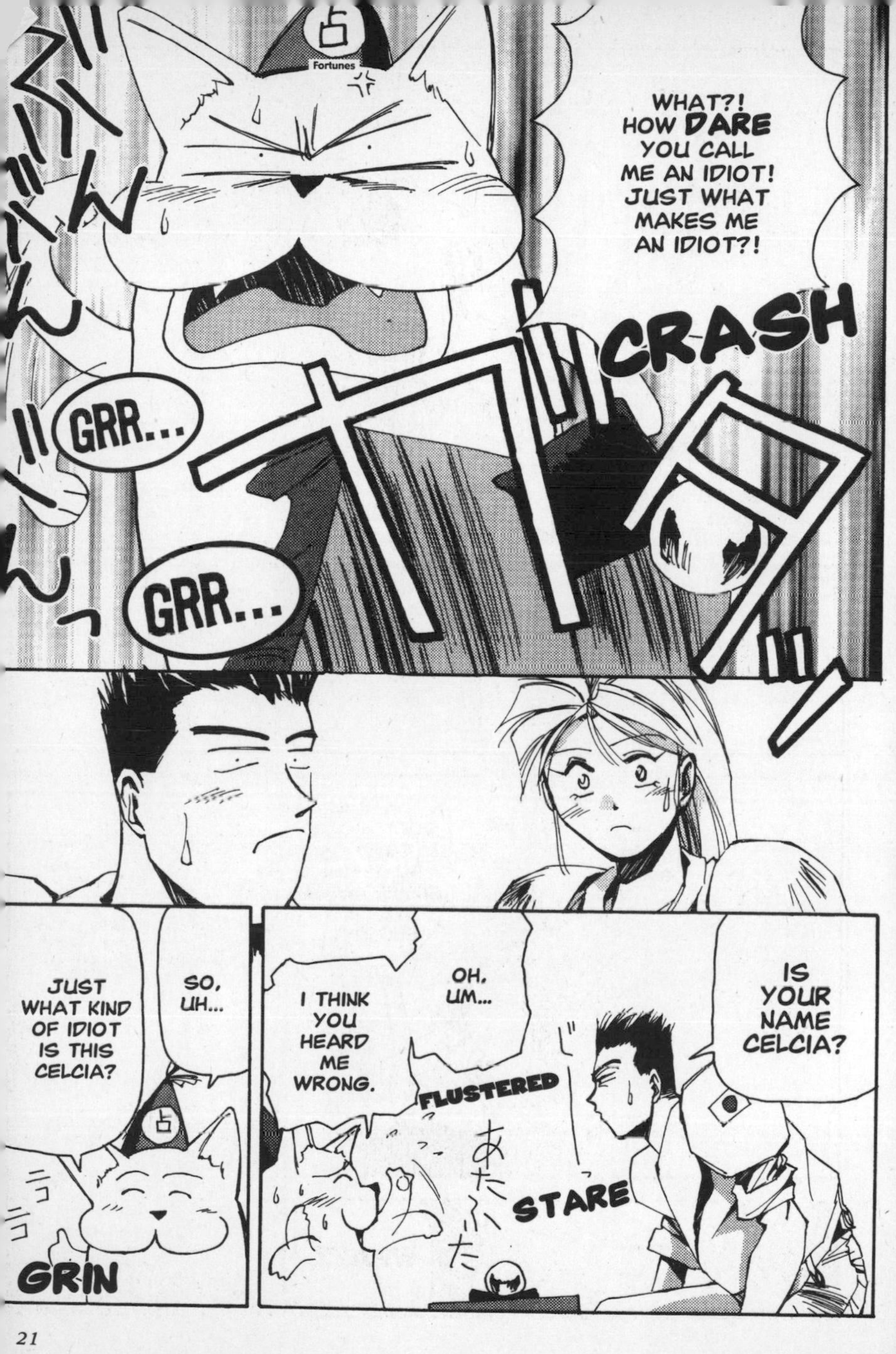
Fortunes
WHAT?! HOW DARE YOU CALL ME AN IDIOT! JUST WHAT MAKES ME AN IDIOT?!
CRASH
GRR...
GRR...
IS YOUR NAME CELCIA?
STARE
OH, UM...
I THINK YOU HEARD ME WRONG.
FLUSTERED
あたふた
SO, UH...
JUST WHAT KIND OF IDIOT IS THIS CELCIA?
GRIN

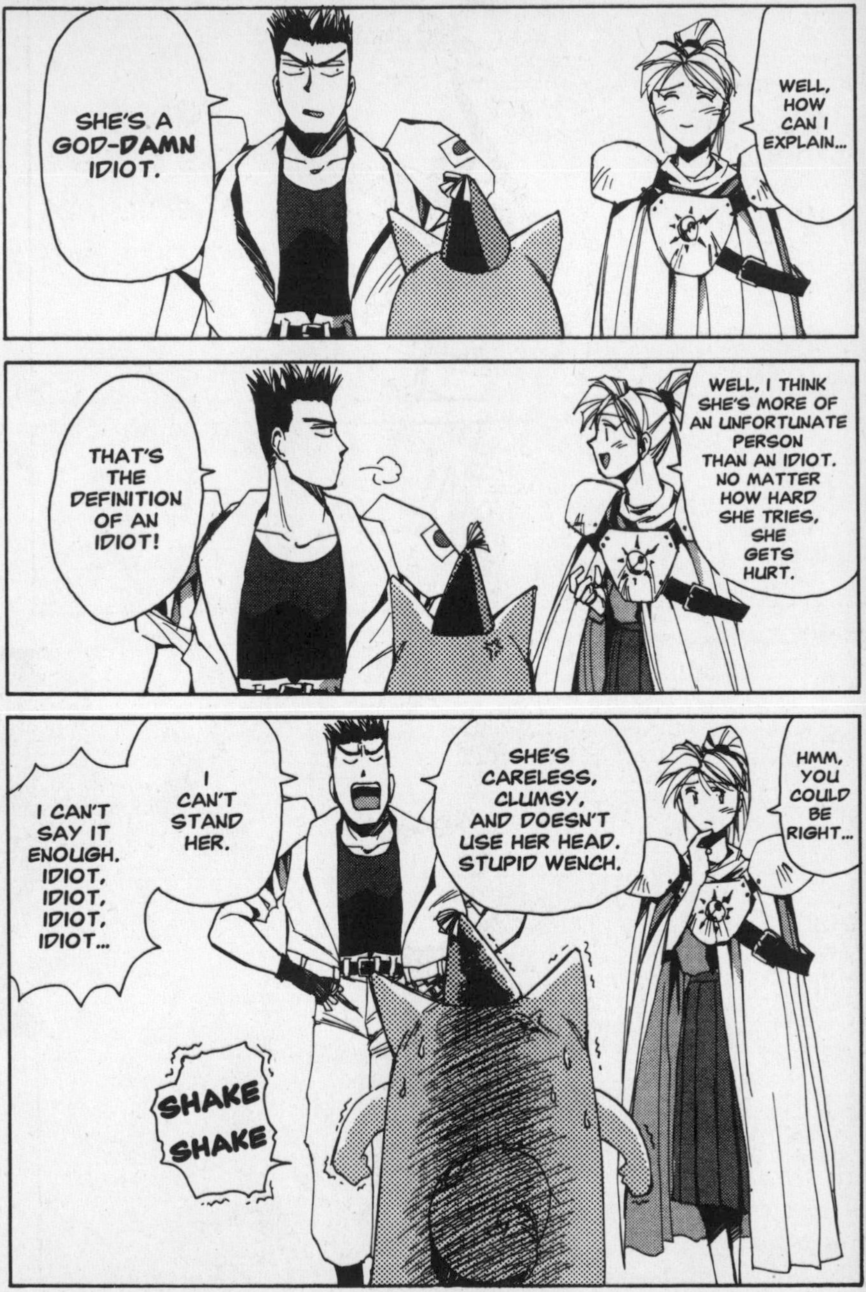
WELL, HOW CAN I EXPLAIN...
SHE'S A GOD-DAMN IDIOT.
WELL, I THINK SHE'S MORE OF AN UNFORTUNATE PERSON THAN AN IDIOT. NO MATTER HOW HARD SHE TRIES, SHE GETS HURT.
THAT'S THE DEFINITION OF AN IDIOT!
HMM, YOU COULD BE RIGHT...
SHE'S CARELESS, CLUMSY, AND DOESN'T USE HER HEAD. STUPID WENCH.
I CAN'T STAND HER.
I CAN'T SAY IT ENOUGH. IDIOT, IDIOT, IDIOT, IDIOT...
SHAKE SHAKE

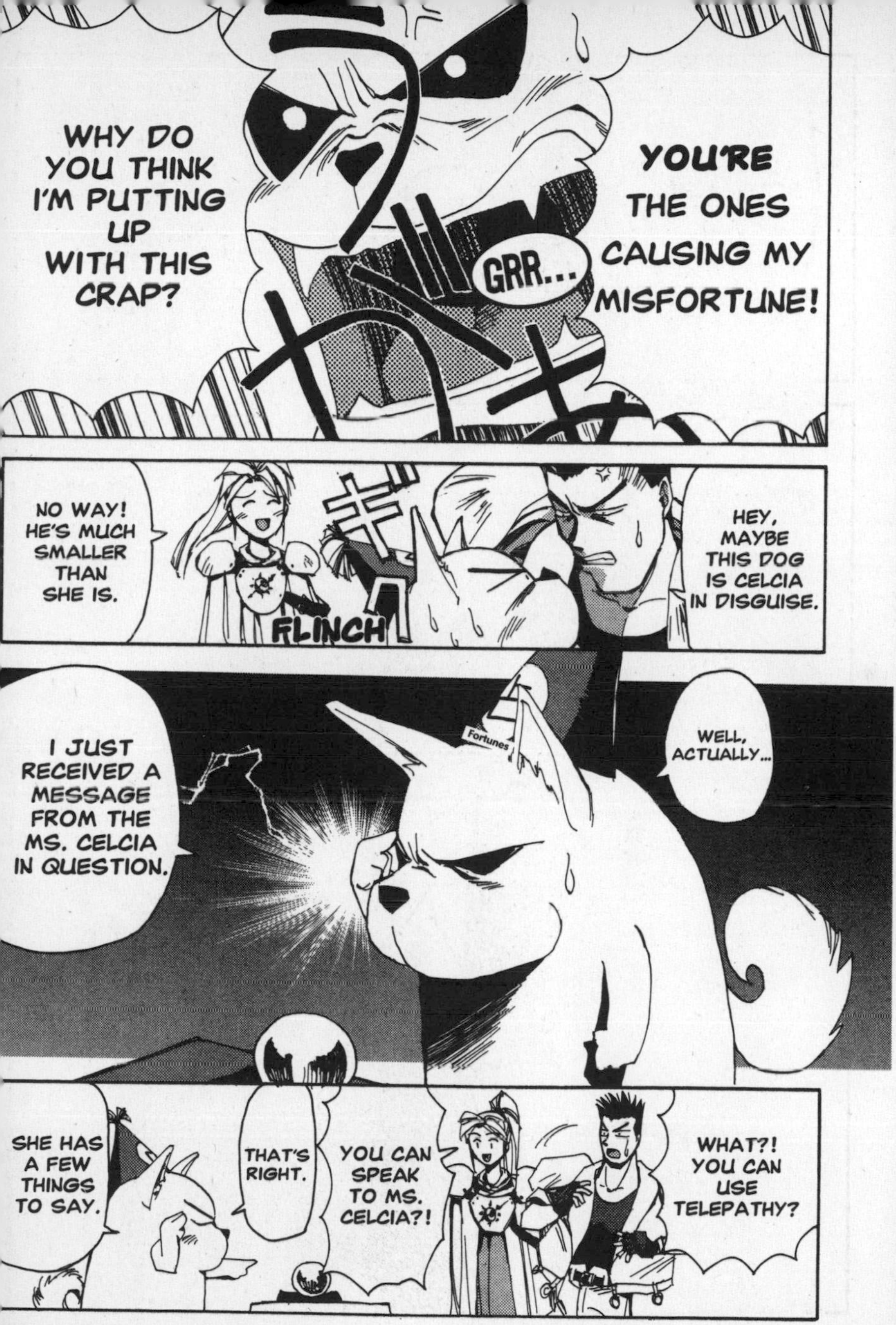
GRR...
WHY DO YOU THINK I'M PUTTING UP WITH THIS CRAP?
YOU'RE THE ONES CAUSING MY MISFORTUNE!
HEY, MAYBE THIS DOG IS CELCIA IN DISGUISE.
FLINCH
NO WAY! HE'S MUCH SMALLER THAN SHE IS.
Fortunes
WELL, ACTUALLY...
I JUST RECEIVED A MESSAGE FROM THE MS. CELCIA IN QUESTION.
WHAT?! YOU CAN USE TELEPATHY?
YOU CAN SPEAK TO MS. CELCIA?!
THAT'S RIGHT.
SHE HAS A FEW THINGS TO SAY.

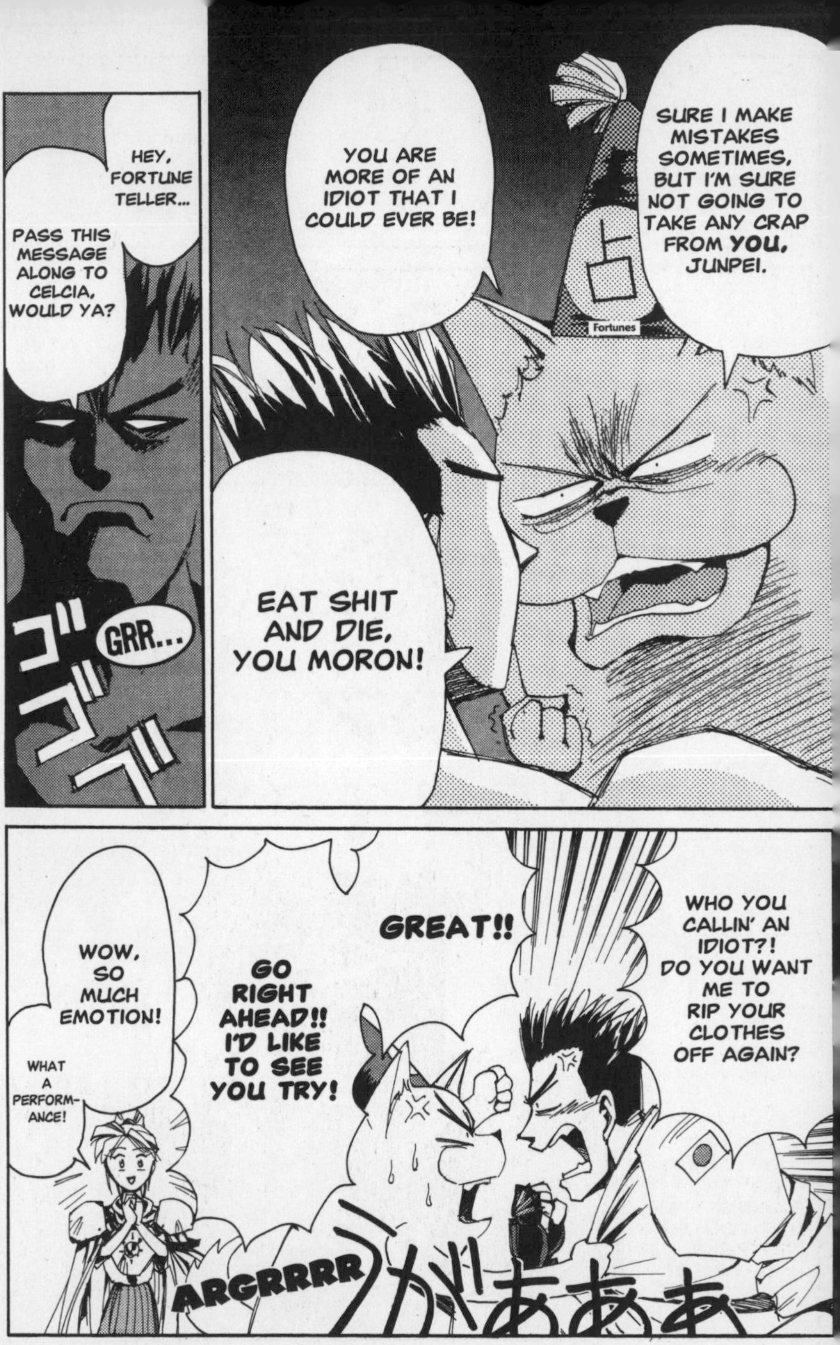
SURE I MAKE MISTAKES SOMETIMES, BUT I'M SURE NOT GOING TO TAKE ANY CRAP FROM **YOU,** JUNPEI.
Fortunes
YOU ARE MORE OF AN IDIOT THAT I COULD EVER BE!
EAT SHIT AND DIE, YOU MORON!
HEY, FORTUNE TELLER...
PASS THIS MESSAGE ALONG TO CELCIA, WOULD YA?
GRR...
ゴゴゴ
WHO YOU CALLIN' AN IDIOT?! DO YOU WANT ME TO RIP YOUR CLOTHES OFF AGAIN?
GREAT!!
GO RIGHT AHEAD!! I'D LIKE TO SEE YOU TRY!
WOW, SO MUCH EMOTION!
WHAT A PERFORM-ANCE!
ARGRRRR
うがあああ

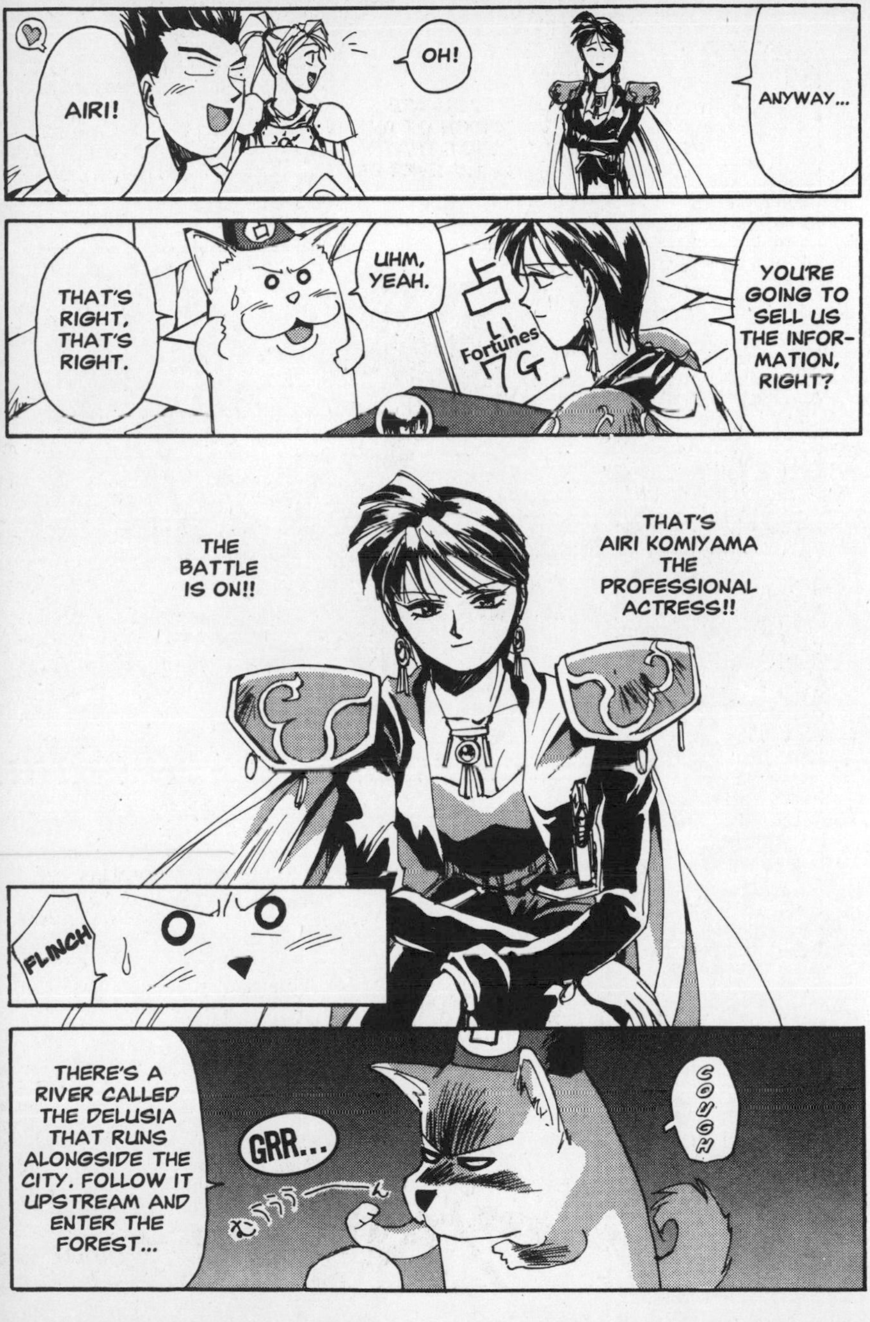

ANYWAY...
OH!
AIRI!
YOU'RE GOING TO SELL US THE INFORMATION, RIGHT?
占い
Fortunes
UHM, YEAH.
THAT'S RIGHT, THAT'S RIGHT.
THAT'S AIRI KOMIYAMA THE PROFESSIONAL ACTRESS!!
THE BATTLE IS ON!!
FLINCH
COUGH
GRR...
THERE'S A RIVER CALLED THE DELUSIA THAT RUNS ALONGSIDE THE CITY. FOLLOW IT UPSTREAM AND ENTER THE FOREST...

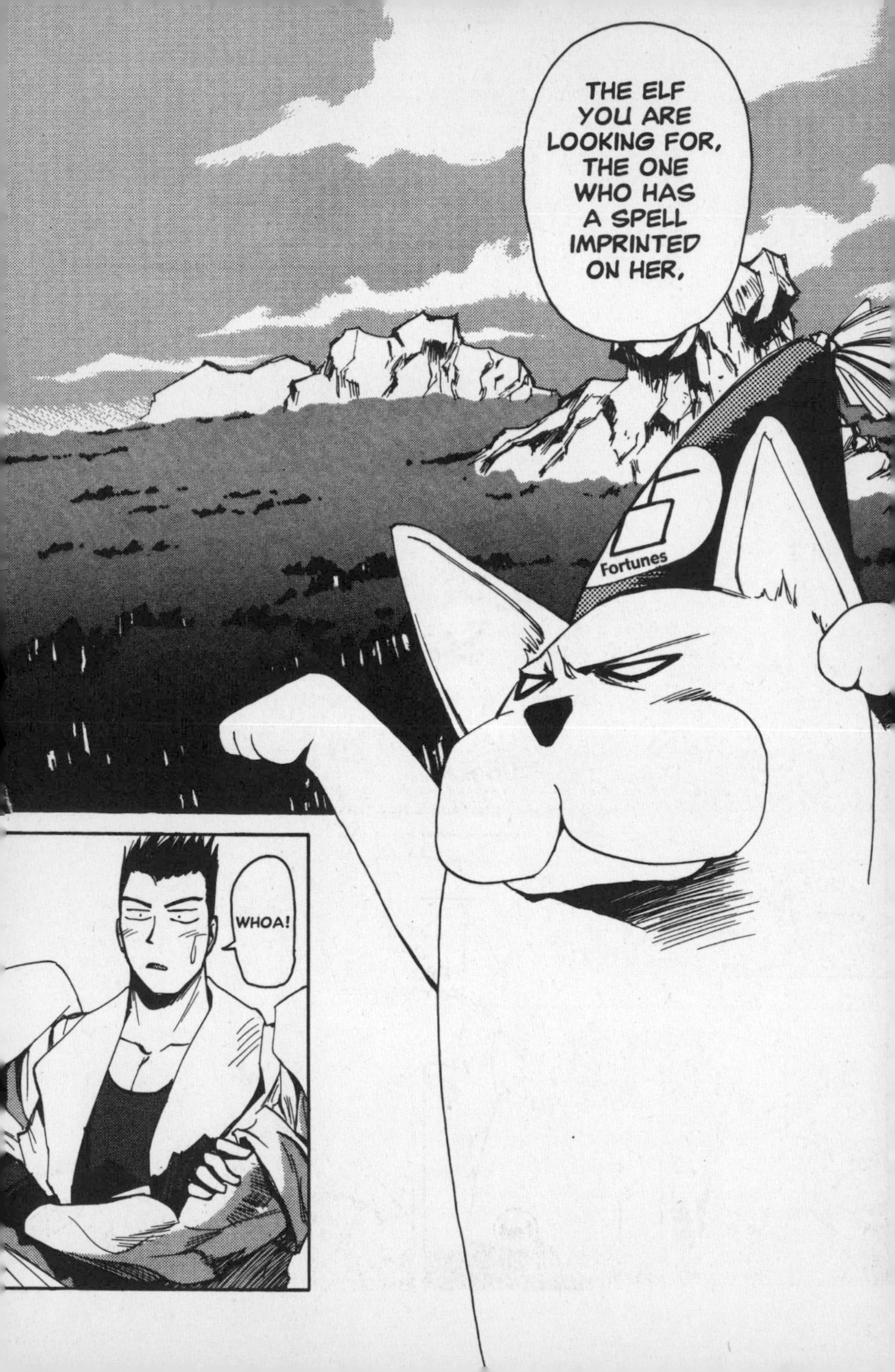
THE ELF YOU ARE LOOKING FOR, THE ONE WHO HAS A SPELL IMPRINTED ON HER,
Fortunes
WHOA!

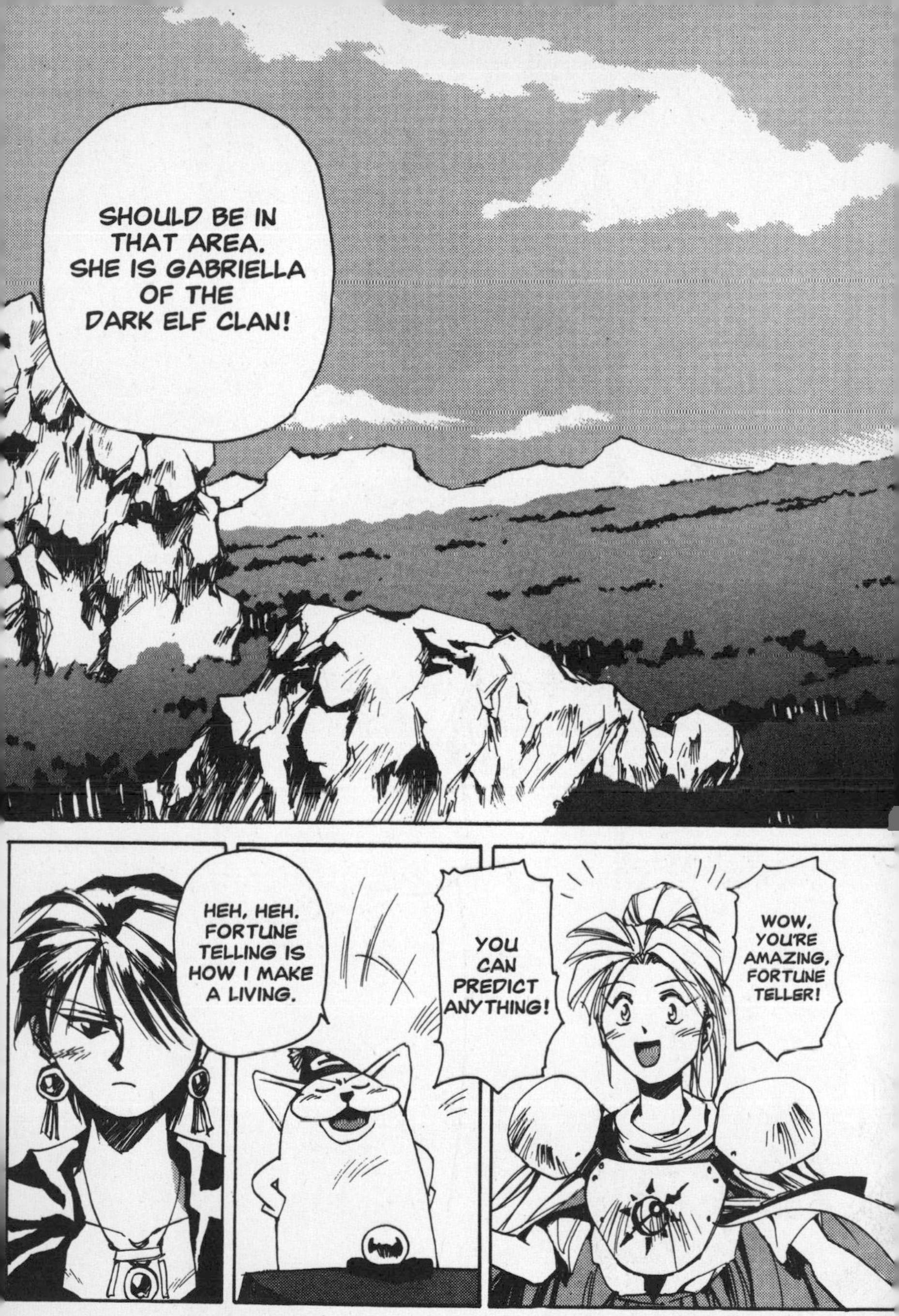
SHOULD BE IN THAT AREA. SHE IS GABRIELLA OF THE DARK ELF CLAN!
WOW, YOU'RE AMAZING, FORTUNE TELLER!
YOU CAN PREDICT ANYTHING!
HEH, HEH. FORTUNE TELLING IS HOW I MAKE A LIVING.

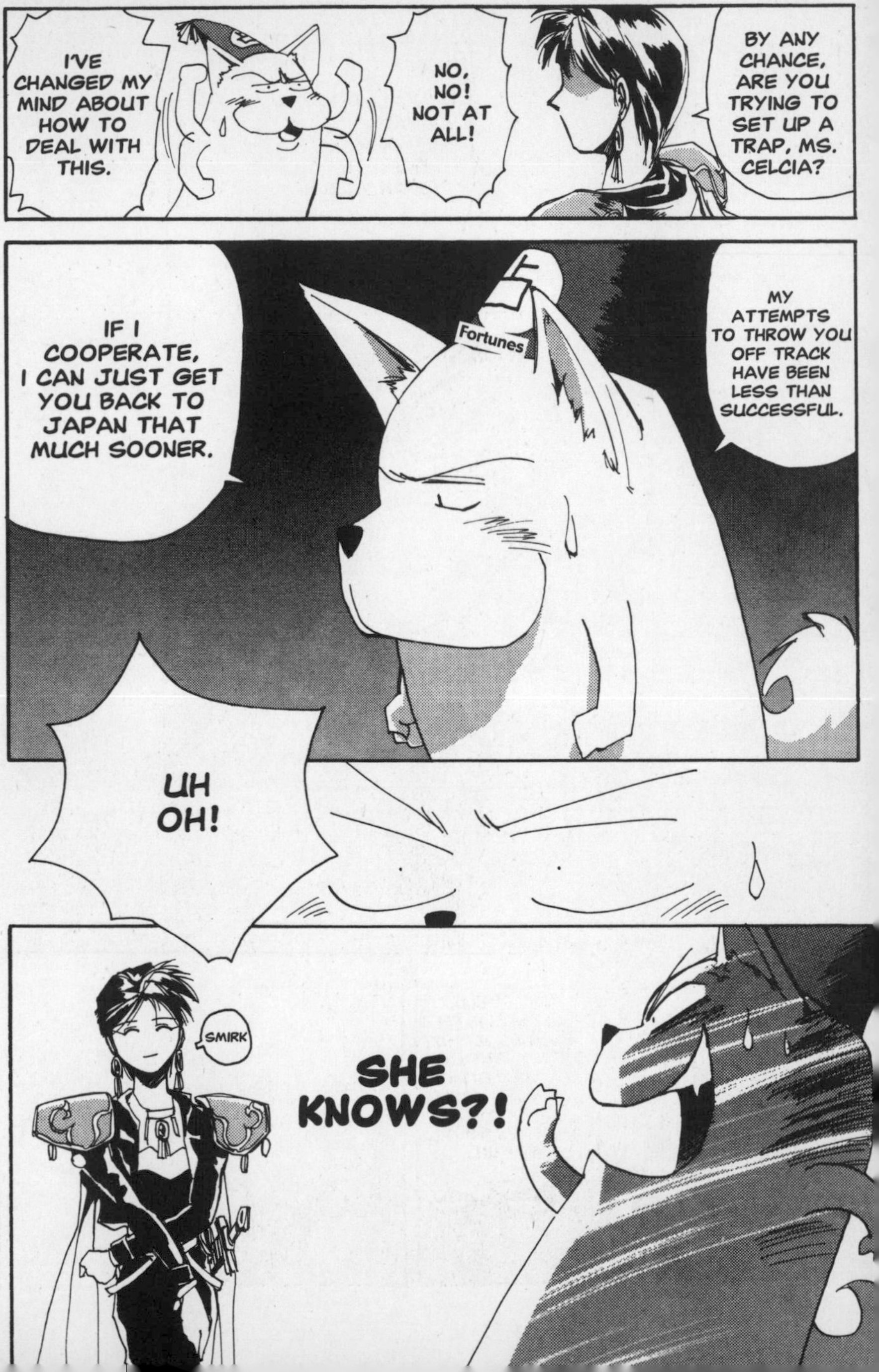

BY ANY CHANCE, ARE YOU TRYING TO SET UP A TRAP, MS. CELCIA?
NO, NO! NOT AT ALL!
I'VE CHANGED MY MIND ABOUT HOW TO DEAL WITH THIS.
Fortunes
MY ATTEMPTS TO THROW YOU OFF TRACK HAVE BEEN LESS THAN SUCCESSFUL.
IF I COOPERATE, I CAN JUST GET YOU BACK TO JAPAN THAT MUCH SOONER.
UH OH!
SMIRK
SHE KNOWS?!

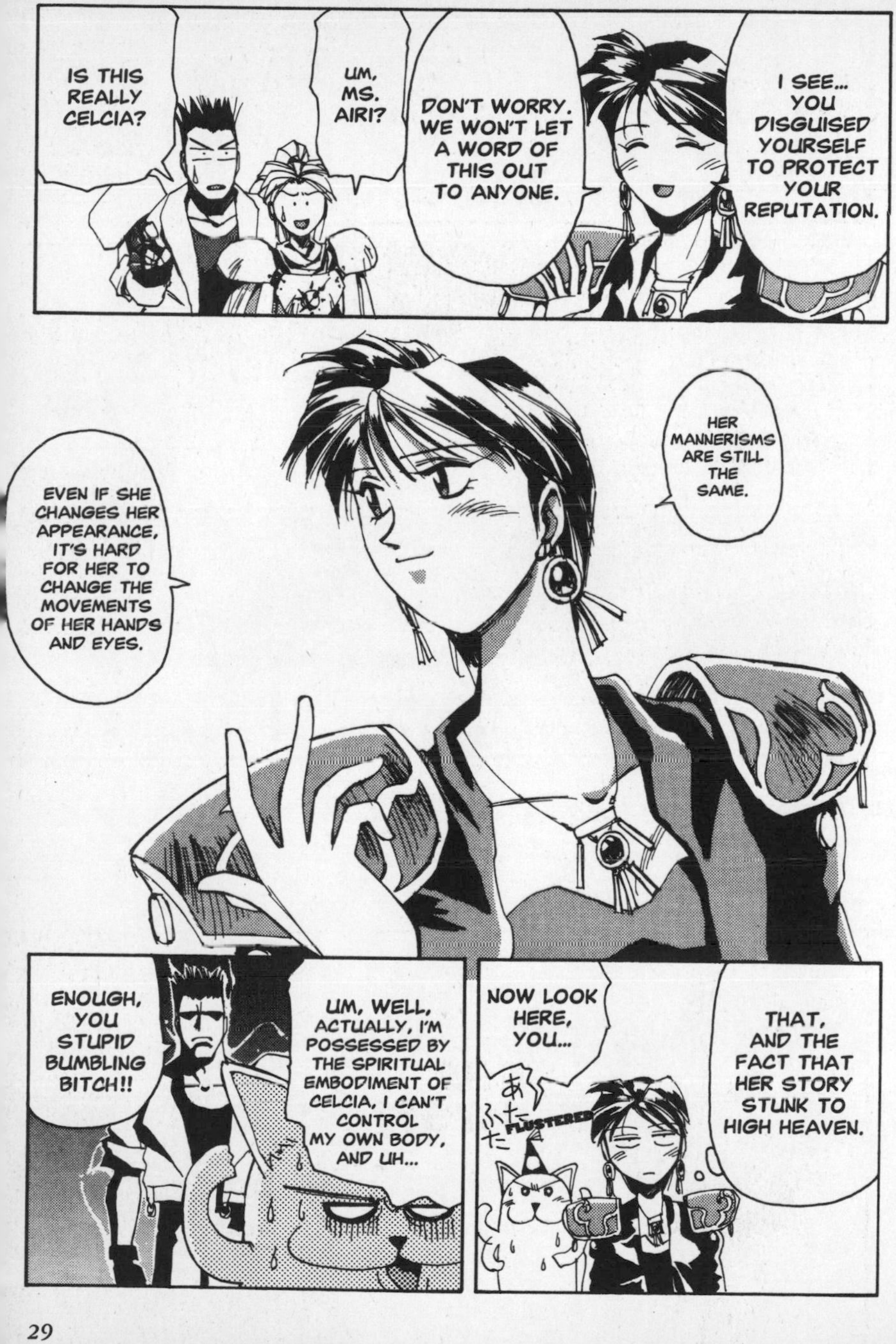
I SEE... YOU DISGUISED YOURSELF TO PROTECT YOUR REPUTATION.
DON'T WORRY. WE WON'T LET A WORD OF THIS OUT TO ANYONE.
UM, MS. AIRI?
IS THIS REALLY CELCIA?
HER MANNERISMS ARE STILL THE SAME.
EVEN IF SHE CHANGES HER APPEARANCE, IT'S HARD FOR HER TO CHANGE THE MOVEMENTS OF HER HANDS AND EYES.
THAT, AND THE FACT THAT HER STORY STUNK TO HIGH HEAVEN.
NOW LOOK HERE, YOU...
あたふた
FLUSTERED
UM, WELL, ACTUALLY, I'M POSSESSED BY THE SPIRITUAL EMBODIMENT OF CELCIA, I CAN'T CONTROL MY OWN BODY, AND UH...
ENOUGH, YOU STUPID BUMBLING BITCH!!

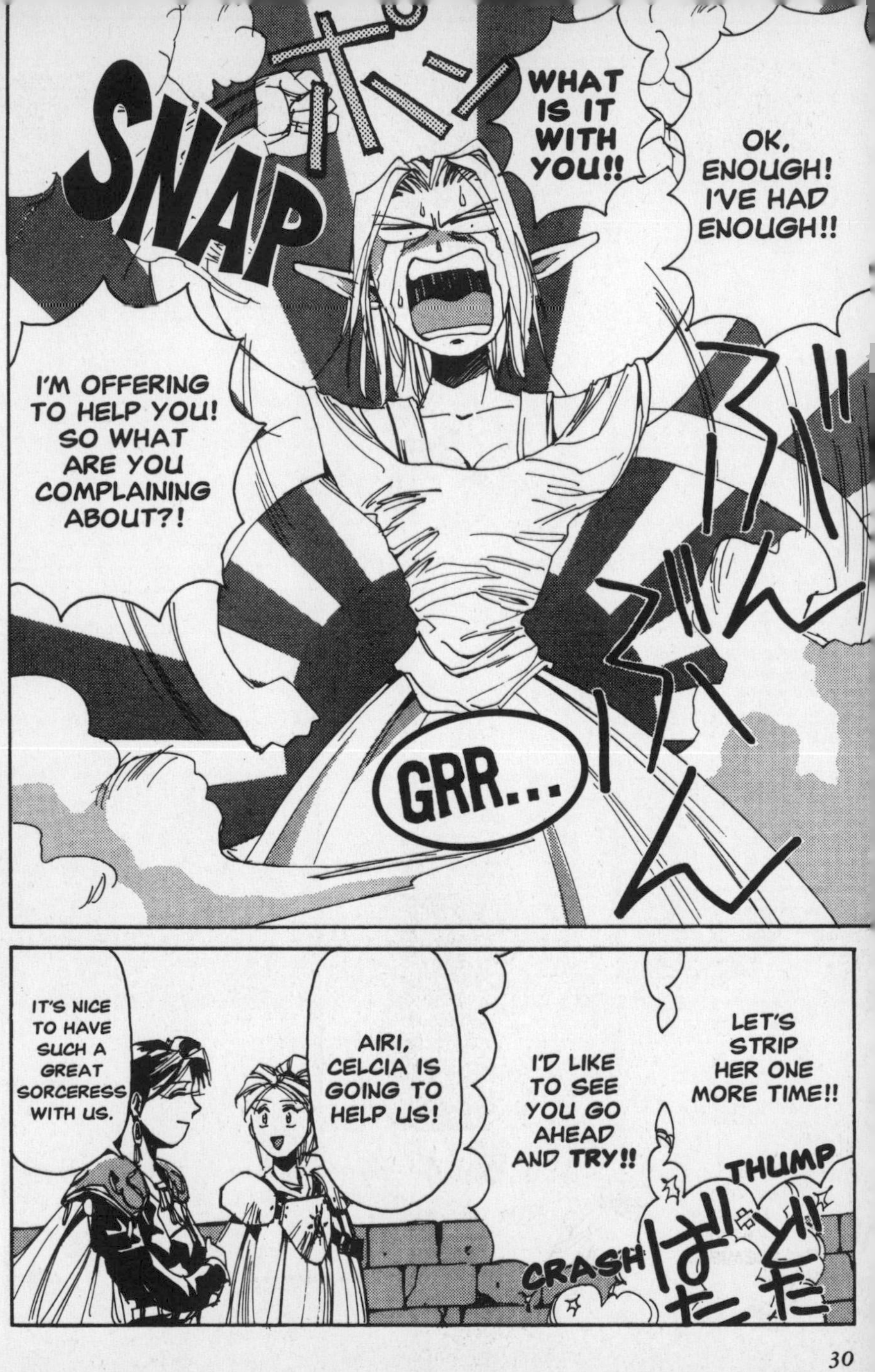

OK, ENOUGH! I'VE HAD ENOUGH!!
WHAT IS IT WITH YOU!!
SNAP
I'M OFFERING TO HELP YOU! SO WHAT ARE YOU COMPLAINING ABOUT?!
GRR...
LET'S STRIP HER ONE MORE TIME!!
I'D LIKE TO SEE YOU GO AHEAD AND TRY!!
THUMP
CRASH
AIRI, CELCIA IS GOING TO HELP US!
IT'S NICE TO HAVE SUCH A GREAT SORCERESS WITH US.

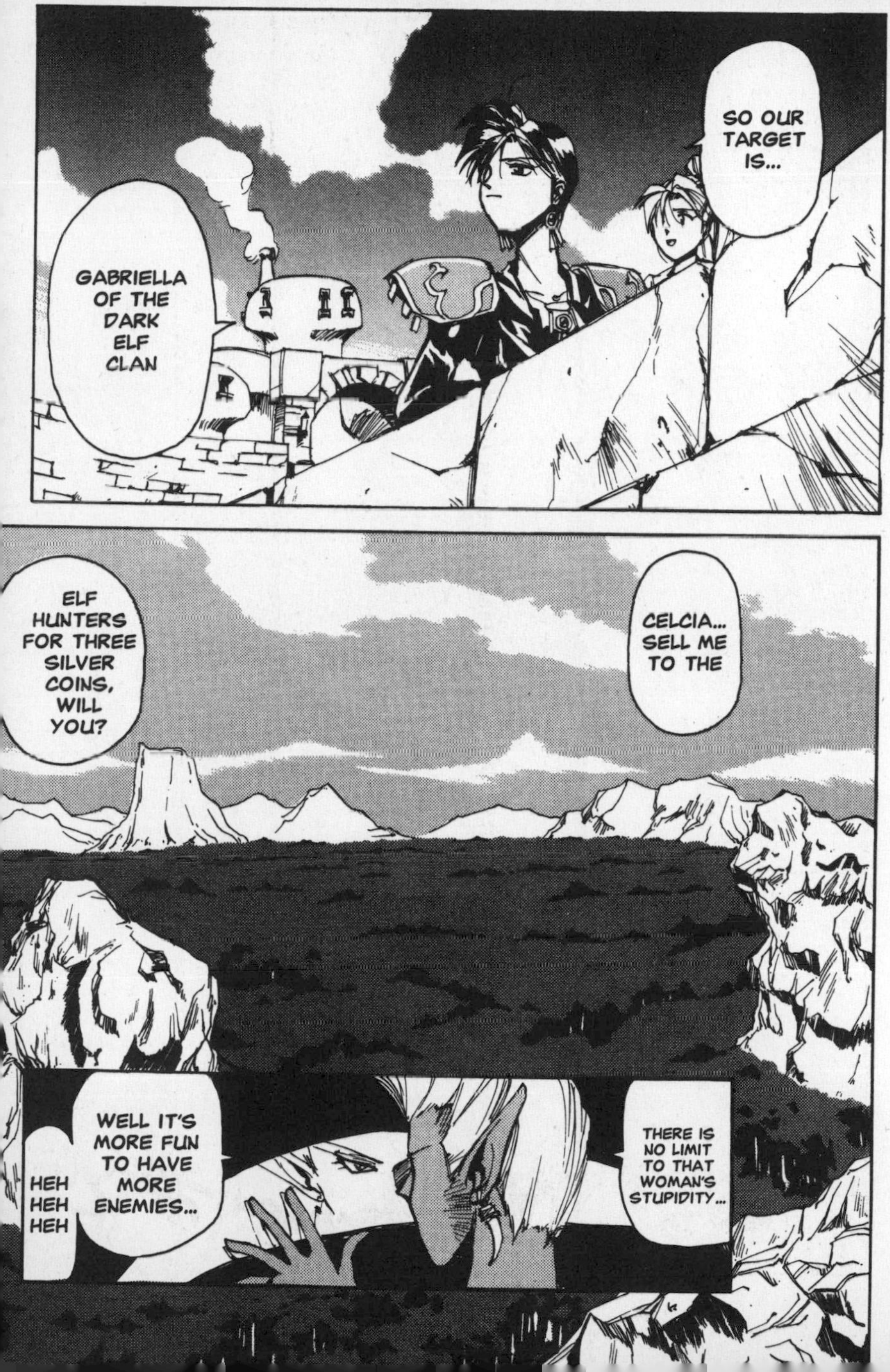
SO OUR TARGET IS...
GABRIELLA OF THE DARK ELF CLAN
CELCIA... SELL ME TO THE
ELF HUNTERS FOR THREE SILVER COINS, WILL YOU?
THERE IS NO LIMIT TO THAT WOMAN'S STUPIDITY...
WELL IT'S MORE FUN TO HAVE MORE ENEMIES...
HEH HEH HEH

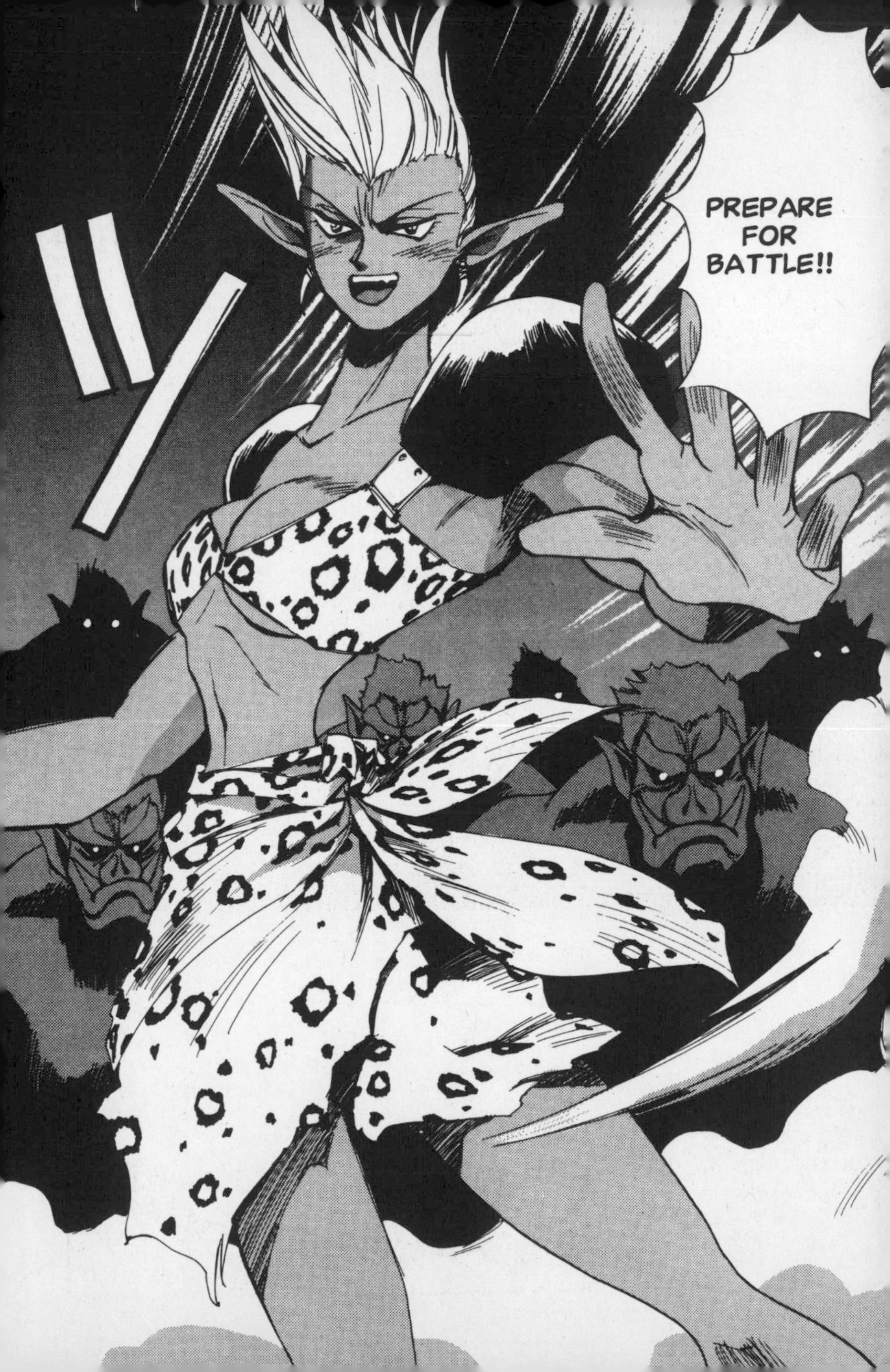
PREPARE FOR BATTLE!!

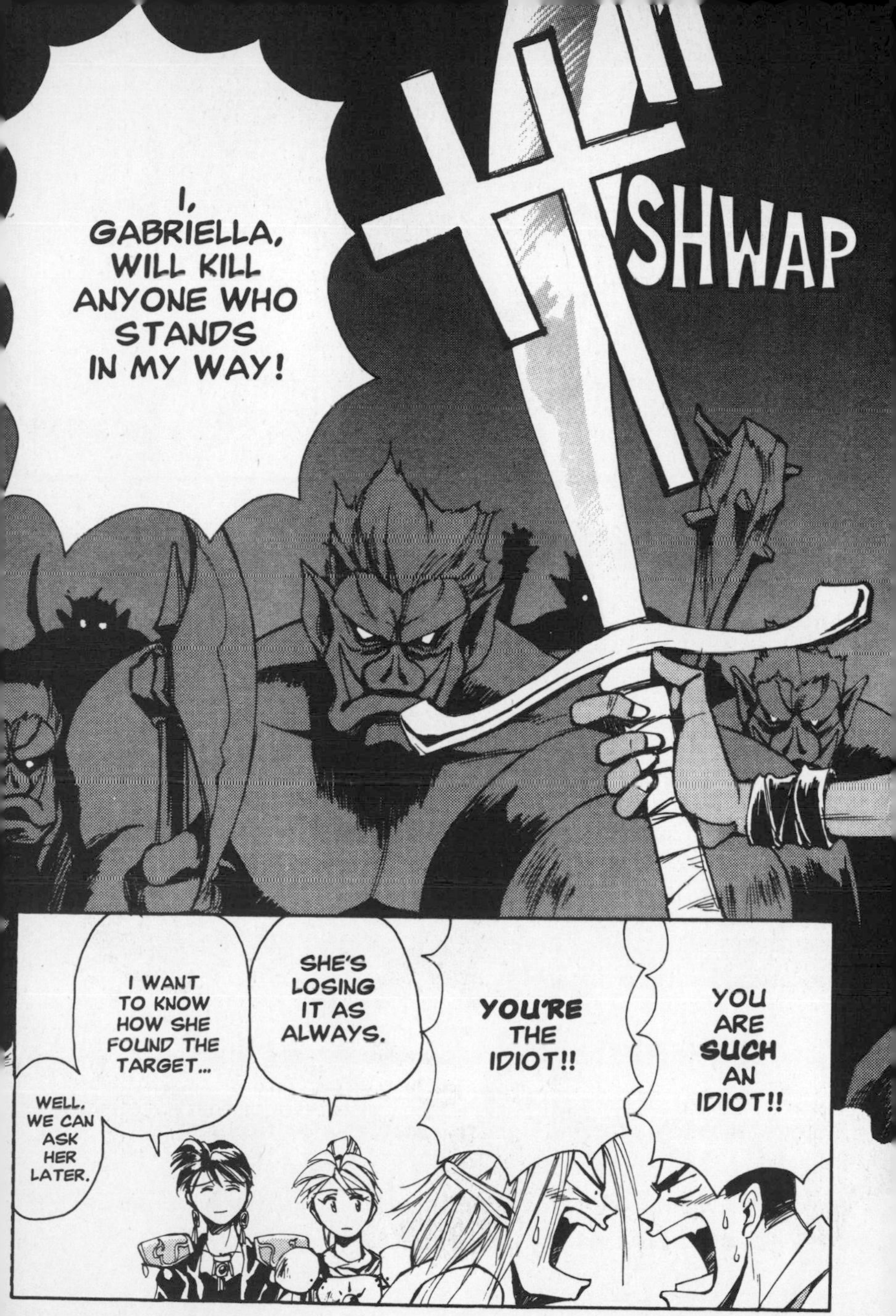
I, GABRIELLA, WILL KILL ANYONE WHO STANDS IN MY WAY!
SHWAP
YOU ARE SUCH AN IDIOT!!
YOU'RE THE IDIOT!!
SHE'S LOSING IT AS ALWAYS.
I WANT TO KNOW HOW SHE FOUND THE TARGET...
WELL. WE CAN ASK HER LATER.

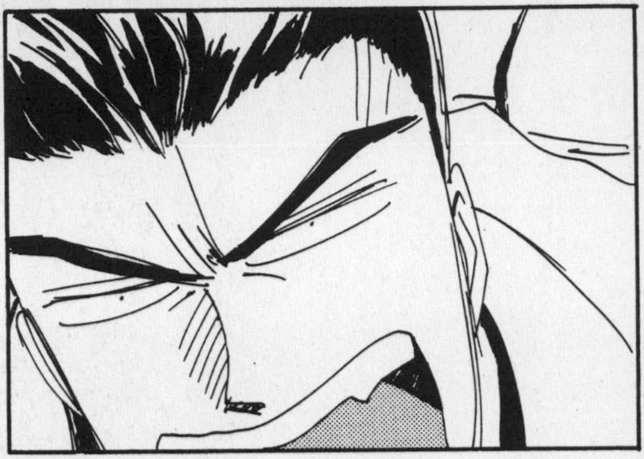

Character Profile (1)

Junpei Ryuzoji

Age: 19
Blood Type: B
Sign: Virgo
Personality: Shallow and stupid

A total loser. He failed his college entrance exams and is currently trying to be a professional fighter. His less-than-average intelligence is compensated by a terrific fighting sense, and the fights he got into in his high school days are legendary. He is a big fan of Airi, the movie star, and he's devoted his life to pursuing her. Junpei's favorite dish is curry rice and he can actually cook it himself.

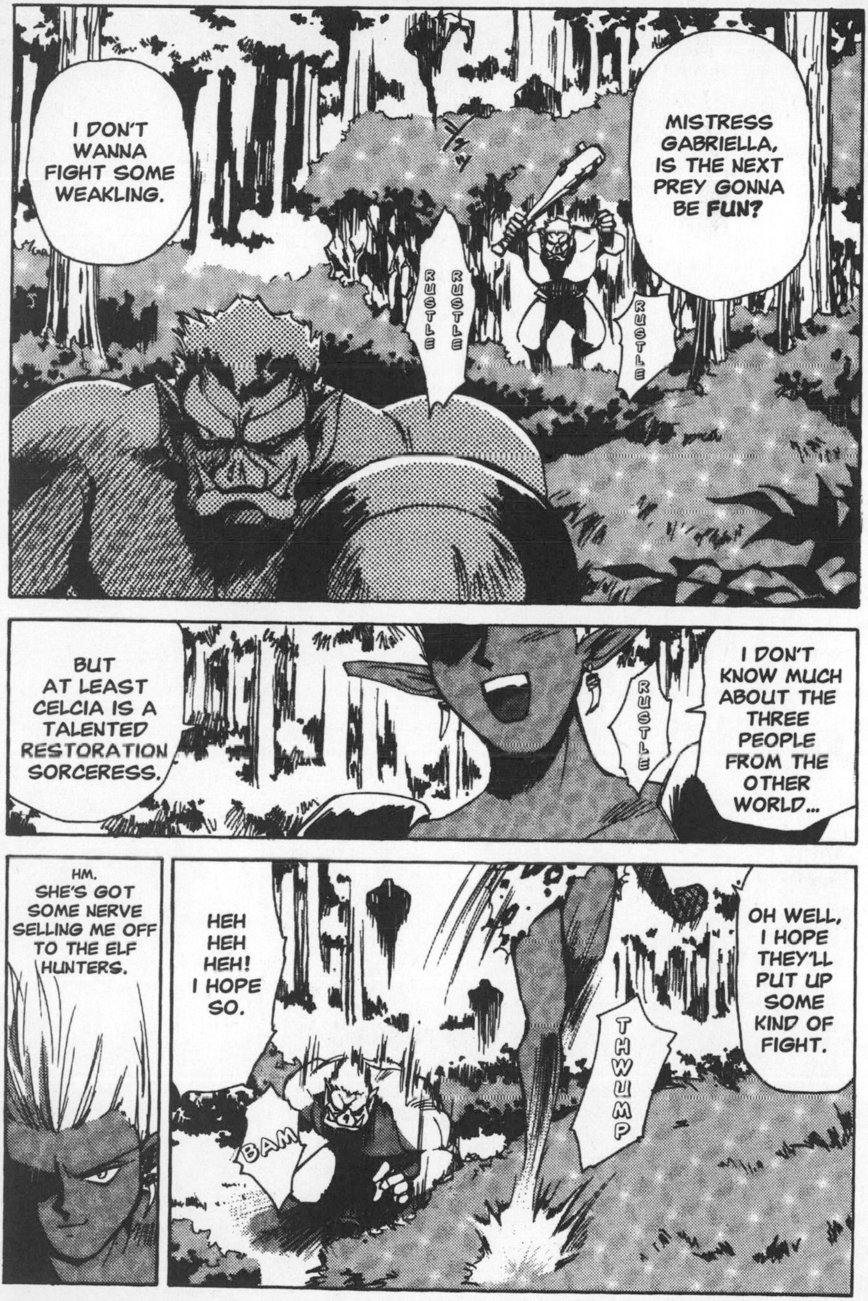
MISTRESS GABRIELLA, IS THE NEXT PREY GONNA BE FUN?
RUSTLE
RUSTLE
RUSTLE
I DON'T WANNA FIGHT SOME WEAKLING.
I DON'T KNOW MUCH ABOUT THE THREE PEOPLE FROM THE OTHER WORLD...
RUSTLE
BUT AT LEAST CELCIA IS A TALENTED RESTORATION SORCERESS.
OH WELL, I HOPE THEY'LL PUT UP SOME KIND OF FIGHT.
THWUMP
HEH HEH HEH! I HOPE SO.
BAM
HM. SHE'S GOT SOME NERVE SELLING ME OFF TO THE ELF HUNTERS.

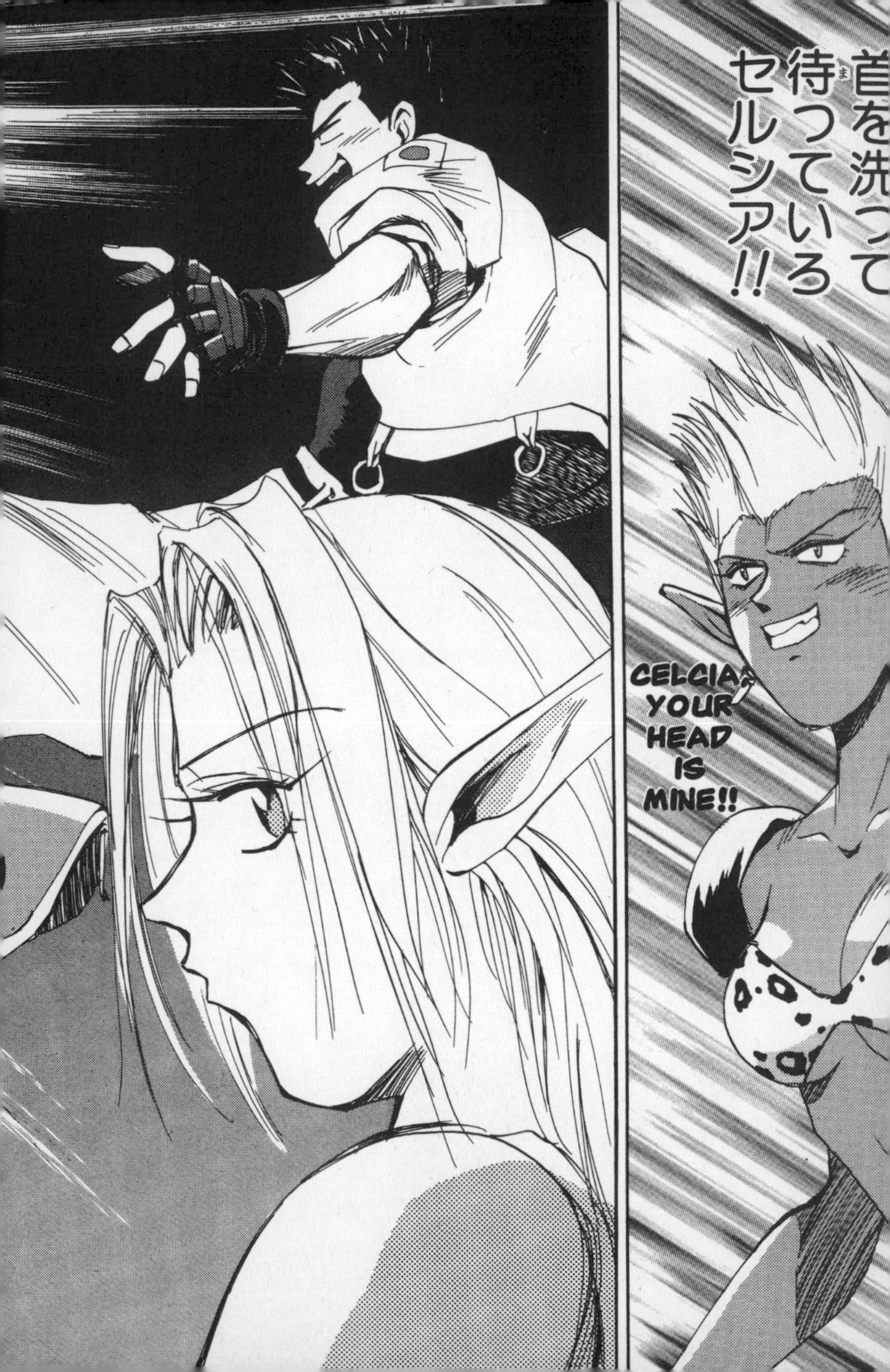
首を洗って待っていろセルシア!!
CELCIA, YOUR HEAD IS MINE!!

#2 Target Acquisition [Part 2]

2 目標完全捕捉!!〔後編〕

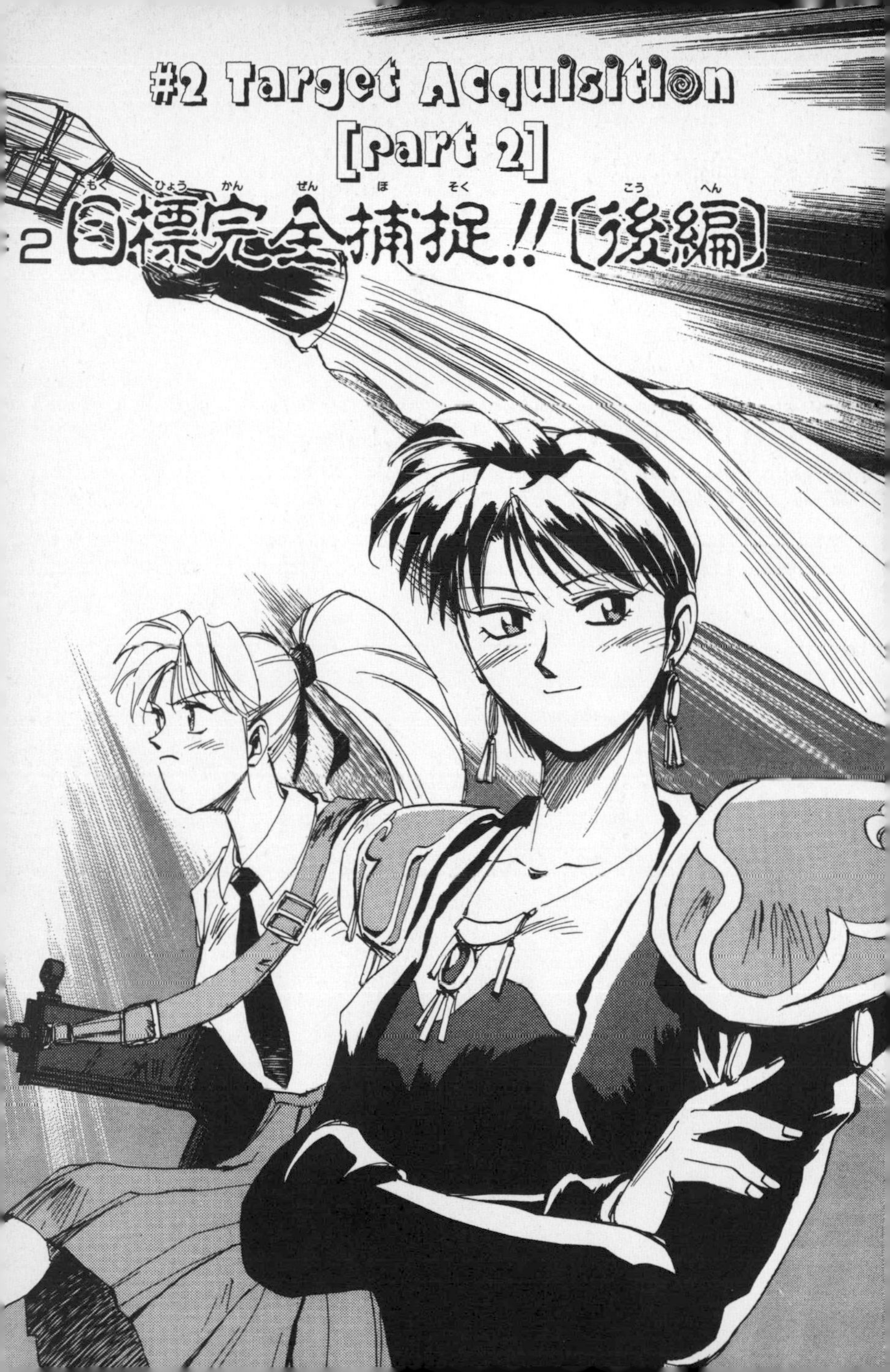

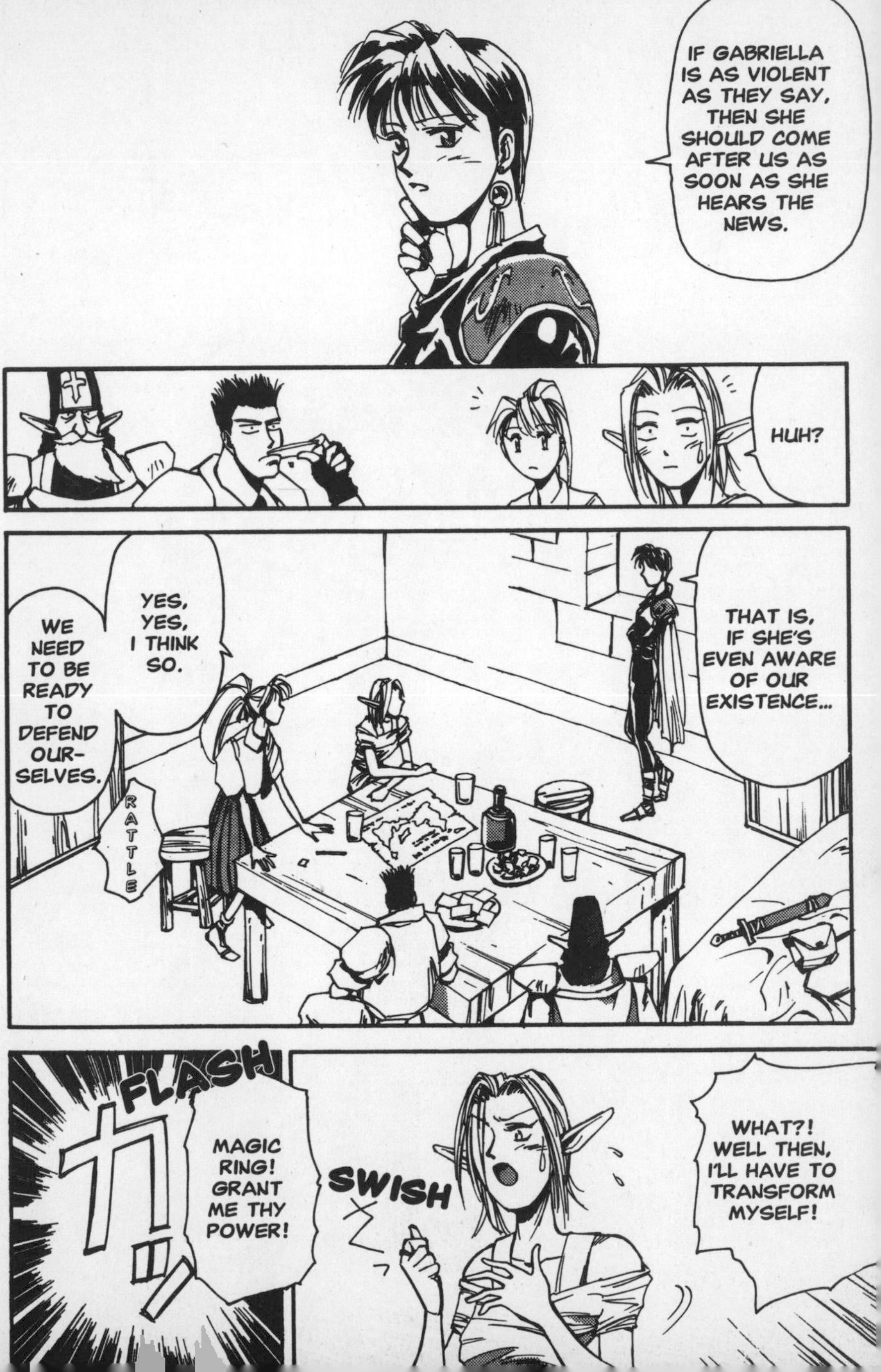
IF GABRIELLA IS AS VIOLENT AS THEY SAY, THEN SHE SHOULD COME AFTER US AS SOON AS SHE HEARS THE NEWS.
HUH?
THAT IS, IF SHE'S EVEN AWARE OF OUR EXISTENCE...
YES, YES, I THINK SO.
WE NEED TO BE READY TO DEFEND OUR-SELVES.
RATTLE
WHAT?! WELL THEN, I'LL HAVE TO TRANSFORM MYSELF!
SWISH
MAGIC RING! GRANT ME THY POWER!
FLASH

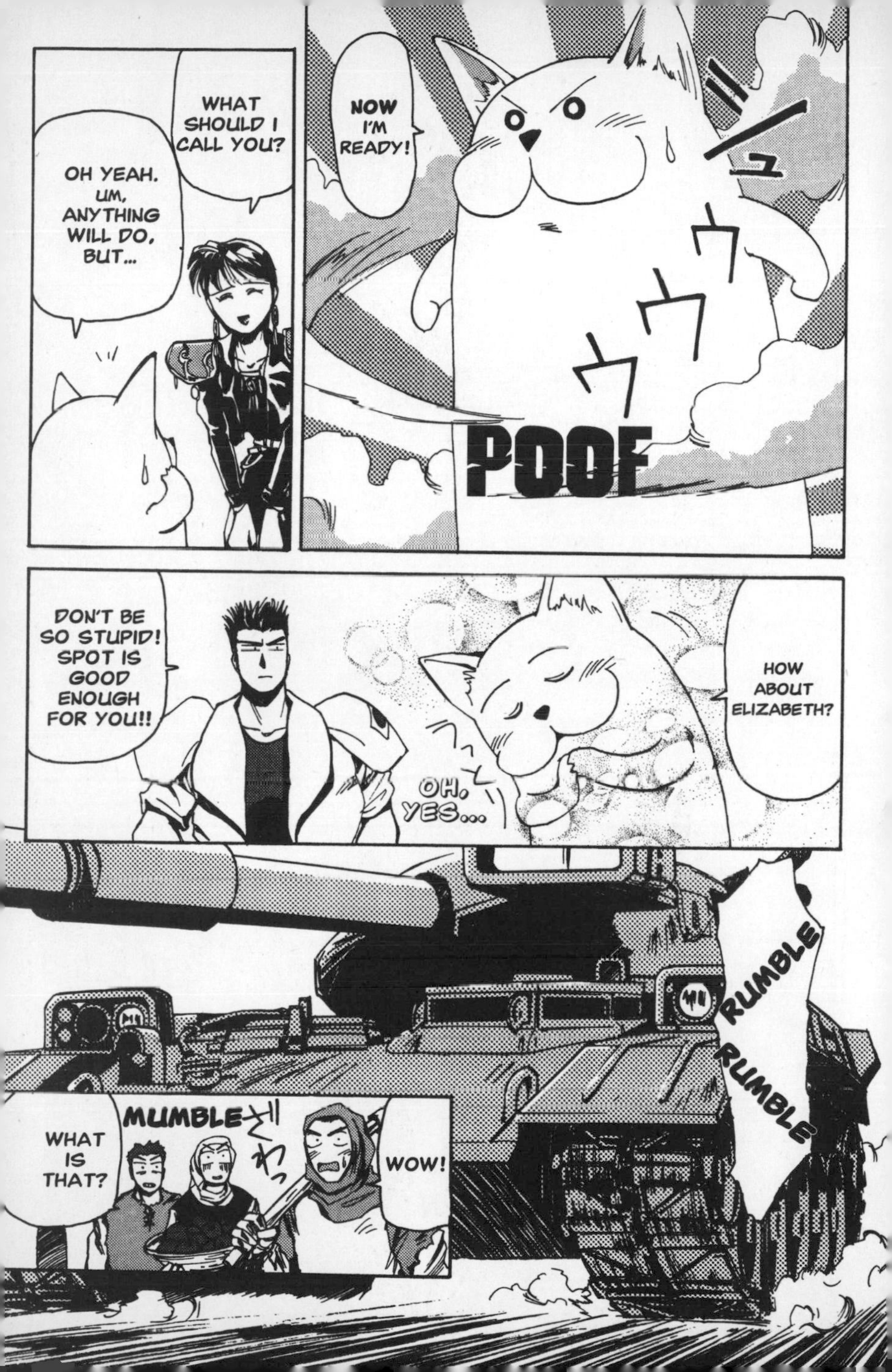
NOW I'M READY!
POOF
WHAT SHOULD I CALL YOU?
OH YEAH. UM, ANYTHING WILL DO, BUT...
HOW ABOUT ELIZABETH?
DON'T BE SO STUPID! SPOT IS GOOD ENOUGH FOR YOU!!
OH. YES...
RUMBLE
RUMBLE
WOW!
MUMBLE
WHAT IS THAT?

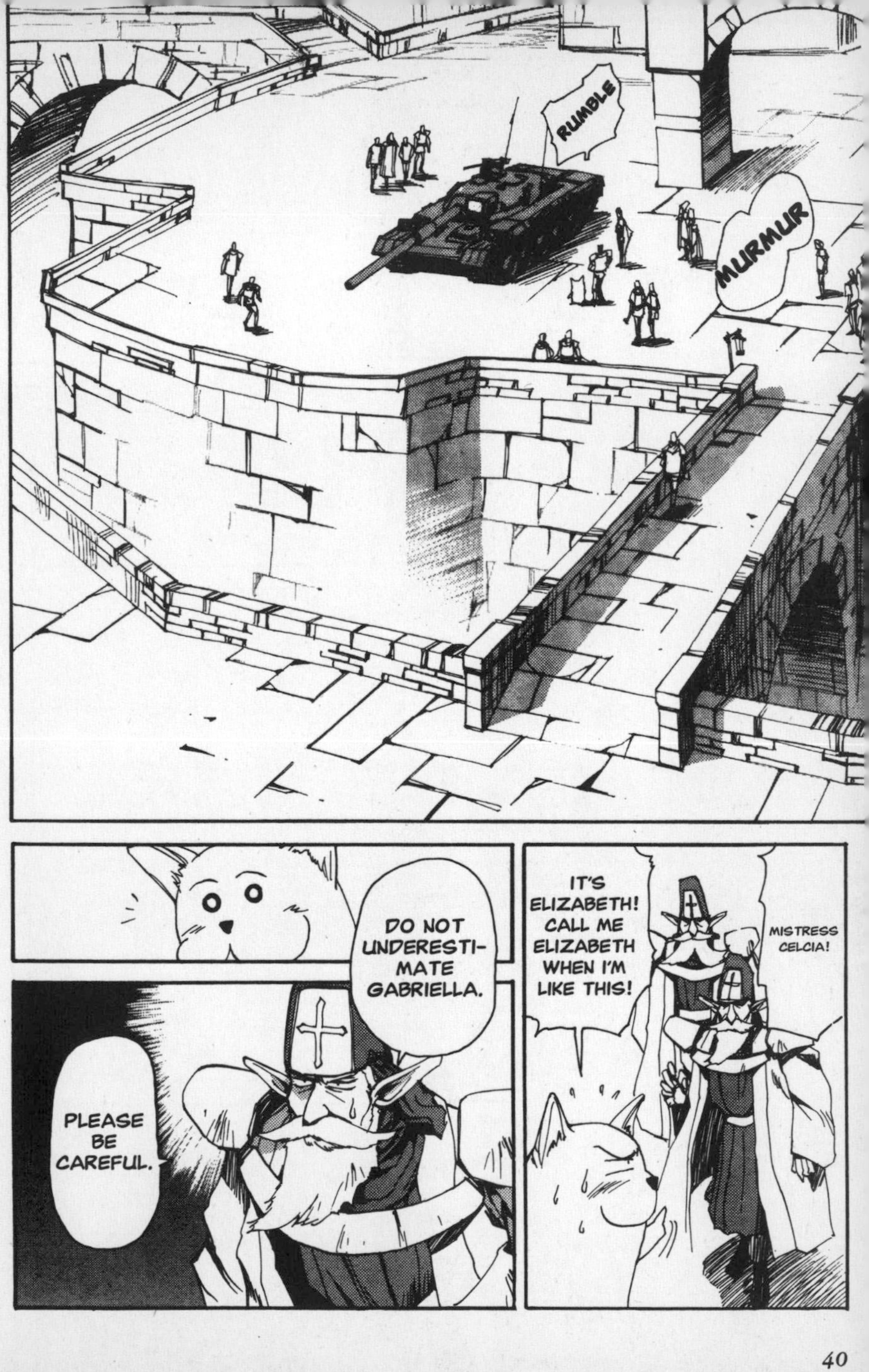
RUMBLE
MURMUR
MISTRESS CELCIA!
IT'S ELIZABETH! CALL ME ELIZABETH WHEN I'M LIKE THIS!
PLEASE BE CAREFUL.
DO NOT UNDERESTI- MATE GABRIELLA.

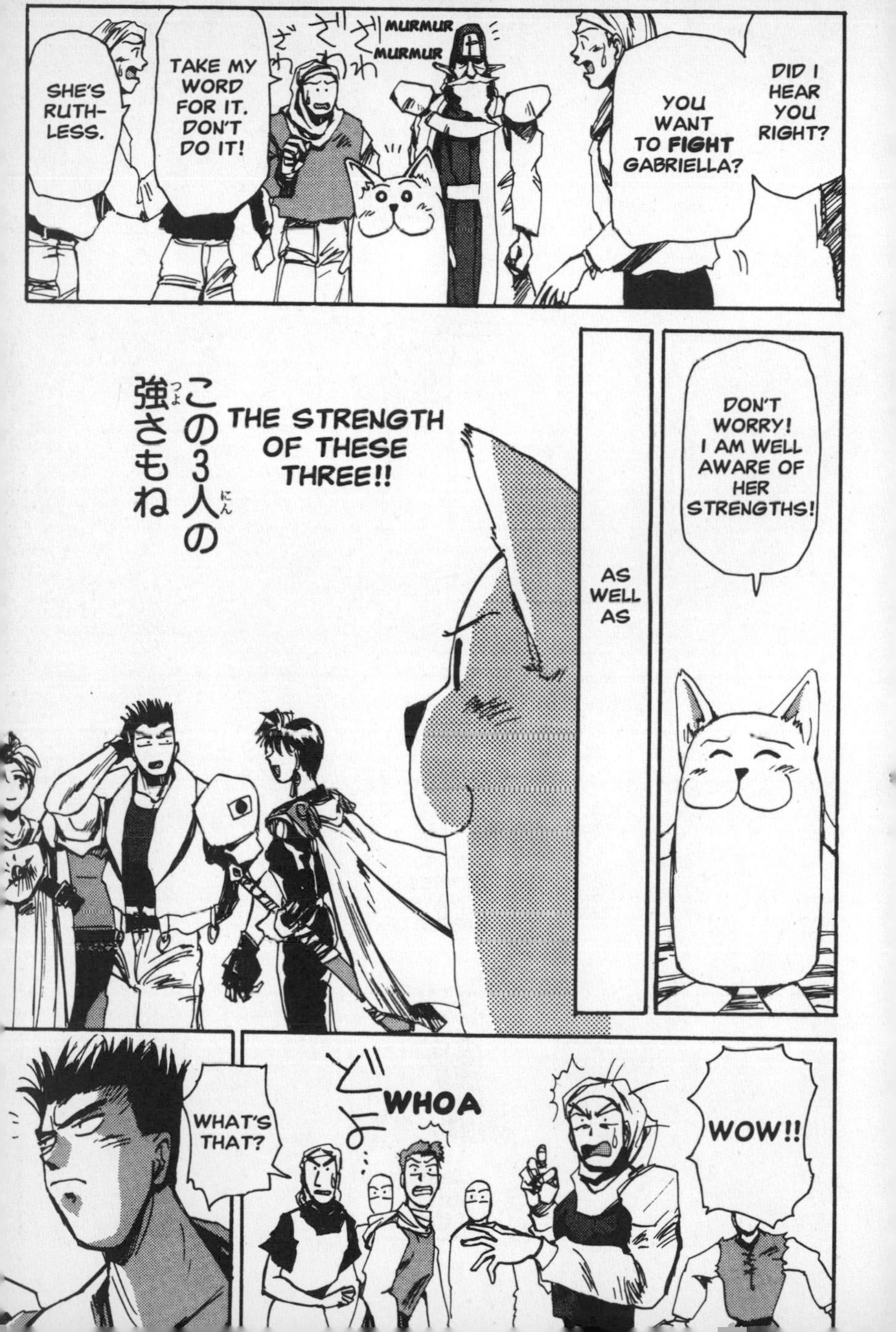
DID I HEAR YOU RIGHT?
YOU WANT TO FIGHT GABRIELLA?
ざわ ざわ
MURMUR MURMUR
TAKE MY WORD FOR IT. DON'T DO IT!
SHE'S RUTHLESS.
DON'T WORRY! I AM WELL AWARE OF HER STRENGTHS!
AS WELL AS
この3人の強さもね
THE STRENGTH OF THESE THREE!!
WOW!!
どよ
WHOA
WHAT'S THAT?

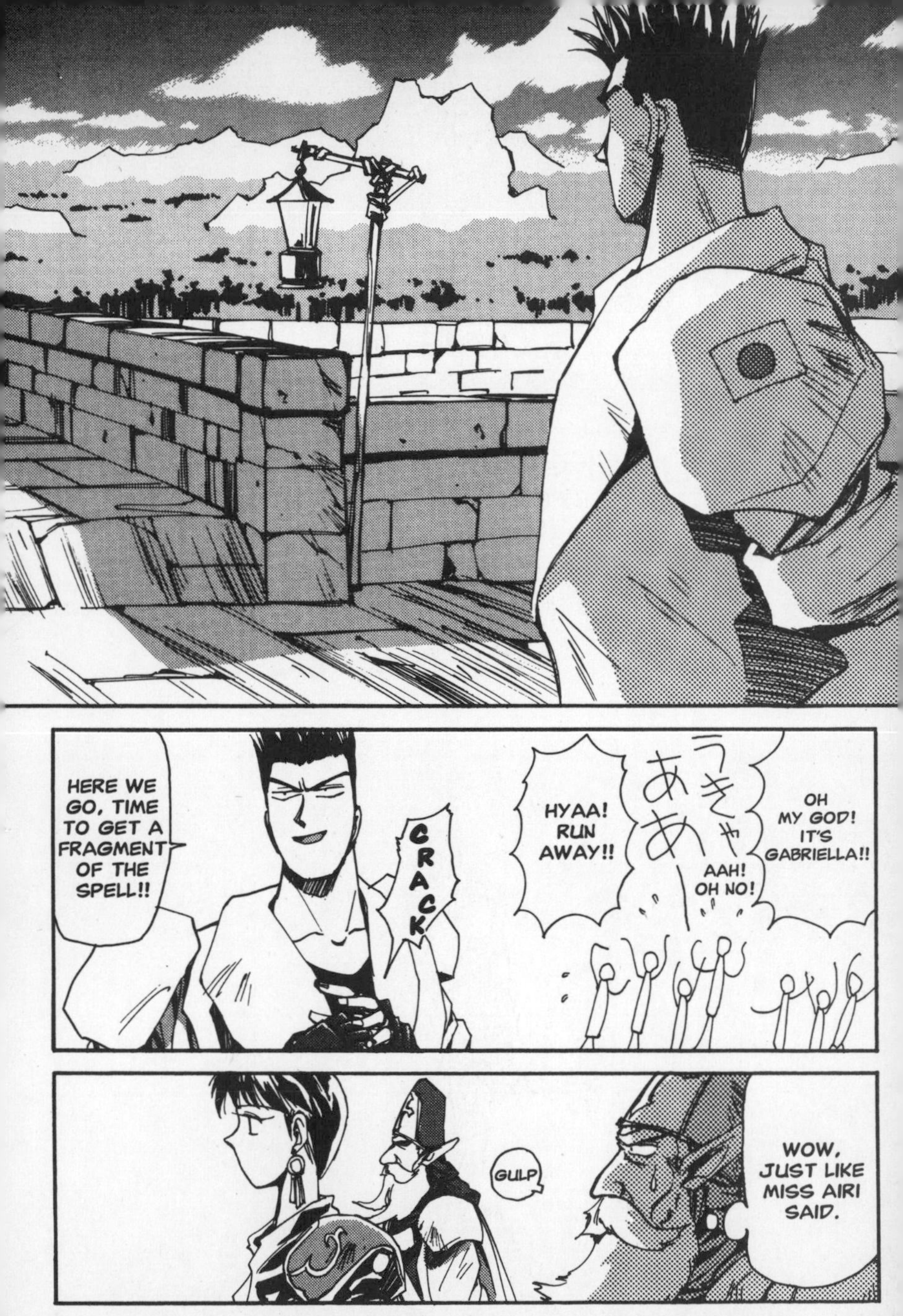
HERE WE GO, TIME TO GET A FRAGMENT OF THE SPELL!!
CRACK
HYAA! RUN AWAY!!
うきゃああ
AAH! OH NO!
OH MY GOD! IT'S GABRIELLA!!
GULP
WOW, JUST LIKE MISS AIRI SAID.

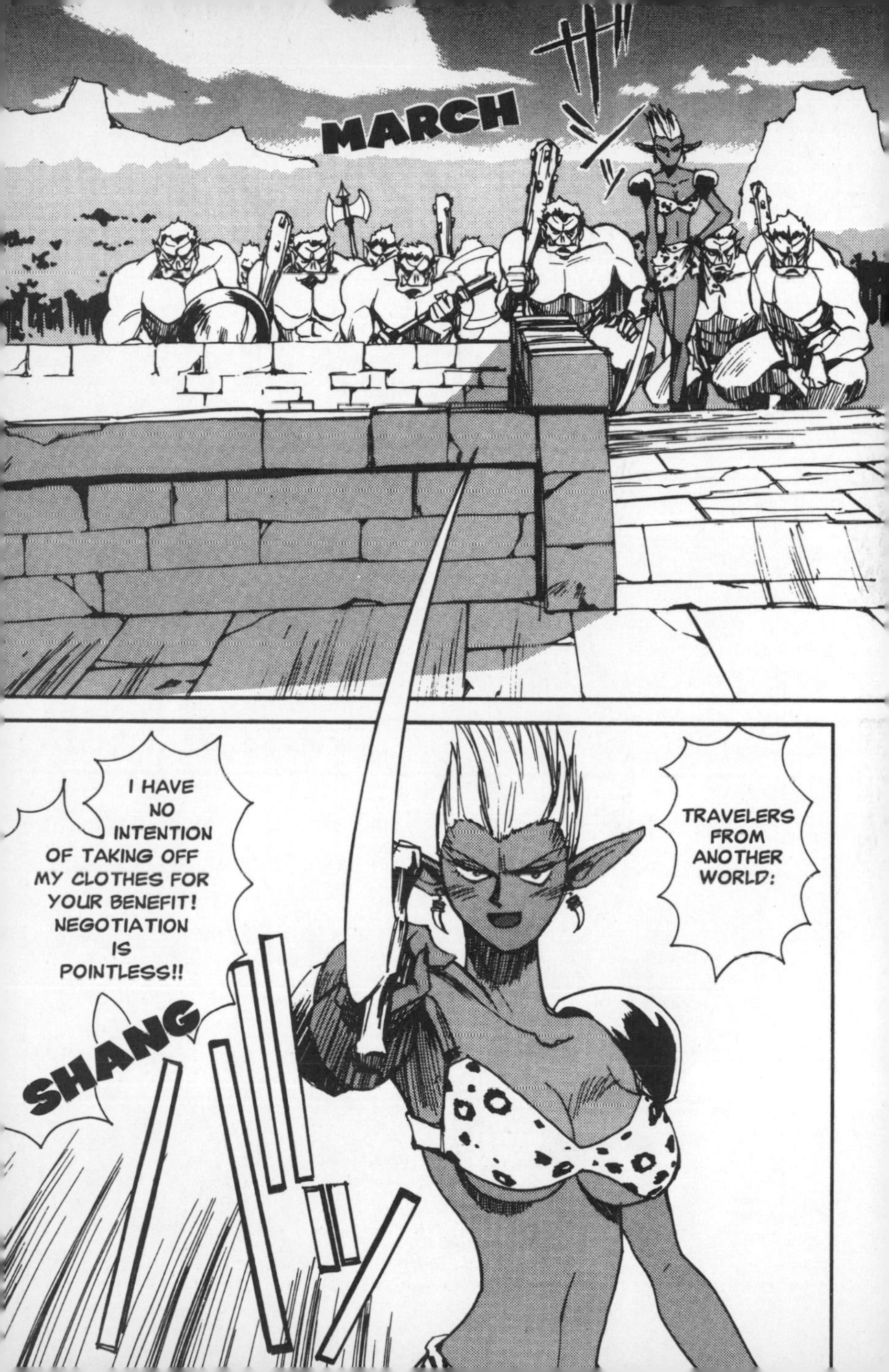
MARCH
TRAVELERS FROM ANOTHER WORLD:
I HAVE NO INTENTION OF TAKING OFF MY CLOTHES FOR YOUR BENEFIT! NEGOTIATION IS POINTLESS!!
SHANG

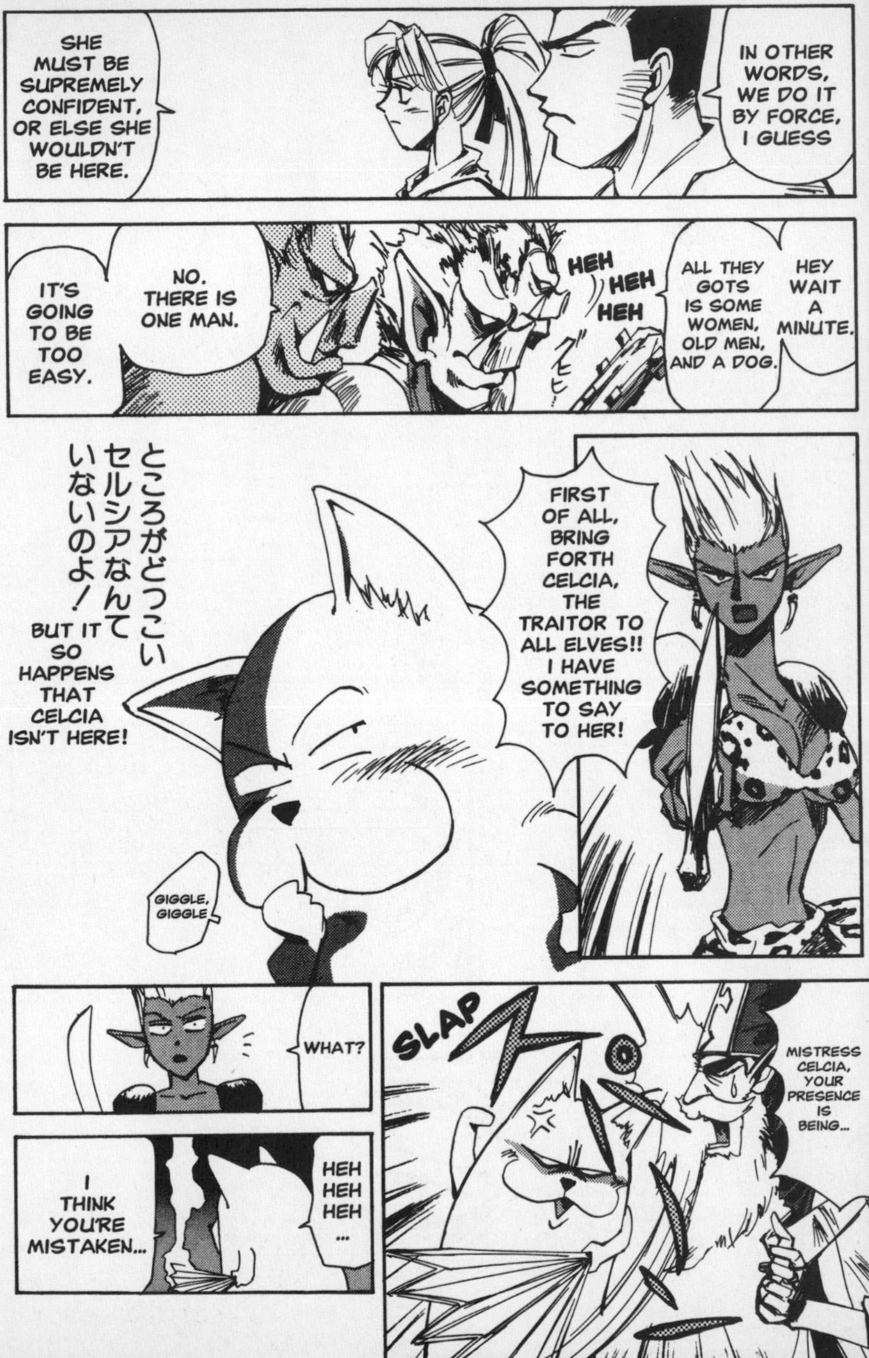
SHE MUST BE SUPREMELY CONFIDENT, OR ELSE SHE WOULDN'T BE HERE.
IN OTHER WORDS, WE DO IT BY FORCE, I GUESS
IT'S GOING TO BE TOO EASY.
NO. THERE IS ONE MAN.
HEH HEH HEH
ALL THEY GOTS IS SOME WOMEN, OLD MEN, AND A DOG.
HEY WAIT A MINUTE.
ところがどっこいセルシアなんていないのよ！
BUT IT SO HAPPENS THAT CELCIA ISN'T HERE!
FIRST OF ALL, BRING FORTH CELCIA, THE TRAITOR TO ALL ELVES!! I HAVE SOMETHING TO SAY TO HER!
GIGGLE, GIGGLE
WHAT?
I THINK YOU'RE MISTAKEN...
HEH HEH HEH ...
SLAP
MISTRESS CELCIA, YOUR PRESENCE IS BEING...

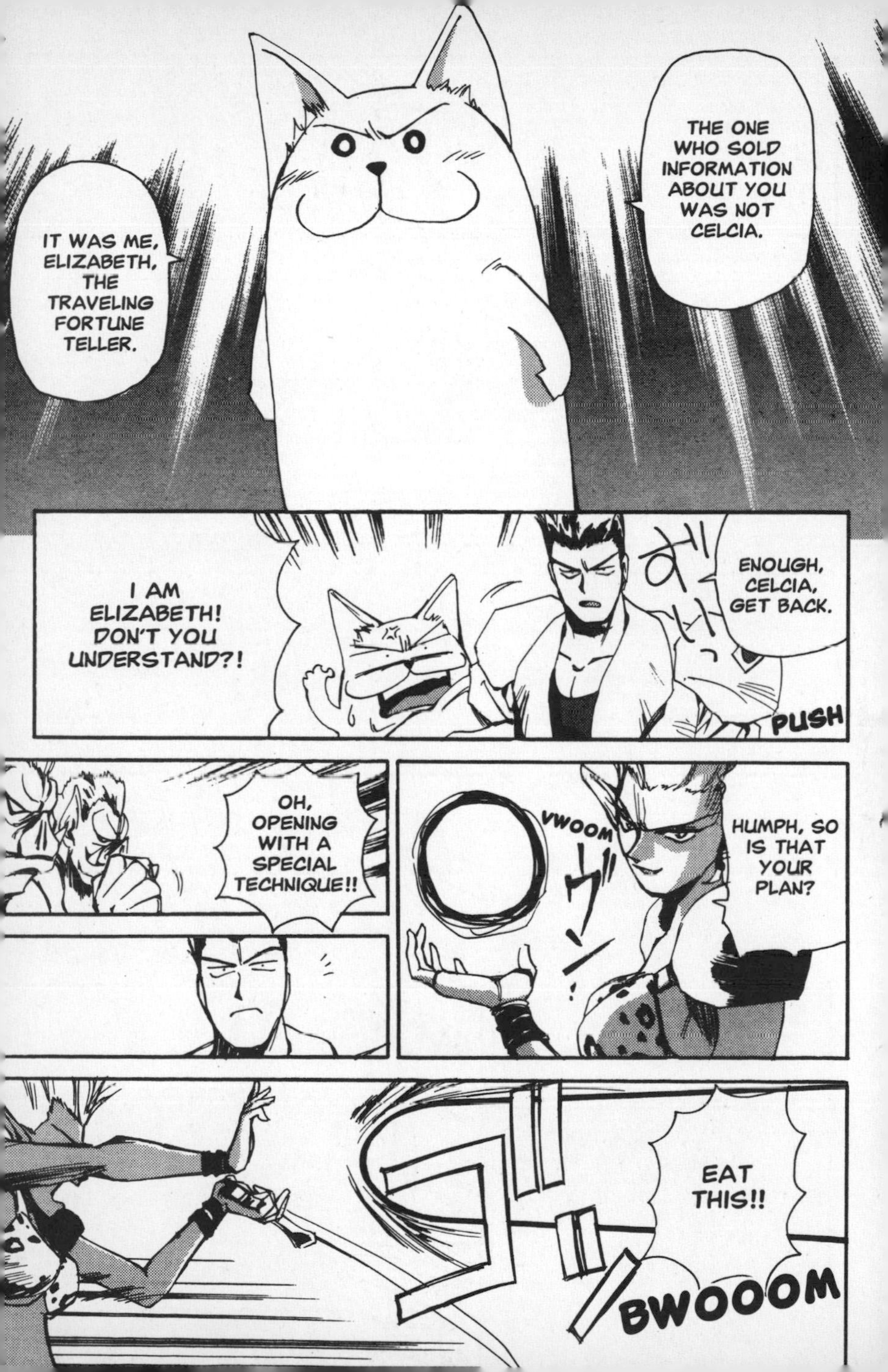
THE ONE WHO SOLD INFORMATION ABOUT YOU WAS NOT CELCIA.
IT WAS ME, ELIZABETH, THE TRAVELING FORTUNE TELLER.
ENOUGH, CELCIA, GET BACK.
PUSH
I AM ELIZABETH! DON'T YOU UNDERSTAND?!
HUMPH, SO IS THAT YOUR PLAN?
VWOOM
OH, OPENING WITH A SPECIAL TECHNIQUE!!
EAT THIS!!
BWOOOM

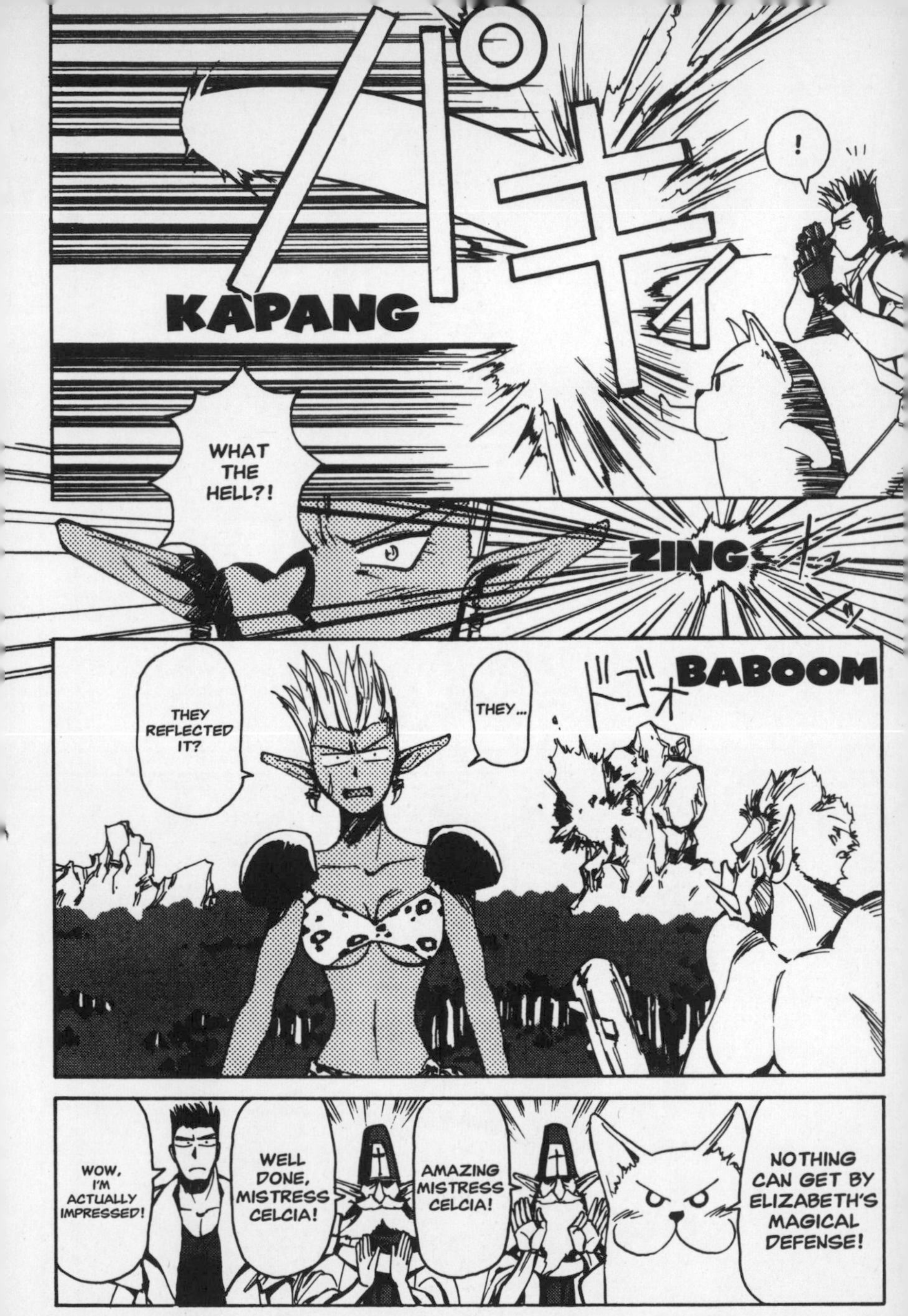
KAPANG
!
WHAT THE HELL?!
ZING
BABOOM
THEY...
THEY REFLECTED IT?
NOTHING CAN GET BY ELIZABETH'S MAGICAL DEFENSE!
AMAZING MISTRESS CELCIA!
WELL DONE, MISTRESS CELCIA!
WOW, I'M ACTUALLY IMPRESSED!

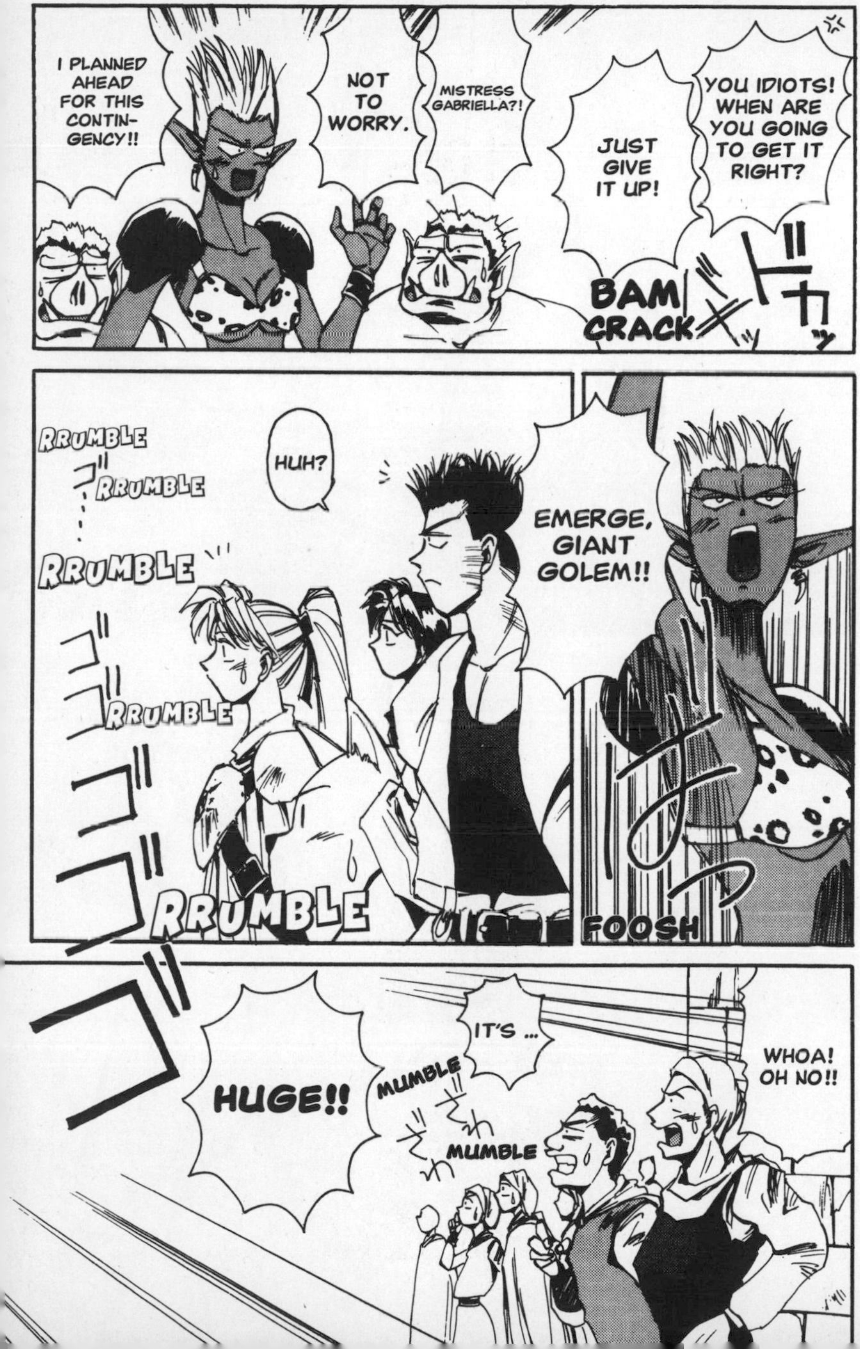
YOU IDIOTS! WHEN ARE YOU GOING TO GET IT RIGHT?
JUST GIVE IT UP!
BAM
CRACK
MISTRESS GABRIELLA?!
NOT TO WORRY.
I PLANNED AHEAD FOR THIS CONTIN-GENCY!!
EMERGE, GIANT GOLEM!!
FOOSH
HUH?
RRUMBLE
RRUMBLE
RRUMBLE
RRUMBLE
RRUMBLE
WHOA! OH NO!!
IT'S ...
MUMBLE
MUMBLE
HUGE!!

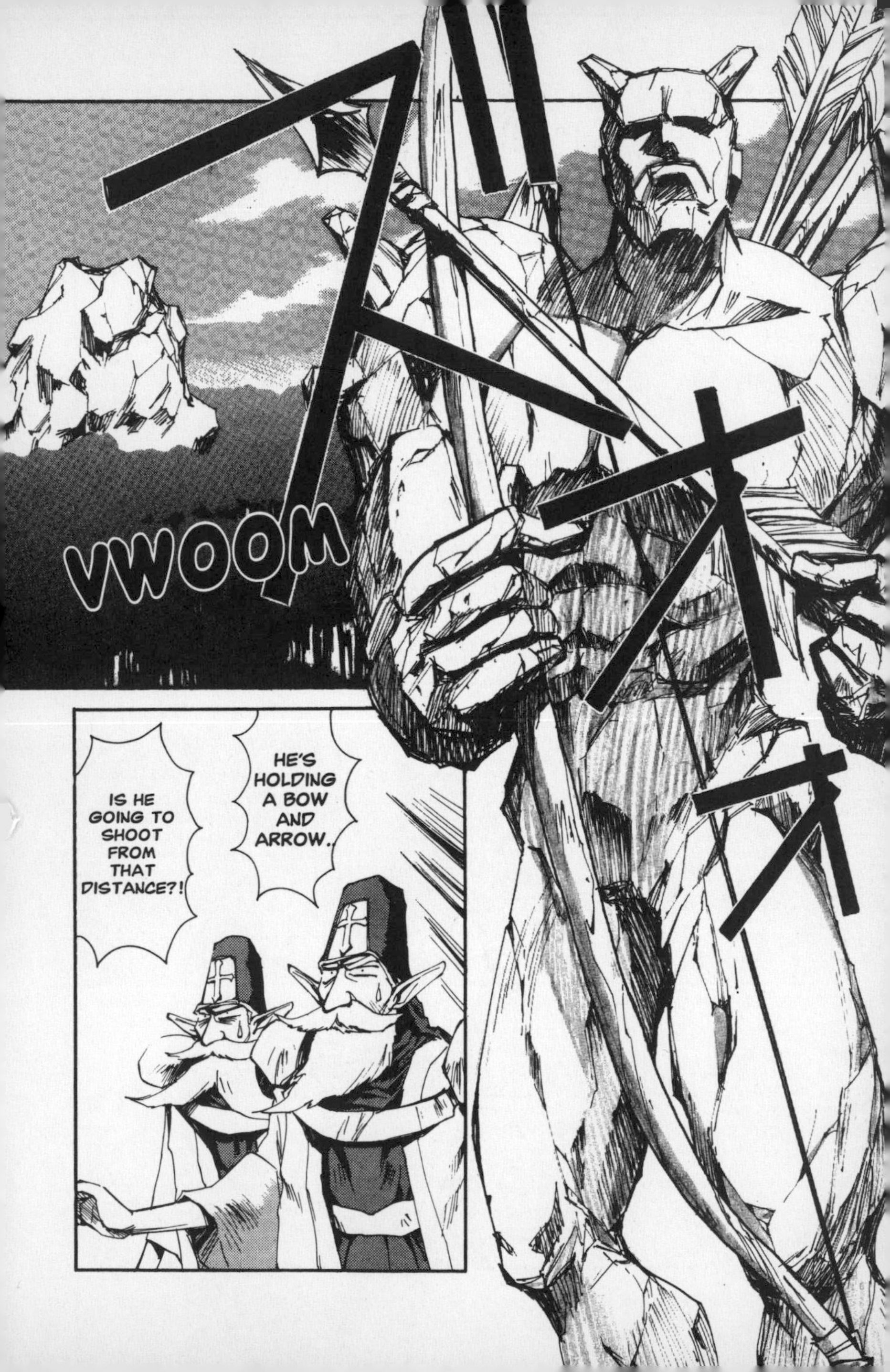
VWOOM
HE'S HOLDING A BOW AND ARROW..
IS HE GOING TO SHOOT FROM THAT DISTANCE?!

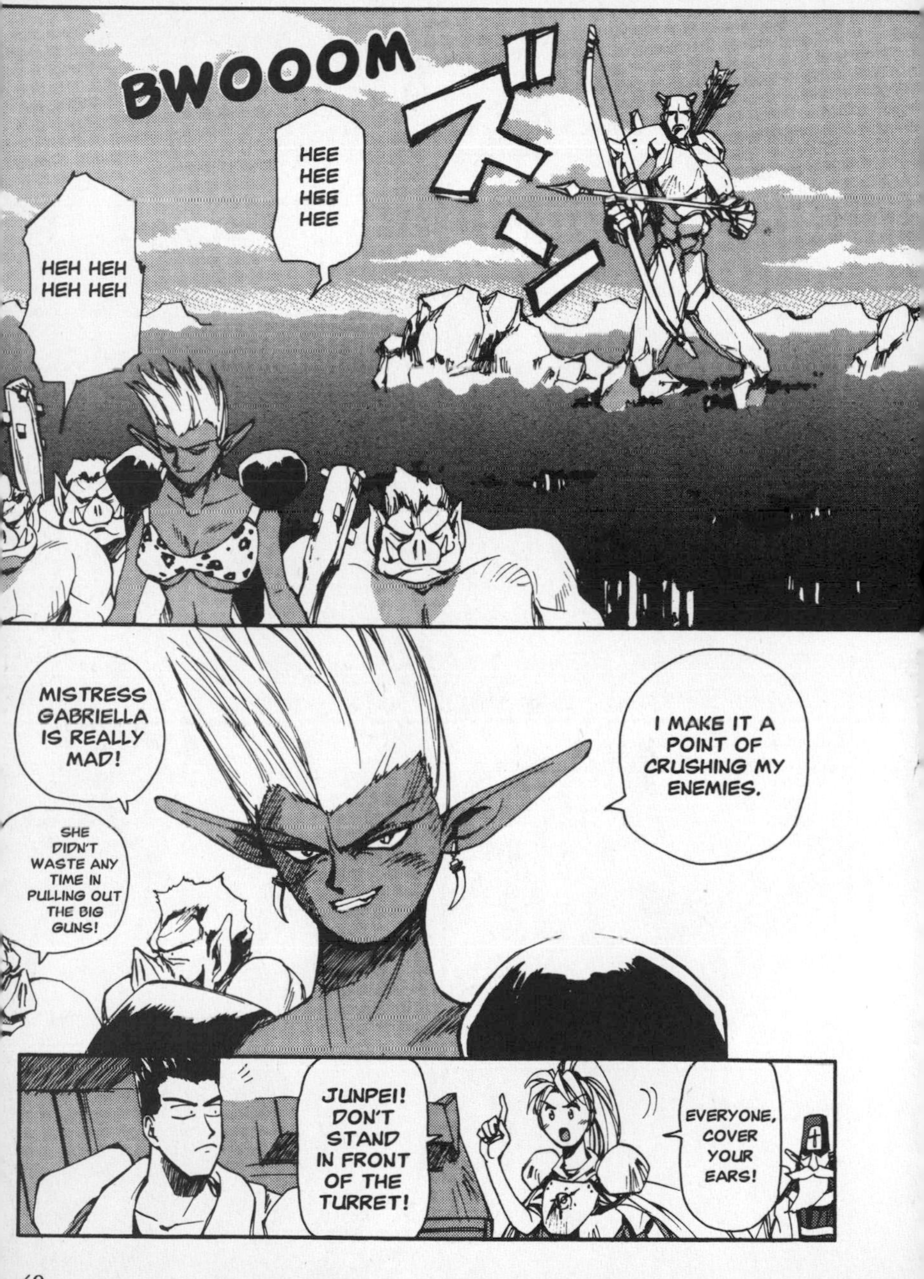
BWOOOM
HEH HEH HEH HEH
HEE HEE HEE HEE
MISTRESS GABRIELLA IS REALLY MAD!
SHE DIDN'T WASTE ANY TIME IN PULLING OUT THE BIG GUNS!
I MAKE IT A POINT OF CRUSHING MY ENEMIES.
JUNPEI! DON'T STAND IN FRONT OF THE TURRET!
EVERYONE, COVER YOUR EARS!

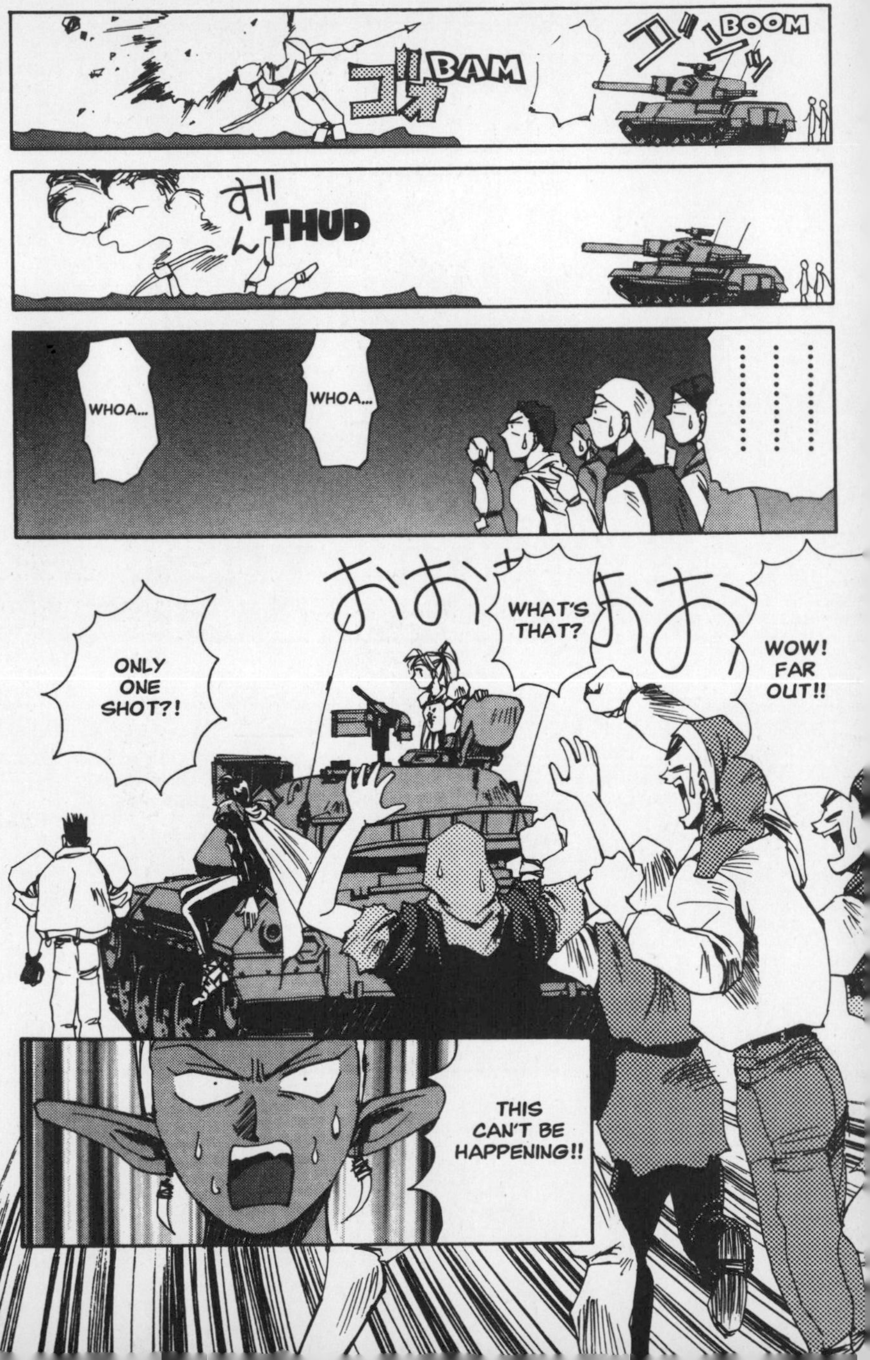
BOOM
BAM
ずん
THUD
......
WHOA...
WHOA...
WOW! FAR OUT!!
おお
WHAT'S THAT?
おお
ONLY ONE SHOT?!
THIS CAN'T BE HAPPENING!!

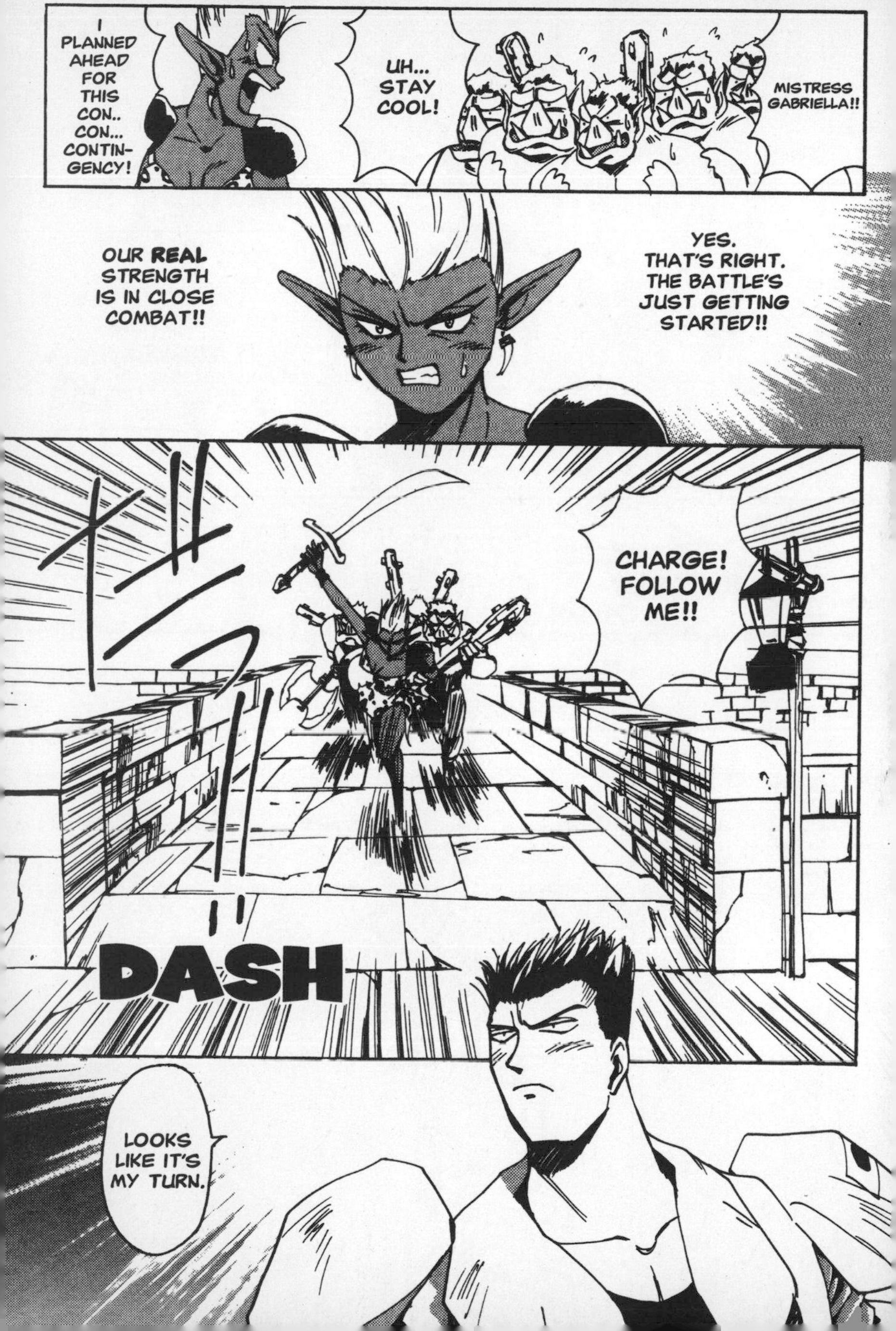
I PLANNED AHEAD FOR THIS CON.. CON... CONTIN-GENCY!
UH... STAY COOL!
MISTRESS GABRIELLA!!
OUR REAL STRENGTH IS IN CLOSE COMBAT!!
YES. THAT'S RIGHT. THE BATTLE'S JUST GETTING STARTED!!
CHARGE! FOLLOW ME!!
DASH
LOOKS LIKE IT'S MY TURN.

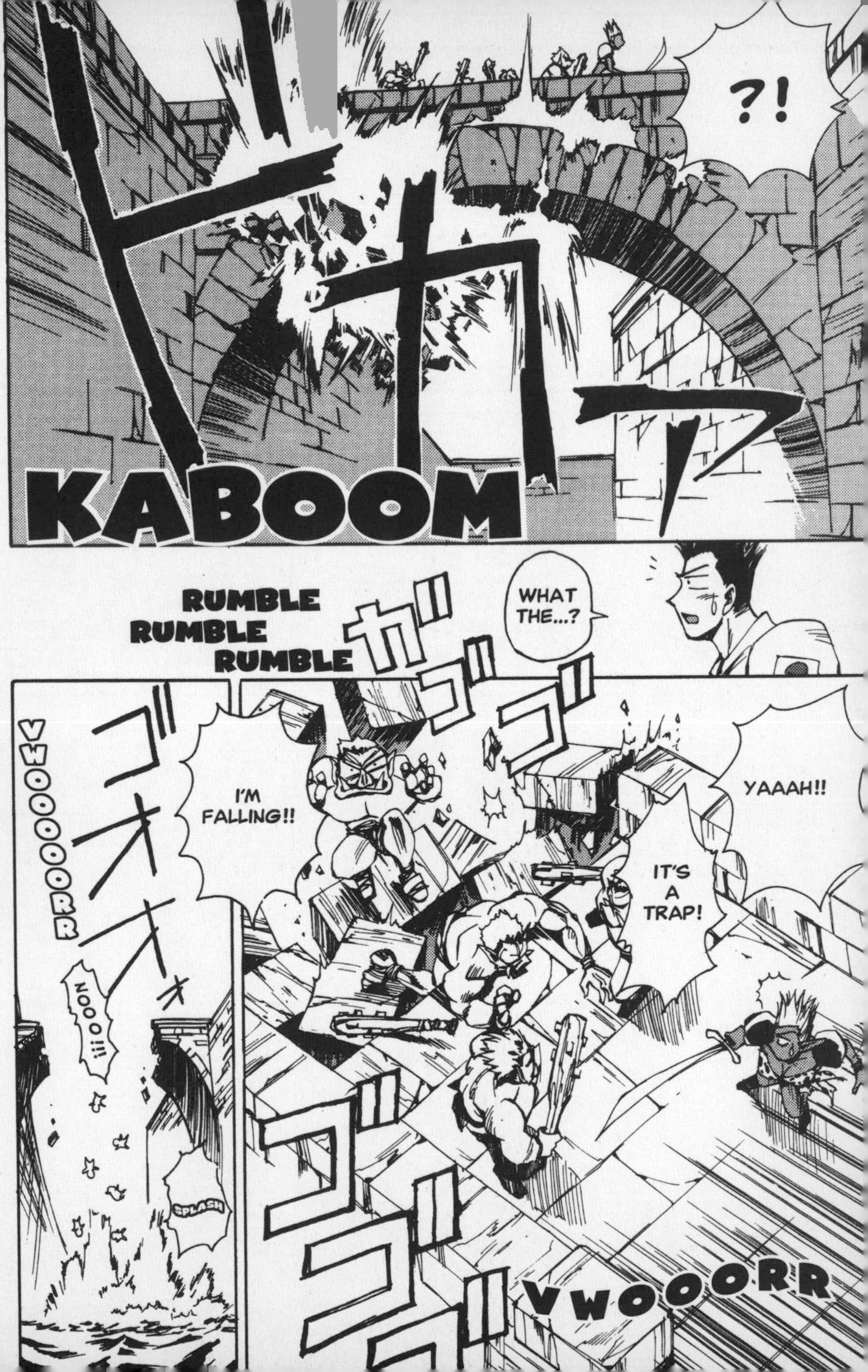
?!
KABOOM
WHAT THE...?
RUMBLE
RUMBLE
RUMBLE
YAAAH!!
IT'S A TRAP!
I'M FALLING!!
VWOOORR
VWOOOOOORR
NOOOO!!!
SPLASH

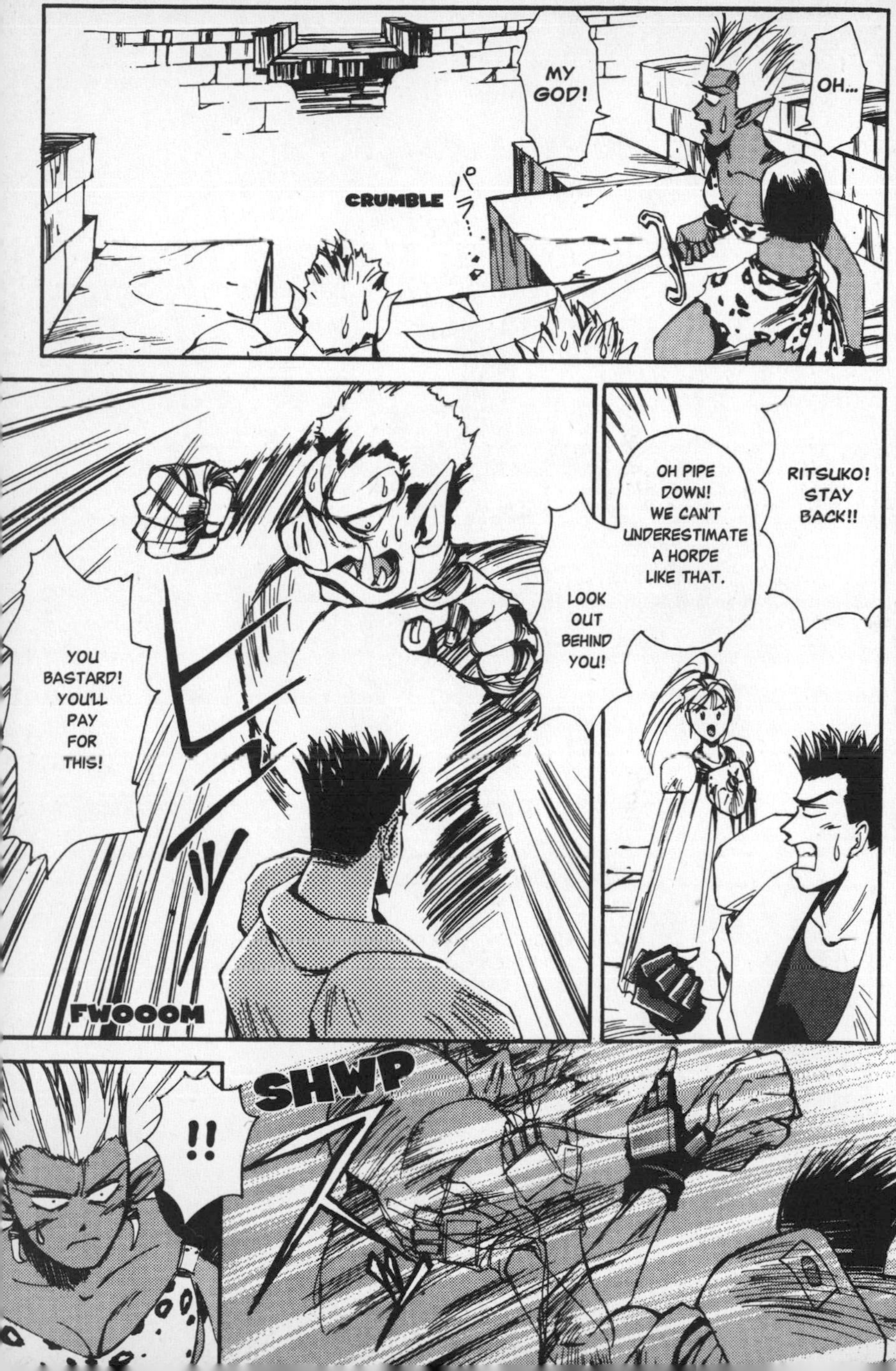
OH...
MY GOD!
CRUMBLE
パラ・・・
RITSUKO! STAY BACK!!
OH PIPE DOWN! WE CAN'T UNDERESTIMATE A HORDE LIKE THAT.
LOOK OUT BEHIND YOU!
YOU BASTARD! YOU'LL PAY FOR THIS!
FWOOOM
SHWP
!!

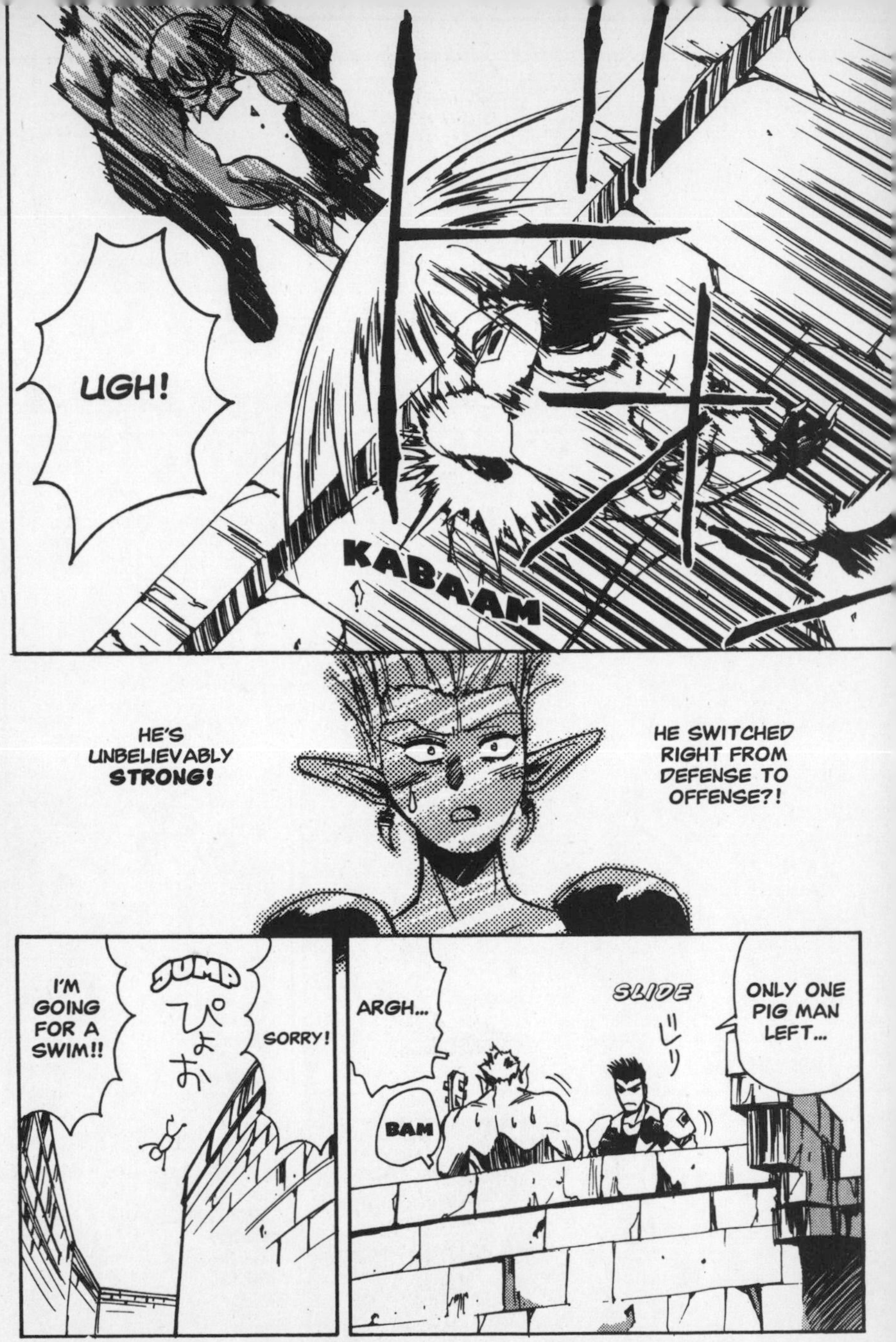
UGH!
KABAAM
HE'S UNBELIEVABLY STRONG!
HE SWITCHED RIGHT FROM DEFENSE TO OFFENSE?!
I'M GOING FOR A SWIM!!
JUMP
ぴょお
SORRY!
ARGH...
BAM
SLIDE
ジリ
ONLY ONE PIG MAN LEFT...

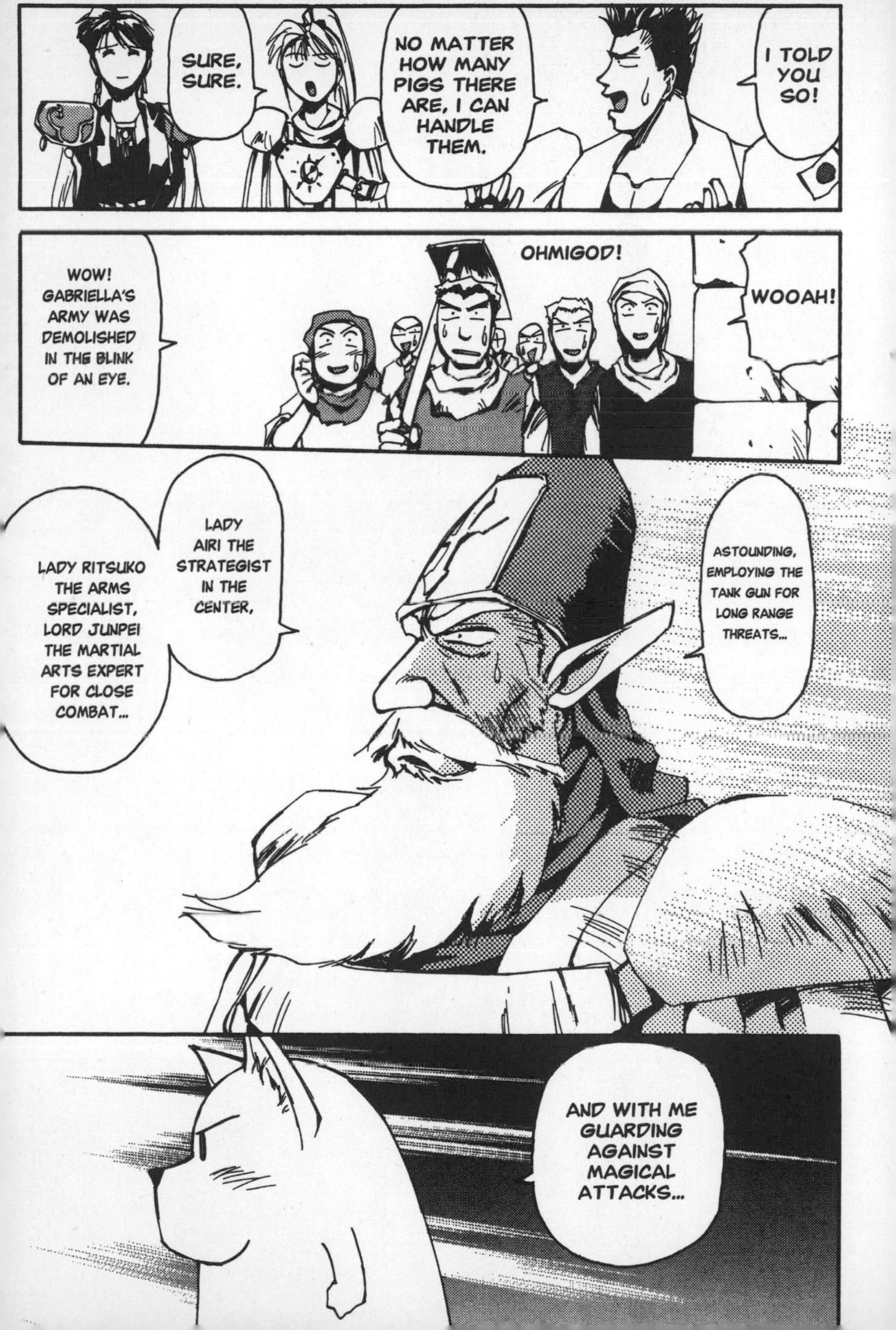
I TOLD YOU SO!
NO MATTER HOW MANY PIGS THERE ARE, I CAN HANDLE THEM.
SURE, SURE.
WOOAH!
OHMIGOD!
WOW! GABRIELLA'S ARMY WAS DEMOLISHED IN THE BLINK OF AN EYE.
ASTOUNDING, EMPLOYING THE TANK GUN FOR LONG RANGE THREATS...
LADY AIRI THE STRATEGIST IN THE CENTER,
LADY RITSUKO THE ARMS SPECIALIST, LORD JUNPEI THE MARTIAL ARTS EXPERT FOR CLOSE COMBAT...
AND WITH ME GUARDING AGAINST MAGICAL ATTACKS...

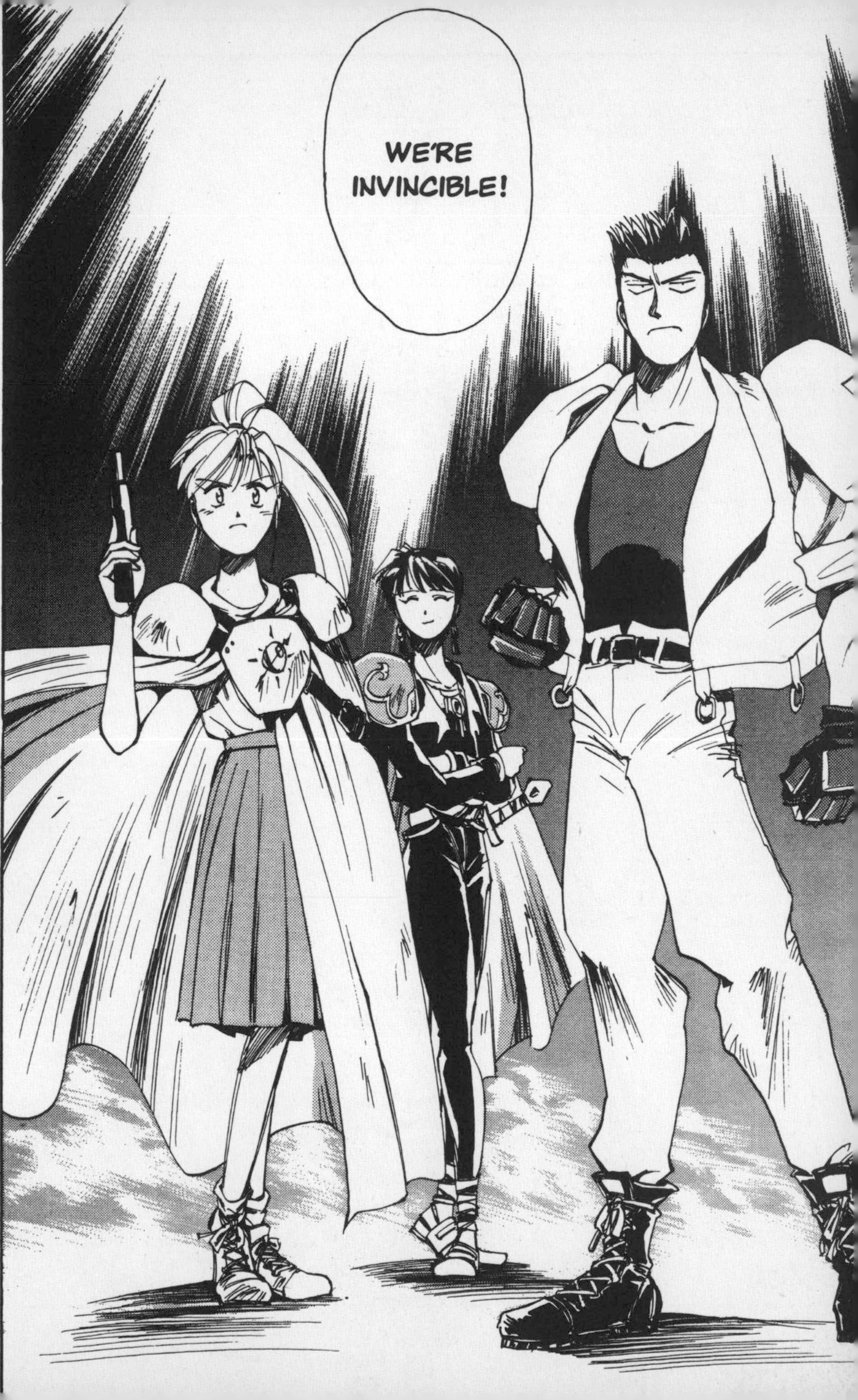
WE'RE
INVINCIBLE!

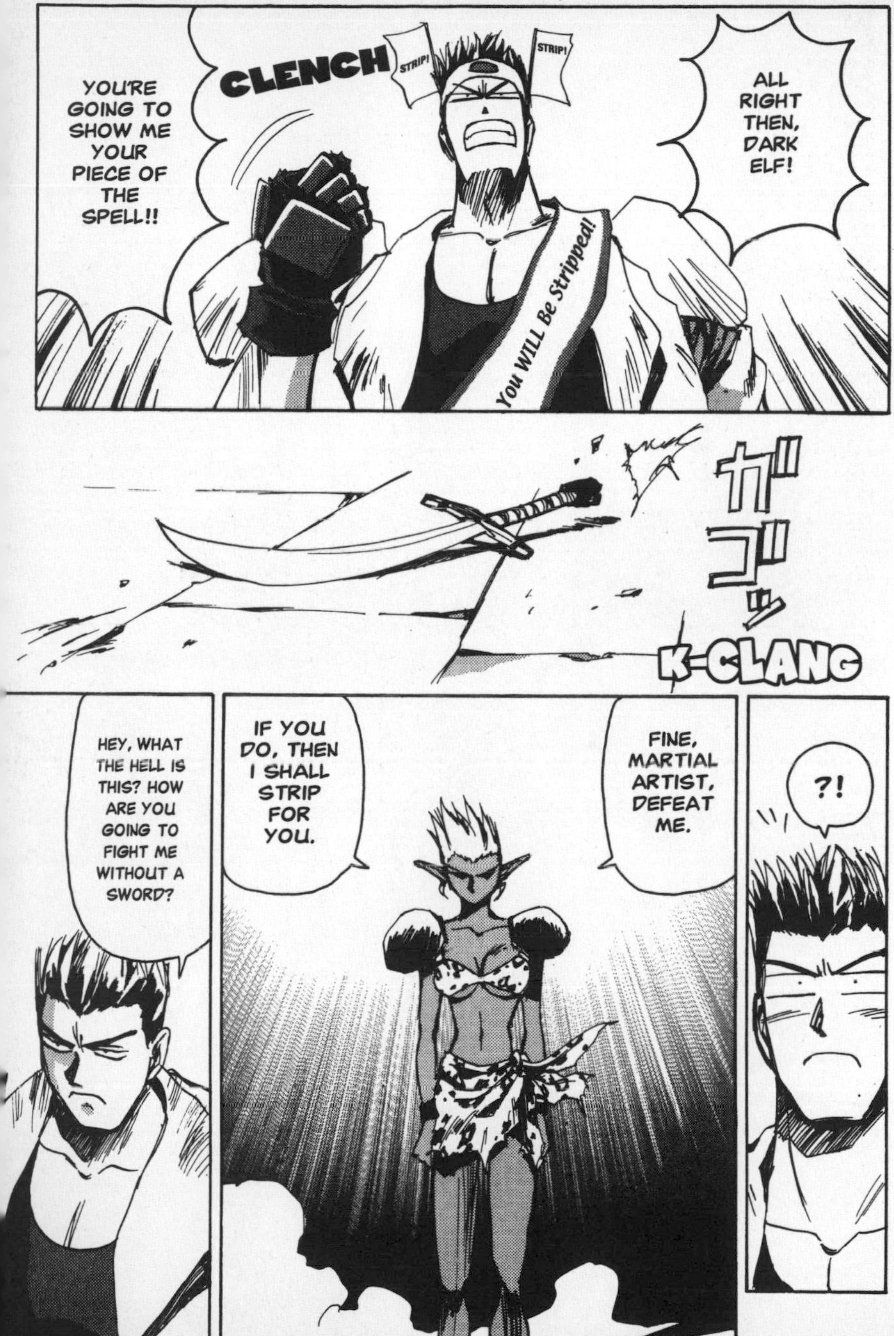
ALL RIGHT THEN, DARK ELF!
CLENCH
STRIP!
STRIP!
YOU'RE GOING TO SHOW ME YOUR PIECE OF THE SPELL!!
You WILL Be Stripped!
ガゴッ
K-CLANG
?!
FINE, MARTIAL ARTIST, DEFEAT ME.
IF YOU DO, THEN I SHALL STRIP FOR YOU.
HEY, WHAT THE HELL IS THIS? HOW ARE YOU GOING TO FIGHT ME WITHOUT A SWORD?

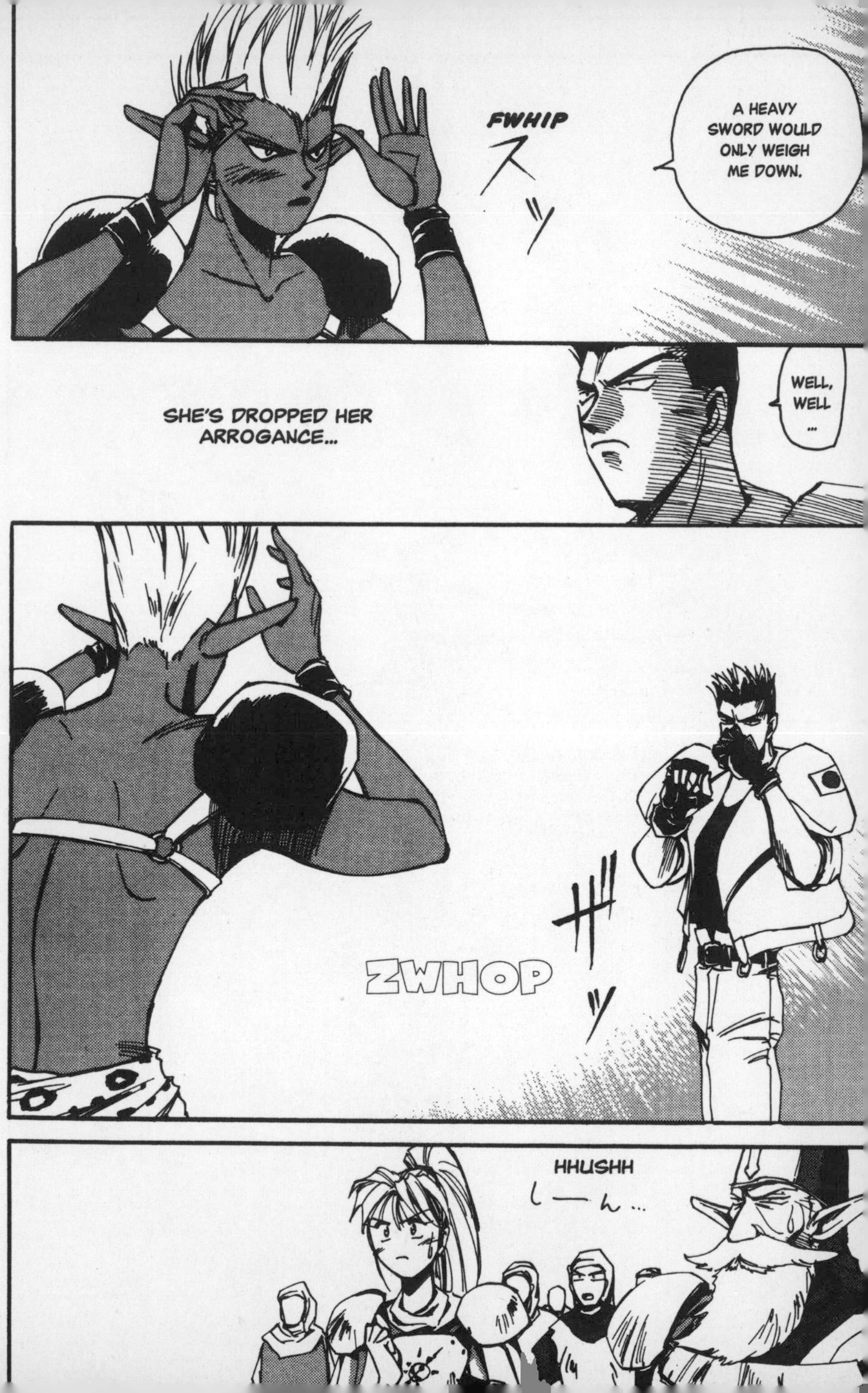
A HEAVY SWORD WOULD ONLY WEIGH ME DOWN.
FWHIP
ス
ッ
WELL, WELL ...
SHE'S DROPPED HER ARROGANCE...
ZWHOP
HHUSHH
しーん...

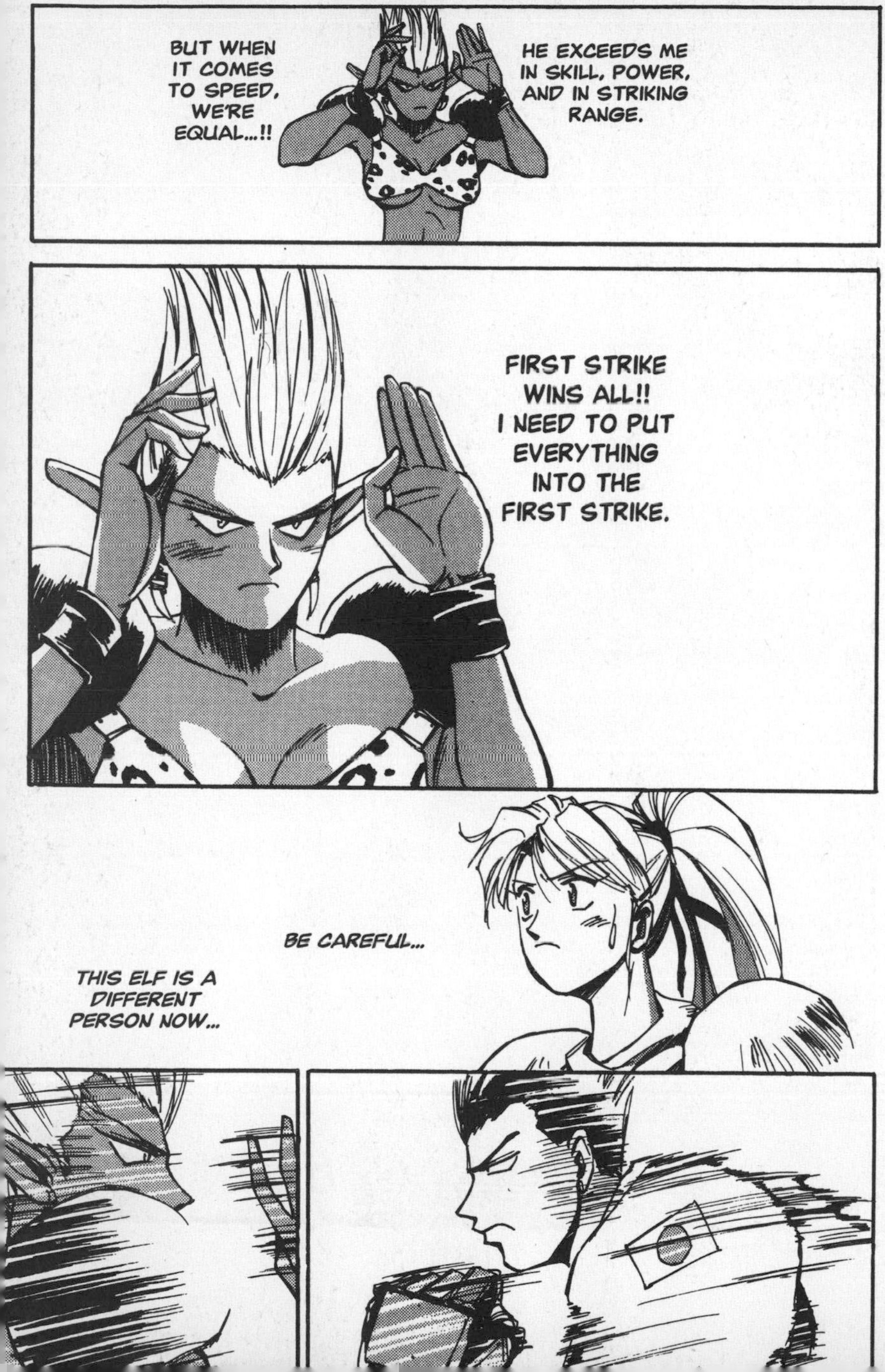
HE EXCEEDS ME IN SKILL, POWER, AND IN STRIKING RANGE.
BUT WHEN IT COMES TO SPEED, WE'RE EQUAL...!!
FIRST STRIKE WINS ALL!! I NEED TO PUT EVERYTHING INTO THE FIRST STRIKE.
BE CAREFUL...
THIS ELF IS A DIFFERENT PERSON NOW...

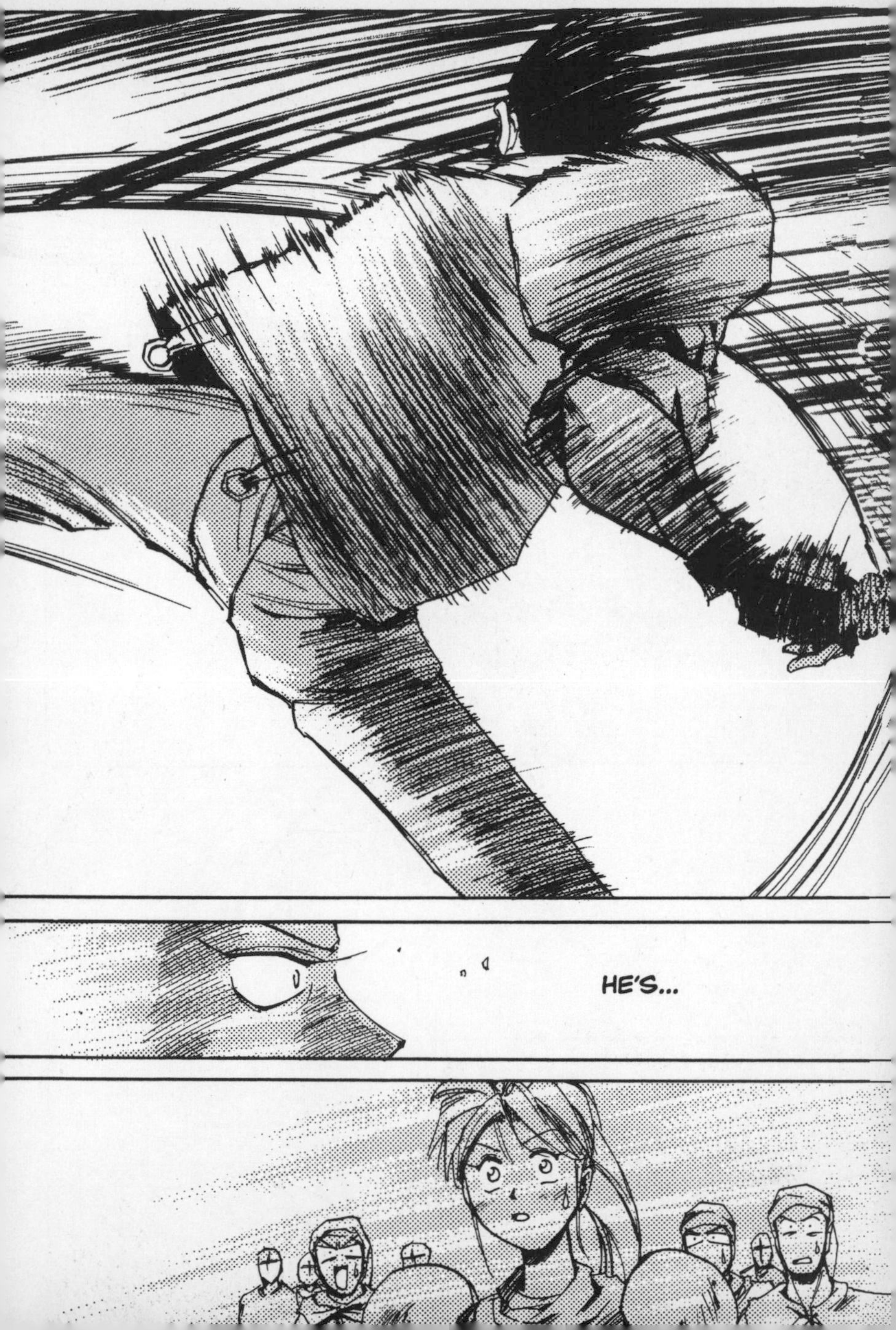
HE'S...

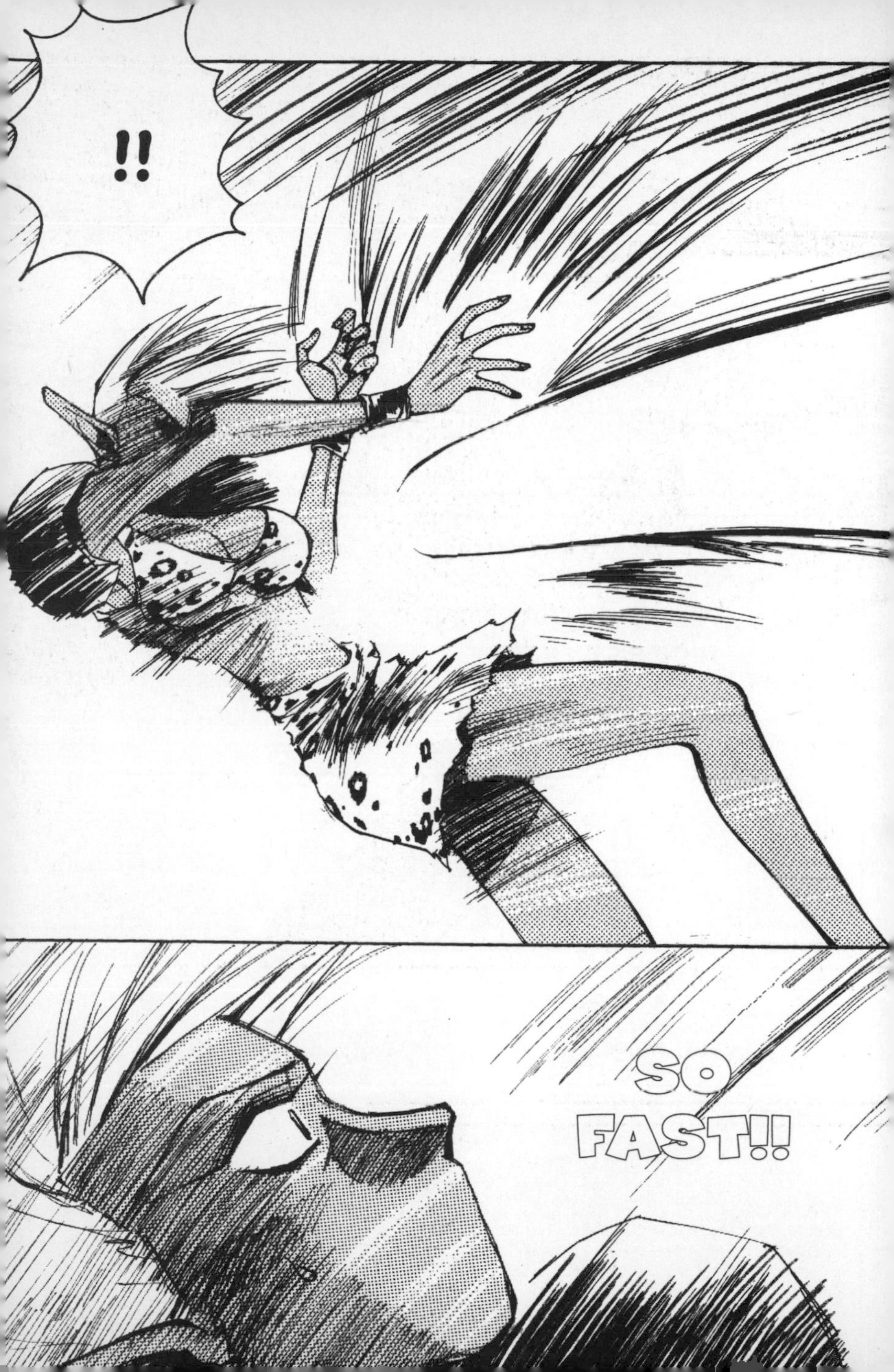
!!
SO FAST!!

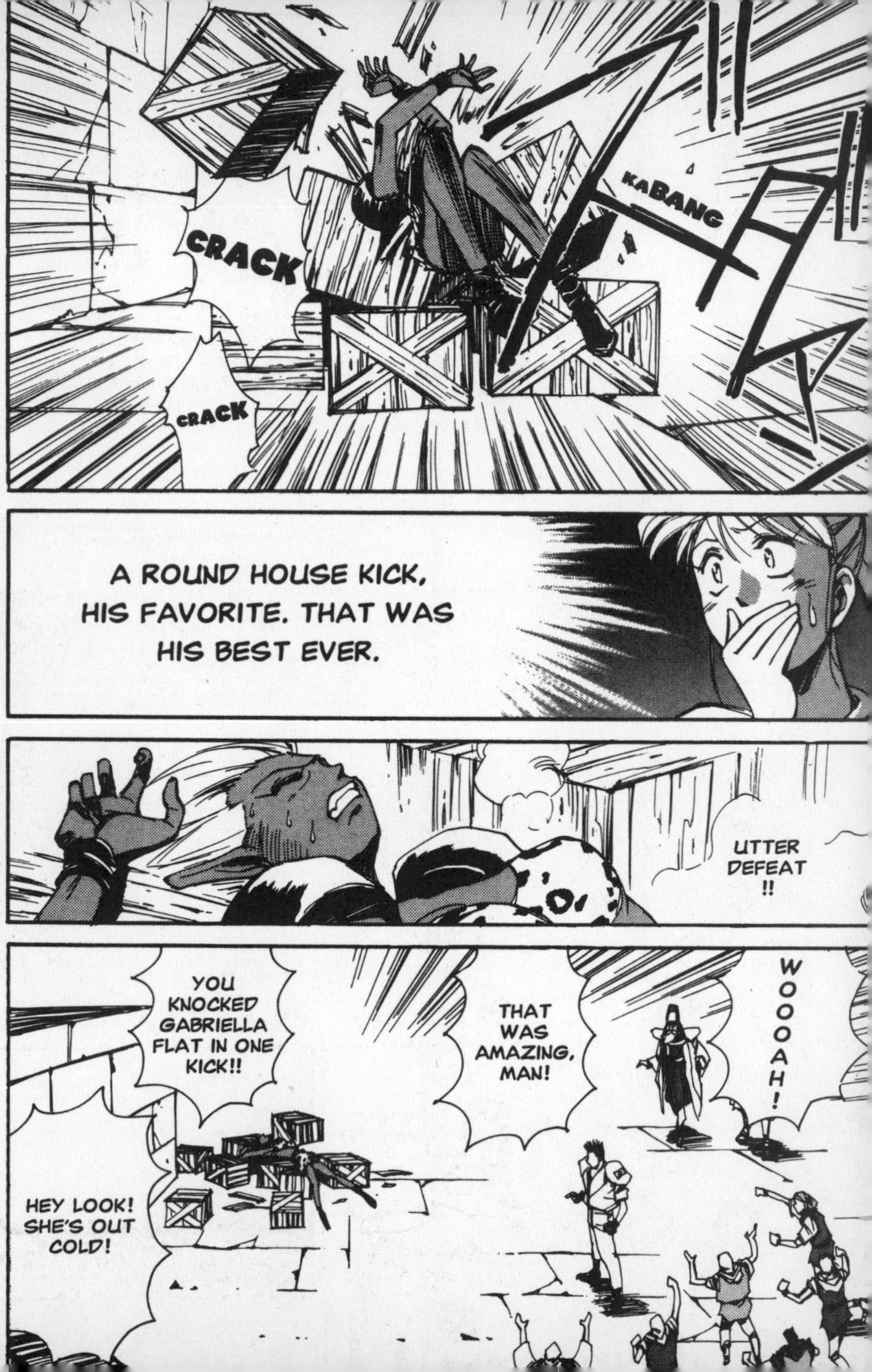
CRACK
CRACK
KABANG
A ROUND HOUSE KICK, HIS FAVORITE. THAT WAS HIS BEST EVER.
UTTER DEFEAT !!
YOU KNOCKED GABRIELLA FLAT IN ONE KICK!!
THAT WAS AMAZING, MAN!
WOOOOAH!
HEY LOOK! SHE'S OUT COLD!

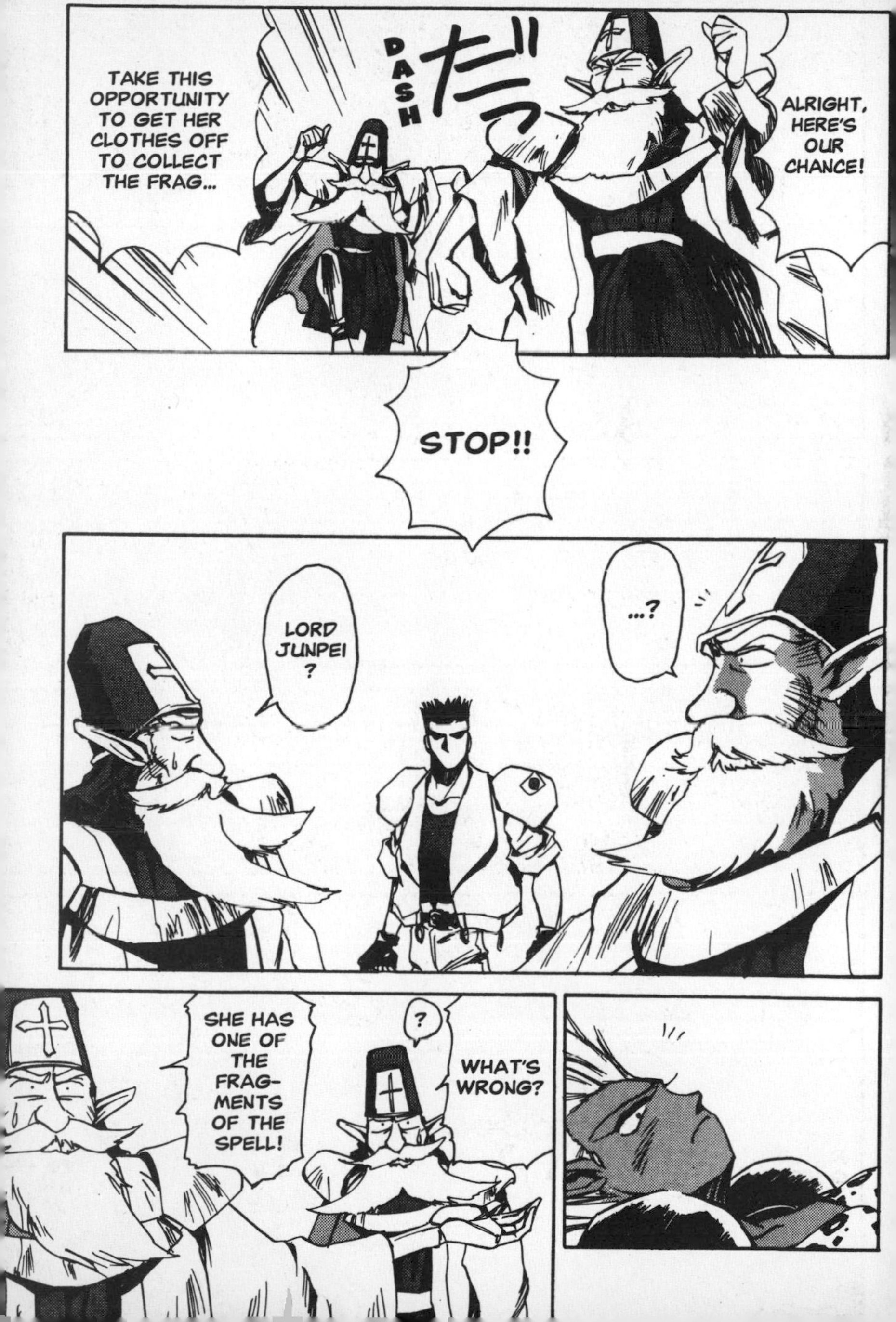
ALRIGHT, HERE'S OUR CHANCE!
DASH
TAKE THIS OPPORTUNITY TO GET HER CLOTHES OFF TO COLLECT THE FRAG...
STOP!!
...?
LORD JUNPEI ?
?
WHAT'S WRONG?
SHE HAS ONE OF THE FRAG-MENTS OF THE SPELL!

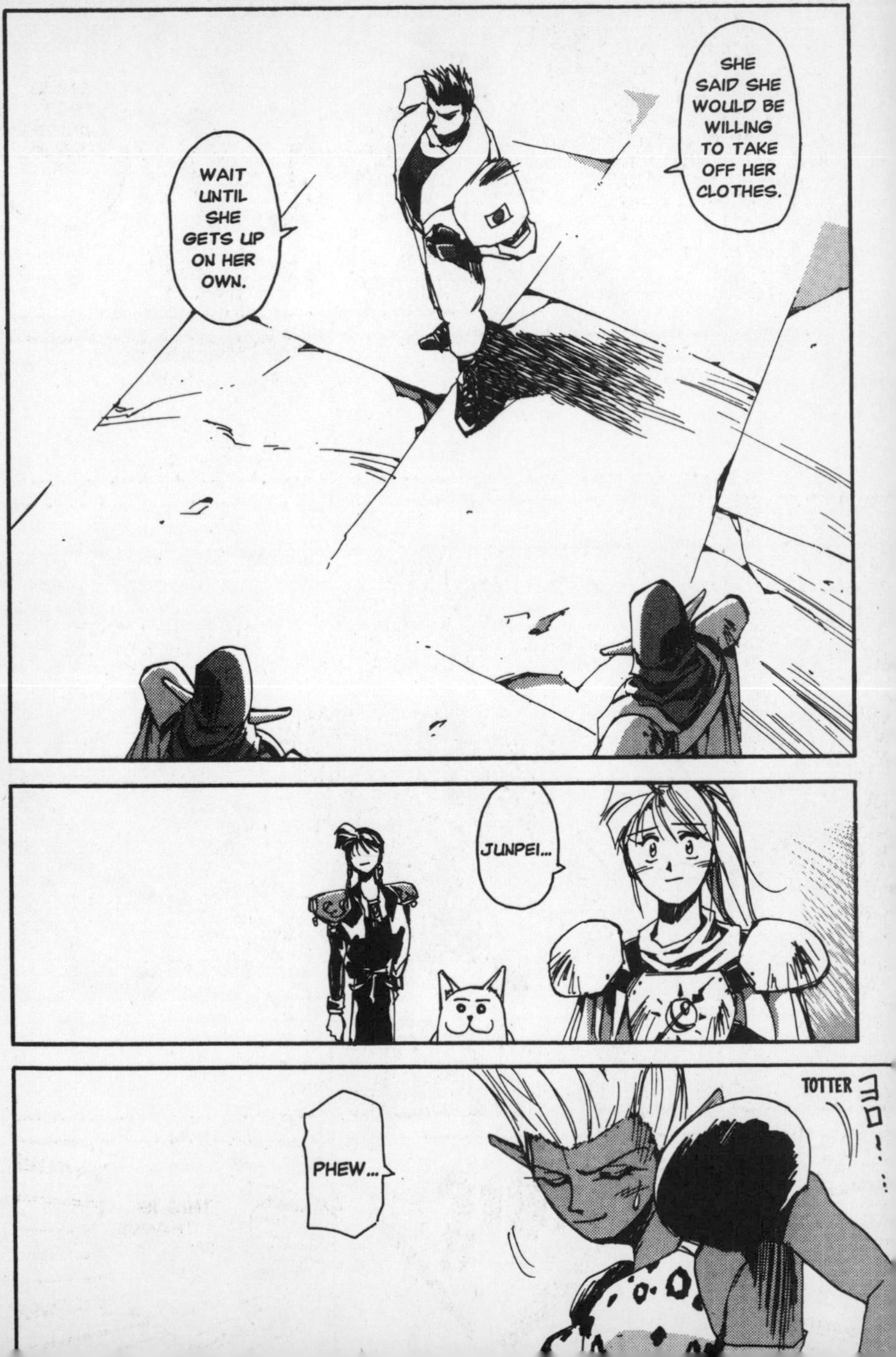
SHE SAID SHE WOULD BE WILLING TO TAKE OFF HER CLOTHES.
WAIT UNTIL SHE GETS UP ON HER OWN.
JUNPEI...
TOTTER
PHEW...

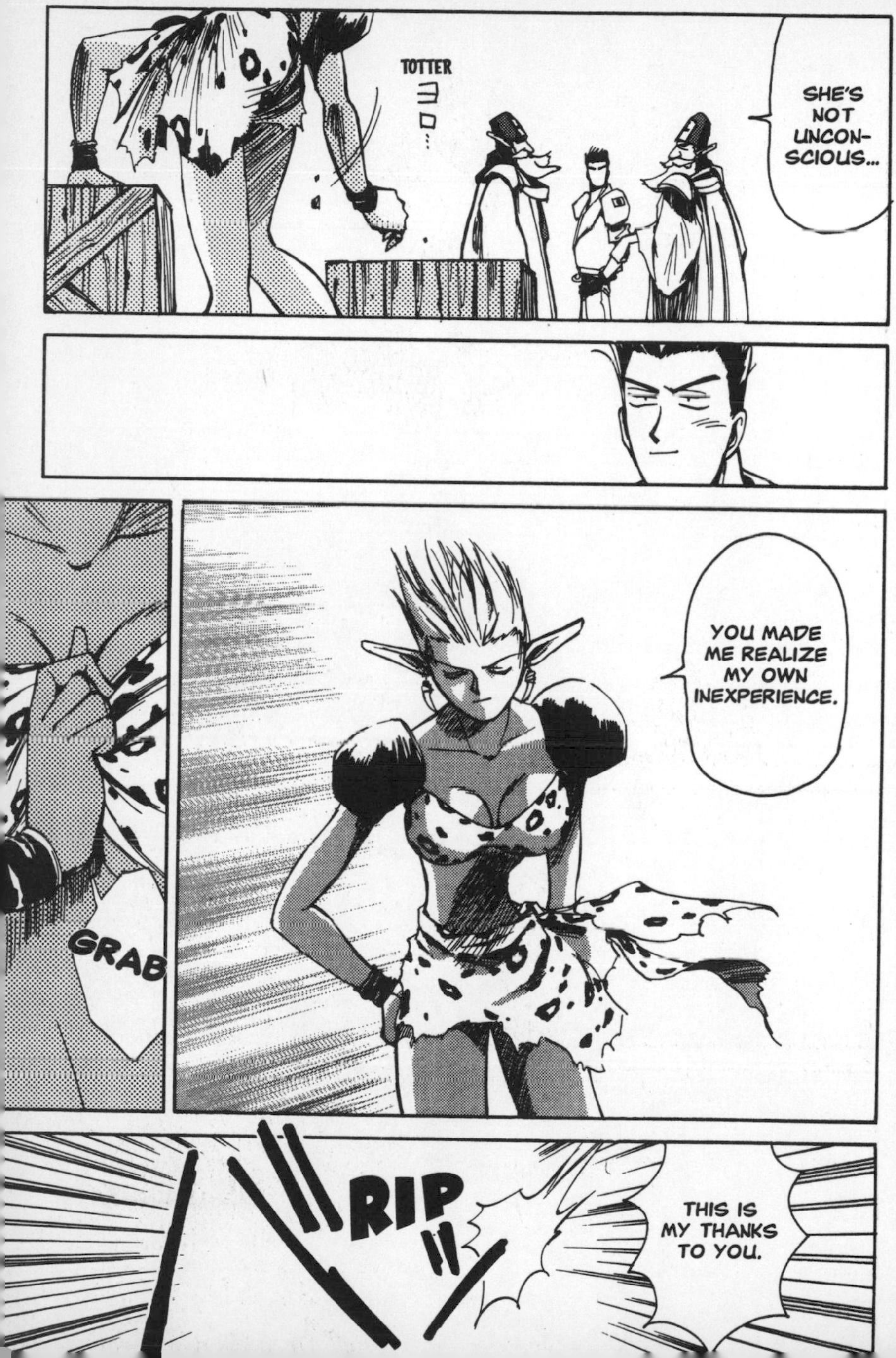
SHE'S NOT UNCON-SCIOUS...
TOTTER
ヨロ...
YOU MADE ME REALIZE MY OWN INEXPERIENCE.
GRAB
THIS IS MY THANKS TO YOU.
RIP!!

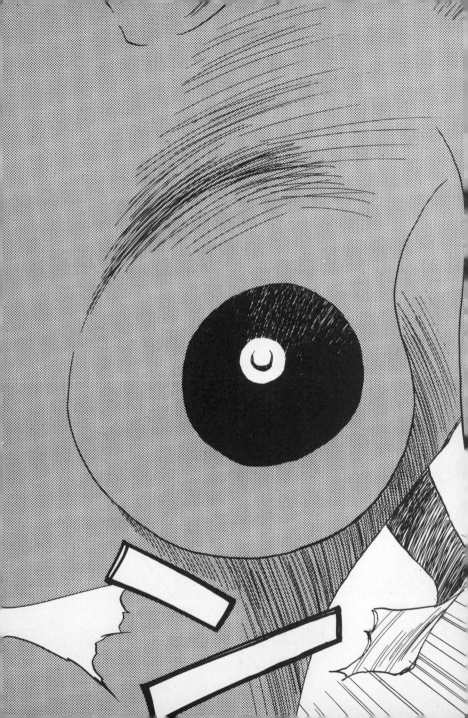

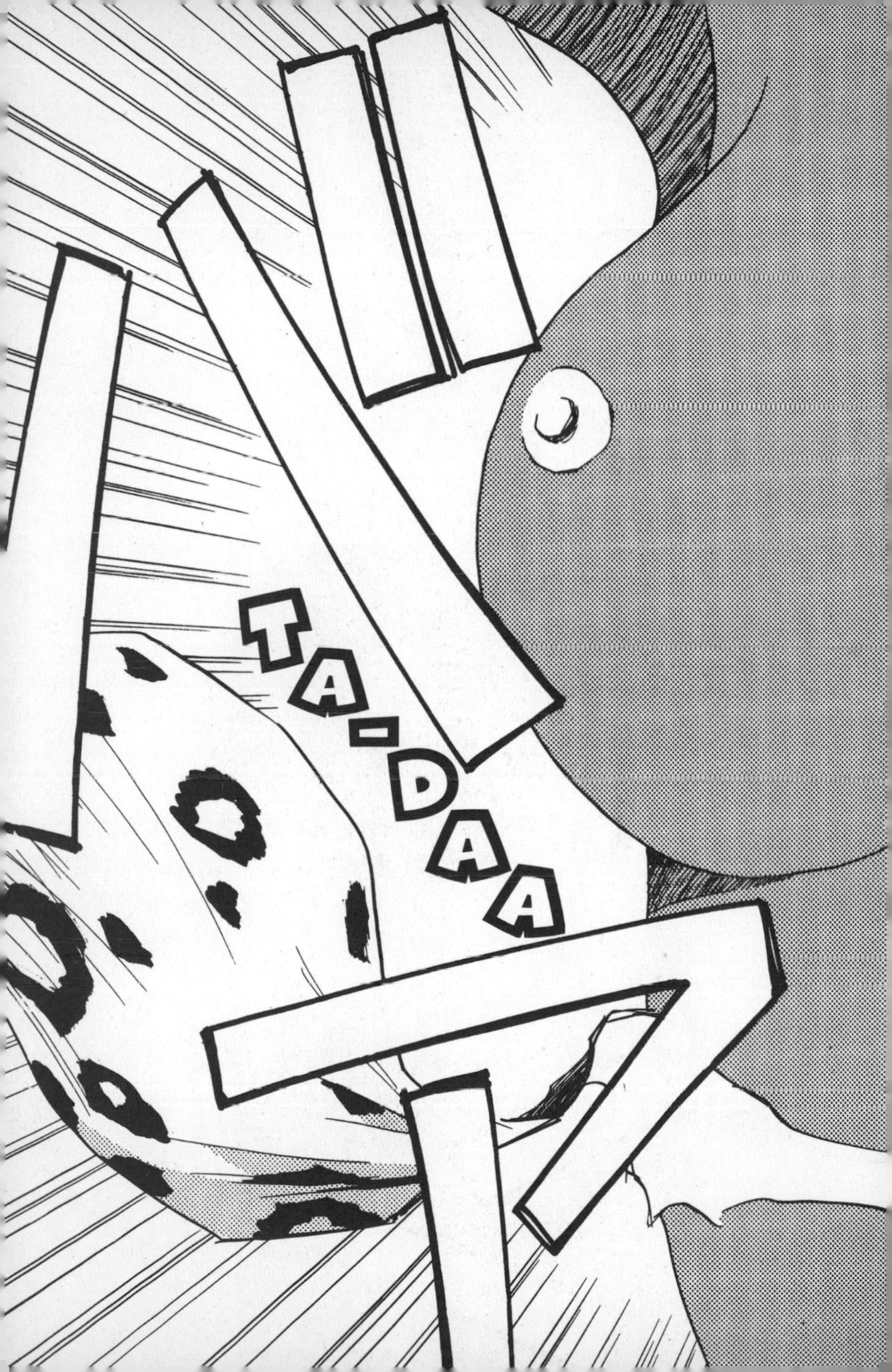
TA-DAAA

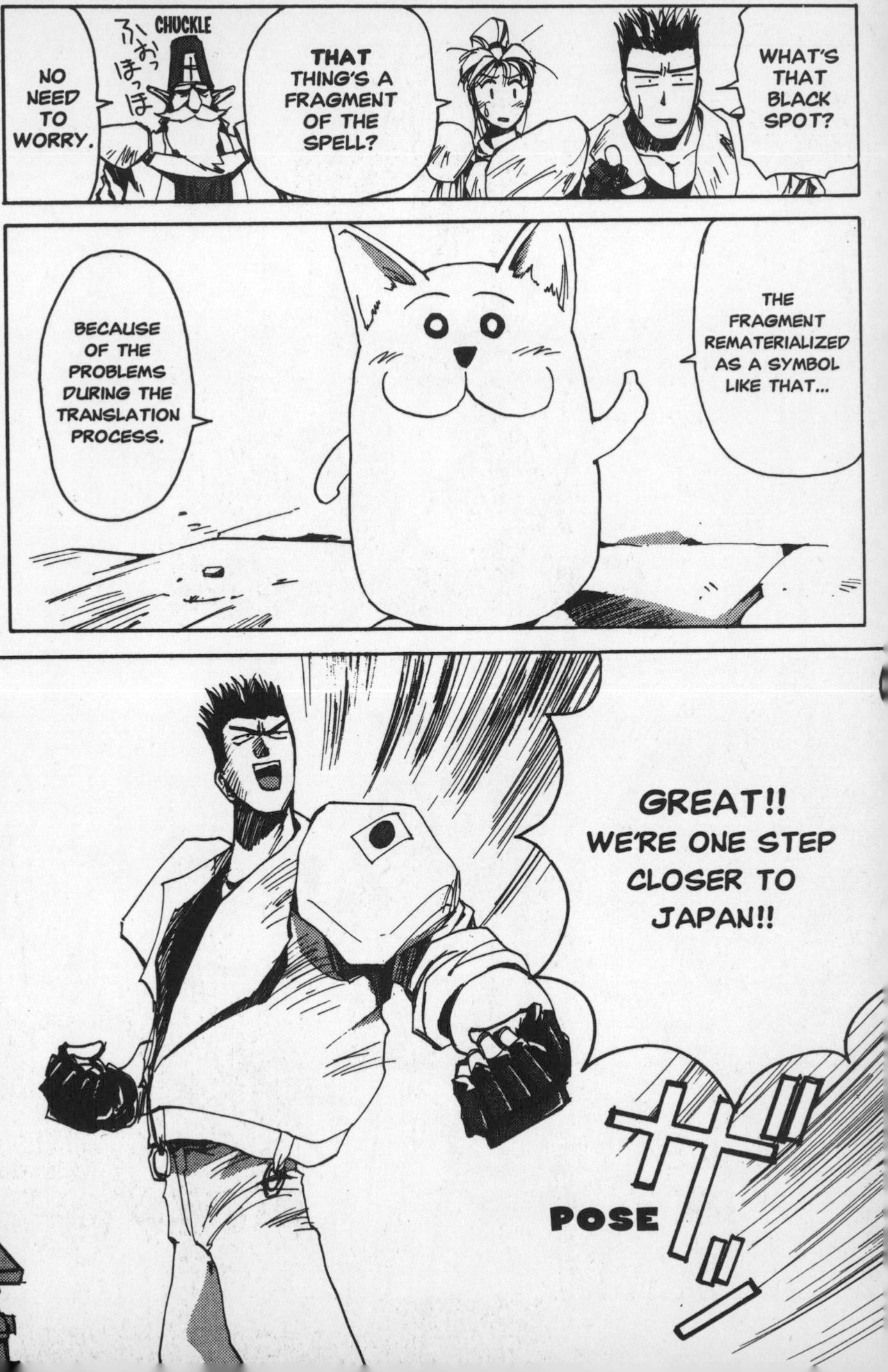

WHAT'S THAT BLACK SPOT?
THAT THING'S A FRAGMENT OF THE SPELL?
ふおっほっほ
CHUCKLE
NO NEED TO WORRY.
THE FRAGMENT REMATERIALIZED AS A SYMBOL LIKE THAT...
BECAUSE OF THE PROBLEMS DURING THE TRANSLATION PROCESS.
GREAT!! WE'RE ONE STEP CLOSER TO JAPAN!!
POSE

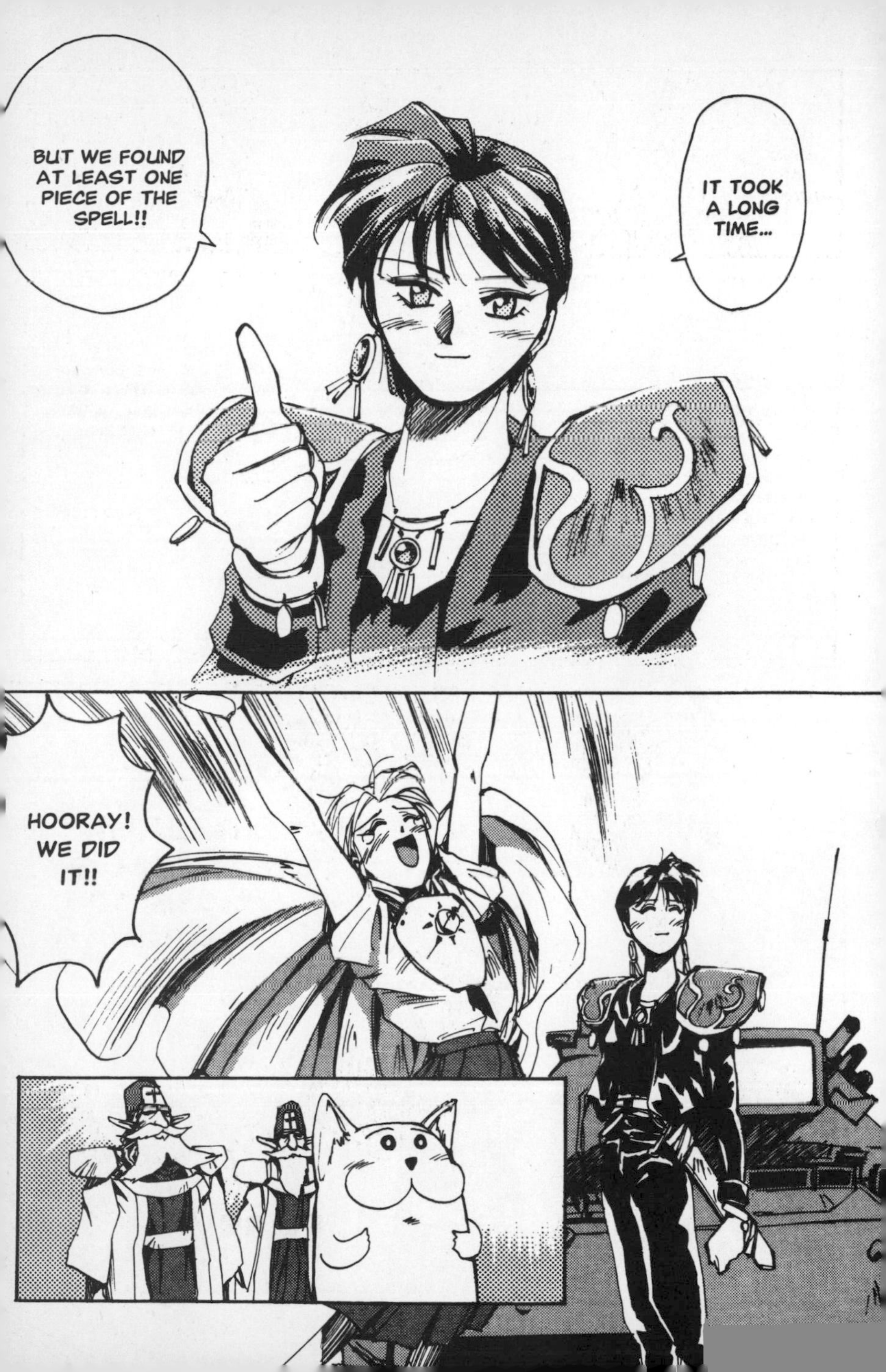
IT TOOK A LONG TIME...
BUT WE FOUND AT LEAST ONE PIECE OF THE SPELL!!
HOORAY! WE DID IT!!

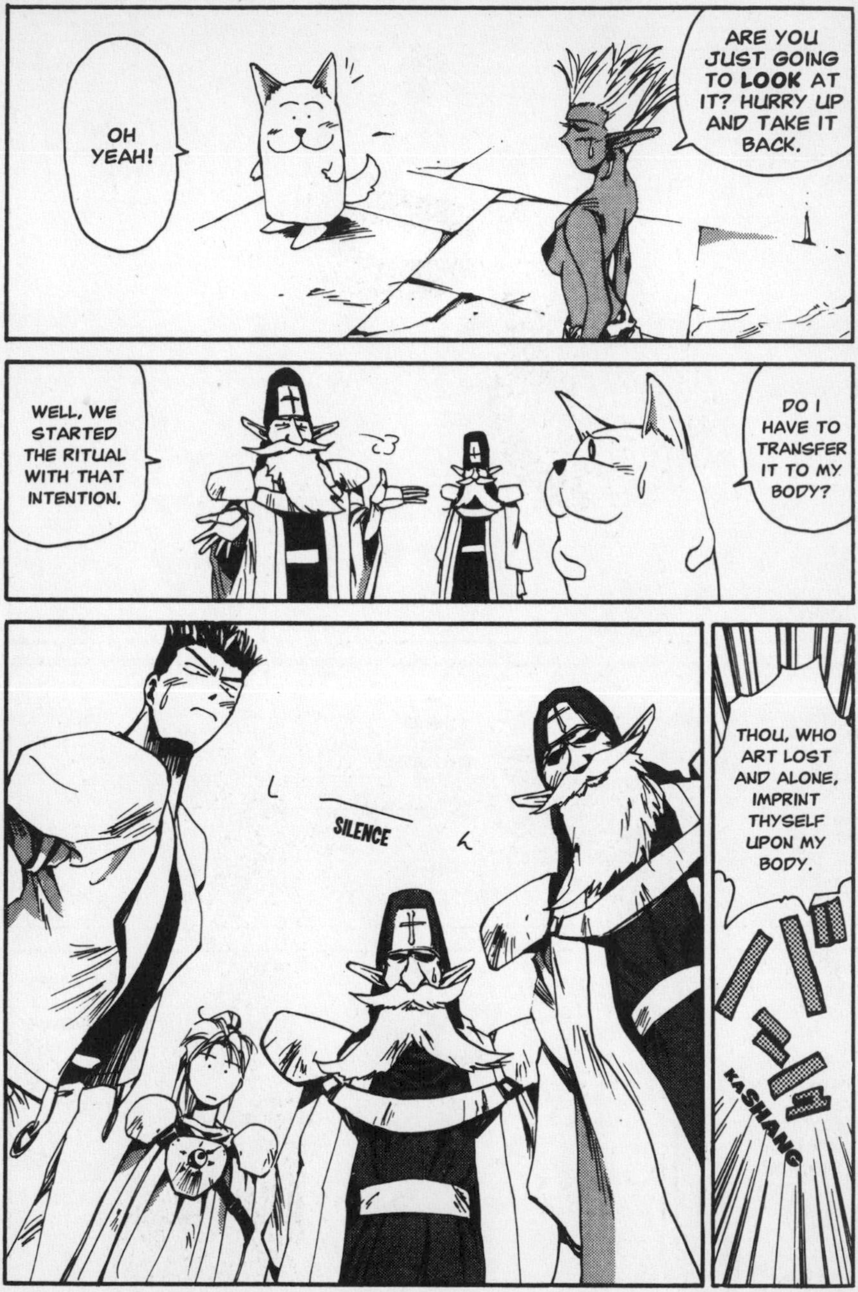
ARE YOU JUST GOING TO LOOK AT IT? HURRY UP AND TAKE IT BACK.
OH YEAH!
DO I HAVE TO TRANSFER IT TO MY BODY?
WELL, WE STARTED THE RITUAL WITH THAT INTENTION.
THOU, WHO ART LOST AND ALONE, IMPRINT THYSELF UPON MY BODY.
KASHANG
SILENCE

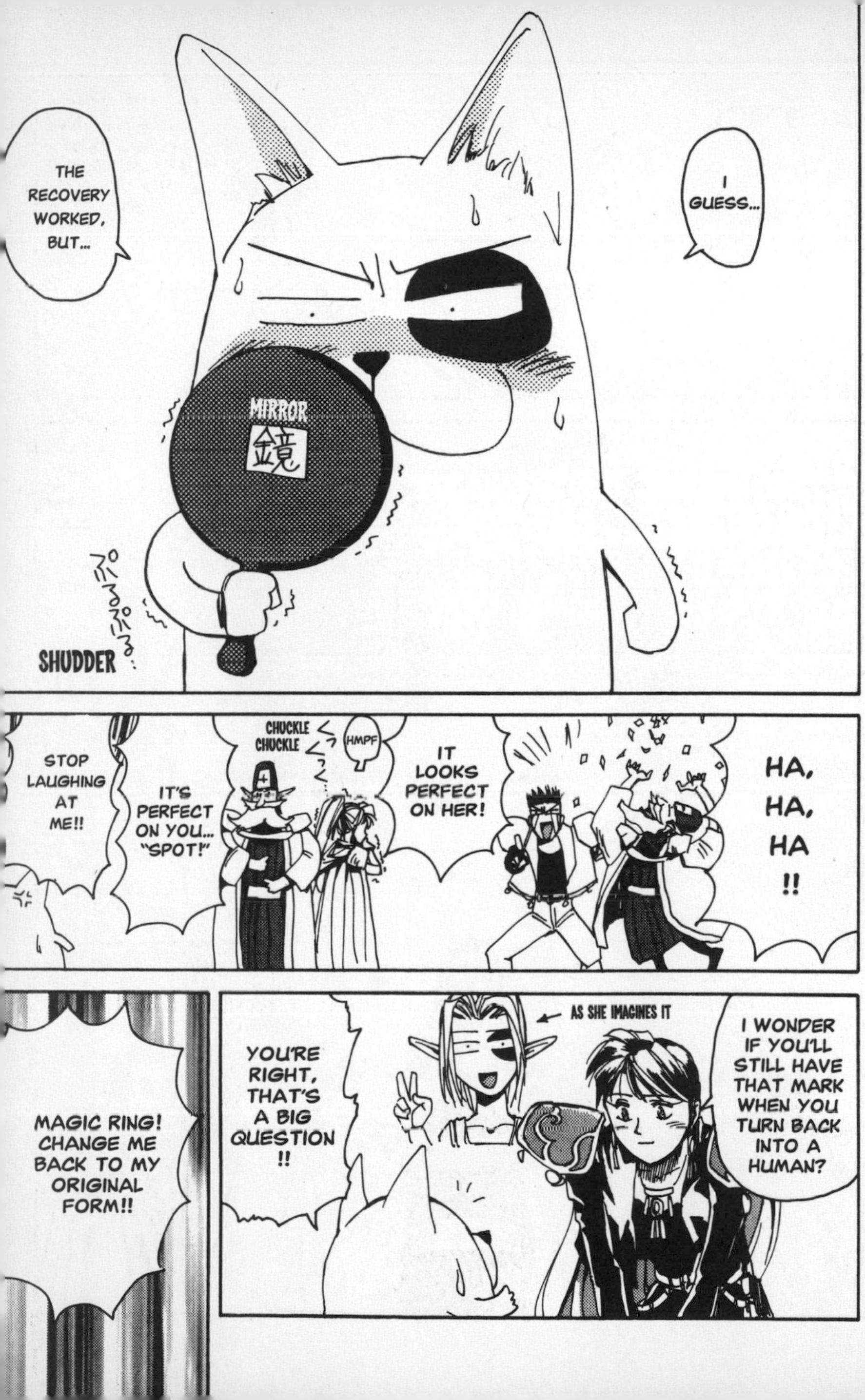
I GUESS...
THE RECOVERY WORKED, BUT...
MIRROR
鏡
SHUDDER
HA, HA, HA !!
IT LOOKS PERFECT ON HER!
HMPF
CHUCKLE CHUCKLE
IT'S PERFECT ON YOU... "SPOT!"
STOP LAUGHING AT ME!!
I WONDER IF YOU'LL STILL HAVE THAT MARK WHEN YOU TURN BACK INTO A HUMAN?
AS SHE IMAGINES IT
YOU'RE RIGHT, THAT'S A BIG QUESTION !!
MAGIC RING! CHANGE ME BACK TO MY ORIGINAL FORM!!

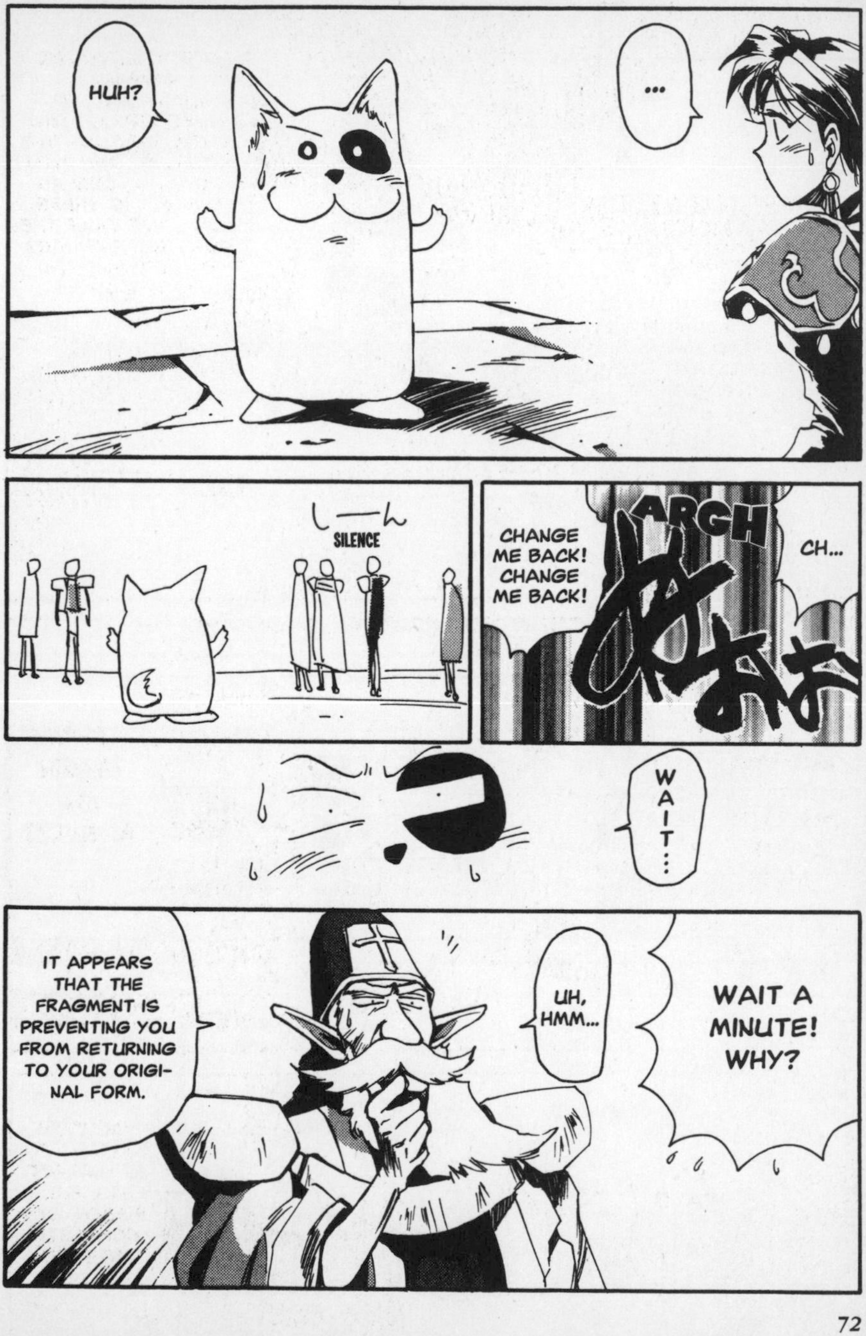
...
HUH?
CH...
ARGH
CHANGE ME BACK! CHANGE ME BACK!
しーん
SILENCE
WAIT...
WAIT A MINUTE! WHY?
UH, HMM...
IT APPEARS THAT THE FRAGMENT IS PREVENTING YOU FROM RETURNING TO YOUR ORIGINAL FORM.

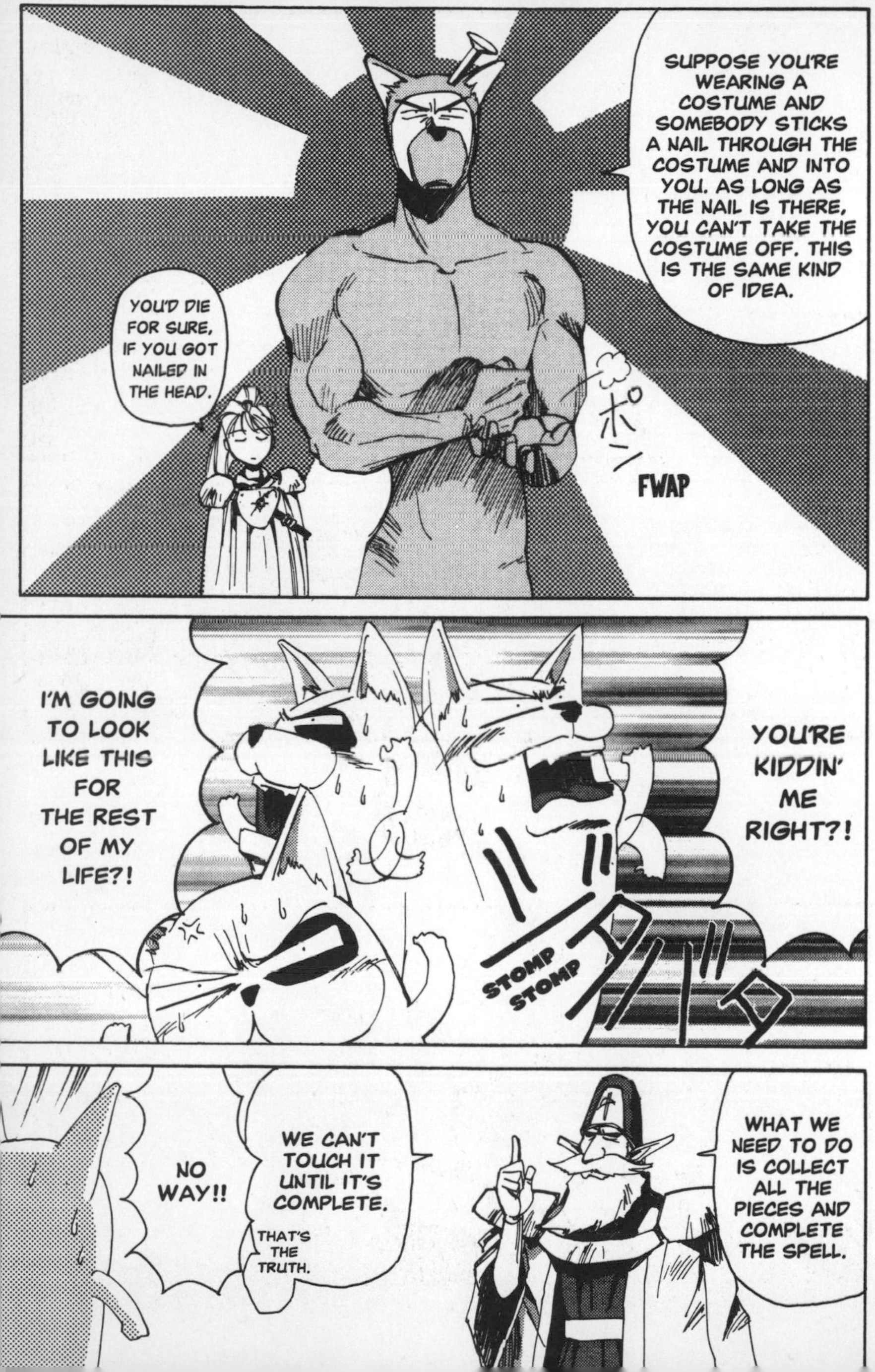
SUPPOSE YOU'RE WEARING A COSTUME AND SOMEBODY STICKS A NAIL THROUGH THE COSTUME AND INTO YOU. AS LONG AS THE NAIL IS THERE, YOU CAN'T TAKE THE COSTUME OFF. THIS IS THE SAME KIND OF IDEA.
YOU'D DIE FOR SURE, IF YOU GOT NAILED IN THE HEAD.
ポン
FWAP
YOU'RE KIDDIN' ME RIGHT?!
I'M GOING TO LOOK LIKE THIS FOR THE REST OF MY LIFE?!
ダダダ
STOMP STOMP
WHAT WE NEED TO DO IS COLLECT ALL THE PIECES AND COMPLETE THE SPELL.
WE CAN'T TOUCH IT UNTIL IT'S COMPLETE.
THAT'S THE TRUTH.
NO WAY!!

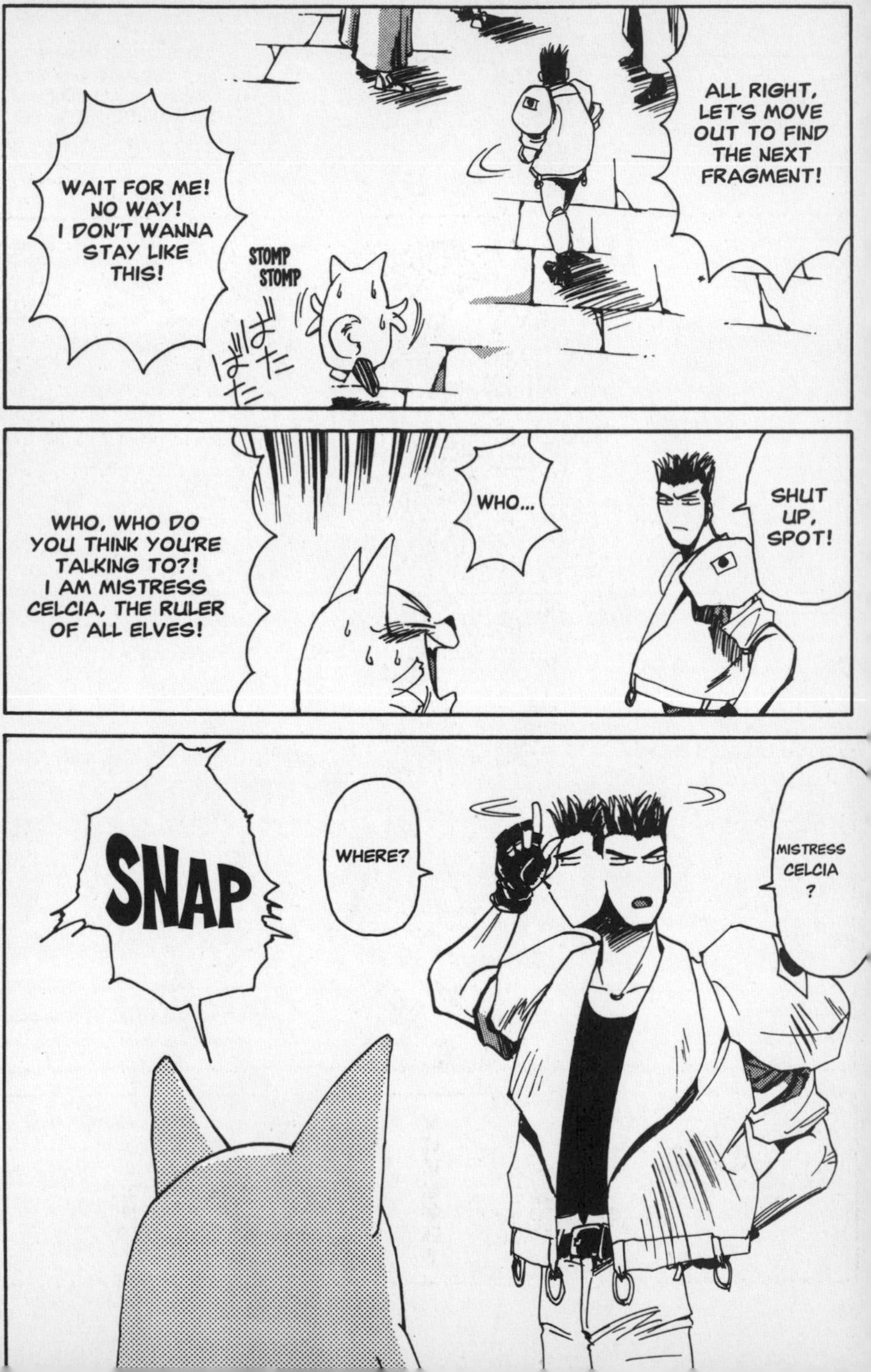
ALL RIGHT, LET'S MOVE OUT TO FIND THE NEXT FRAGMENT!
WAIT FOR ME! NO WAY! I DON'T WANNA STAY LIKE THIS!
STOMP STOMP
ばた ばた
SHUT UP, SPOT!
WHO...
WHO, WHO DO YOU THINK YOU'RE TALKING TO?! I AM MISTRESS CELCIA, THE RULER OF ALL ELVES!
MISTRESS CELCIA ?
WHERE?
SNAP

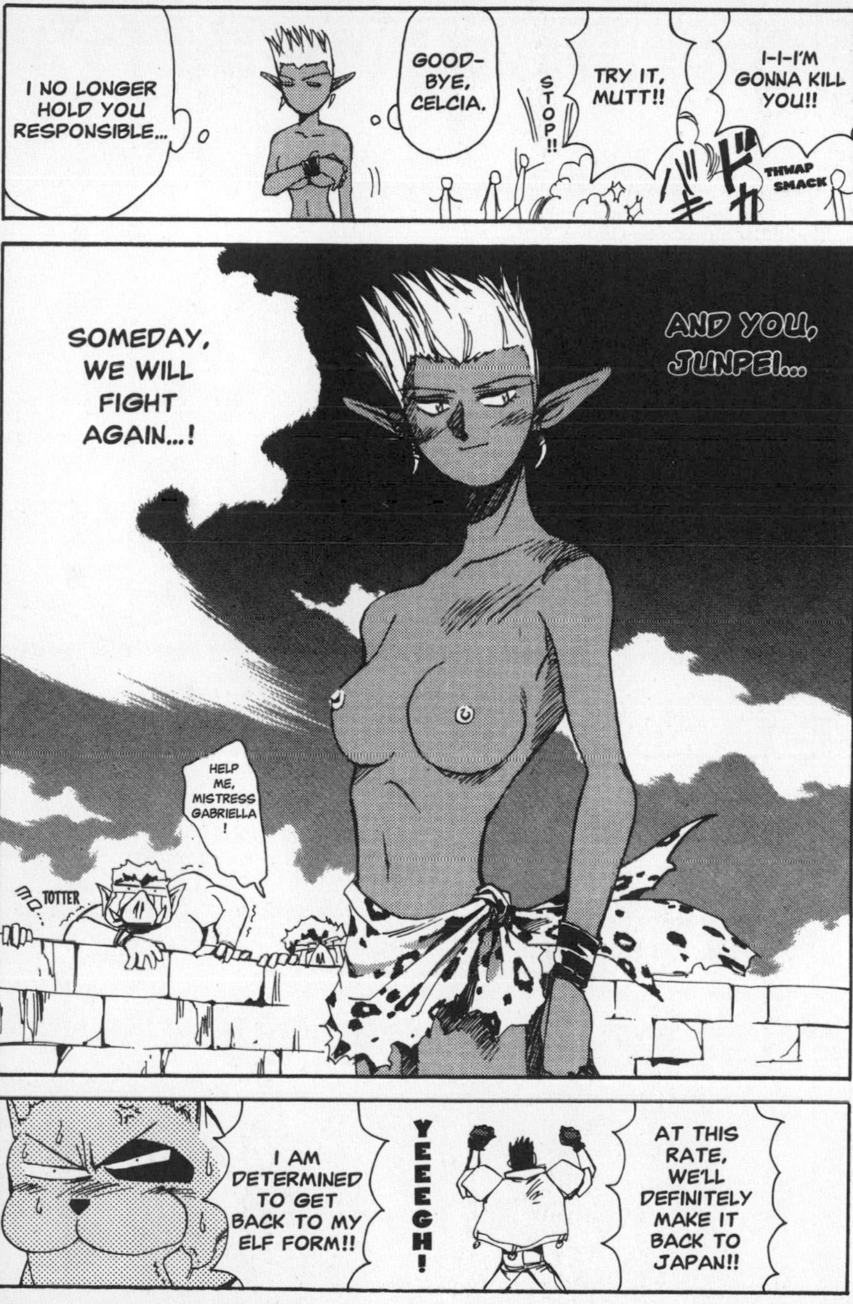

I NO LONGER HOLD YOU RESPONSIBLE...
GOOD-BYE, CELCIA.
STOP!!
TRY IT, MUTT!!
I-I-I'M GONNA KILL YOU!!
バキ
ドカ
THWAP
SMACK
SOMEDAY, WE WILL FIGHT AGAIN...!
AND YOU, JUNPEI...
HELP ME, MISTRESS GABRIELLA!
TOTTER
I AM DETERMINED TO GET BACK TO MY ELF FORM!!
YEEEGH!
AT THIS RATE, WE'LL DEFINITELY MAKE IT BACK TO JAPAN!!

character profile (2)

Airi Komiyama

Age: 24
Blood Type: AB
Sign: Gemini
Personality: Calm and composed

After finishing acting school in the U.S., she immediately started working in Hollywood. Two years later, Airi won the Oscar for Best Leading Actress. Not much is known about her childhood in Japan. She likes taking walks and has a large collection of exotic teas. Airi's favorite thing to do is to relax at luxury hotels.

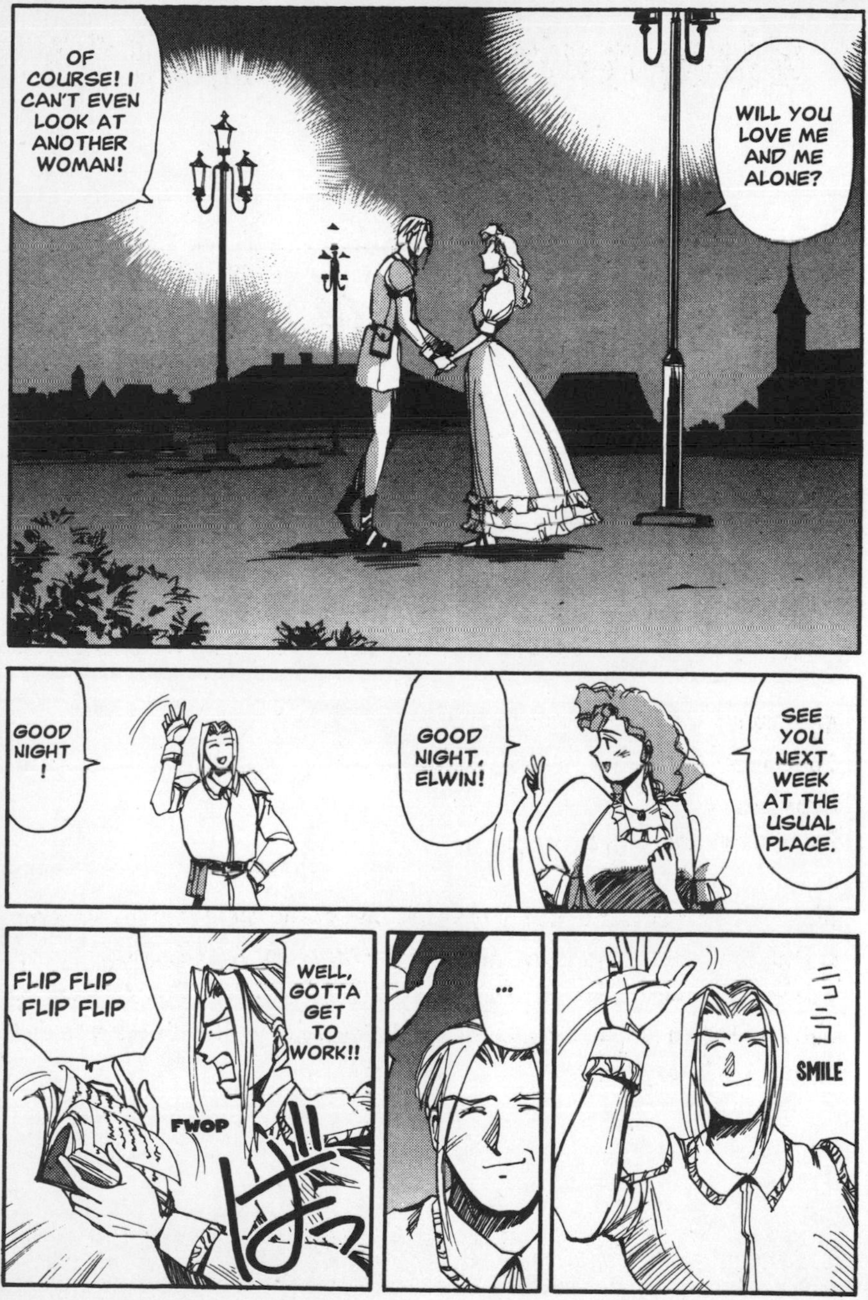
WILL YOU LOVE ME AND ME ALONE?
OF COURSE! I CAN'T EVEN LOOK AT ANOTHER WOMAN!
SEE YOU NEXT WEEK AT THE USUAL PLACE.
GOOD NIGHT, ELWIN!
GOOD NIGHT!
SMILE
...
WELL, GOTTA GET TO WORK!!
FLIP FLIP FLIP FLIP
FWOP

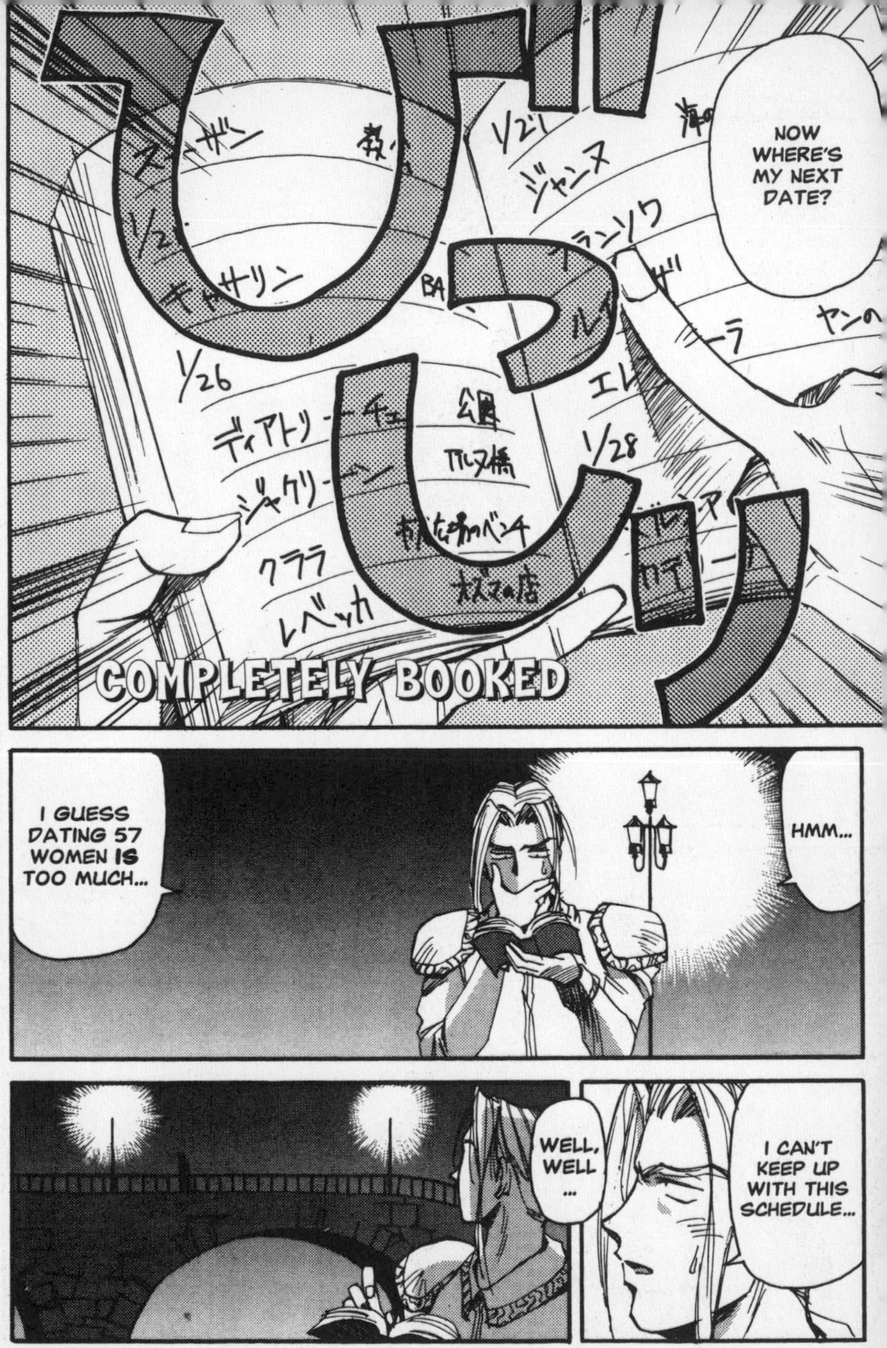
NOW WHERE'S MY NEXT DATE?
COMPLETELY BOOKED
HMM...
I GUESS DATING 57 WOMEN IS TOO MUCH...
I CAN'T KEEP UP WITH THIS SCHEDULE...
WELL, WELL ...

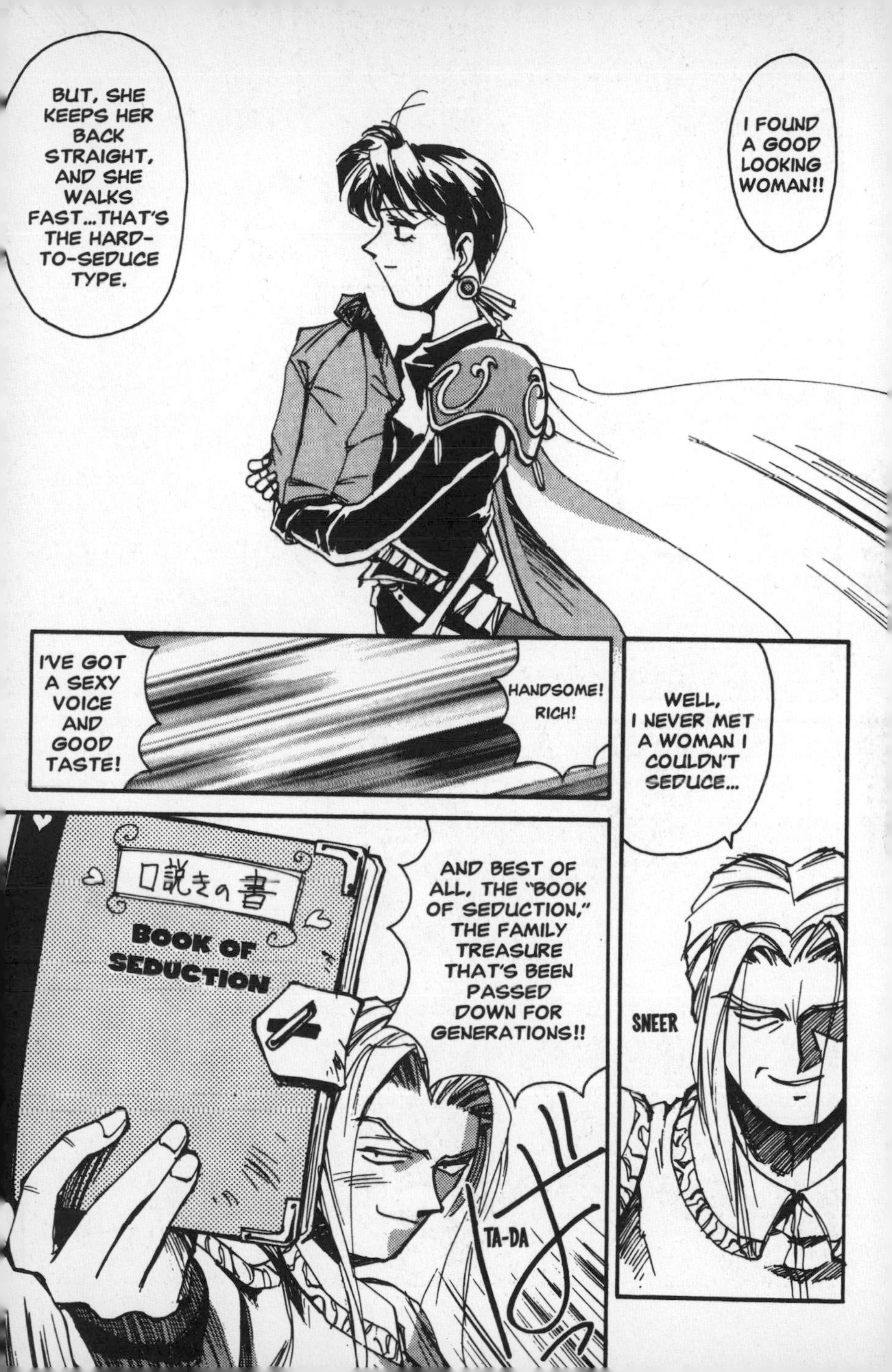
I FOUND A GOOD LOOKING WOMAN!!
BUT, SHE KEEPS HER BACK STRAIGHT, AND SHE WALKS FAST...THAT'S THE HARD-TO-SEDUCE TYPE.
WELL, I NEVER MET A WOMAN I COULDN'T SEDUCE...
HANDSOME! RICH!
I'VE GOT A SEXY VOICE AND GOOD TASTE!
SNEER
AND BEST OF ALL, THE "BOOK OF SEDUCTION," THE FAMILY TREASURE THAT'S BEEN PASSED DOWN FOR GENERATIONS!!
口説きの書
BOOK OF SEDUCTION
TA-DA

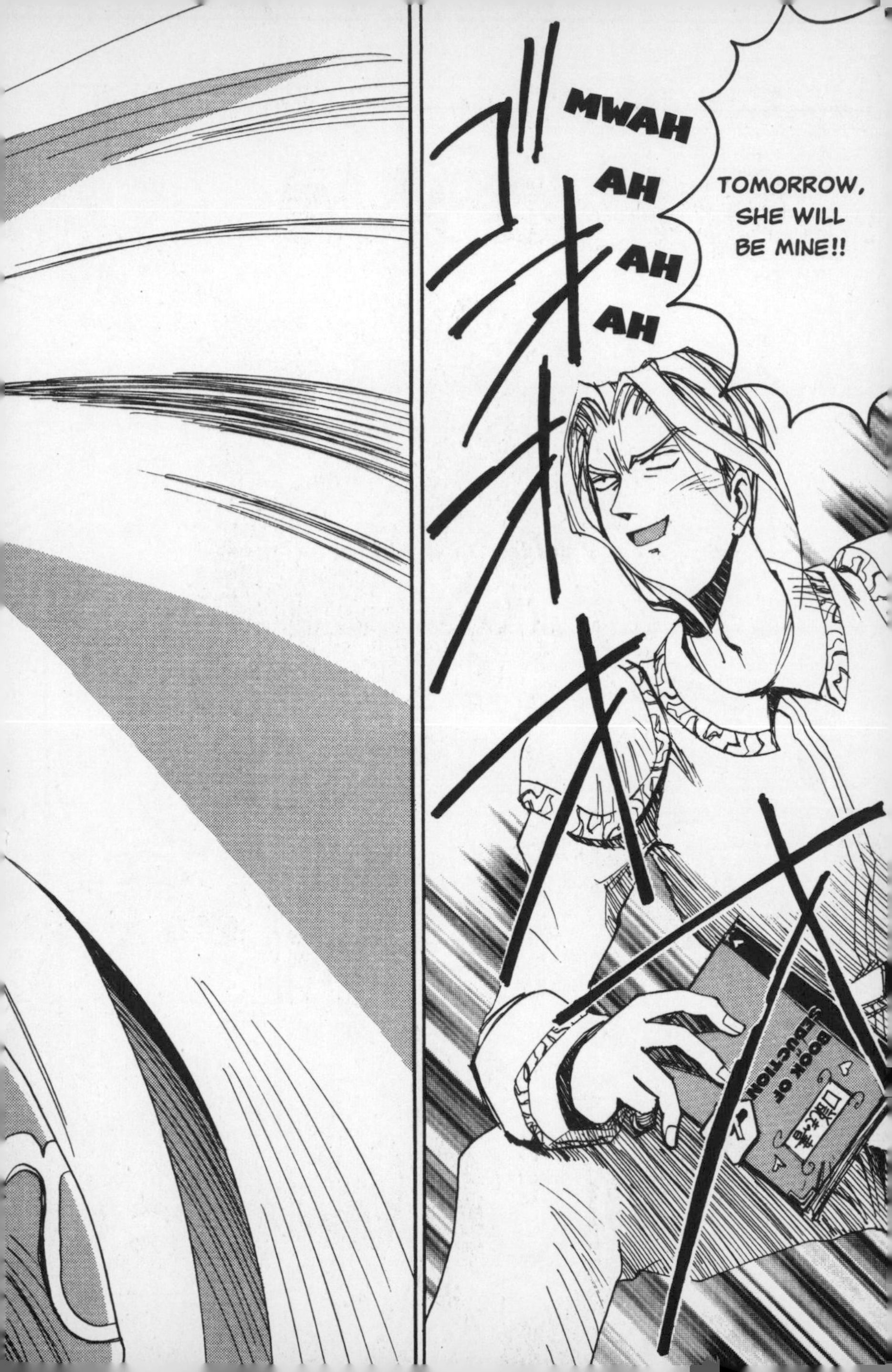
TOMORROW, SHE WILL BE MINE!!
MWAH AH AH AH
BOOK OF SEDUCTION

#3 The Man Who is After Airi

#3 愛理を狙った男

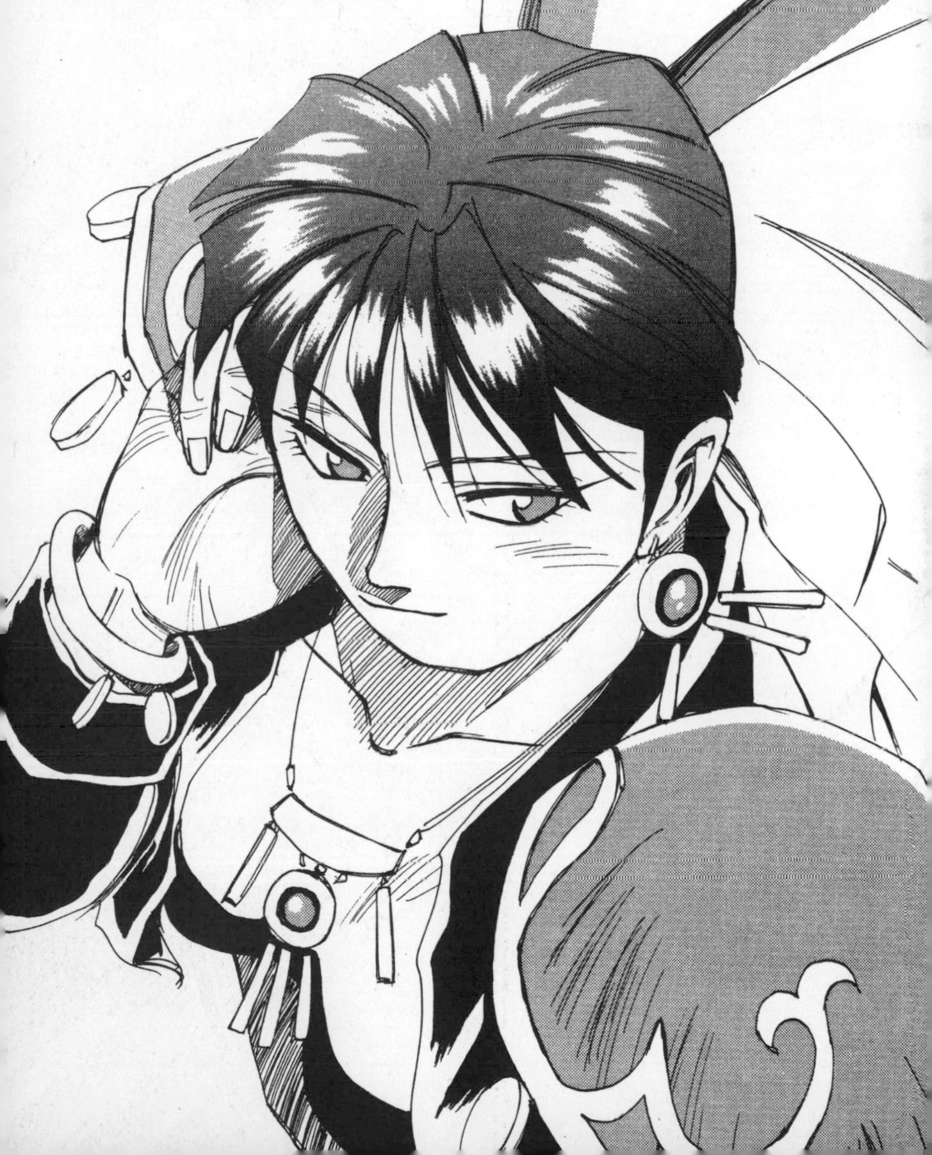

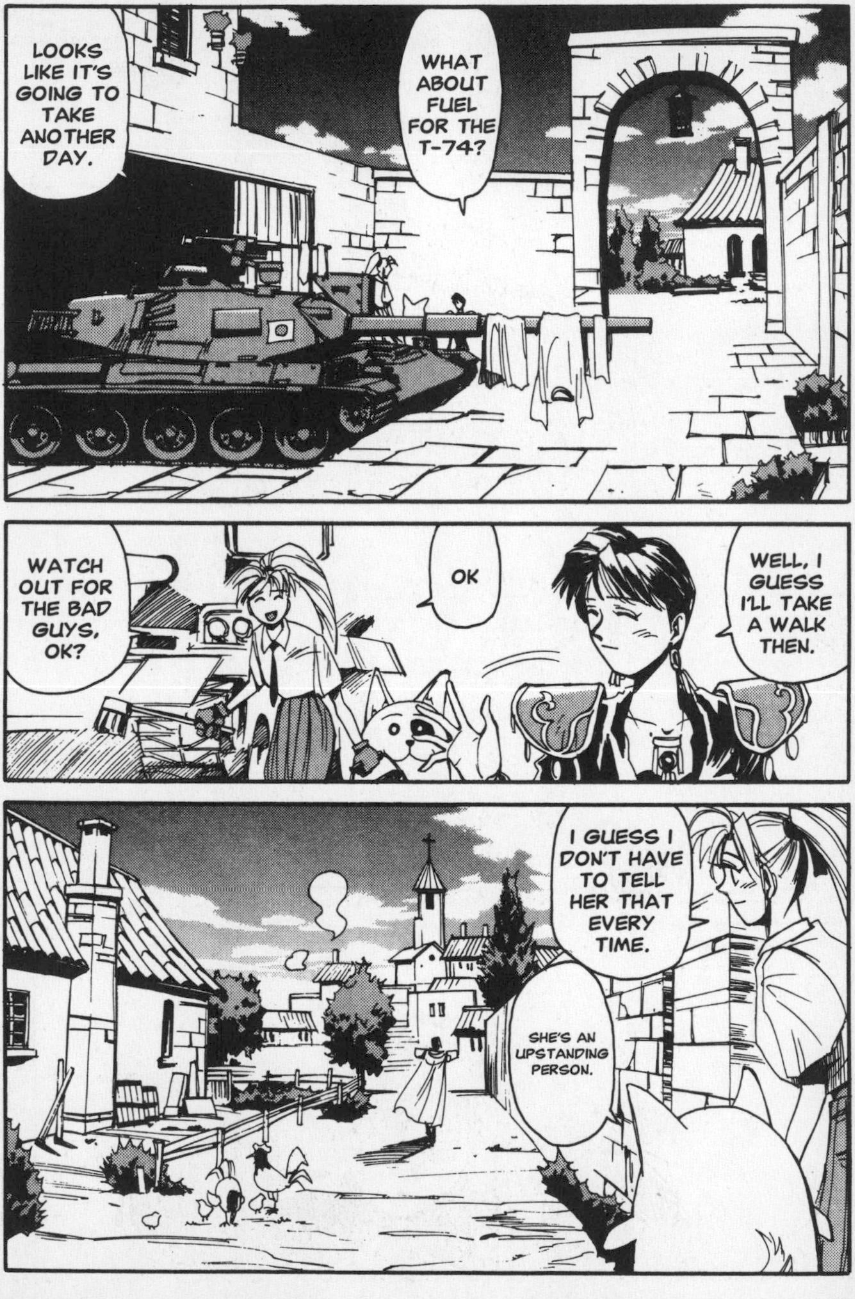
WHAT ABOUT FUEL FOR THE T-74?
LOOKS LIKE IT'S GOING TO TAKE ANOTHER DAY.
WELL, I GUESS I'LL TAKE A WALK THEN.
OK
WATCH OUT FOR THE BAD GUYS, OK?
I GUESS I DON'T HAVE TO TELL HER THAT EVERY TIME.
SHE'S AN UPSTANDING PERSON.

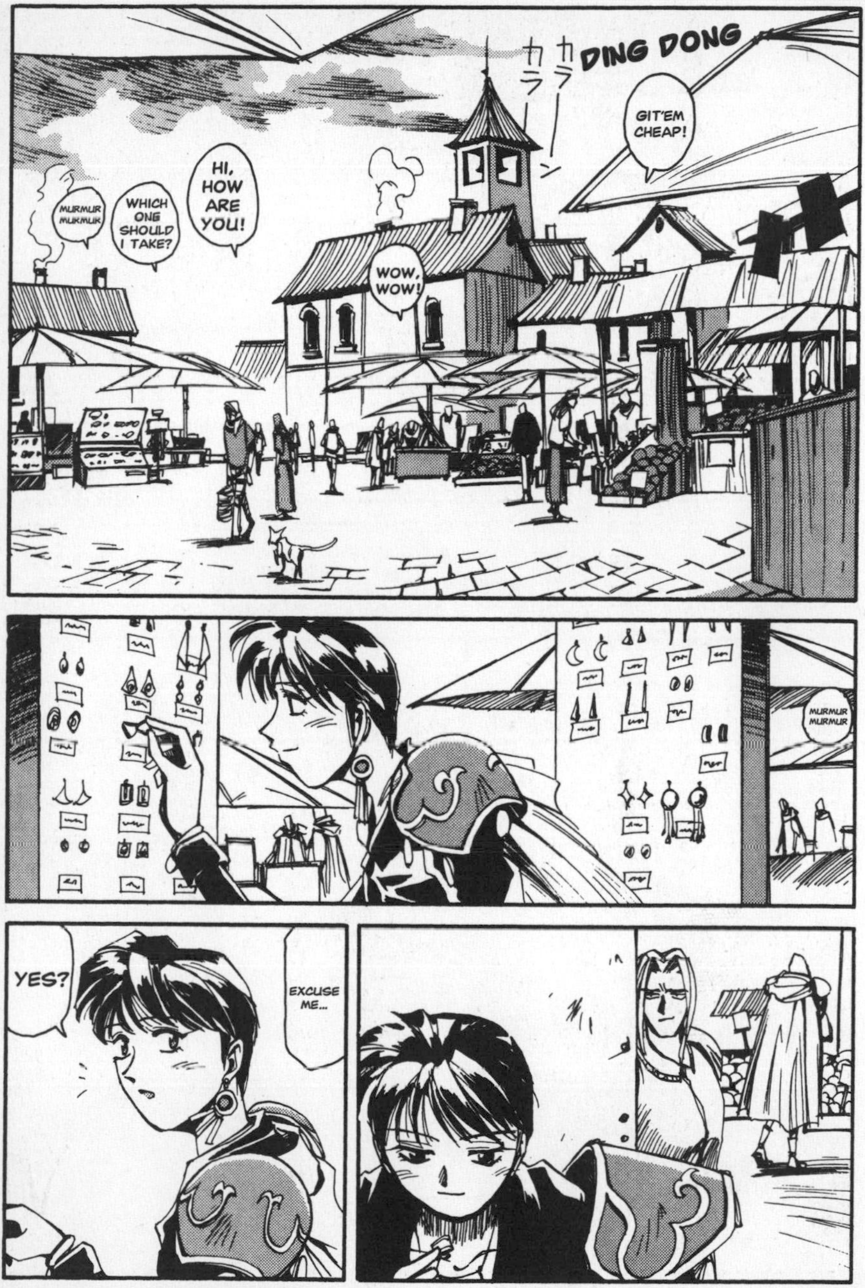

カララン
DING DONG
GIT'EM CHEAP!
HI, HOW ARE YOU!
WHICH ONE SHOULD I TAKE?
MURMUR MUKMUR
WOW, WOW!
MURMUR MURMUR
EXCUSE ME...
YES?

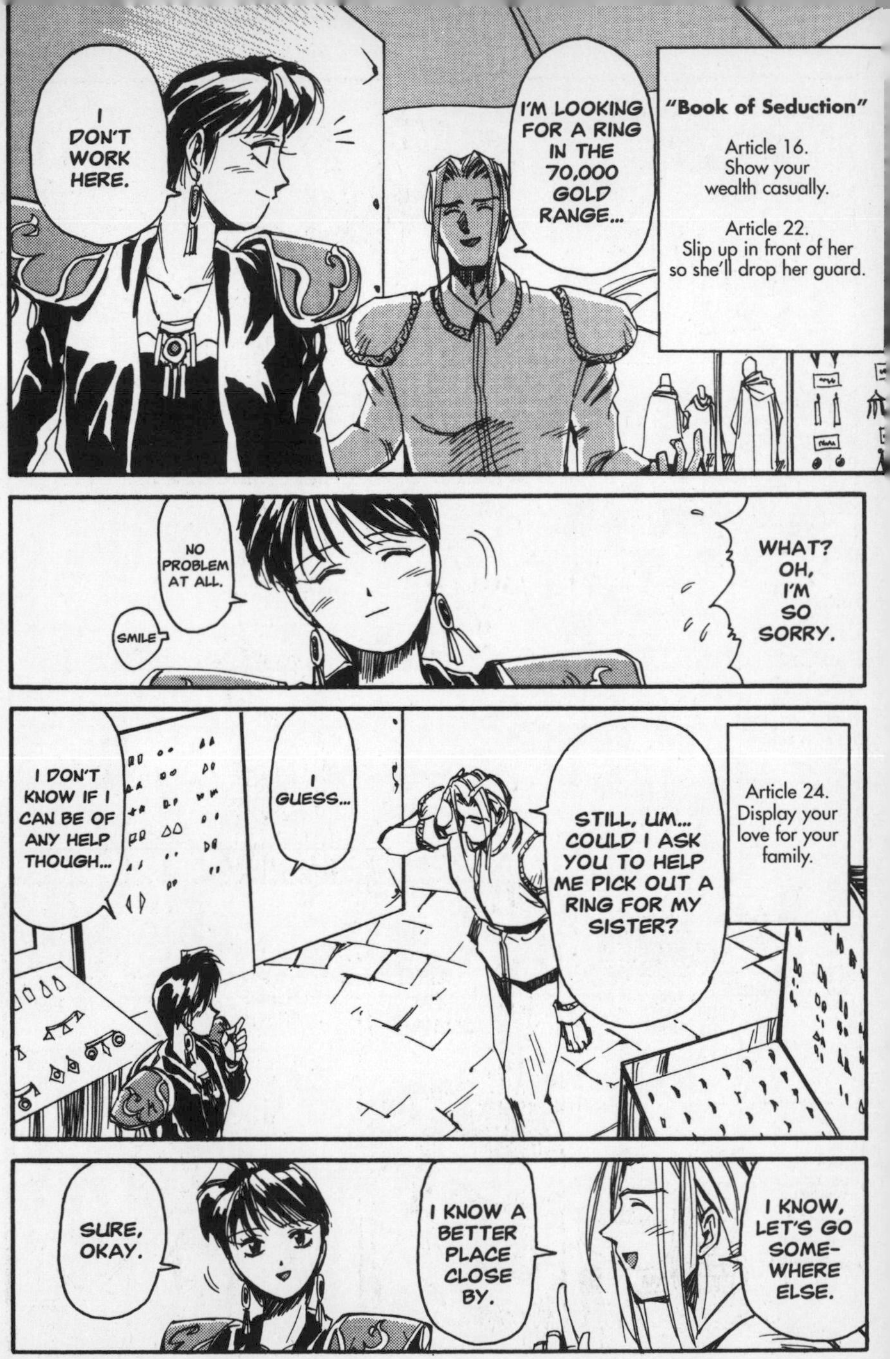
"Book of Seduction"
Article 16. Show your wealth casually.
Article 22. Slip up in front of her so she'll drop her guard.
I'M LOOKING FOR A RING IN THE 70,000 GOLD RANGE...
I DON'T WORK HERE.
WHAT? OH, I'M SO SORRY.
NO PROBLEM AT ALL.
SMILE
Article 24. Display your love for your family.
STILL, UM... COULD I ASK YOU TO HELP ME PICK OUT A RING FOR MY SISTER?
I GUESS...
I DON'T KNOW IF I CAN BE OF ANY HELP THOUGH...
I KNOW, LET'S GO SOMEWHERE ELSE.
I KNOW A BETTER PLACE CLOSE BY.
SURE, OKAY.

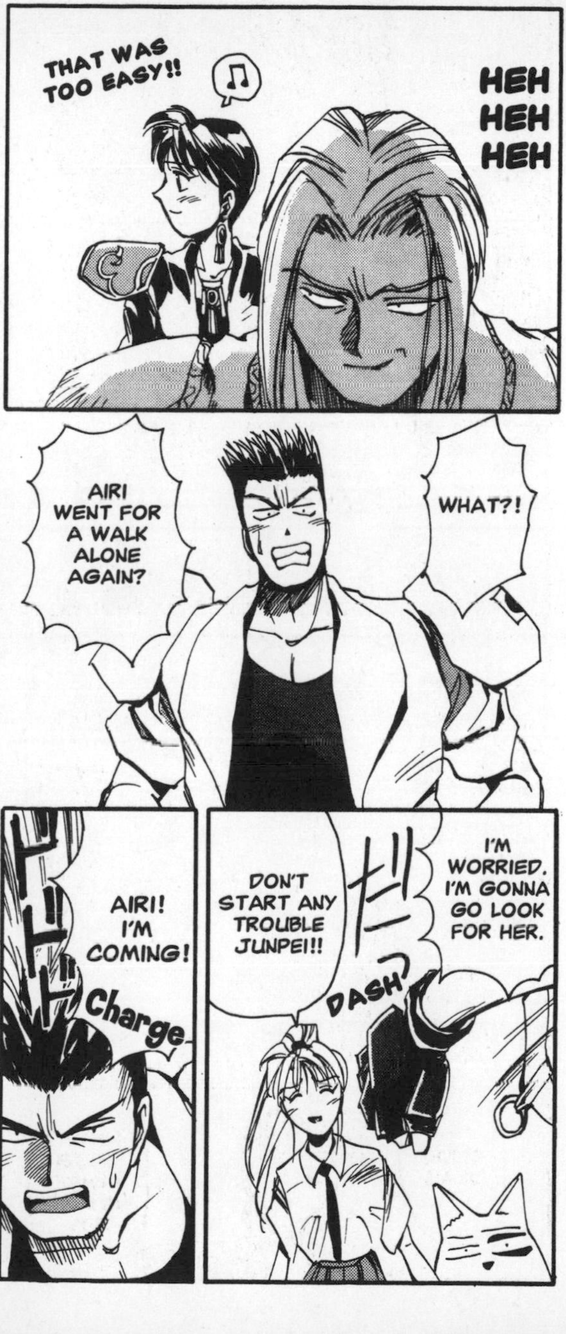

HEH HEH HEH
THAT WAS TOO EASY!!
♪
WHAT?!
AIRI WENT FOR A WALK ALONE AGAIN?
I'M WORRIED. I'M GONNA GO LOOK FOR HER.
DASH
DON'T START ANY TROUBLE JUNPEI!!
AIRI! I'M COMING!
Charge

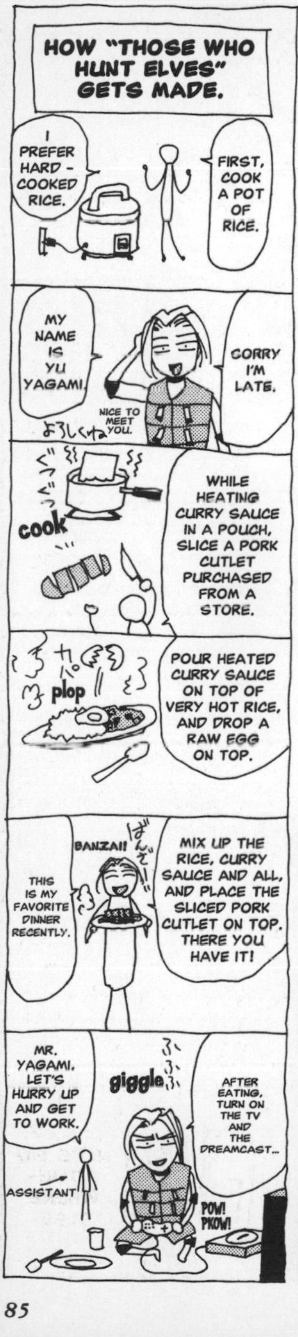

HOW "THOSE WHO HUNT ELVES" GETS MADE.
FIRST, COOK A POT OF RICE.
I PREFER HARD - COOKED RICE.
CORRY I'M LATE.
MY NAME IS YU YAGAMI.
NICE TO MEET YOU.
よろしくね
WHILE HEATING CURRY SAUCE IN A POUCH, SLICE A PORK CUTLET PURCHASED FROM A STORE.
cook
POUR HEATED CURRY SAUCE ON TOP OF VERY HOT RICE, AND DROP A RAW EGG ON TOP.
plop
MIX UP THE RICE, CURRY SAUCE AND ALL, AND PLACE THE SLICED PORK CUTLET ON TOP. THERE YOU HAVE IT!
BANZAI!
THIS IS MY FAVORITE DINNER RECENTLY.
AFTER EATING, TURN ON THE TV AND THE DREAMCAST...
POW! PKOW!
giggle
ふふふ
MR. YAGAMI, LET'S HURRY UP AND GET TO WORK.
ASSISTANT

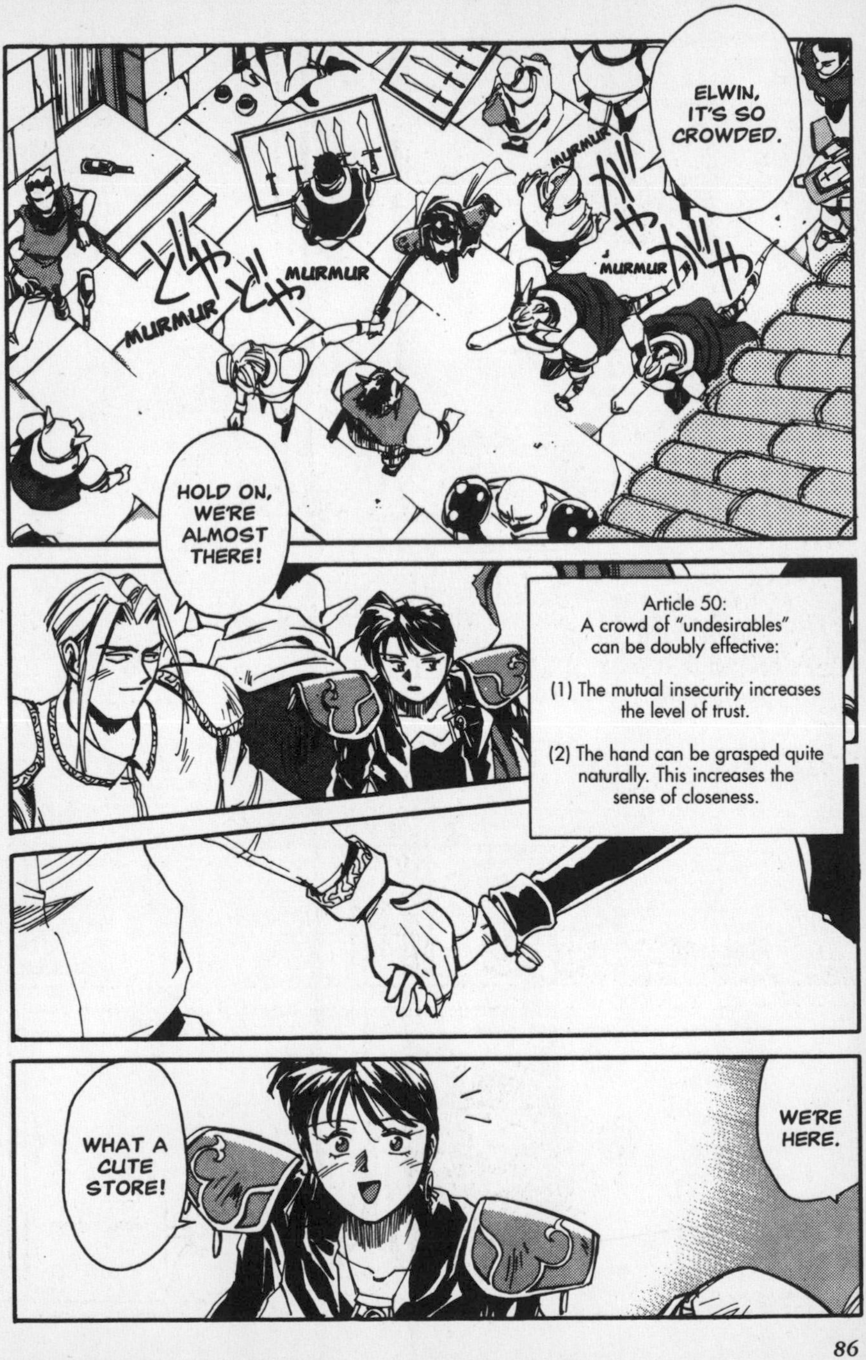
ELWIN, IT'S SO CROWDED.
MURMUR
MURMUR
MURMUR
MURMUR
HOLD ON, WE'RE ALMOST THERE!
Article 50:
A crowd of "undesirables" can be doubly effective:
(1) The mutual insecurity increases the level of trust.
(2) The hand can be grasped quite naturally. This increases the sense of closeness.
WE'RE HERE.
WHAT A CUTE STORE!

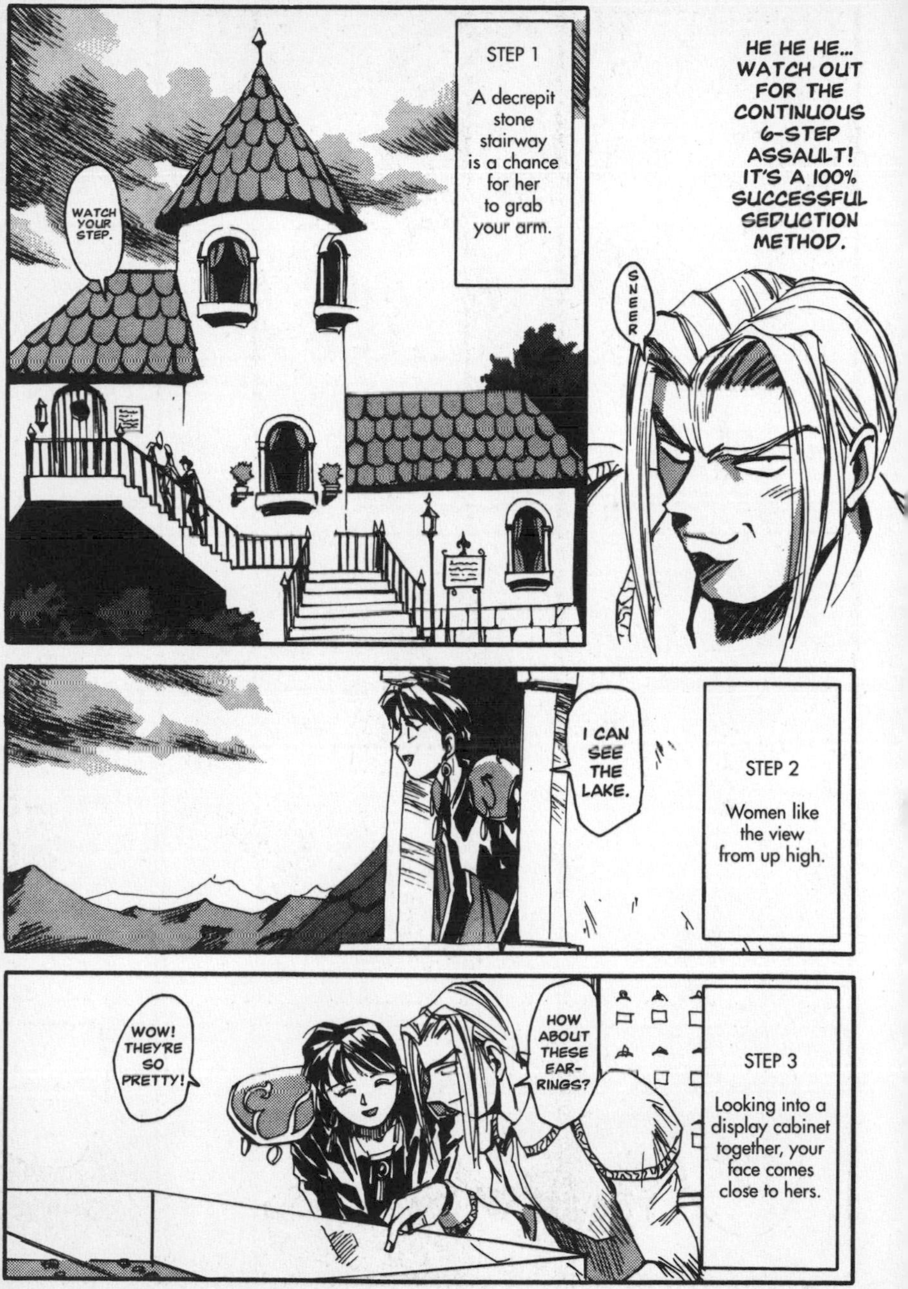
WATCH YOUR STEP.
STEP 1
A decrepit stone stairway is a chance for her to grab your arm.
HE HE HE... WATCH OUT FOR THE CONTINUOUS 6-STEP ASSAULT! IT'S A 100% SUCCESSFUL SEDUCTION METHOD.
SNEER
I CAN SEE THE LAKE.
STEP 2
Women like the view from up high.
WOW! THEY'RE SO PRETTY!
HOW ABOUT THESE EAR-RINGS?
STEP 3
Looking into a display cabinet together, your face comes close to hers.

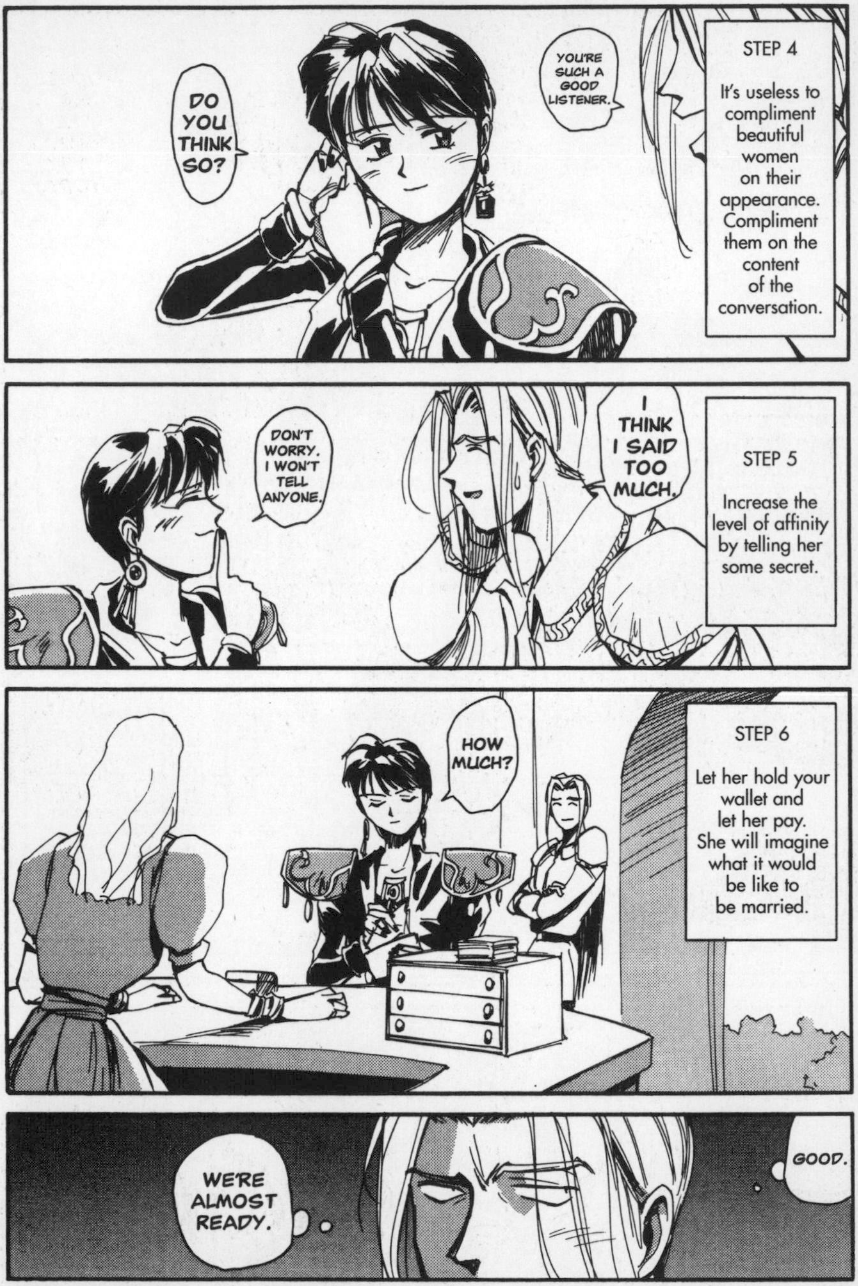
DO YOU THINK SO?
YOU'RE SUCH A GOOD LISTENER.
STEP 4
It's useless to compliment beautiful women on their appearance. Compliment them on the content of the conversation.
DON'T WORRY. I WON'T TELL ANYONE.
I THINK I SAID TOO MUCH.
STEP 5
Increase the level of affinity by telling her some secret.
HOW MUCH?
STEP 6
Let her hold your wallet and let her pay. She will imagine what it would be like to be married.
WE'RE ALMOST READY.
GOOD.

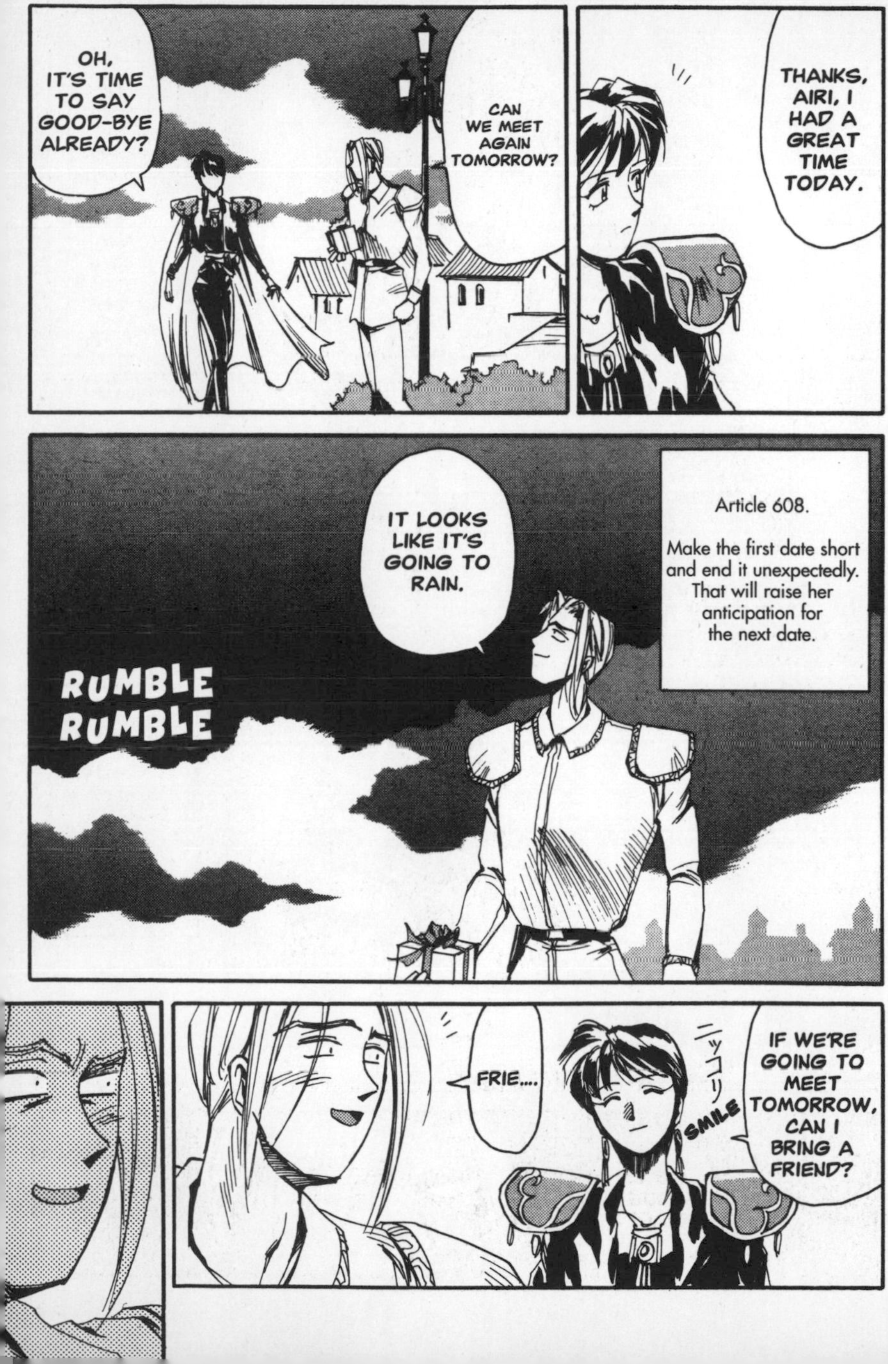
THANKS, AIRI, I HAD A GREAT TIME TODAY.
OH, IT'S TIME TO SAY GOOD-BYE ALREADY?
CAN WE MEET AGAIN TOMORROW?
Article 608.
Make the first date short and end it unexpectedly. That will raise her anticipation for the next date.
IT LOOKS LIKE IT'S GOING TO RAIN.
RUMBLE RUMBLE
IF WE'RE GOING TO MEET TOMORROW, CAN I BRING A FRIEND?
ニッコリ
SMILE
FRIE....

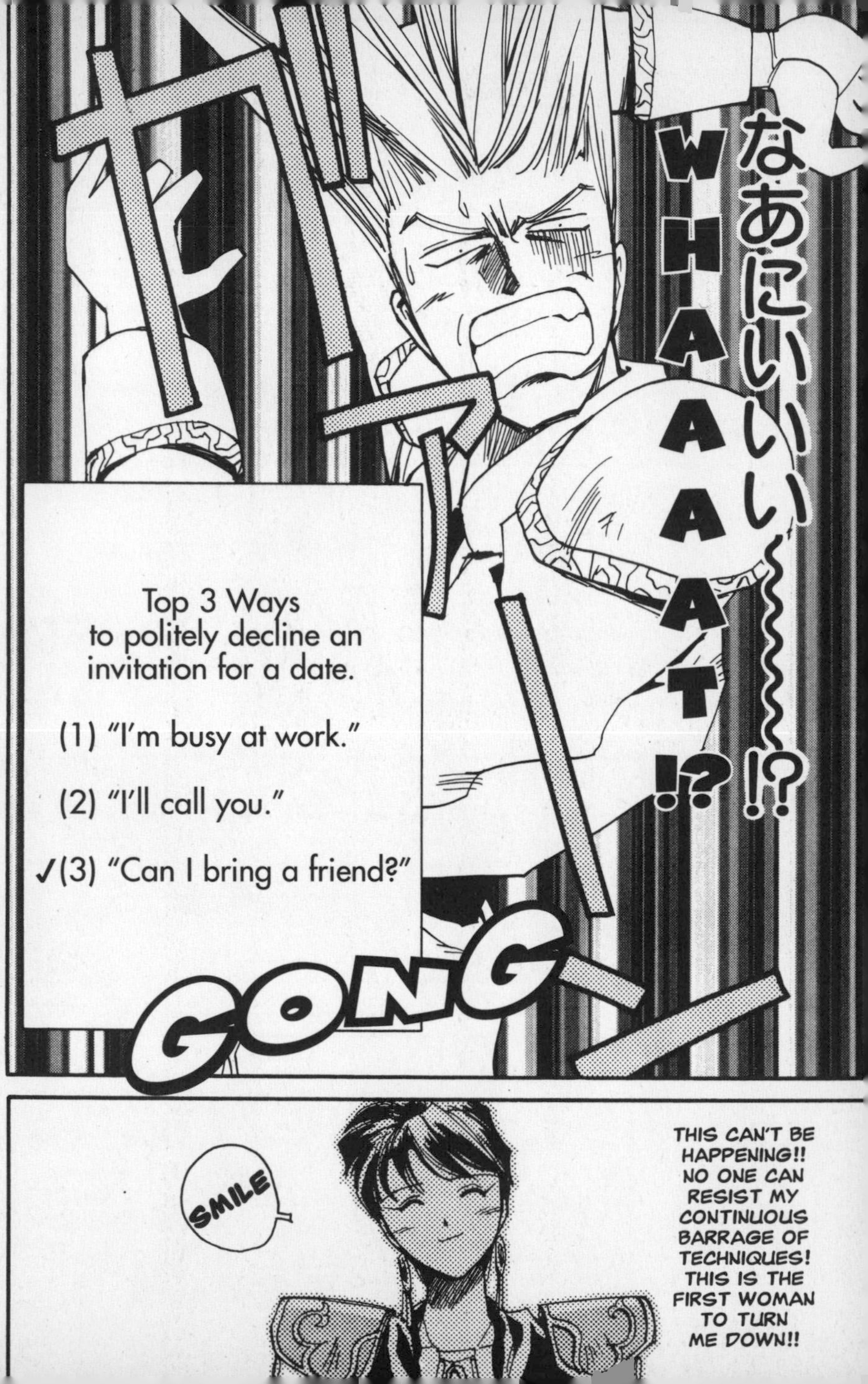

ガー
なあにいいい〜〜〜!?
WHAAAAT!?
Top 3 Ways
to politely decline an
invitation for a date.
(1) "I'm busy at work."
(2) "I'll call you."
✓(3) "Can I bring a friend?"
GONG
SMILE
THIS CAN'T BE HAPPENING!! NO ONE CAN RESIST MY CONTINUOUS BARRAGE OF TECHNIQUES! THIS IS THE FIRST WOMAN TO TURN ME DOWN!!

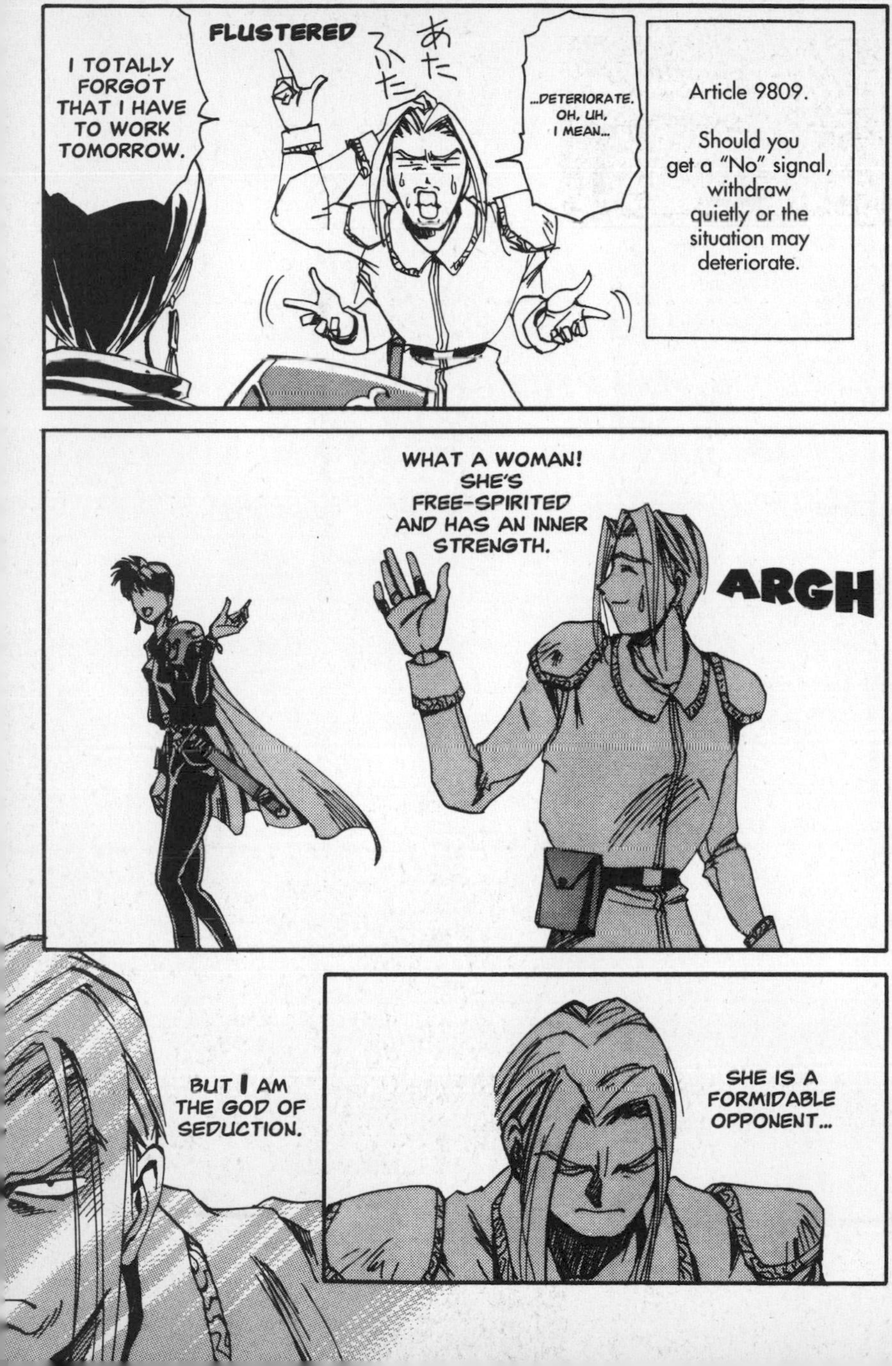
Article 9809.
Should you get a "No" signal, withdraw quietly or the situation may deteriorate.
...DETERIORATE. OH, UH, I MEAN...
あたふた
FLUSTERED
I TOTALLY FORGOT THAT I HAVE TO WORK TOMORROW.
WHAT A WOMAN! SHE'S FREE-SPIRITED AND HAS AN INNER STRENGTH.
ARGH
SHE IS A FORMIDABLE OPPONENT...
BUT I AM THE GOD OF SEDUCTION.

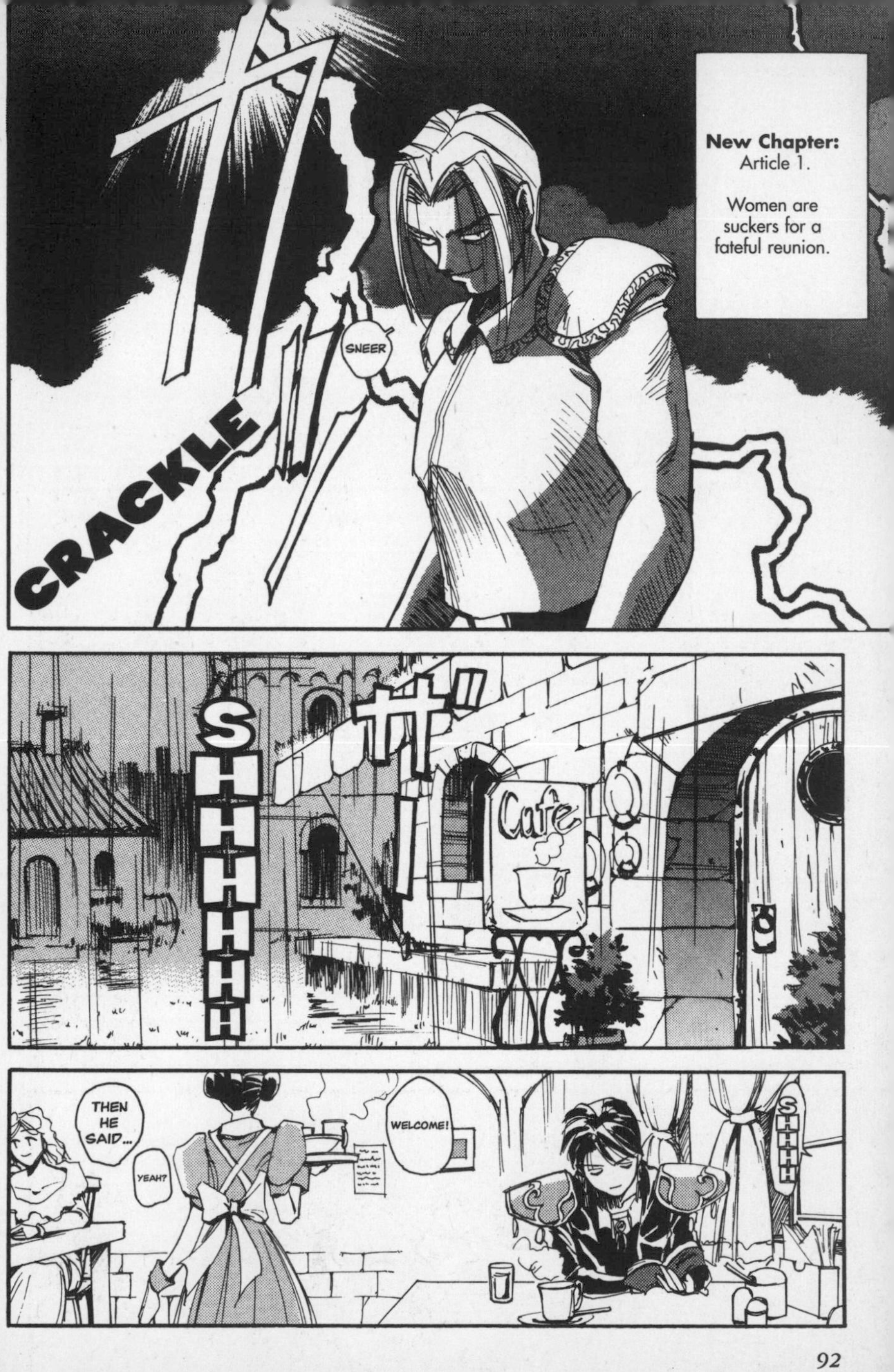
New Chapter:
Article 1.
Women are suckers for a fateful reunion.
SNEER
CRACKLE
SHHHHHHHH
Cafe
THEN HE SAID...
YEAH?
WELCOME!
SHHHH

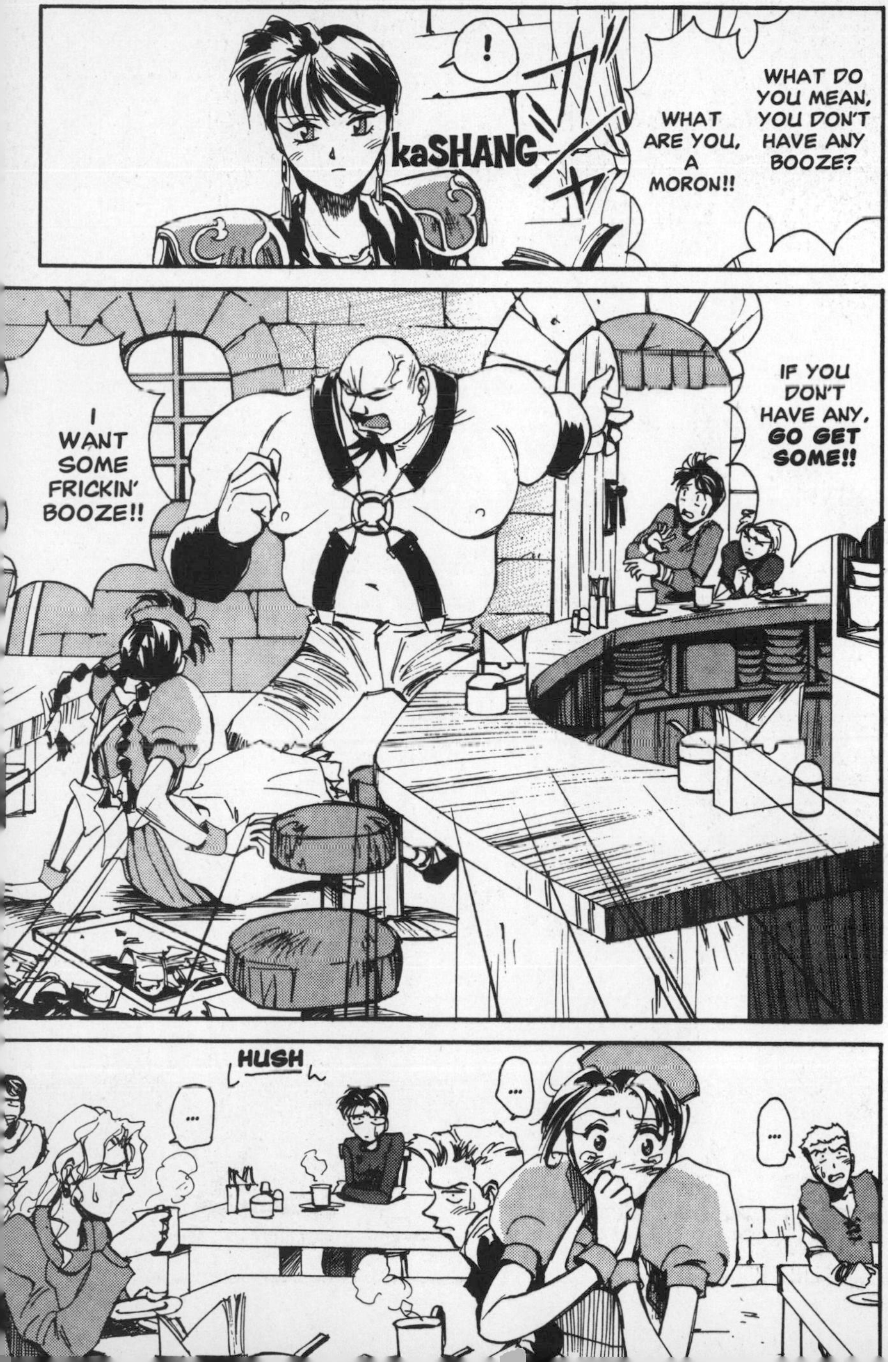
!
WHAT DO YOU MEAN, YOU DON'T HAVE ANY BOOZE?
WHAT ARE YOU, A MORON!!
kaSHANG
IF YOU DON'T HAVE ANY, **GO GET SOME!!**
I WANT SOME FRICKIN' BOOZE!!
...
...
HUSH
...
...

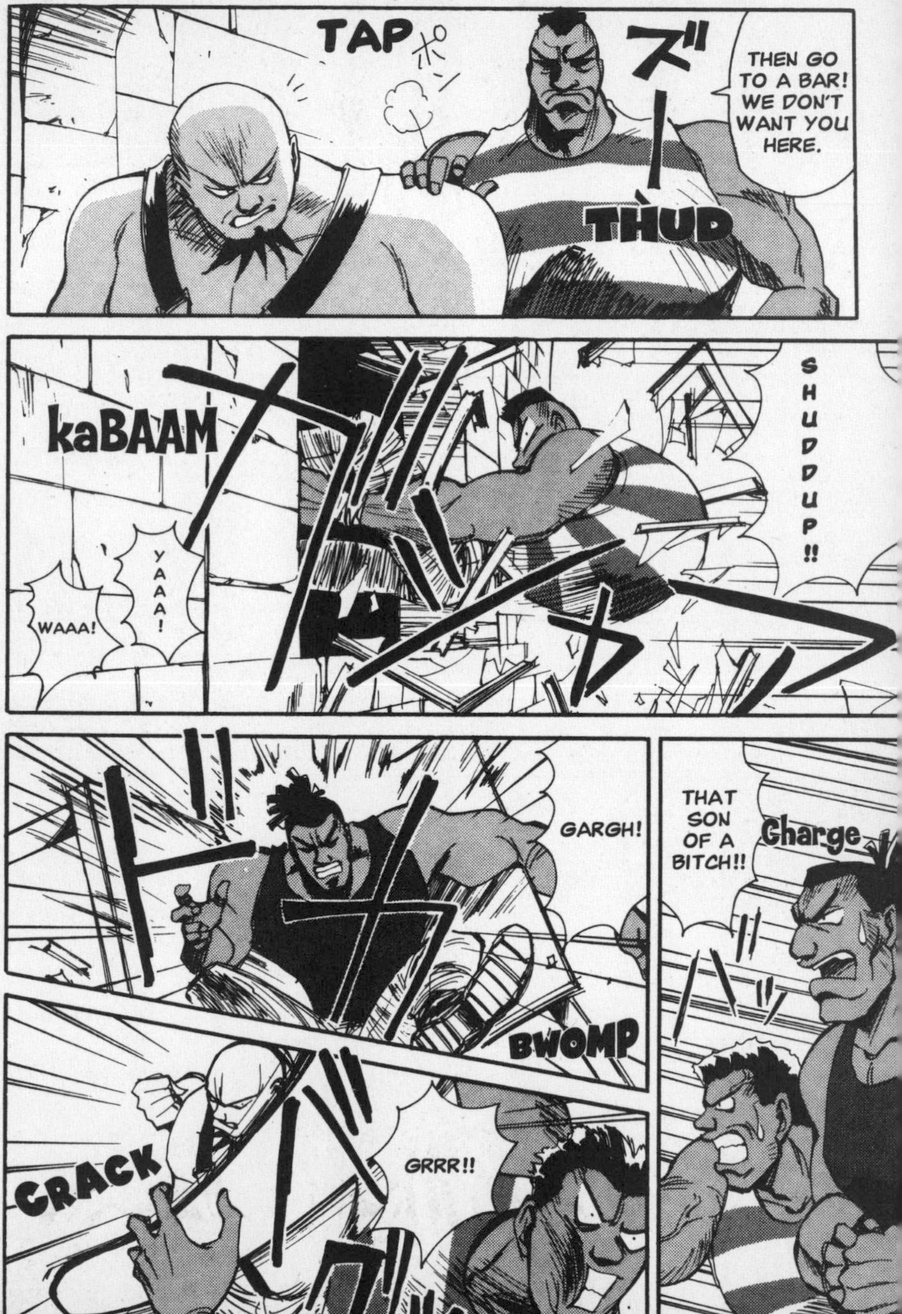
TAP
THEN GO TO A BAR! WE DON'T WANT YOU HERE.
THUD
kaBAAM
SHUDDUP!!
YAAAA!
WAAA!
GARGH!
BWOMP
THAT SON OF A BITCH!!
Charge
CRACK
GRRR!!

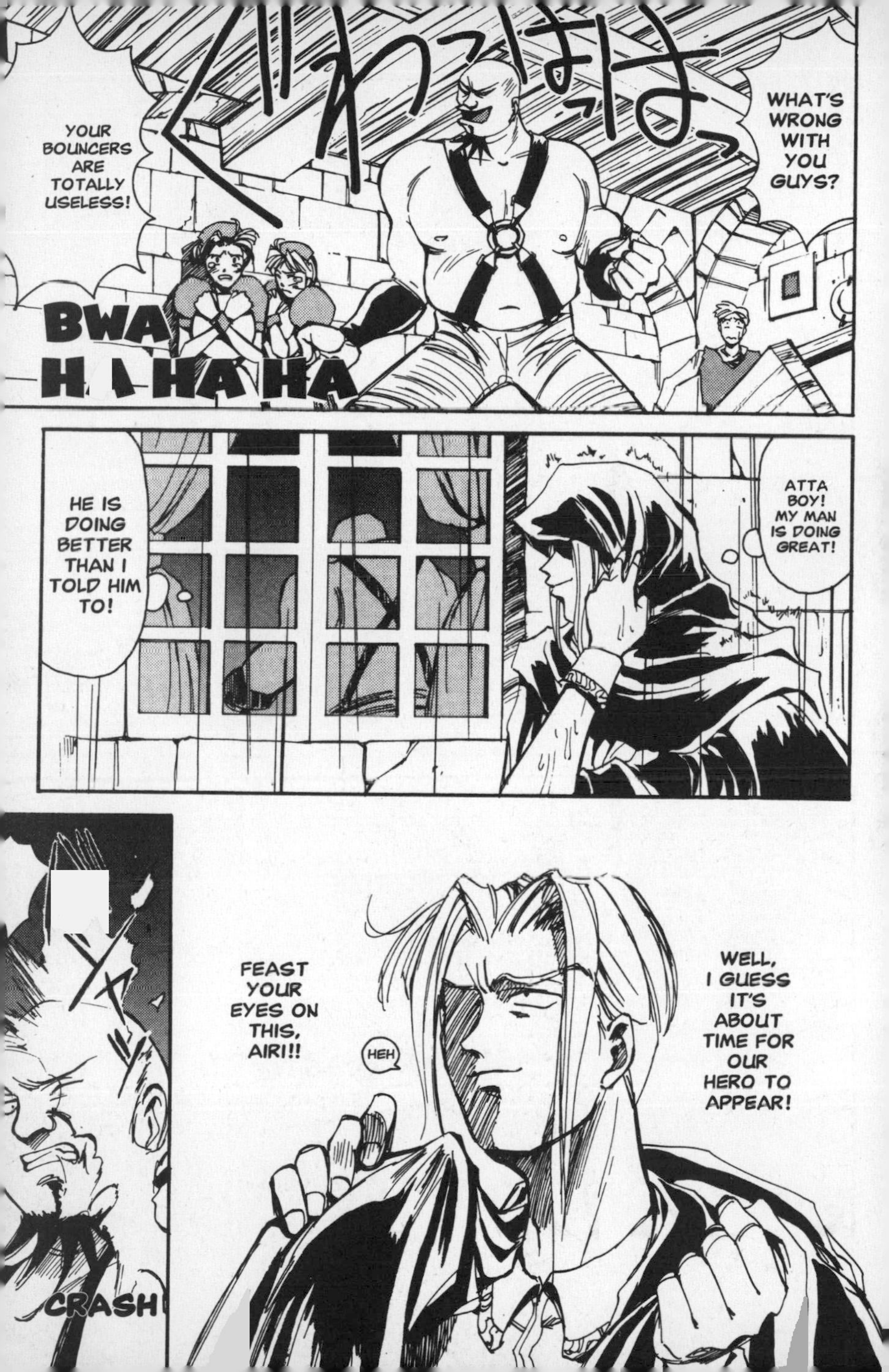

WHAT'S WRONG WITH YOU GUYS?
YOUR BOUNCERS ARE TOTALLY USELESS!
BWA HA HA HA HA
ATTA BOY! MY MAN IS DOING GREAT!
HE IS DOING BETTER THAN I TOLD HIM TO!
WELL, I GUESS IT'S ABOUT TIME FOR OUR HERO TO APPEAR!
HEH
FEAST YOUR EYES ON THIS, AIRI!!
CRASH

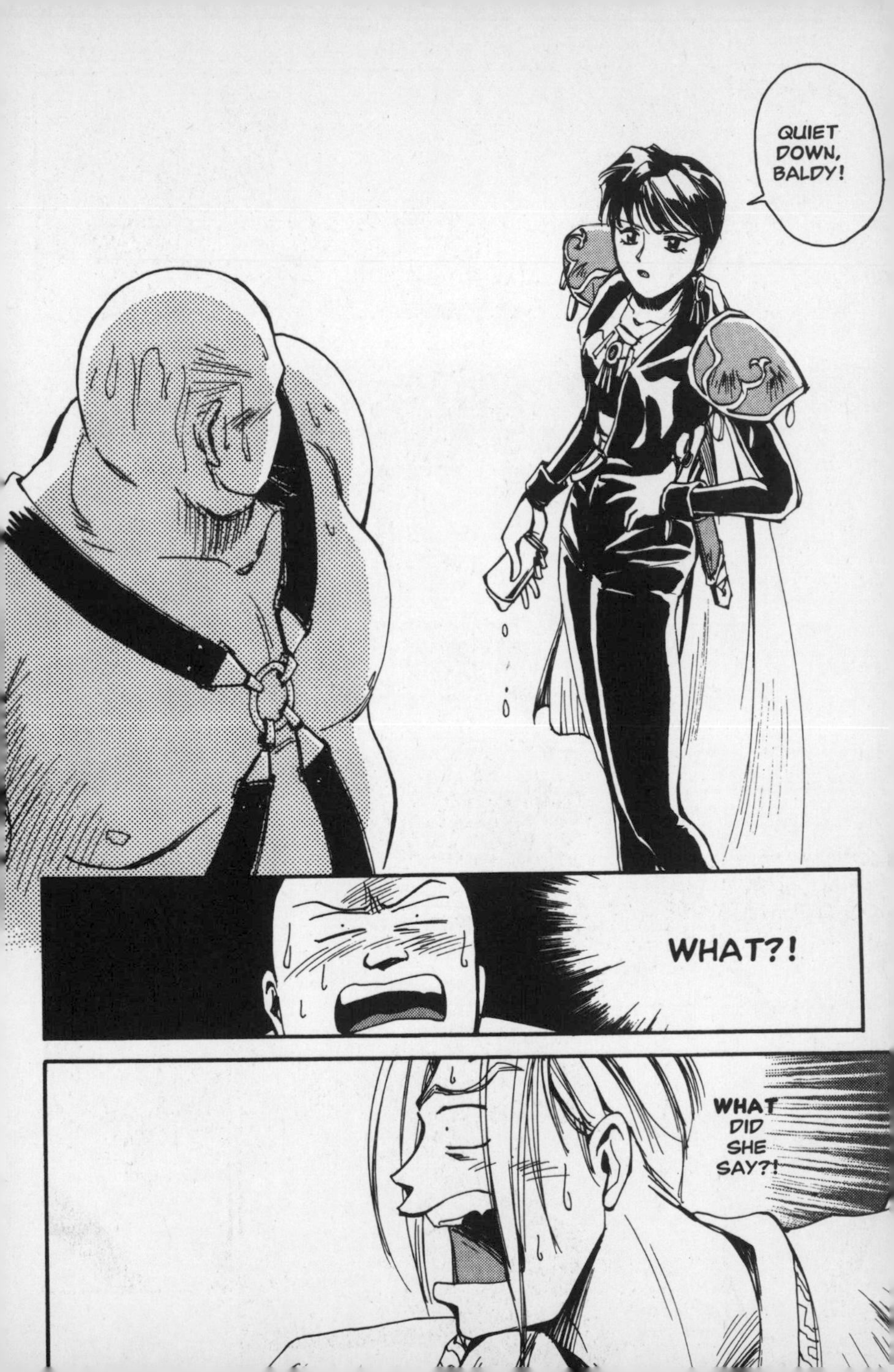
QUIET DOWN, BALDY!
WHAT?!
WHAT DID SHE SAY?!

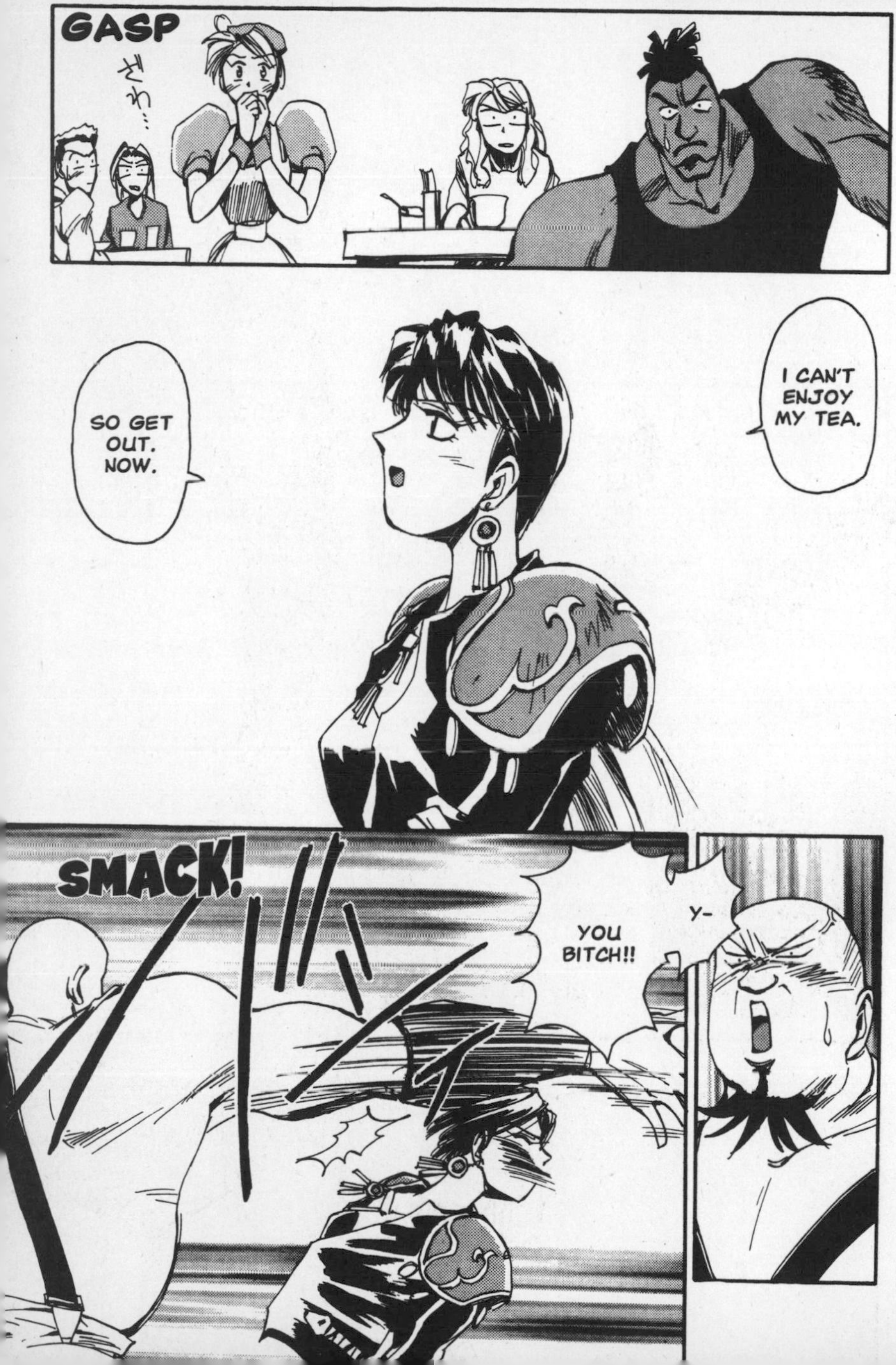
GASP
ざわ…
I CAN'T ENJOY MY TEA.
SO GET OUT. NOW.
Y-
YOU BITCH!!
SMACK!

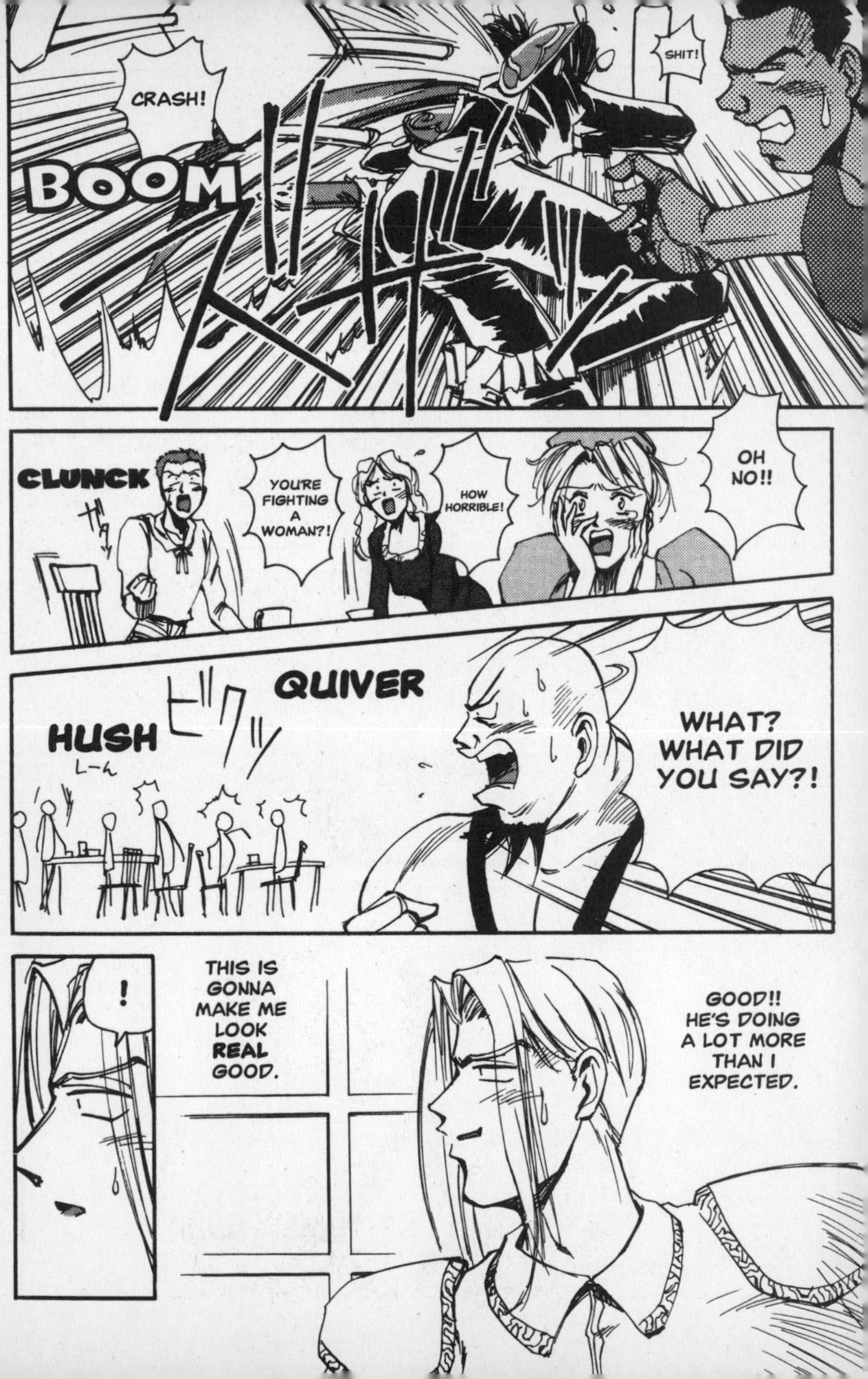
SHIT!
CRASH!
BOOM
OH NO!!
HOW HORRIBLE!
YOU'RE FIGHTING A WOMAN?!
CLUNCK
WHAT? WHAT DID YOU SAY?!
QUIVER
HUSH
GOOD!! HE'S DOING A LOT MORE THAN I EXPECTED.
THIS IS GONNA MAKE ME LOOK REAL GOOD.
!

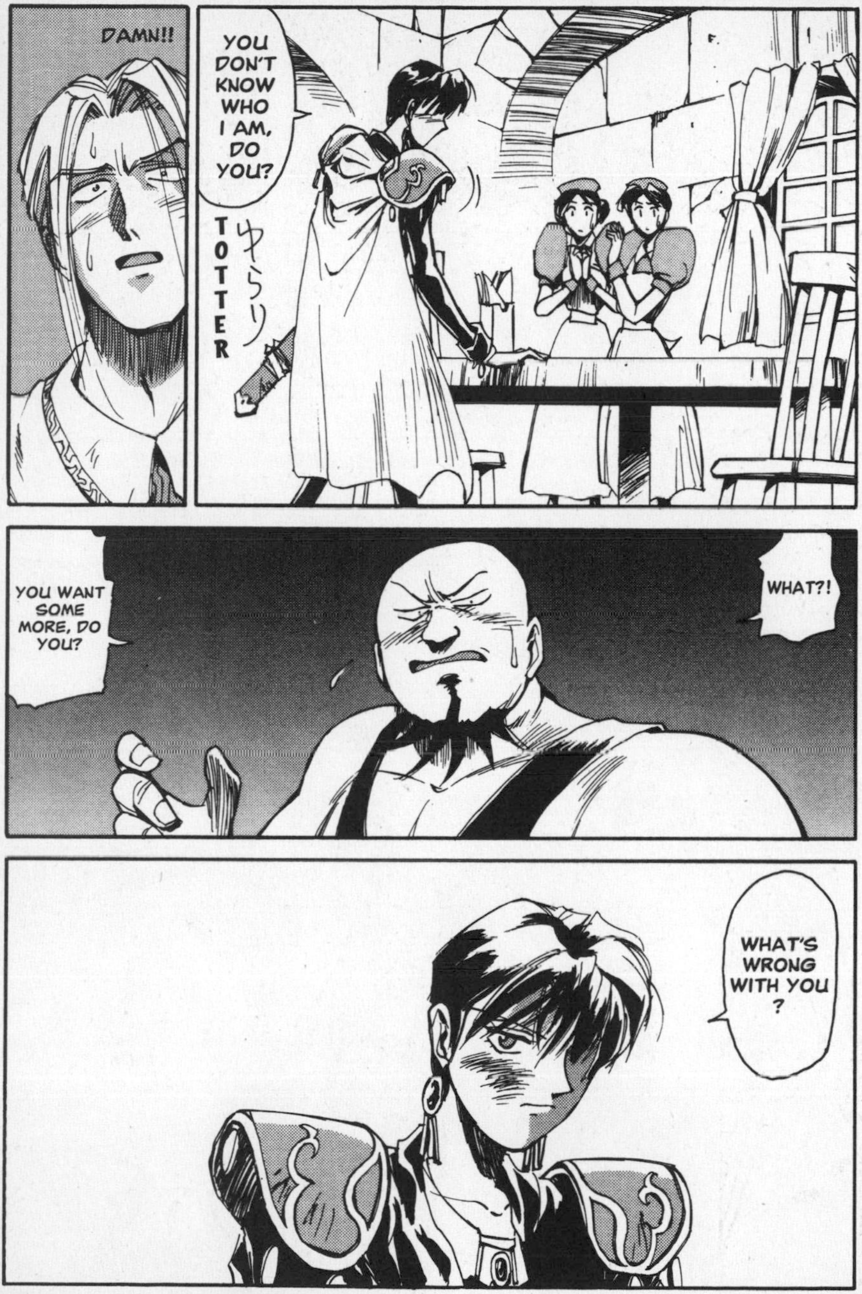
YOU DON'T KNOW WHO I AM, DO YOU?
やらり
TOTTER
DAMN!!
WHAT?!
YOU WANT SOME MORE, DO YOU?
WHAT'S WRONG WITH YOU ?

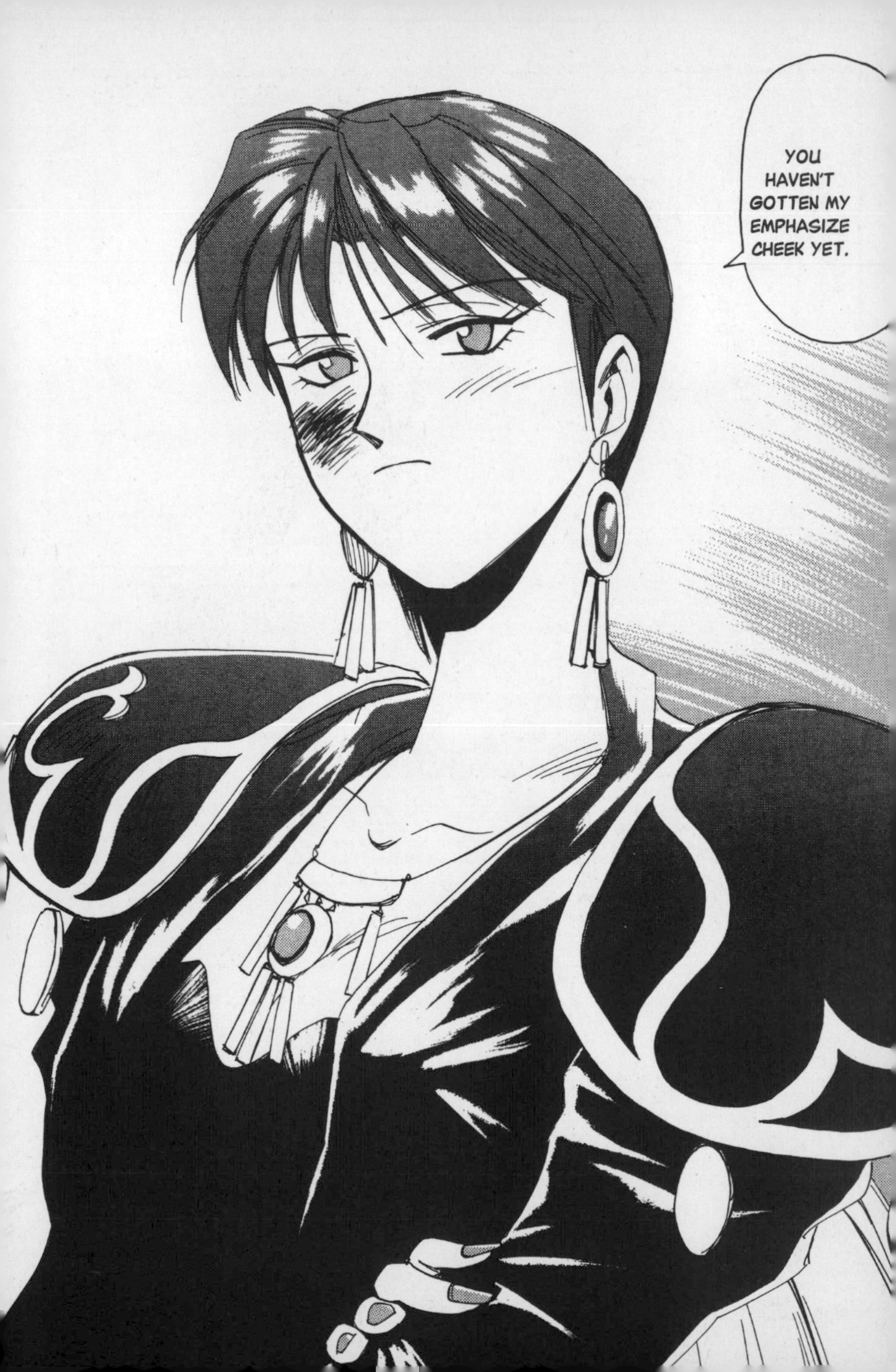
YOU HAVEN'T GOTTEN MY EMPHASIZE CHEEK YET.

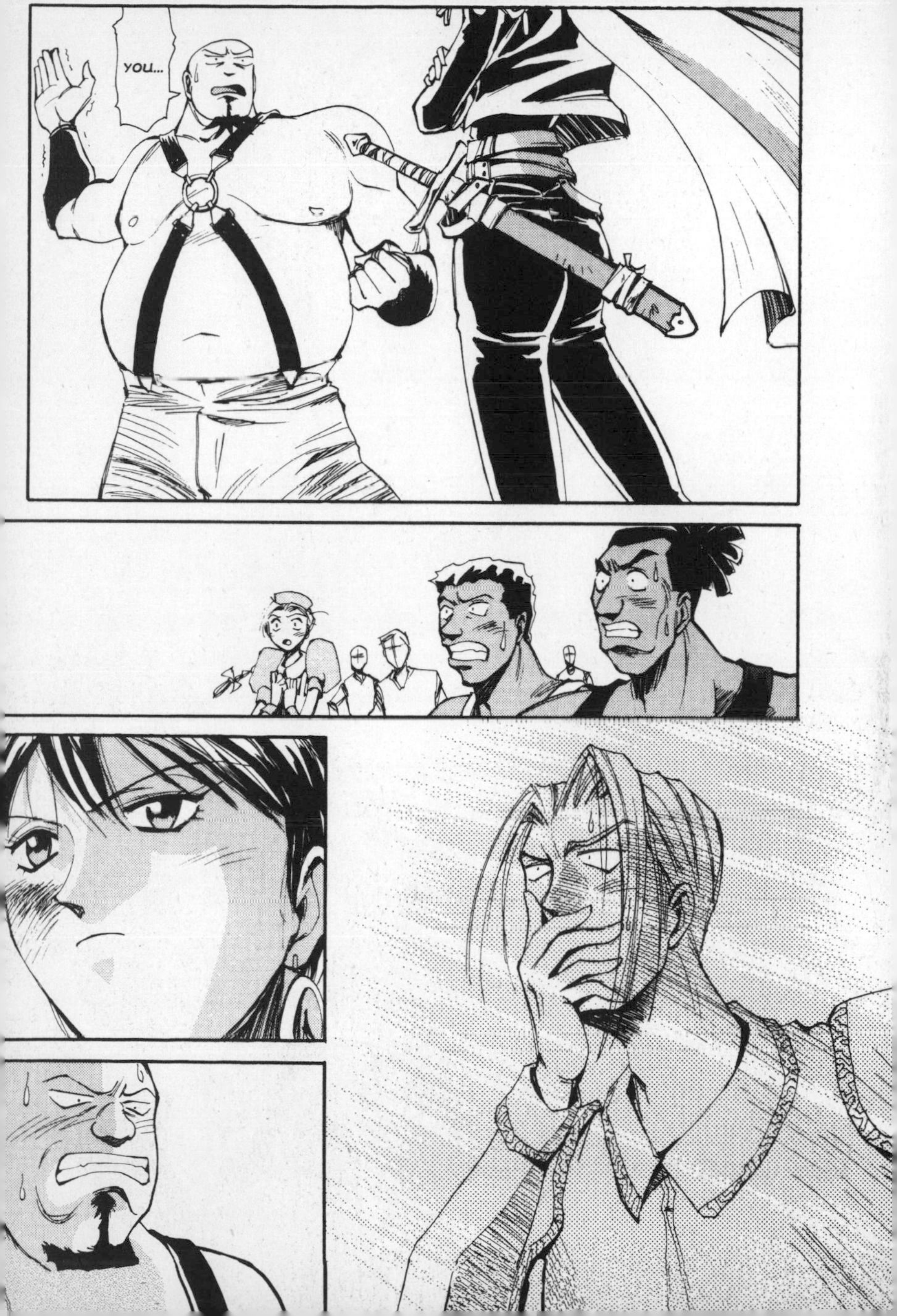
YOU...

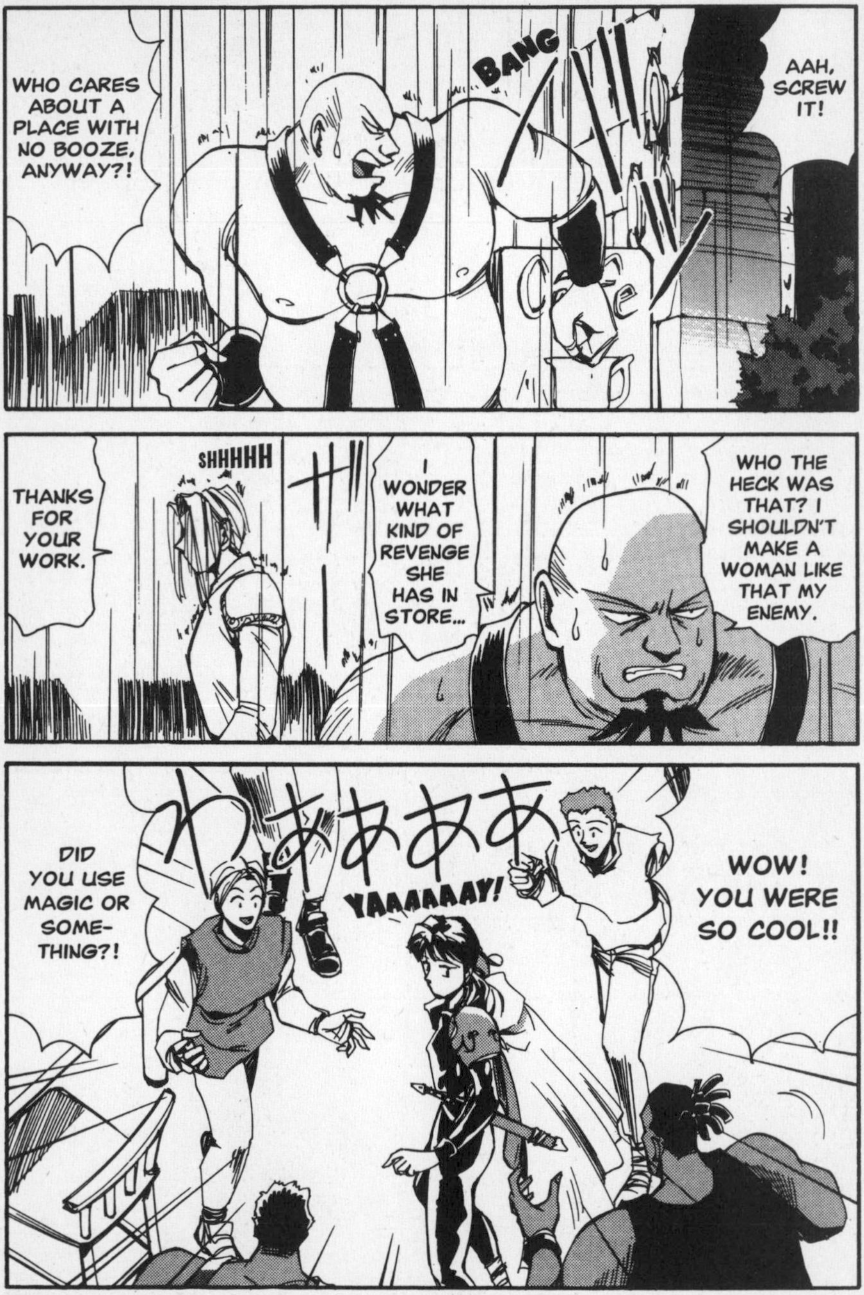
AAH, SCREW IT!
BANG
WHO CARES ABOUT A PLACE WITH NO BOOZE, ANYWAY?!
WHO THE HECK WAS THAT? I SHOULDN'T MAKE A WOMAN LIKE THAT MY ENEMY.
I WONDER WHAT KIND OF REVENGE SHE HAS IN STORE...
SHHHHH
THANKS FOR YOUR WORK.
わあああああ
WOW! YOU WERE SO COOL!!
YAAAAAAY!
DID YOU USE MAGIC OR SOME-THING?!

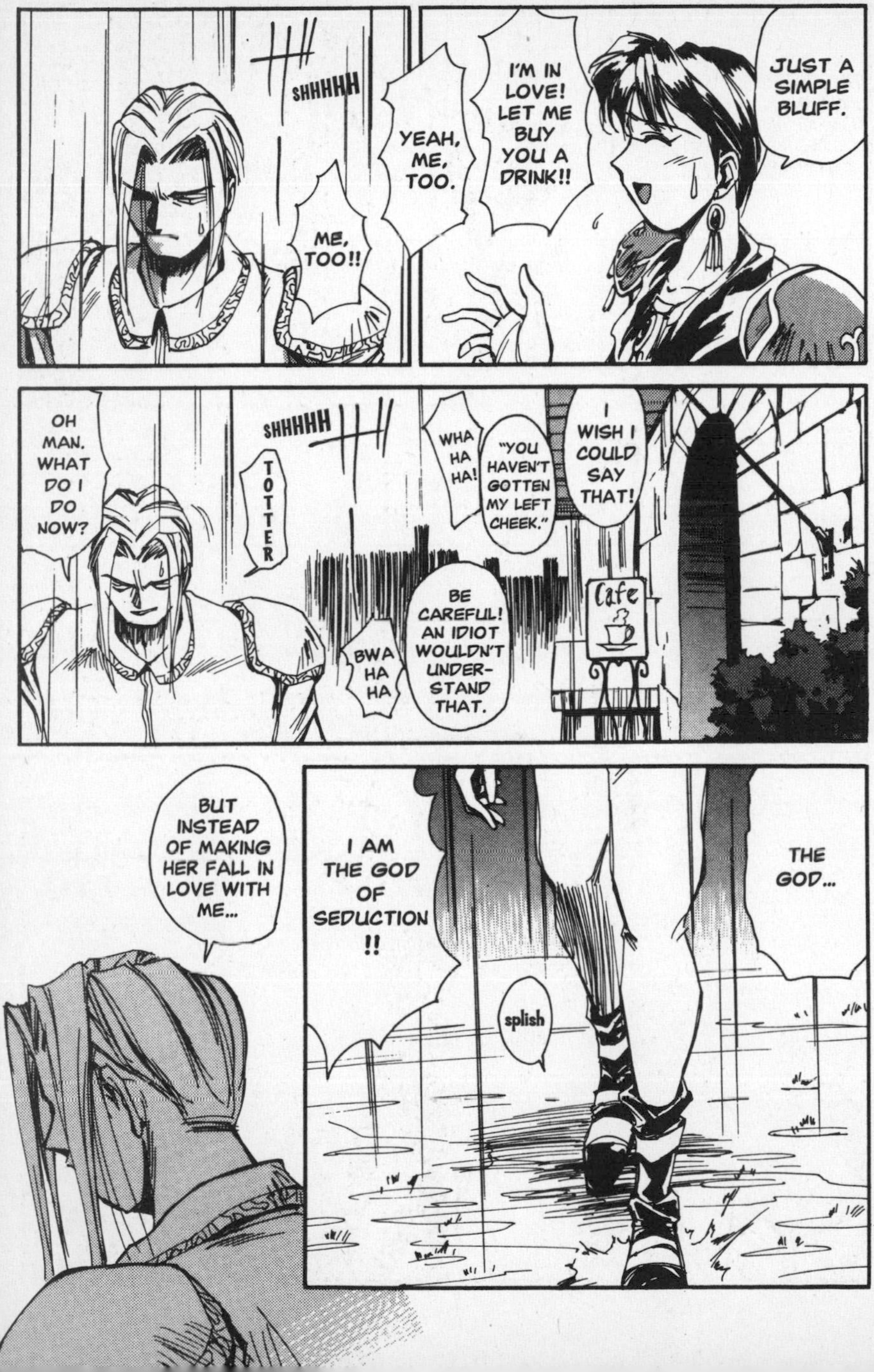
JUST A SIMPLE BLUFF.
I'M IN LOVE! LET ME BUY YOU A DRINK!!
YEAH, ME, TOO.
ME, TOO!!
SHHHHH
I WISH I COULD SAY THAT!
"YOU HAVEN'T GOTTEN MY LEFT CHEEK."
WHA HA HA!
BE CAREFUL! AN IDIOT WOULDN'T UNDER-STAND THAT.
BWA HA HA
Cafe
TOTTER
SHHHHH
OH MAN. WHAT DO I DO NOW?
THE GOD...
I AM THE GOD OF SEDUCTION!!
splish
BUT INSTEAD OF MAKING HER FALL IN LOVE WITH ME...

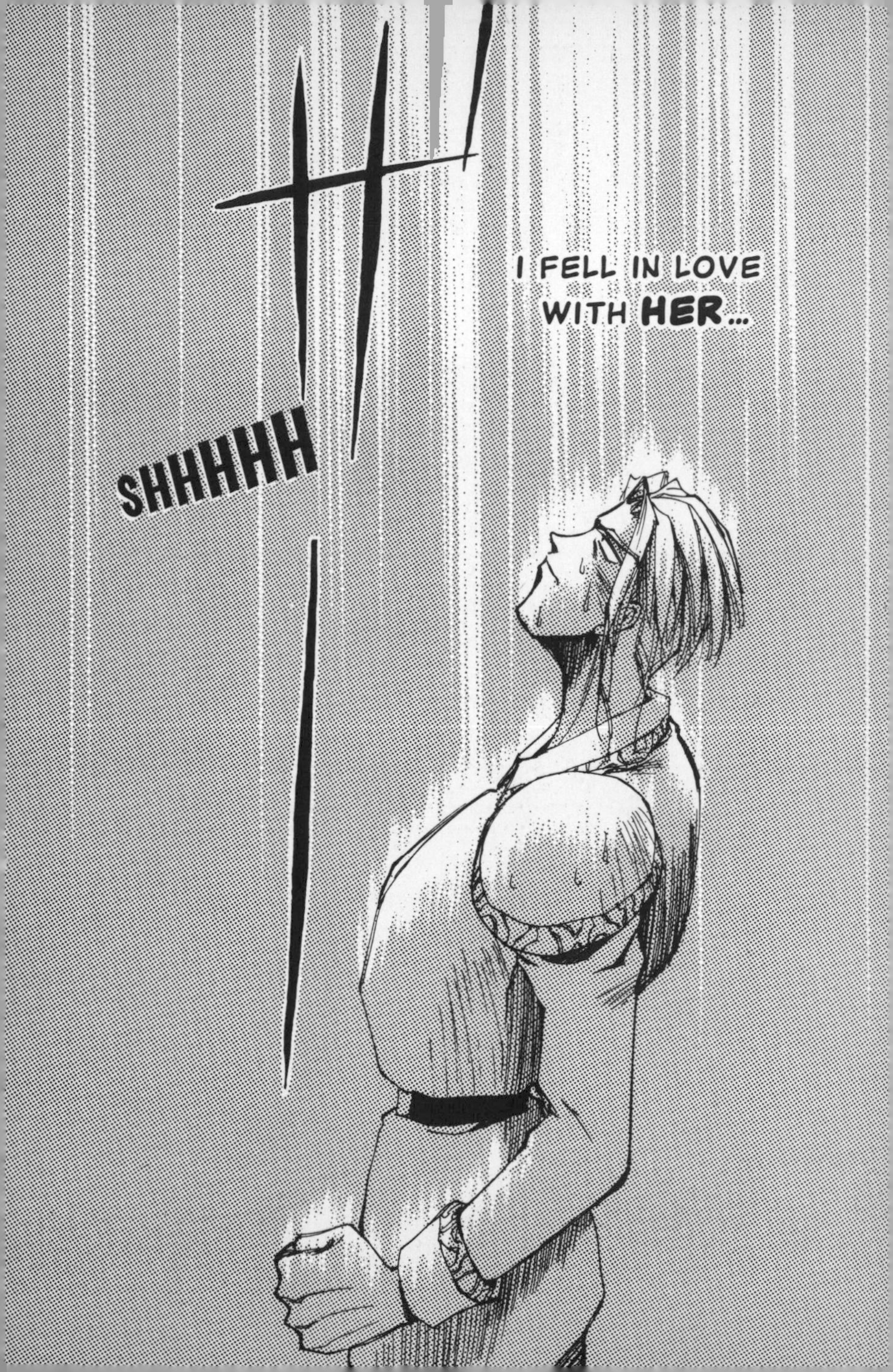
I FELL IN LOVE WITH HER...
SHHHHH

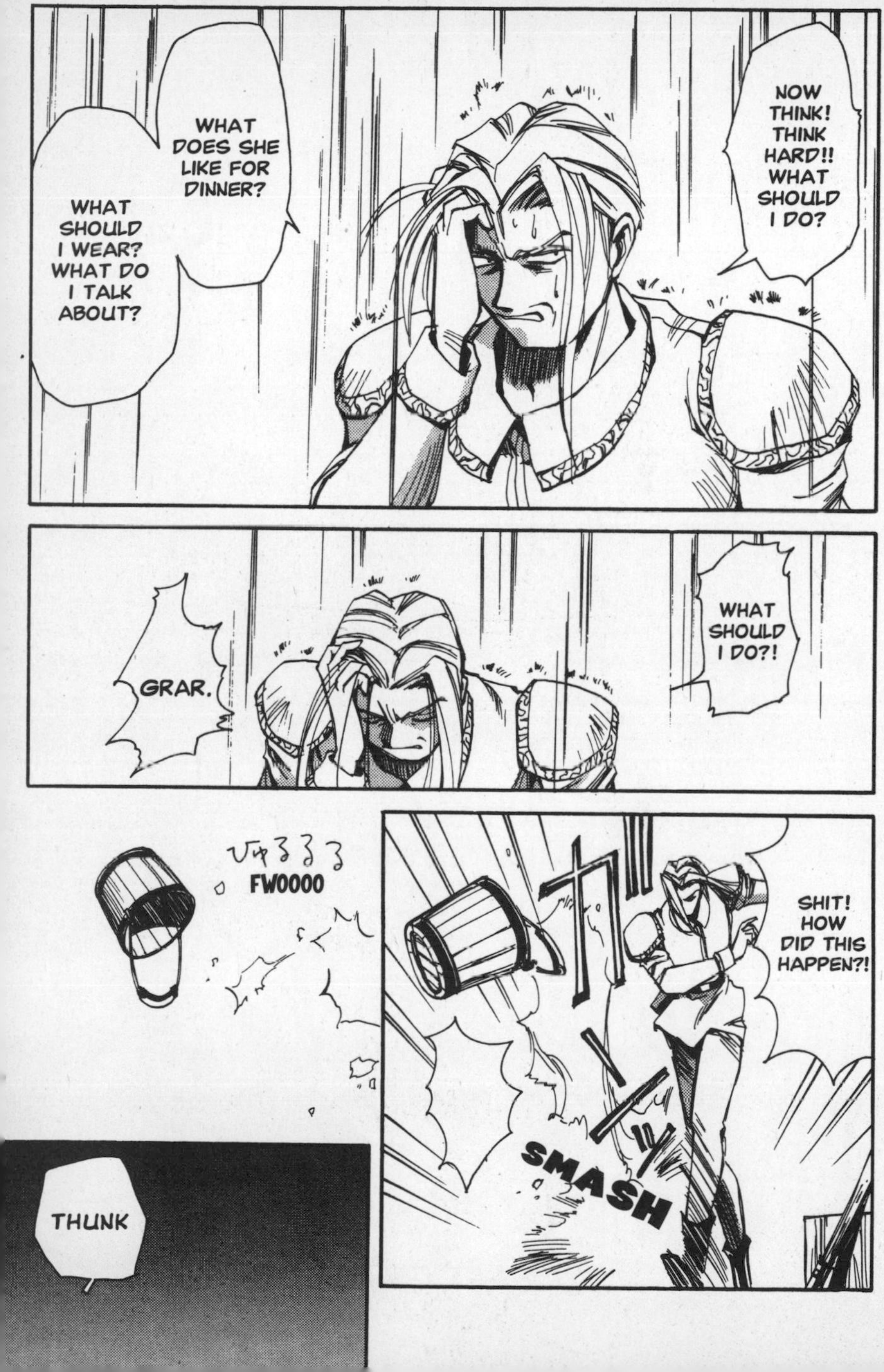
WHAT SHOULD I WEAR? WHAT DO I TALK ABOUT?
WHAT DOES SHE LIKE FOR DINNER?
NOW THINK! THINK HARD!! WHAT SHOULD I DO?
GRAR.
WHAT SHOULD I DO?!
ひゅるるる
FWOOOO
THUNK
SMASH
SHIT! HOW DID THIS HAPPEN?!

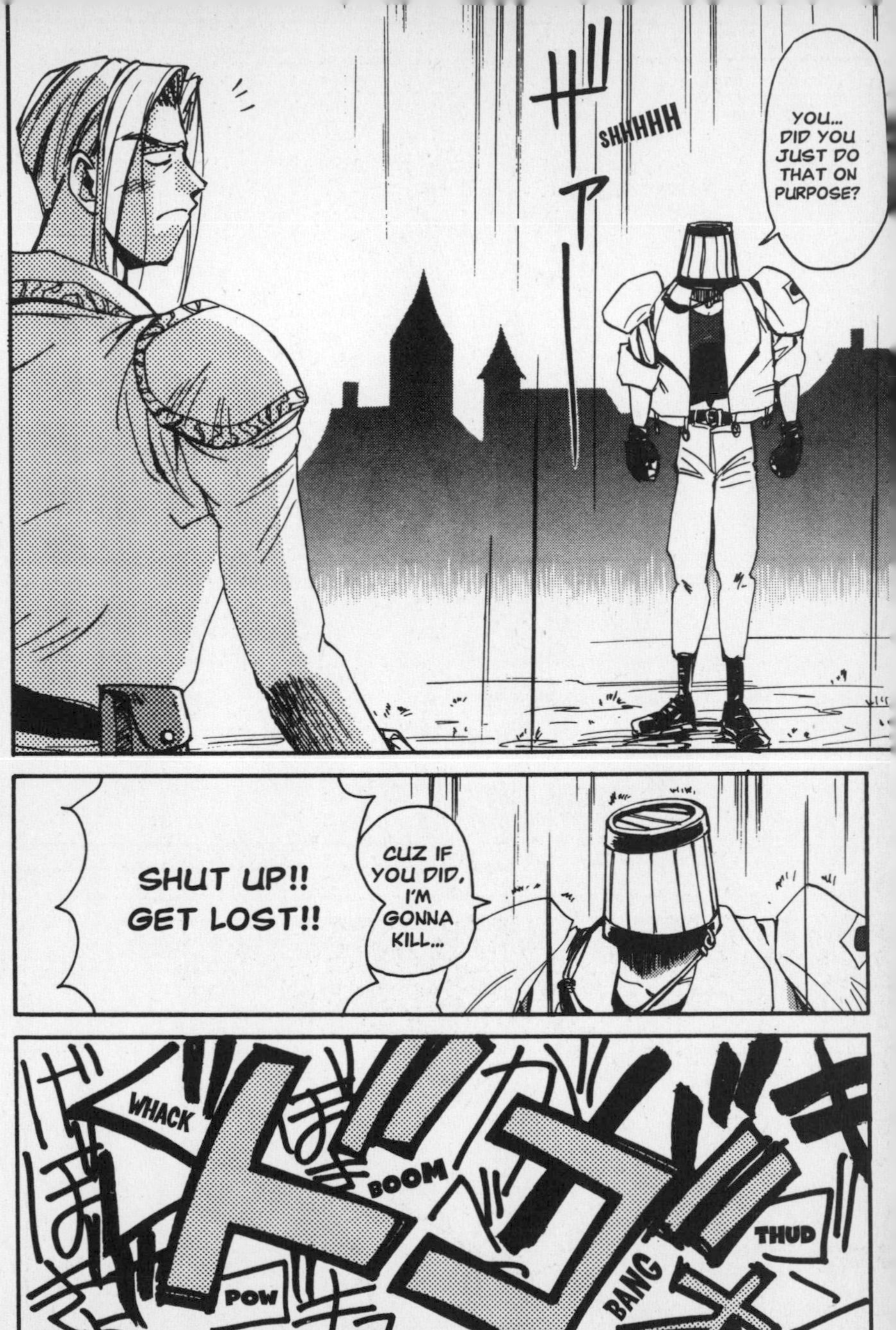
SHHHHH
YOU... DID YOU JUST DO THAT ON PURPOSE?
CUZ IF YOU DID, I'M GONNA KILL...
SHUT UP!! GET LOST!!
THUD
BANG
BOOM
WHACK
POW

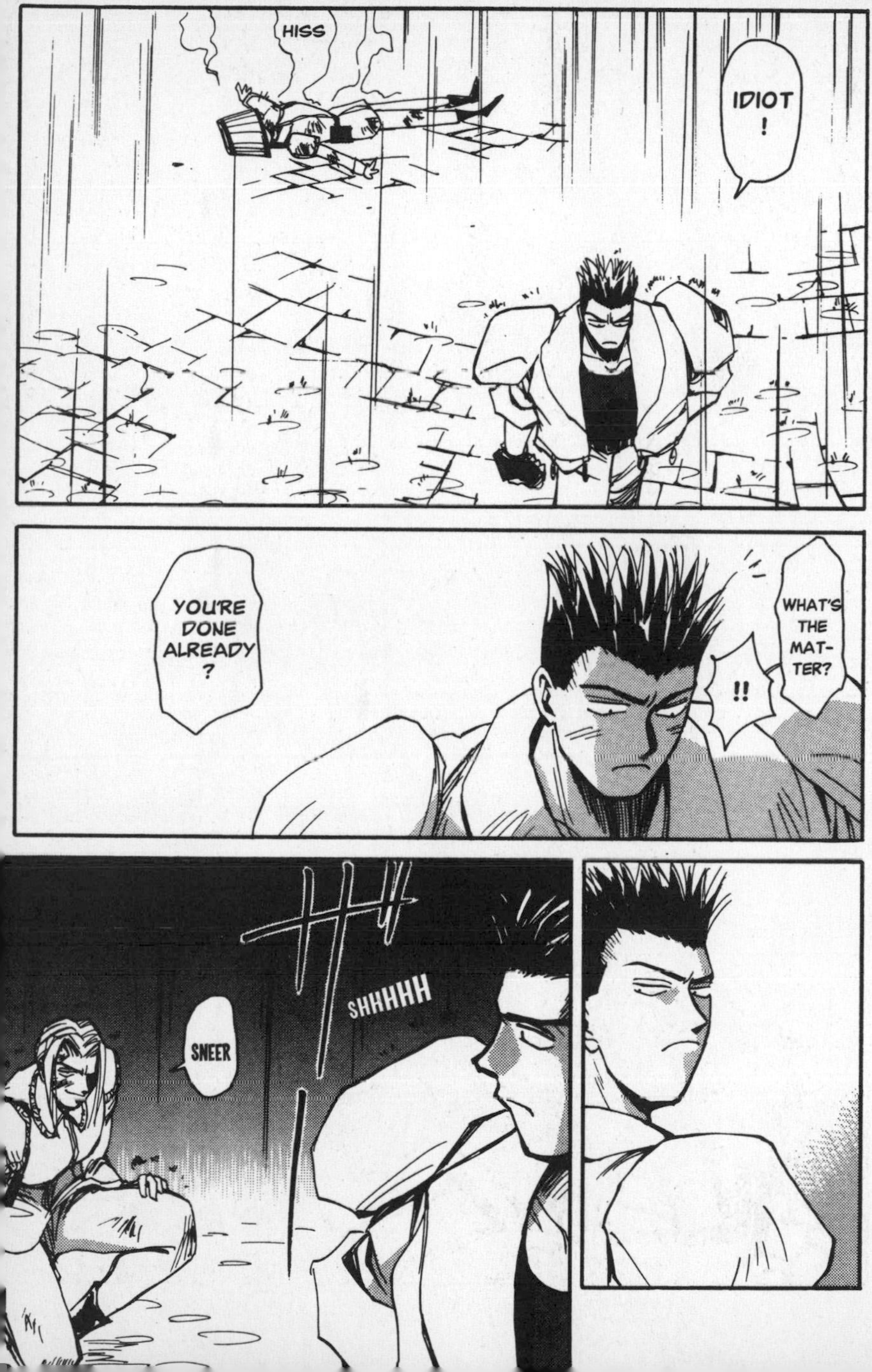
HISS
IDIOT!
YOU'RE DONE ALREADY?
!!
WHAT'S THE MAT-TER?
SNEER
SHHHHH

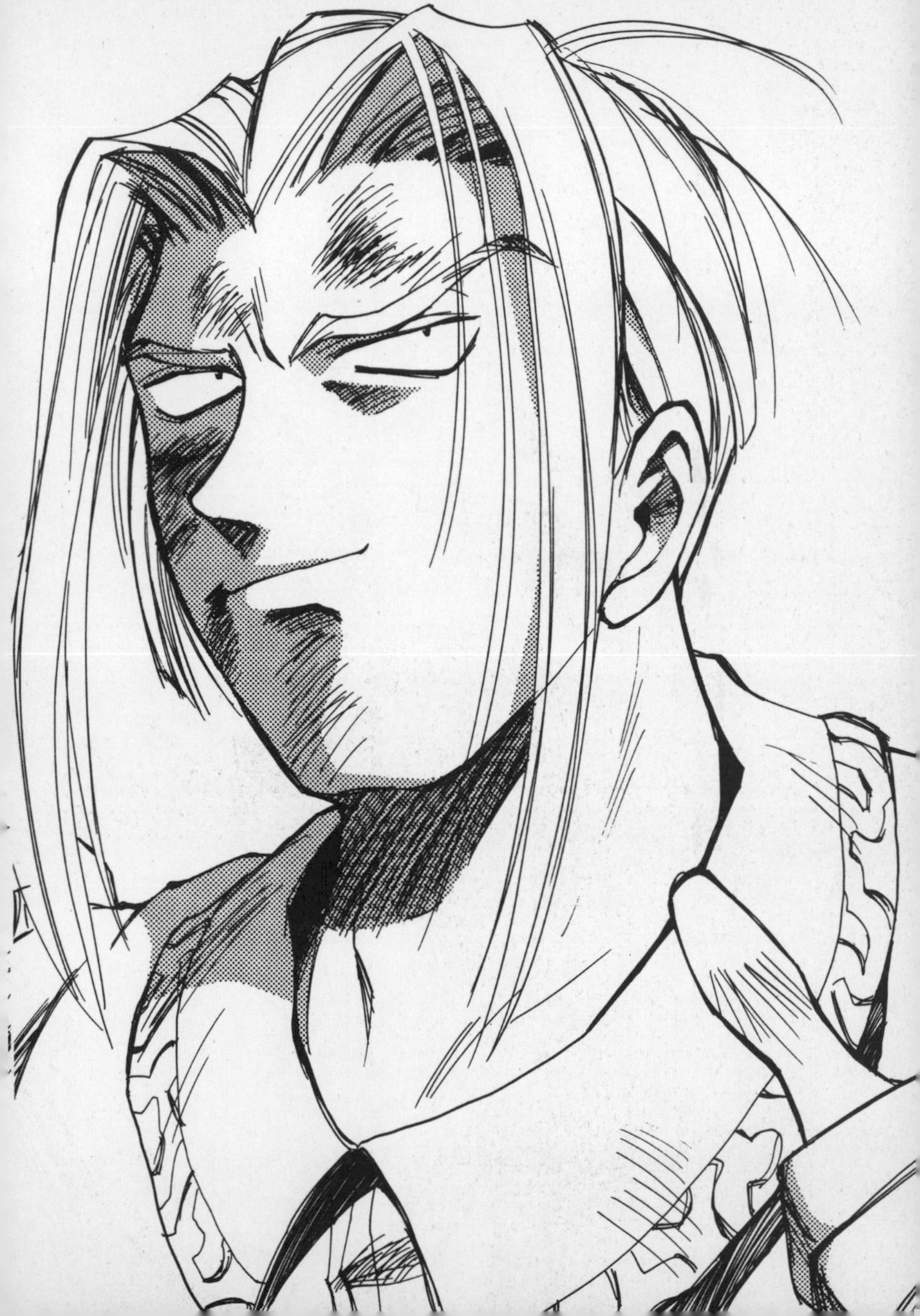

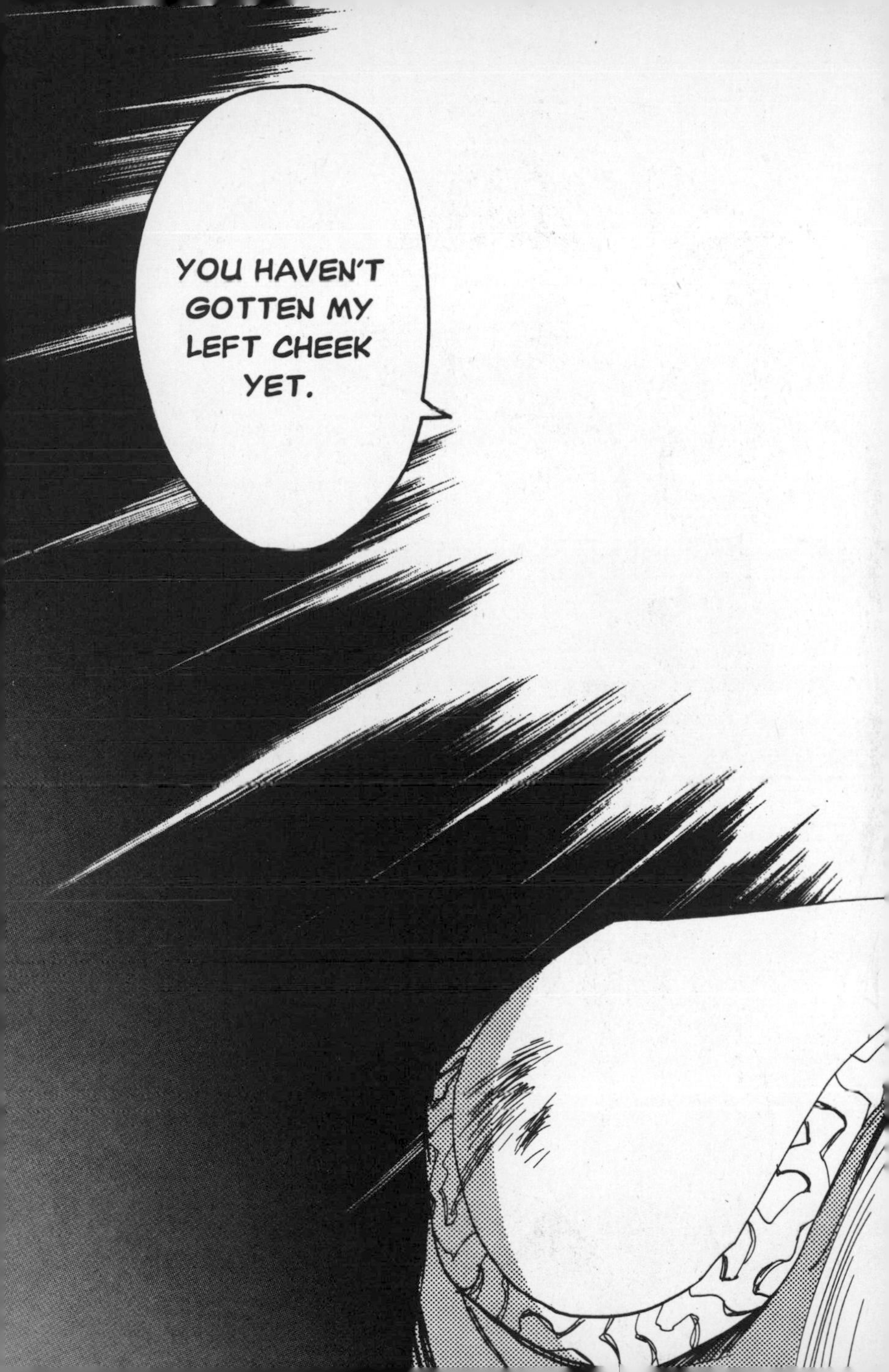
YOU HAVEN'T GOTTEN MY LEFT CHEEK YET.

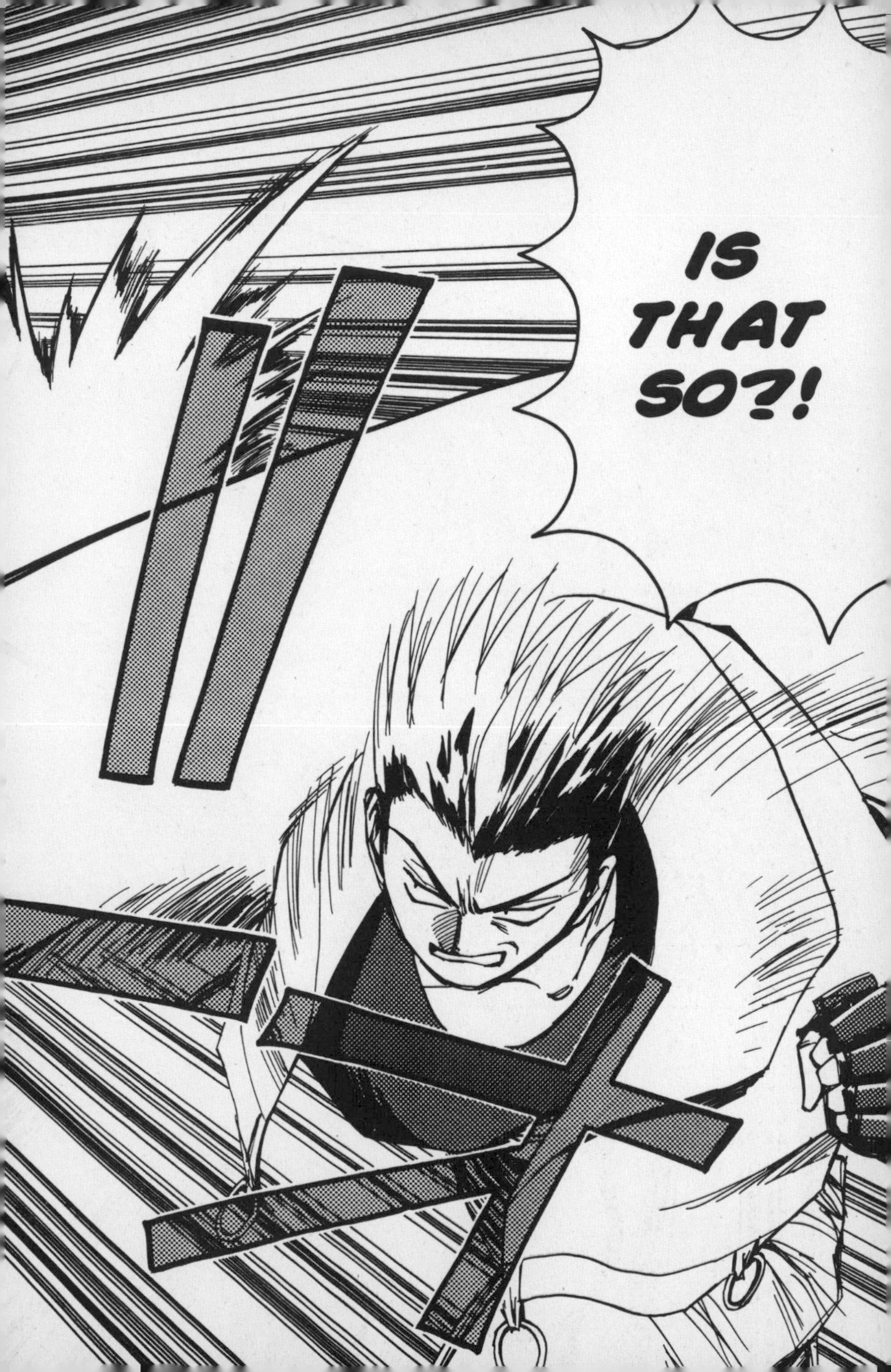
IS THAT SO?!

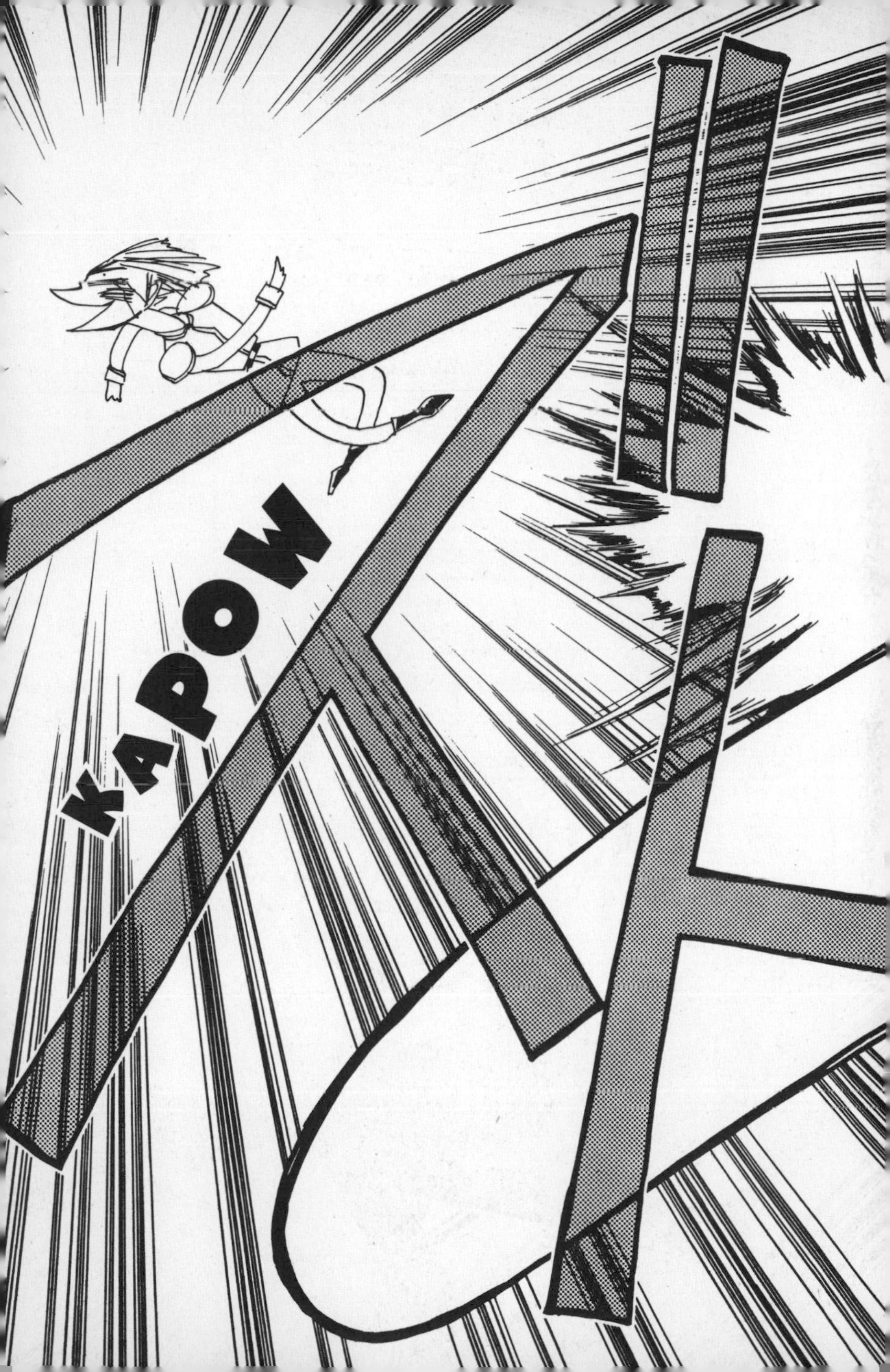
KAPOW

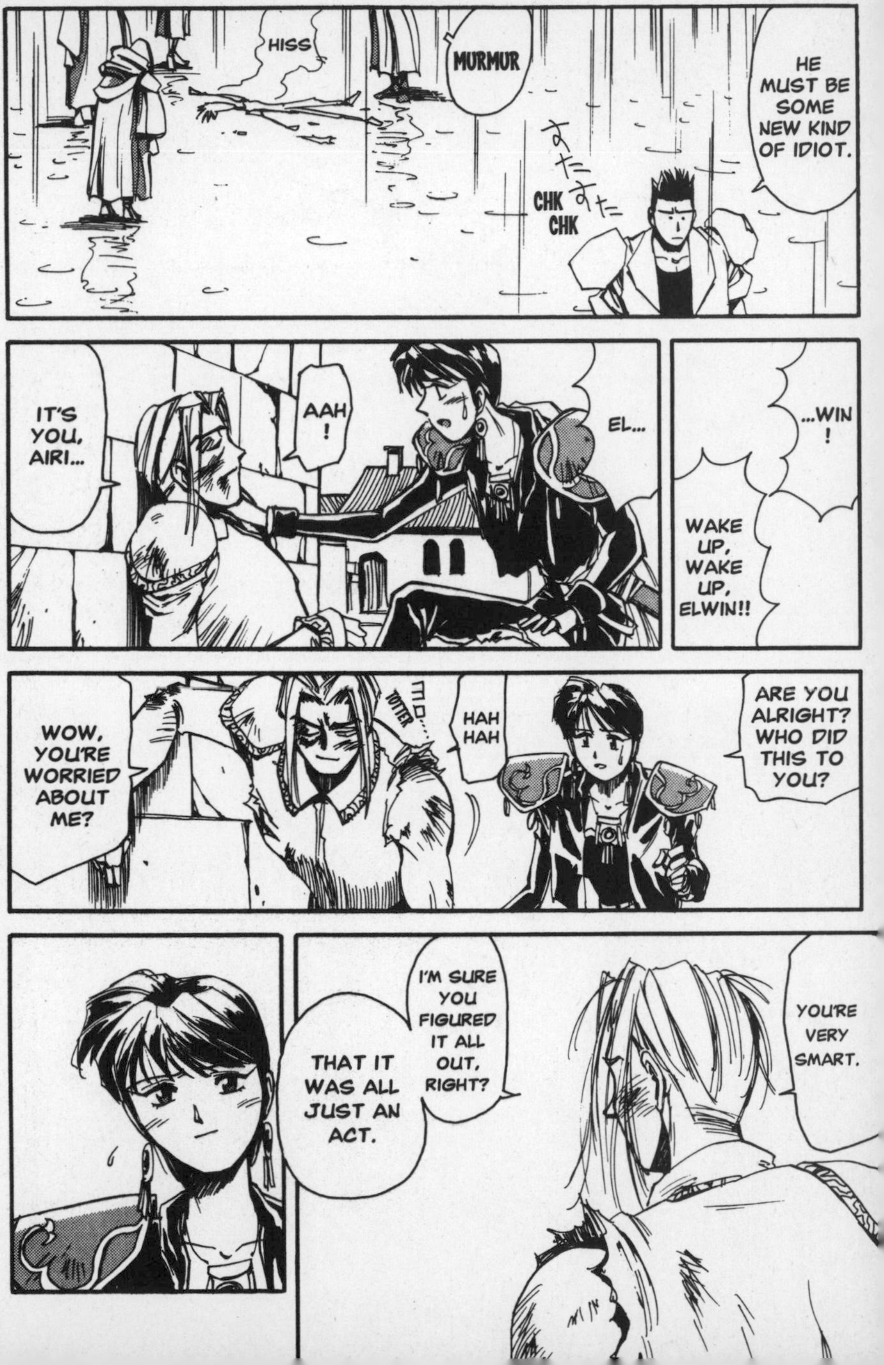
HE MUST BE SOME NEW KIND OF IDIOT.
CHK CHK
すたすた
MURMUR
HISS
...WIN!
WAKE UP, WAKE UP, ELWIN!!
EL...
AAH!
IT'S YOU, AIRI...
ARE YOU ALRIGHT? WHO DID THIS TO YOU?
HAH HAH
TOTTER
WOW, YOU'RE WORRIED ABOUT ME?
YOU'RE VERY SMART.
I'M SURE YOU FIGURED IT ALL OUT, RIGHT?
THAT IT WAS ALL JUST AN ACT.

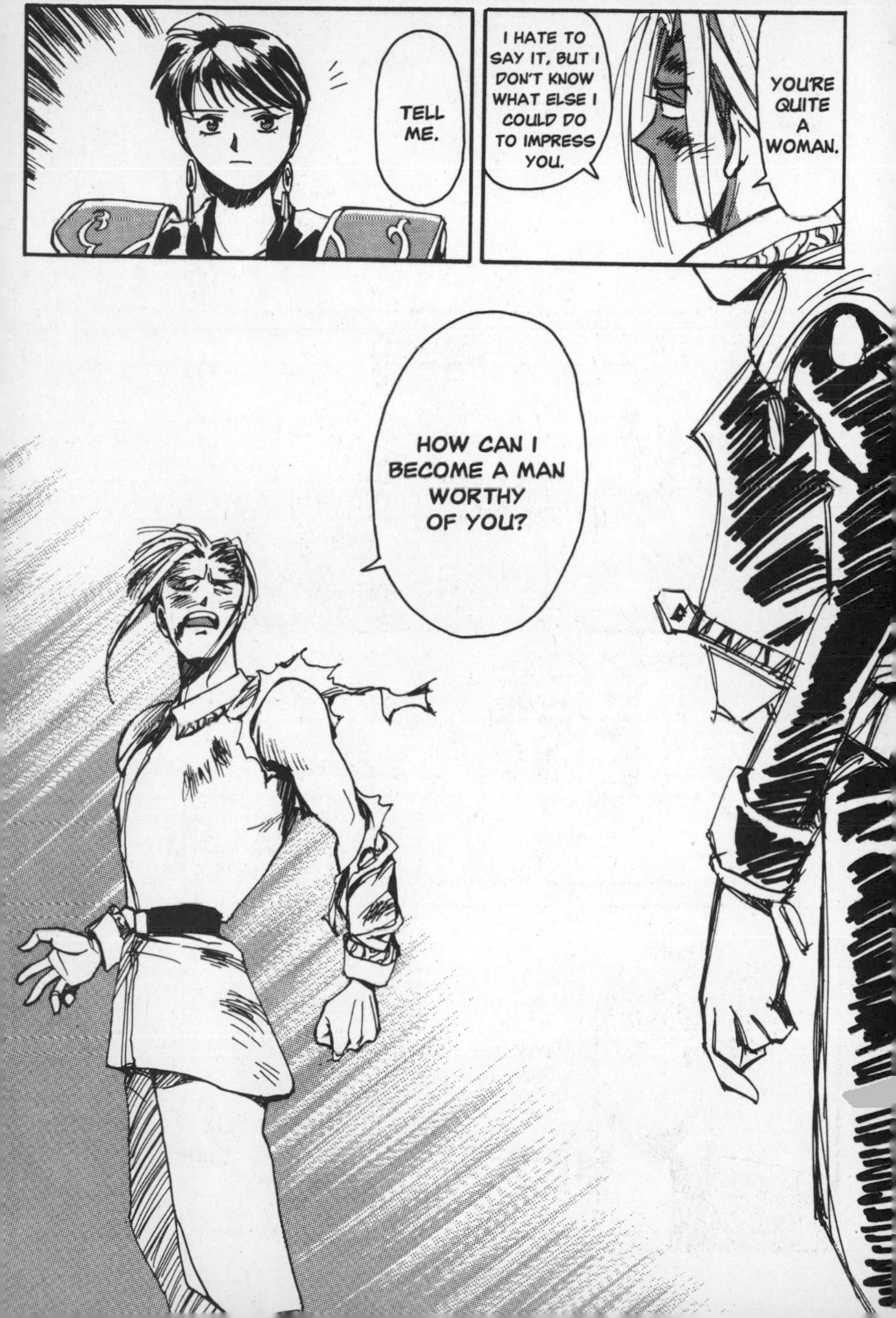
YOU'RE QUITE A WOMAN.
I HATE TO SAY IT, BUT I DON'T KNOW WHAT ELSE I COULD DO TO IMPRESS YOU.
TELL ME.
HOW CAN I BECOME A MAN WORTHY OF YOU?

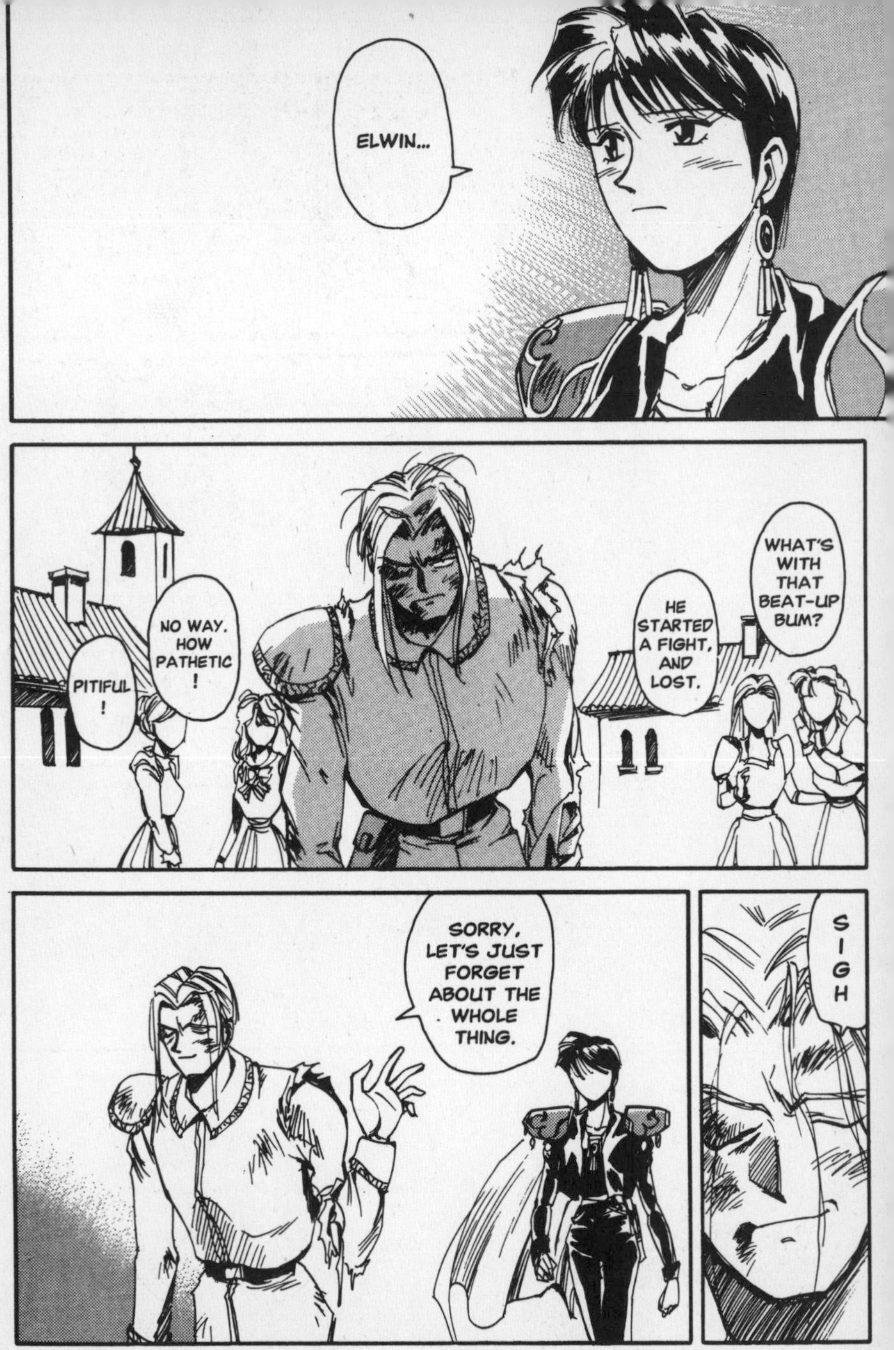
ELWIN...
WHAT'S WITH THAT BEAT-UP BUM?
HE STARTED A FIGHT, AND LOST.
NO WAY. HOW PATHETIC!
PITIFUL!
SORRY, LET'S JUST FORGET ABOUT THE WHOLE THING.
SIGH

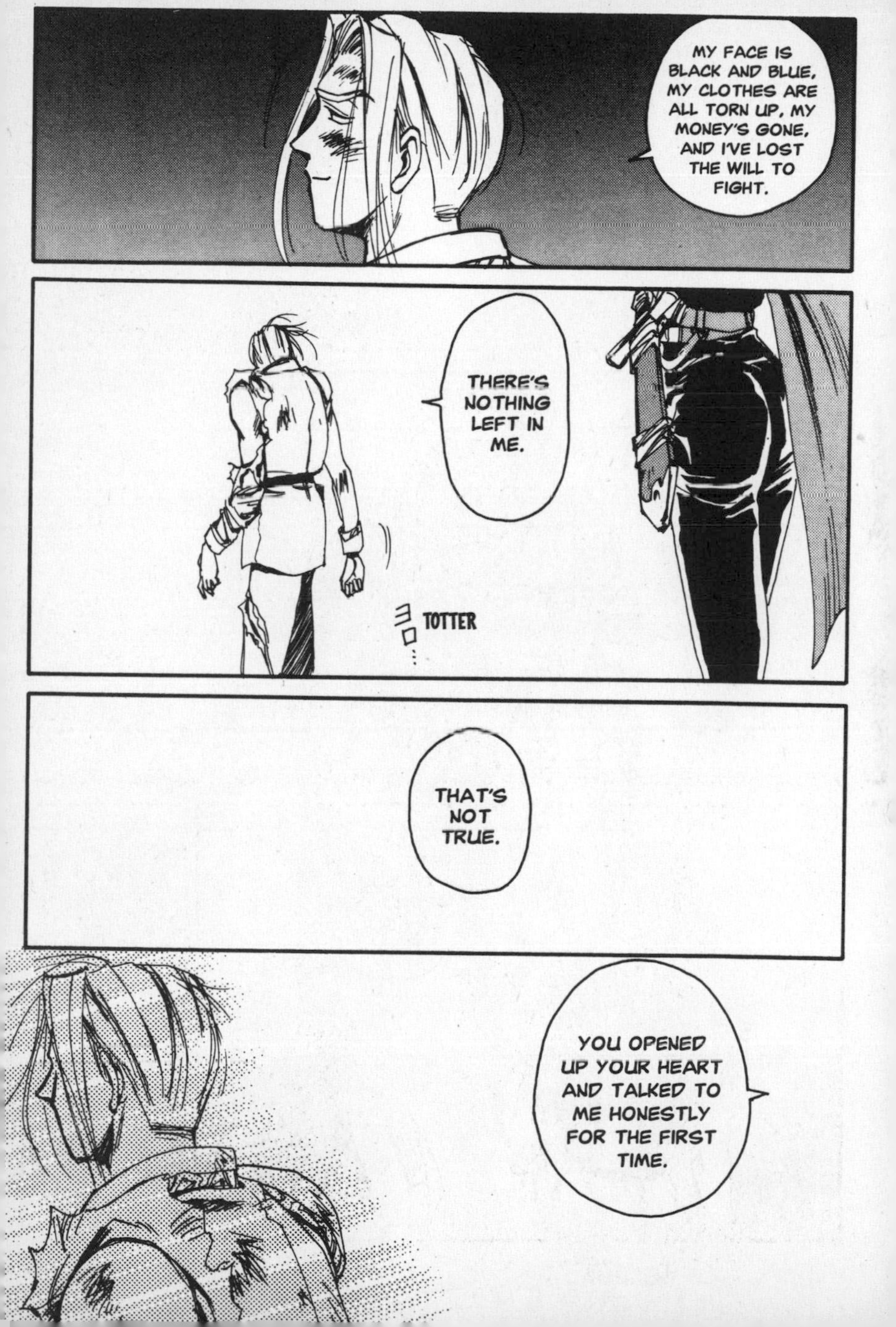
MY FACE IS BLACK AND BLUE, MY CLOTHES ARE ALL TORN UP, MY MONEY'S GONE, AND I'VE LOST THE WILL TO FIGHT.
THERE'S NOTHING LEFT IN ME.
ヨロ…
TOTTER
THAT'S NOT TRUE.
YOU OPENED UP YOUR HEART AND TALKED TO ME HONESTLY FOR THE FIRST TIME.

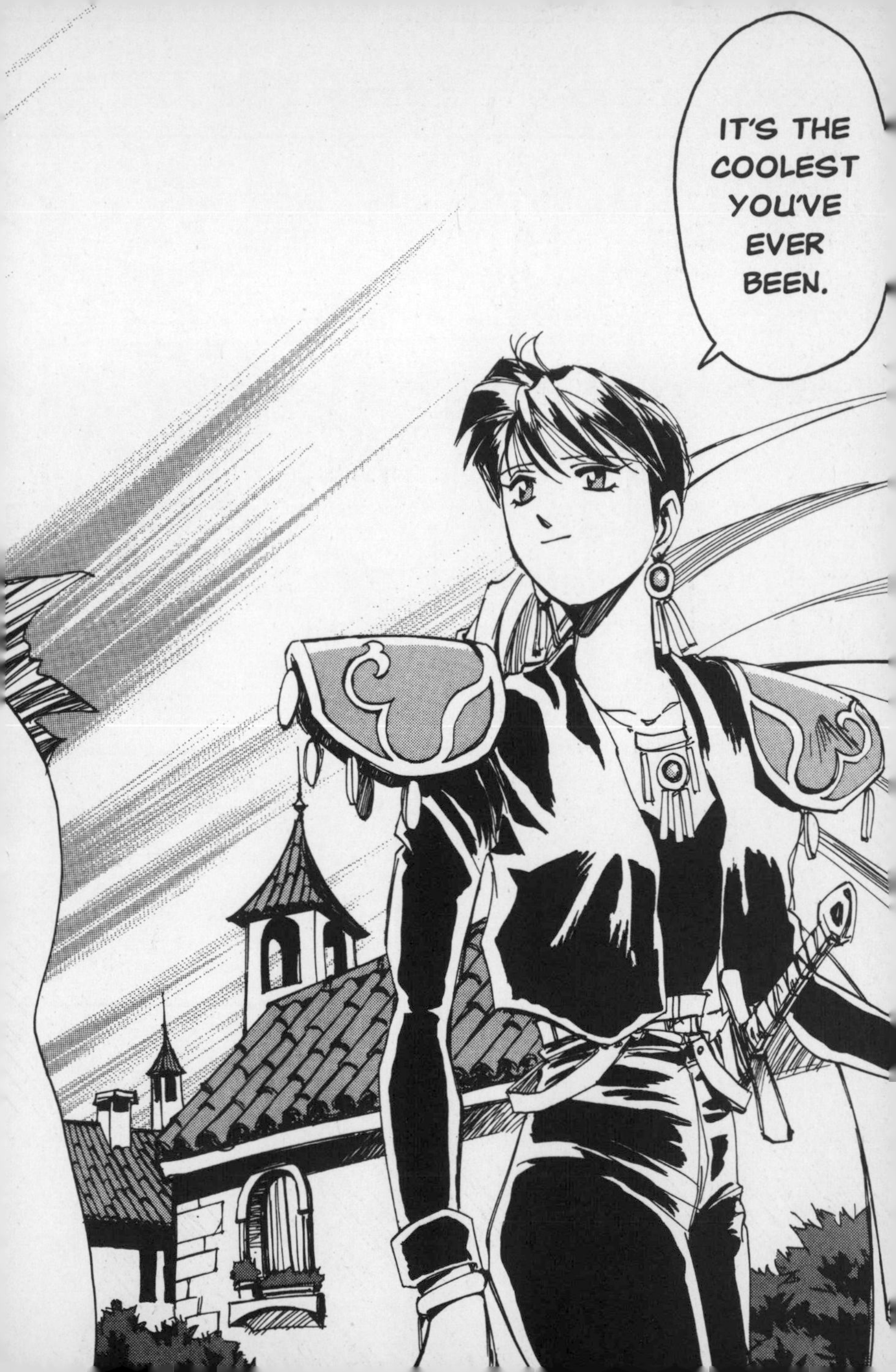
IT'S THE COOLEST YOU'VE EVER BEEN.

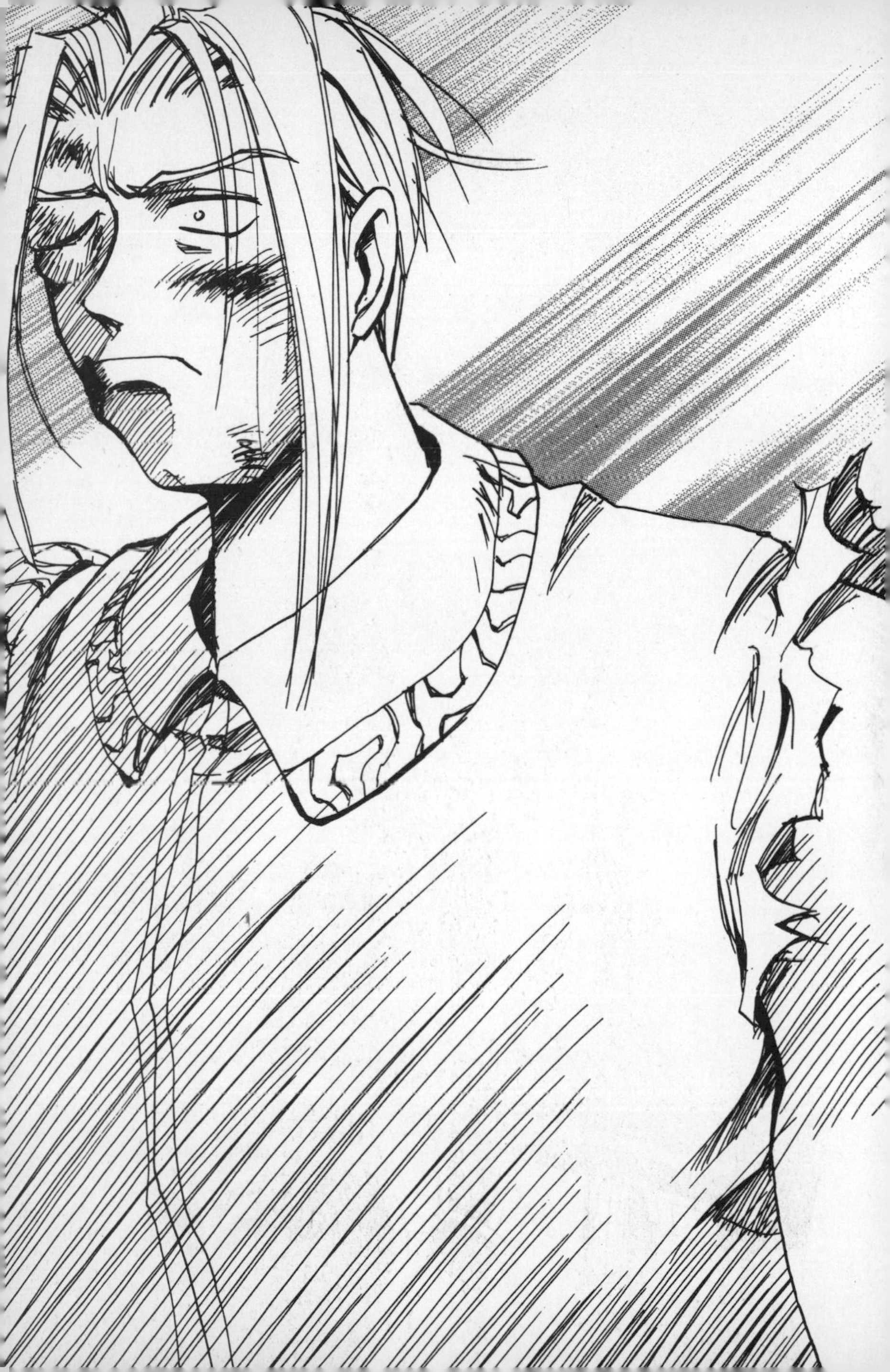

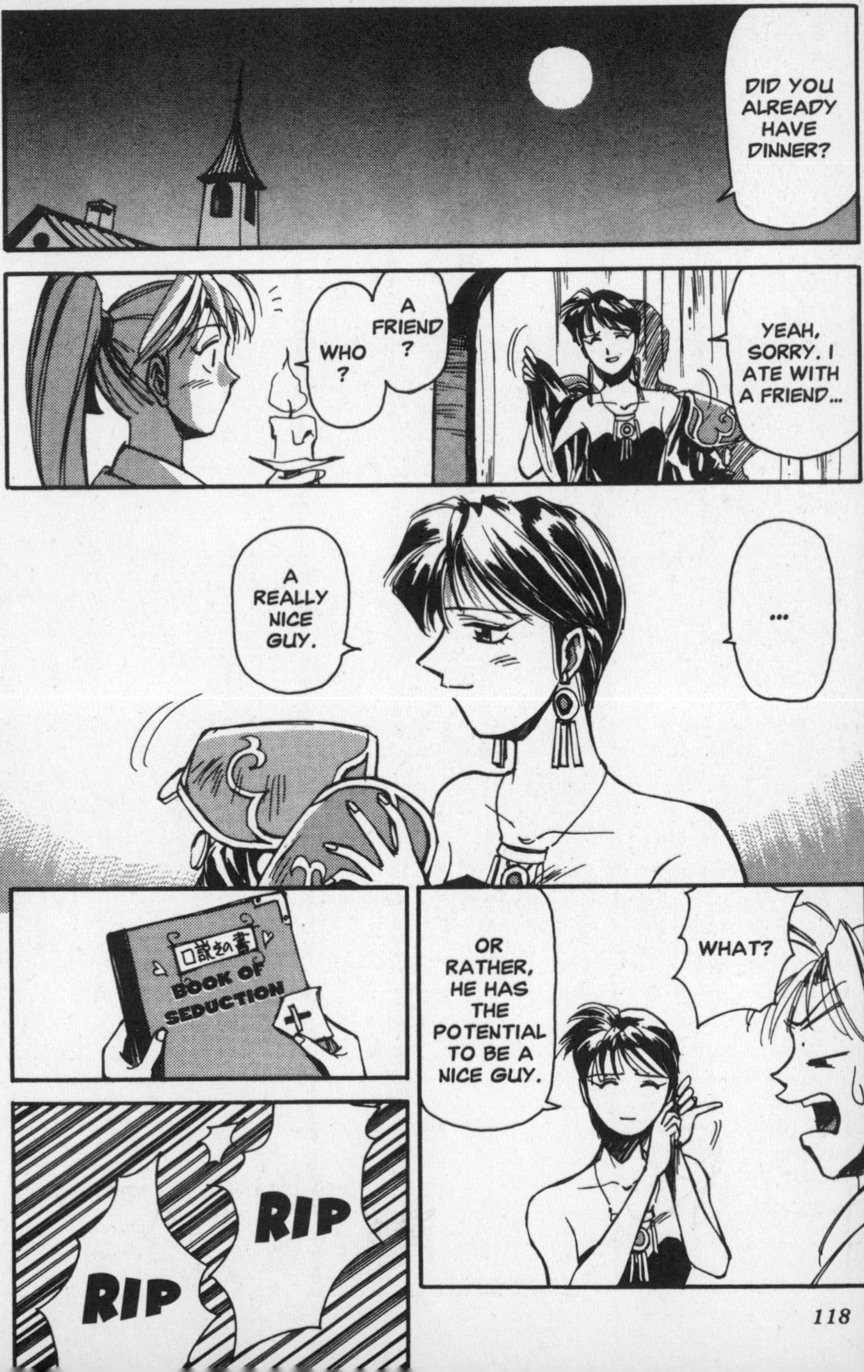
DID YOU ALREADY HAVE DINNER?
YEAH, SORRY. I ATE WITH A FRIEND...
A FRIEND ?
WHO ?
...
A REALLY NICE GUY.
WHAT?
OR RATHER, HE HAS THE POTENTIAL TO BE A NICE GUY.
口説きの書
BOOK OF SEDUCTION
RIP
RIP

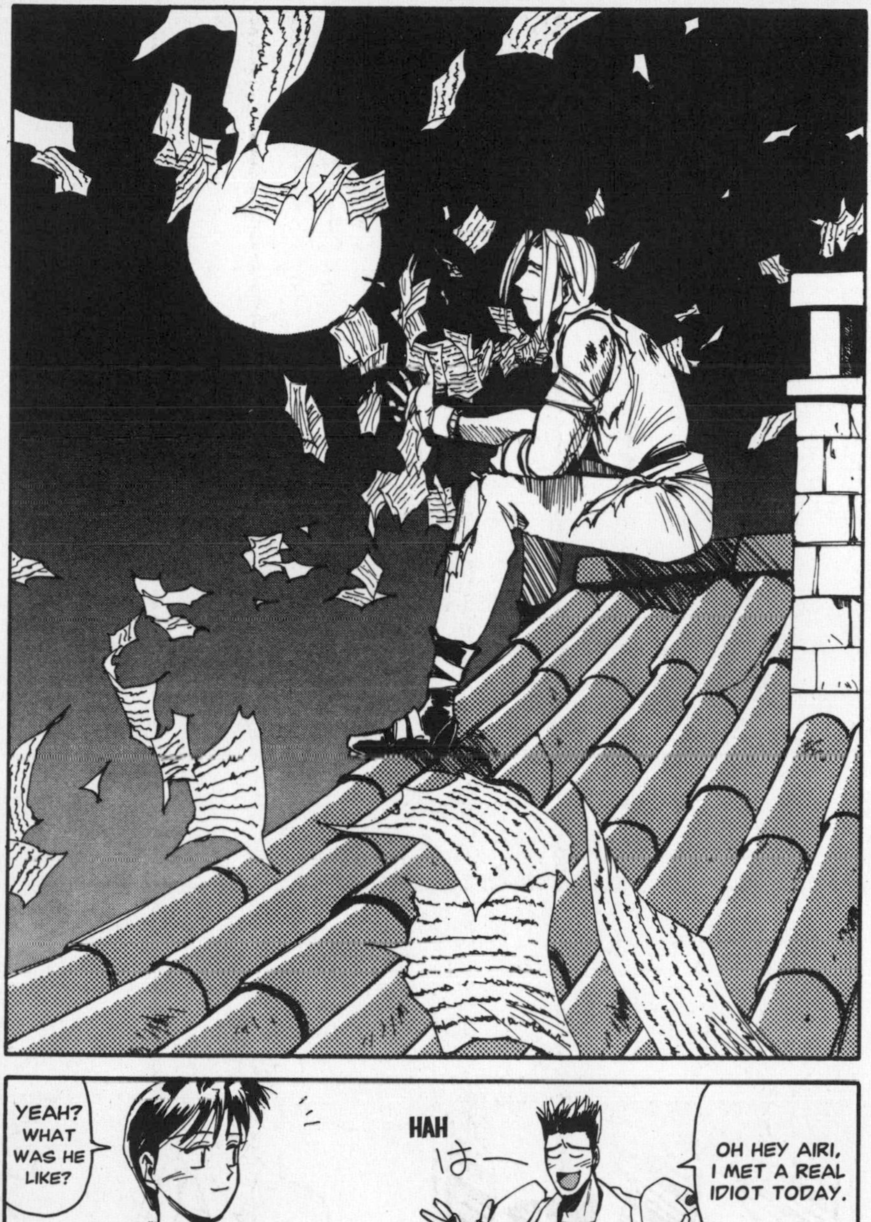
OH HEY AIRI, I MET A REAL IDIOT TODAY.
HAH
はー
YEAH? WHAT WAS HE LIKE?

character profile (3)

Ritsuko Inoue

Age: 17
Blood Type: A
Sign: Pisces
Personality: Bright, loving and nerdy.

Ritsuko is a real military buff, which is rather
unusual for a high school girl. She is particularly knowledgeable about
armored vehicles and tanks, and can keep them in perfect running
order. She even owns a T-74 tank (though it's not clear how she got
it). Other than that, Ritsuko is a normal teenager who loves candy
and Disney Land.

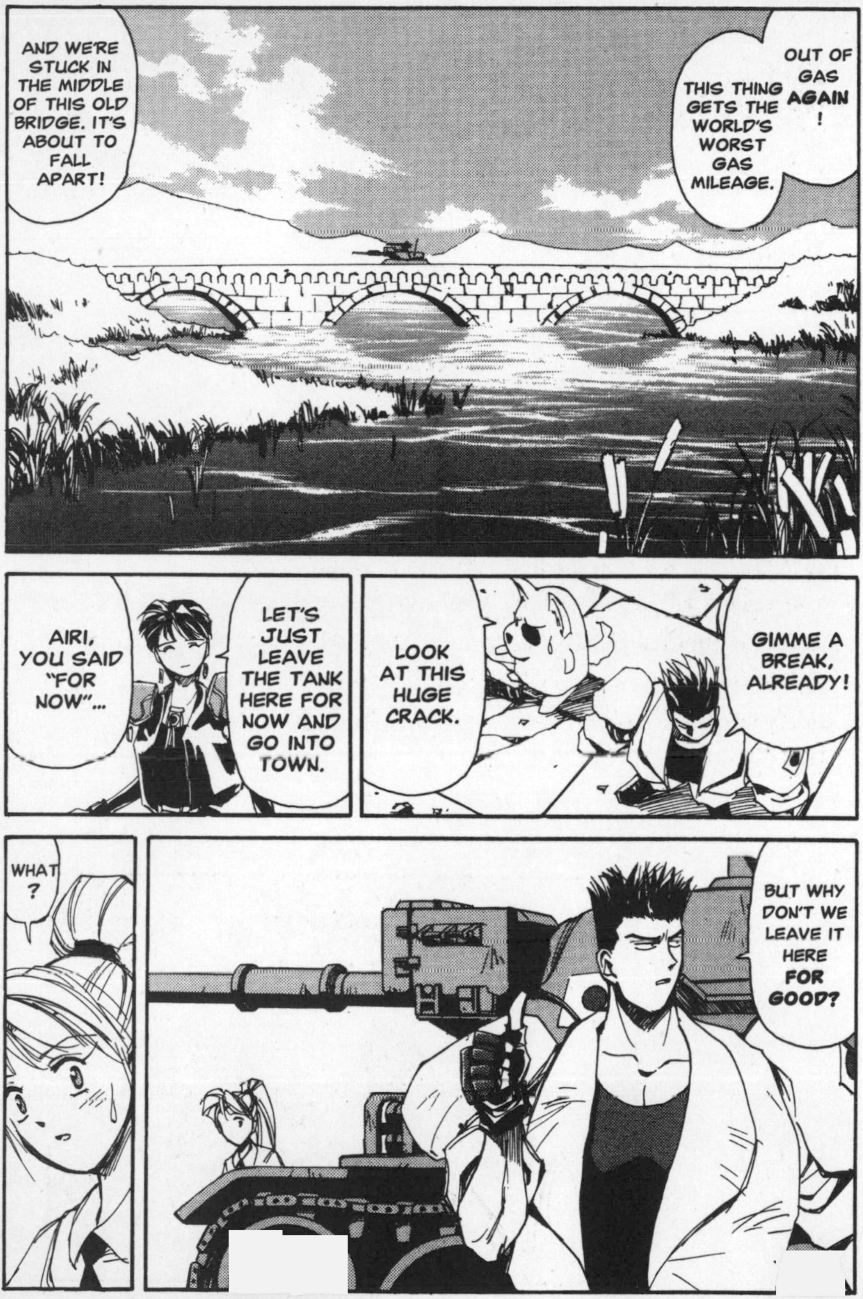
OUT OF GAS AGAIN!
THIS THING GETS THE WORLD'S WORST GAS MILEAGE.
AND WE'RE STUCK IN THE MIDDLE OF THIS OLD BRIDGE. IT'S ABOUT TO FALL APART!
GIMME A BREAK, ALREADY!
LOOK AT THIS HUGE CRACK.
LET'S JUST LEAVE THE TANK HERE FOR NOW AND GO INTO TOWN.
AIRI, YOU SAID "FOR NOW"...
BUT WHY DON'T WE LEAVE IT HERE FOR GOOD?
WHAT?

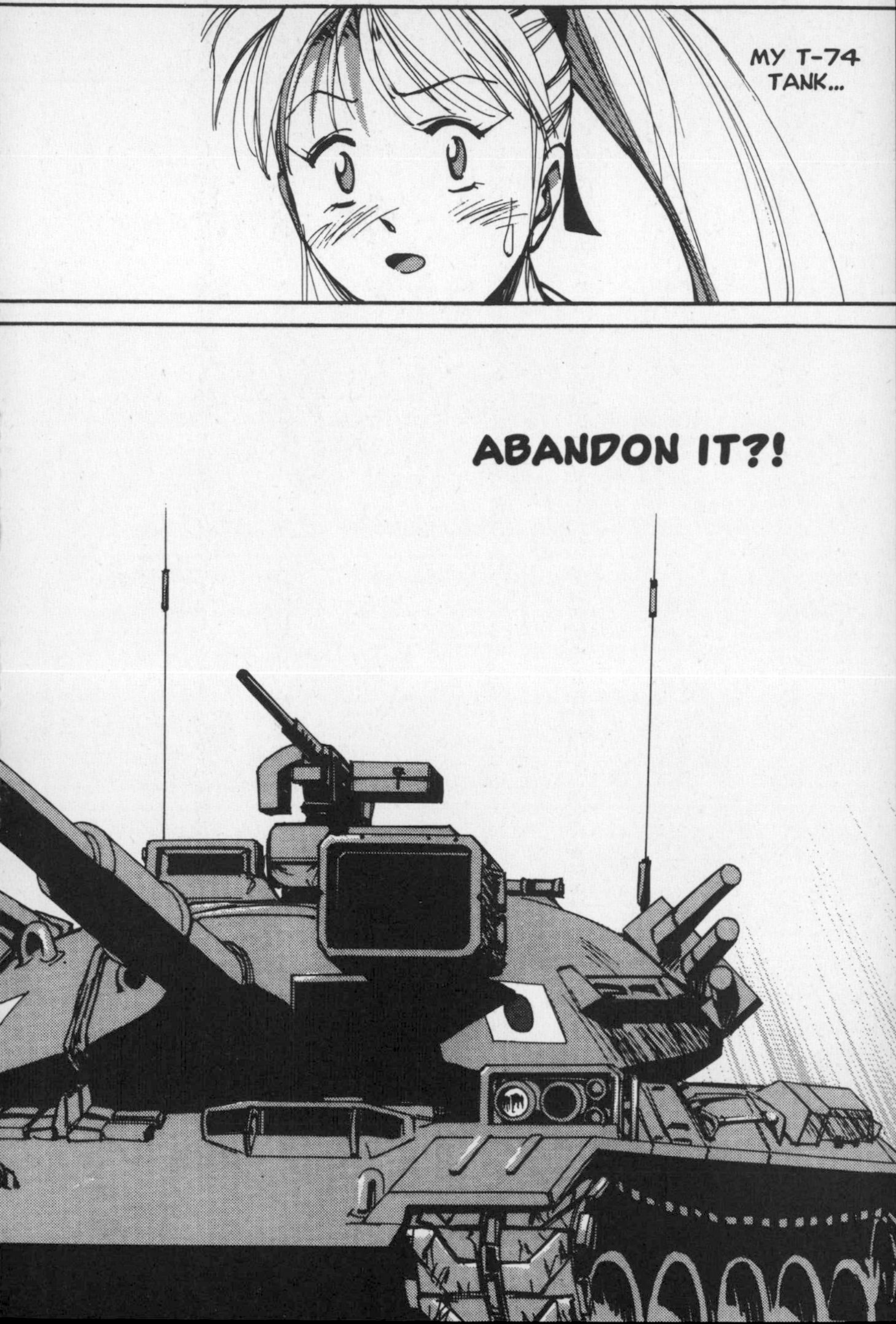
MY T-74
TANK...
ABANDON IT?!

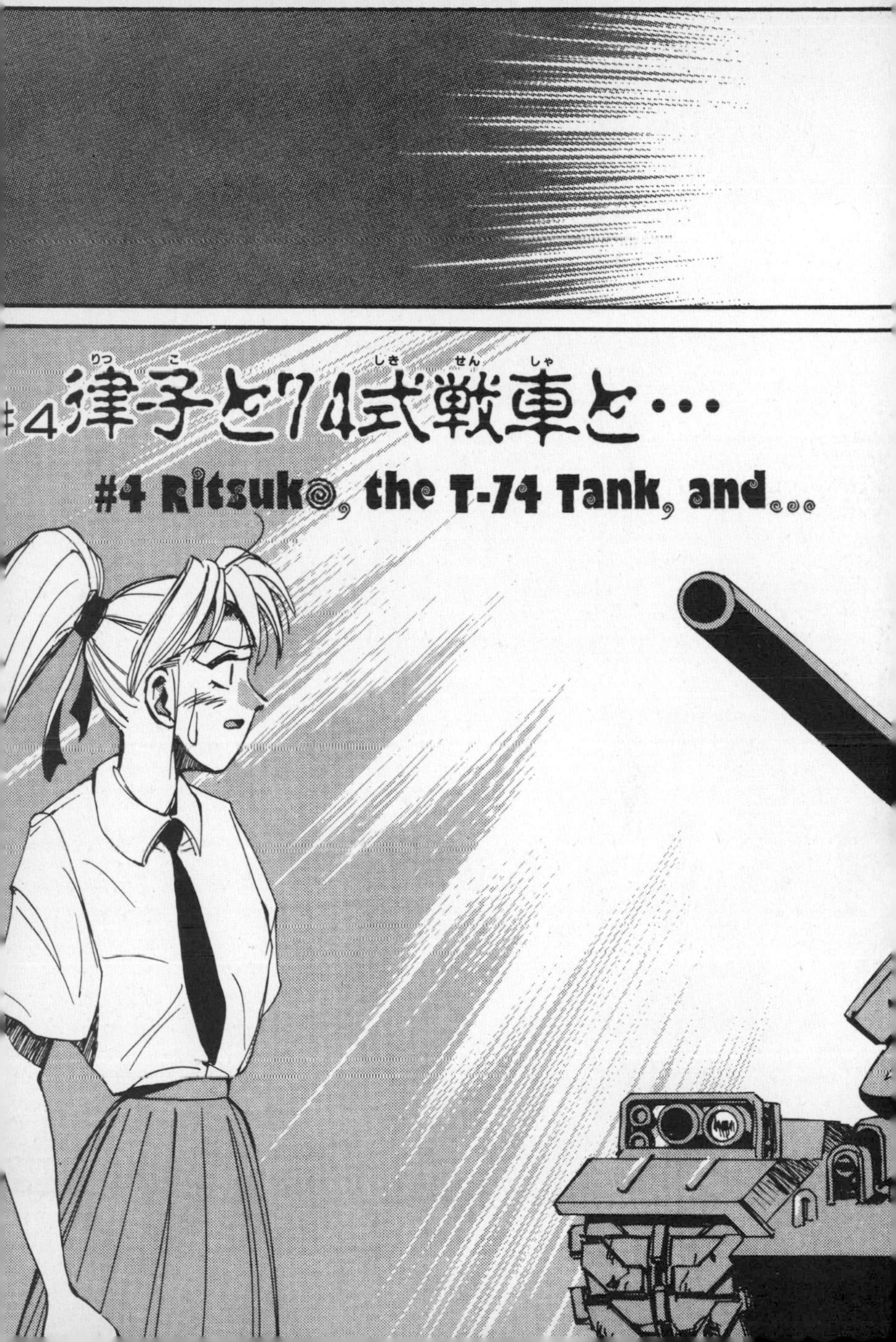
#4 律子と74式戦車と…
#4 Ritsuko, the T-74 Tank, and...

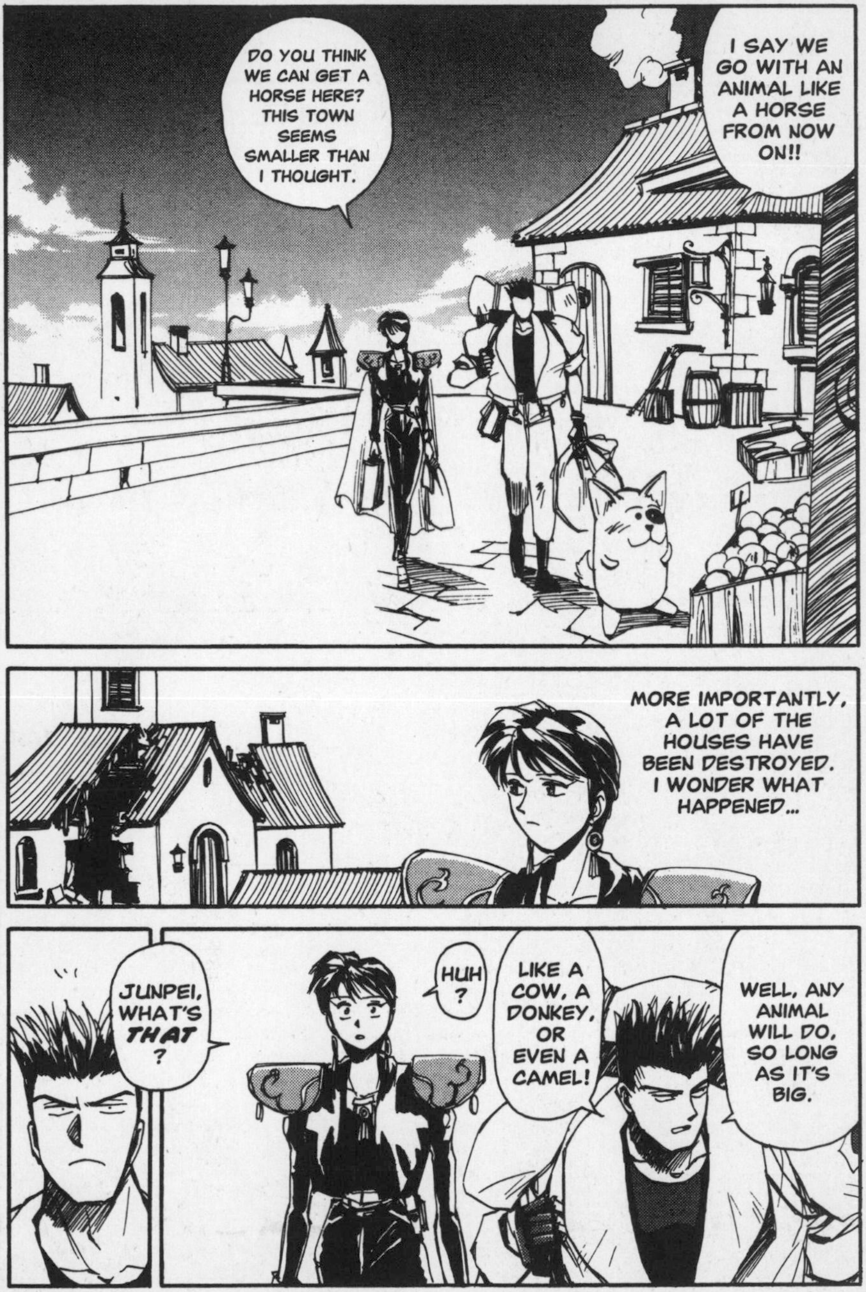
DO YOU THINK WE CAN GET A HORSE HERE? THIS TOWN SEEMS SMALLER THAN I THOUGHT.
I SAY WE GO WITH AN ANIMAL LIKE A HORSE FROM NOW ON!!
MORE IMPORTANTLY, A LOT OF THE HOUSES HAVE BEEN DESTROYED. I WONDER WHAT HAPPENED...
WELL, ANY ANIMAL WILL DO, SO LONG AS IT'S BIG.
LIKE A COW, A DONKEY, OR EVEN A CAMEL!
HUH?
JUNPEI, WHAT'S *THAT*?

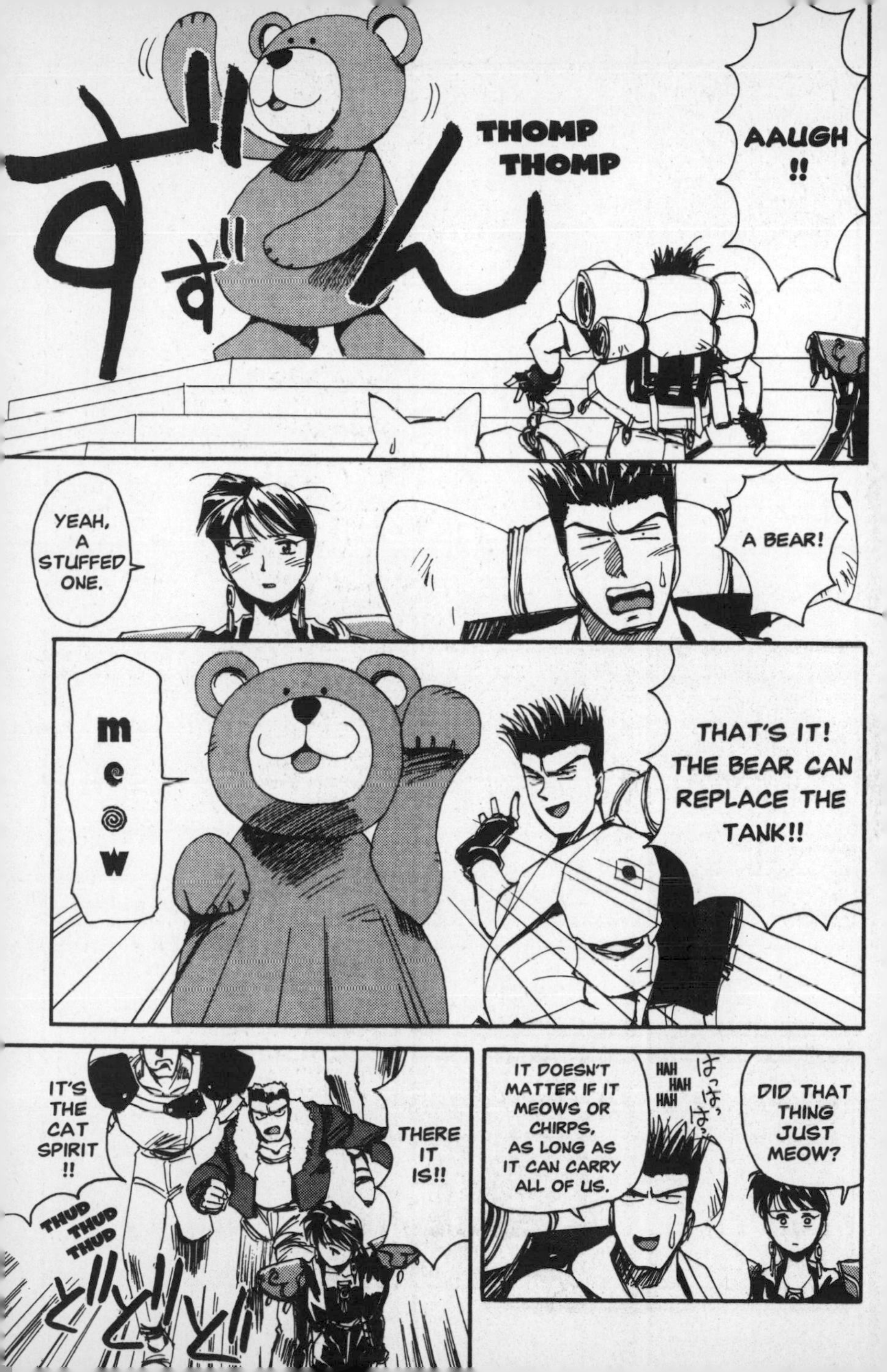
AAUGH !!
THOMP THOMP
すずん
A BEAR!
YEAH, A STUFFED ONE.
THAT'S IT! THE BEAR CAN REPLACE THE TANK!!
meow
DID THAT THING JUST MEOW?
HAH HAH HAH
はっはっはっ
IT DOESN'T MATTER IF IT MEOWS OR CHIRPS, AS LONG AS IT CAN CARRY ALL OF US.
THERE IT IS!!
IT'S THE CAT SPIRIT !!
THUD THUD THUD
どどど

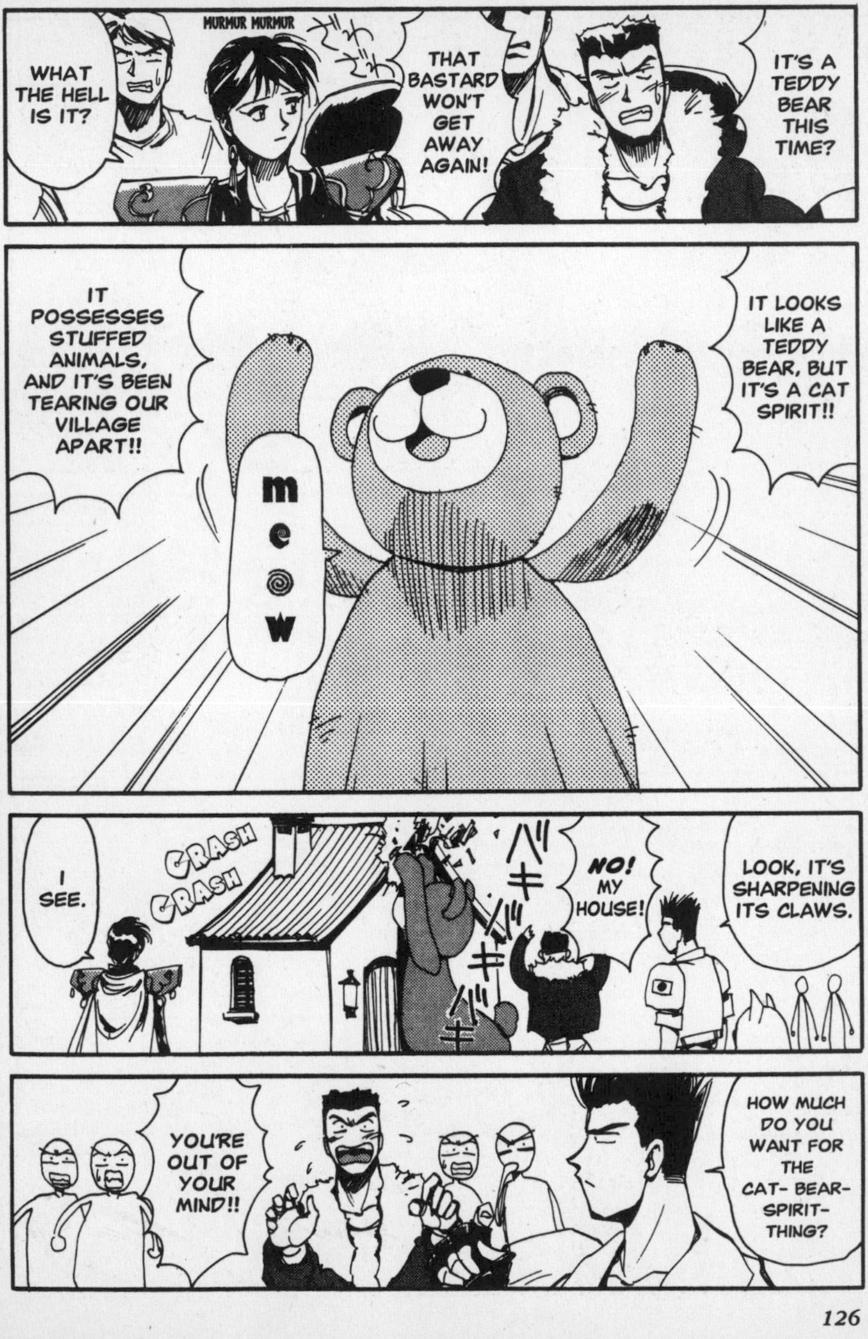
IT'S A TEDDY BEAR THIS TIME?
THAT BASTARD WON'T GET AWAY AGAIN!
MURMUR MURMUR
ざわざわ
WHAT THE HELL IS IT?
IT LOOKS LIKE A TEDDY BEAR, BUT IT'S A CAT SPIRIT!!
meow
IT POSSESSES STUFFED ANIMALS, AND IT'S BEEN TEARING OUR VILLAGE APART!!
LOOK, IT'S SHARPENING ITS CLAWS.
NO! MY HOUSE!
CRASH CRASH
I SEE.
HOW MUCH DO YOU WANT FOR THE CAT- BEAR- SPIRIT- THING?
YOU'RE OUT OF YOUR MIND!!

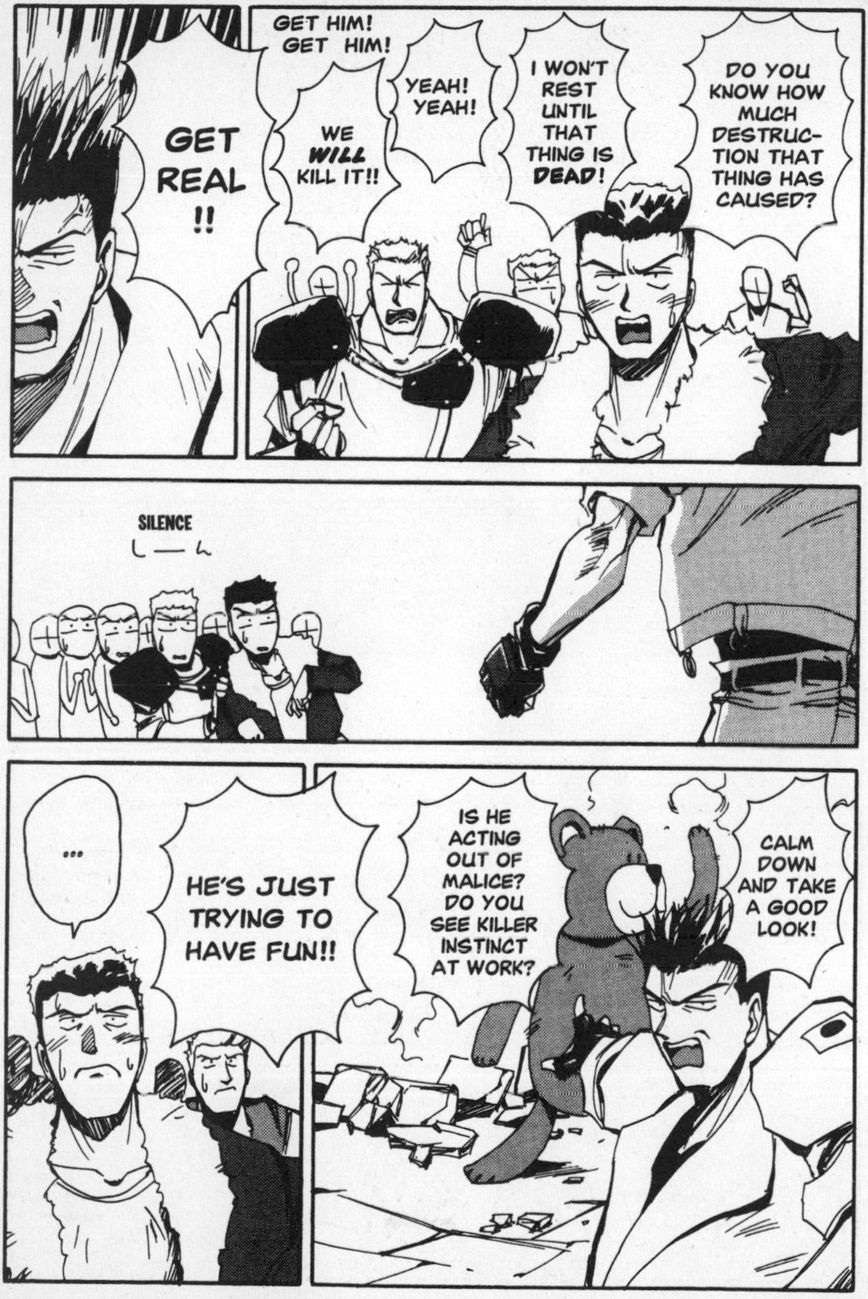
DO YOU KNOW HOW MUCH DESTRUCTION THAT THING HAS CAUSED?
I WON'T REST UNTIL THAT THING IS DEAD!
YEAH! YEAH!
WE WILL KILL IT!!
GET HIM! GET HIM!
GET REAL!!
SILENCE
し―ん
CALM DOWN AND TAKE A GOOD LOOK!
IS HE ACTING OUT OF MALICE? DO YOU SEE KILLER INSTINCT AT WORK?
HE'S JUST TRYING TO HAVE FUN!!
...

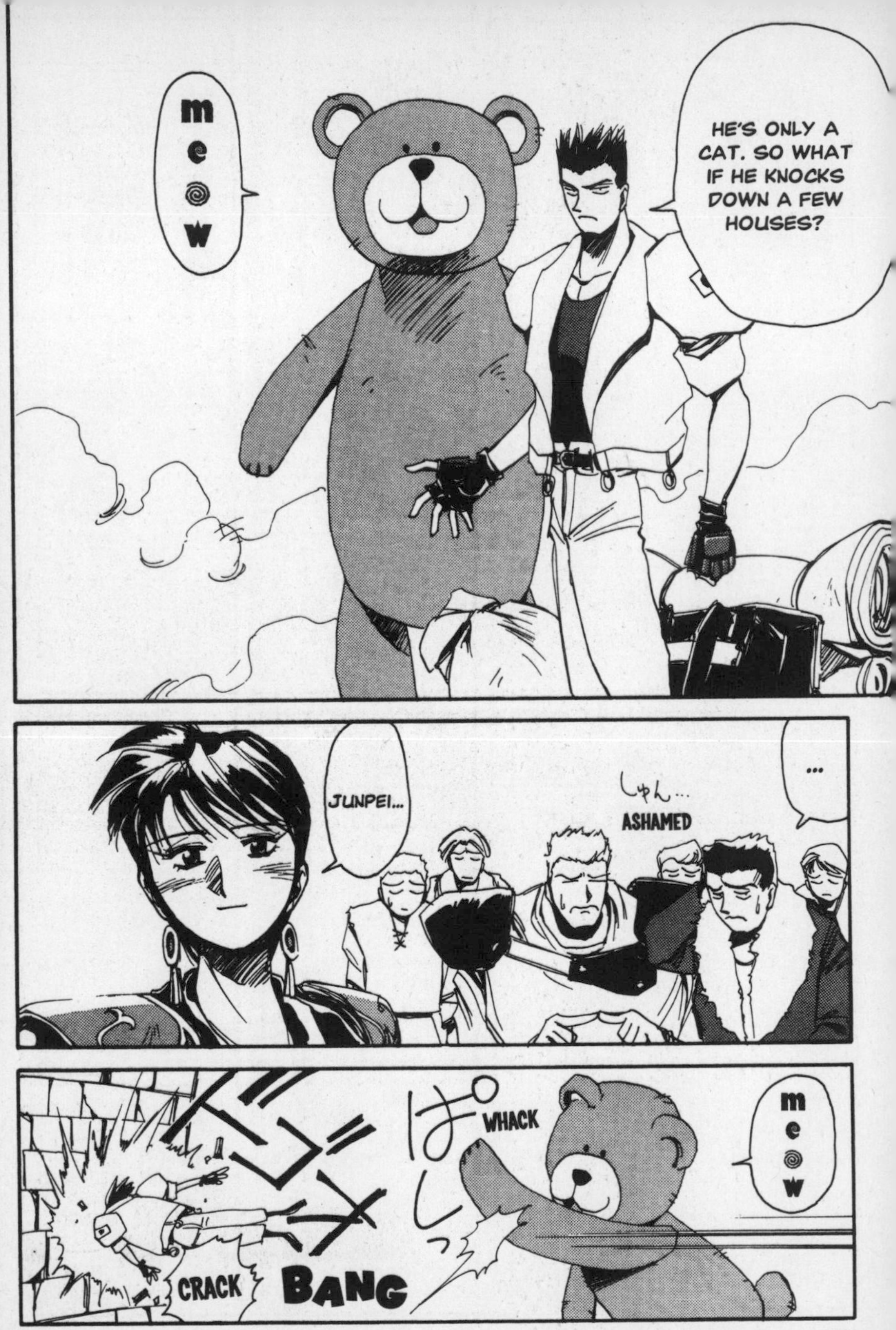
HE'S ONLY A CAT. SO WHAT IF HE KNOCKS DOWN A FEW HOUSES?
meow
...
しゅん...
ASHAMED
JUNPEI...
meow
ぱしっ
WHACK
BANG
CRACK

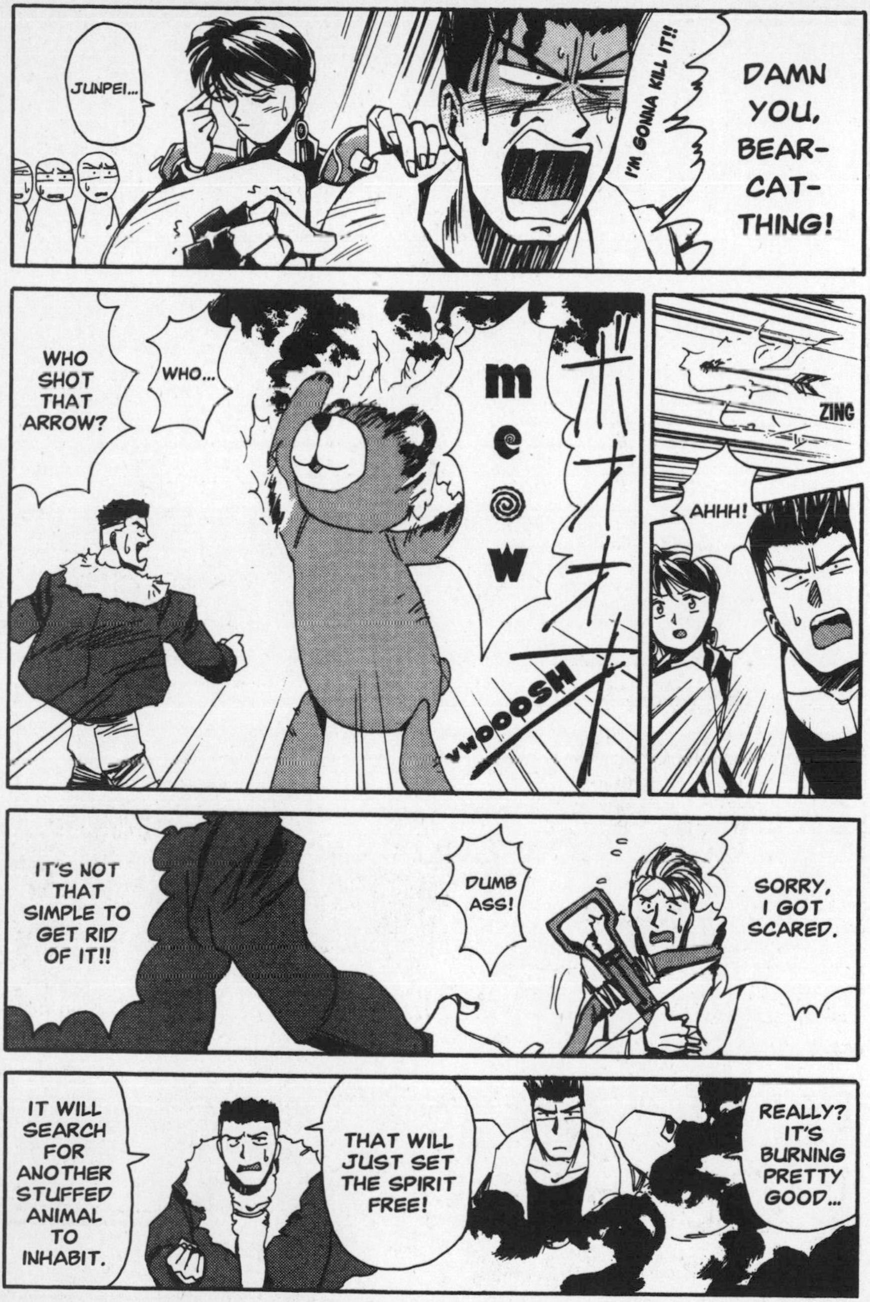

DAMN YOU, BEAR-CAT-THING!
I'M GONNA KILL IT!!
JUNPEI...
ZING
AHHH!
mew
VWOOOSH
WHO...
WHO SHOT THAT ARROW?
SORRY, I GOT SCARED.
DUMB ASS!
IT'S NOT THAT SIMPLE TO GET RID OF IT!!
REALLY? IT'S BURNING PRETTY GOOD...
THAT WILL JUST SET THE SPIRIT FREE!
IT WILL SEARCH FOR ANOTHER STUFFED ANIMAL TO INHABIT.

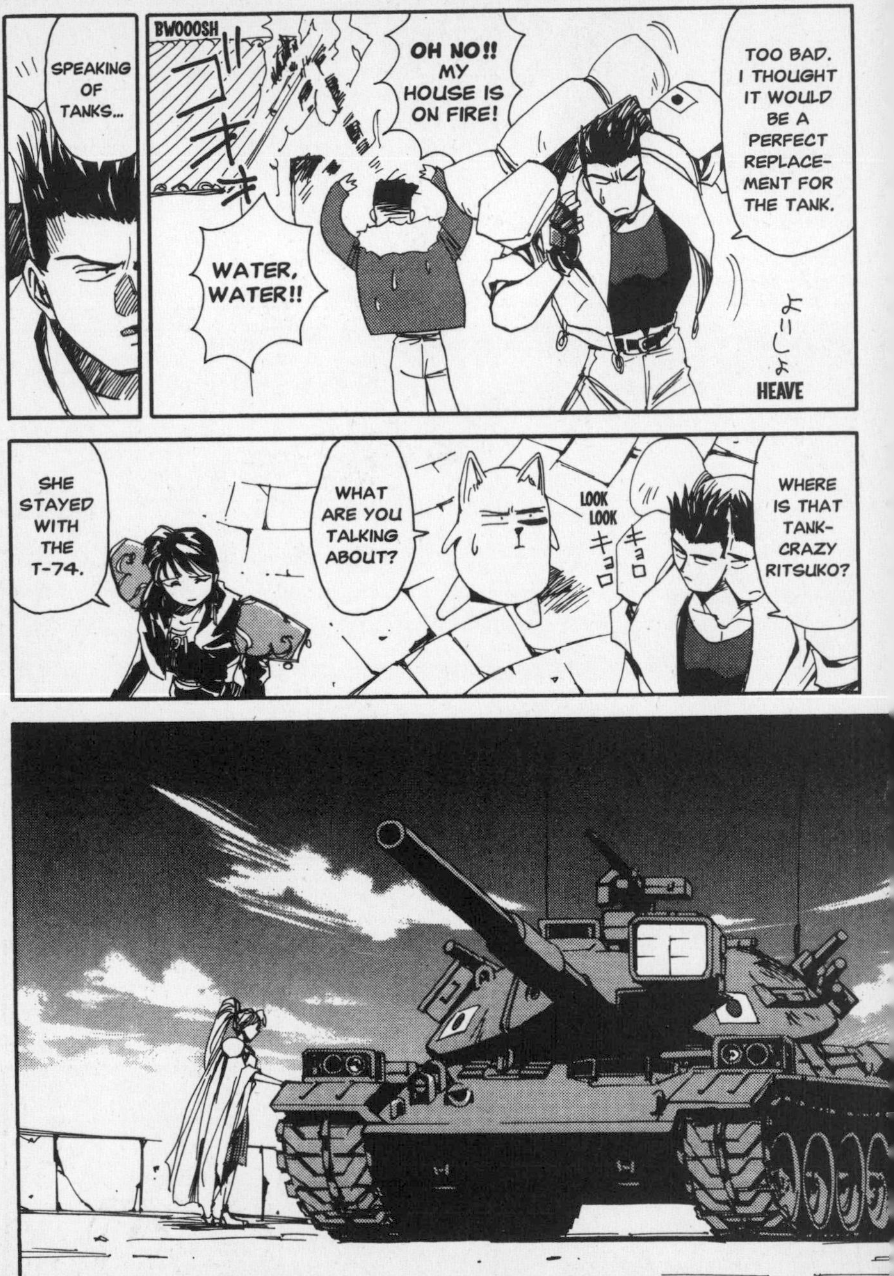
TOO BAD. I THOUGHT IT WOULD BE A PERFECT REPLACEMENT FOR THE TANK.
よいしょ
HEAVE
OH NO!! MY HOUSE IS ON FIRE!
BWOOOSH
WATER, WATER!!
SPEAKING OF TANKS...
WHERE IS THAT TANK-CRAZY RITSUKO?
キョロ キョロ
LOOK LOOK
WHAT ARE YOU TALKING ABOUT?
SHE STAYED WITH THE T-74.

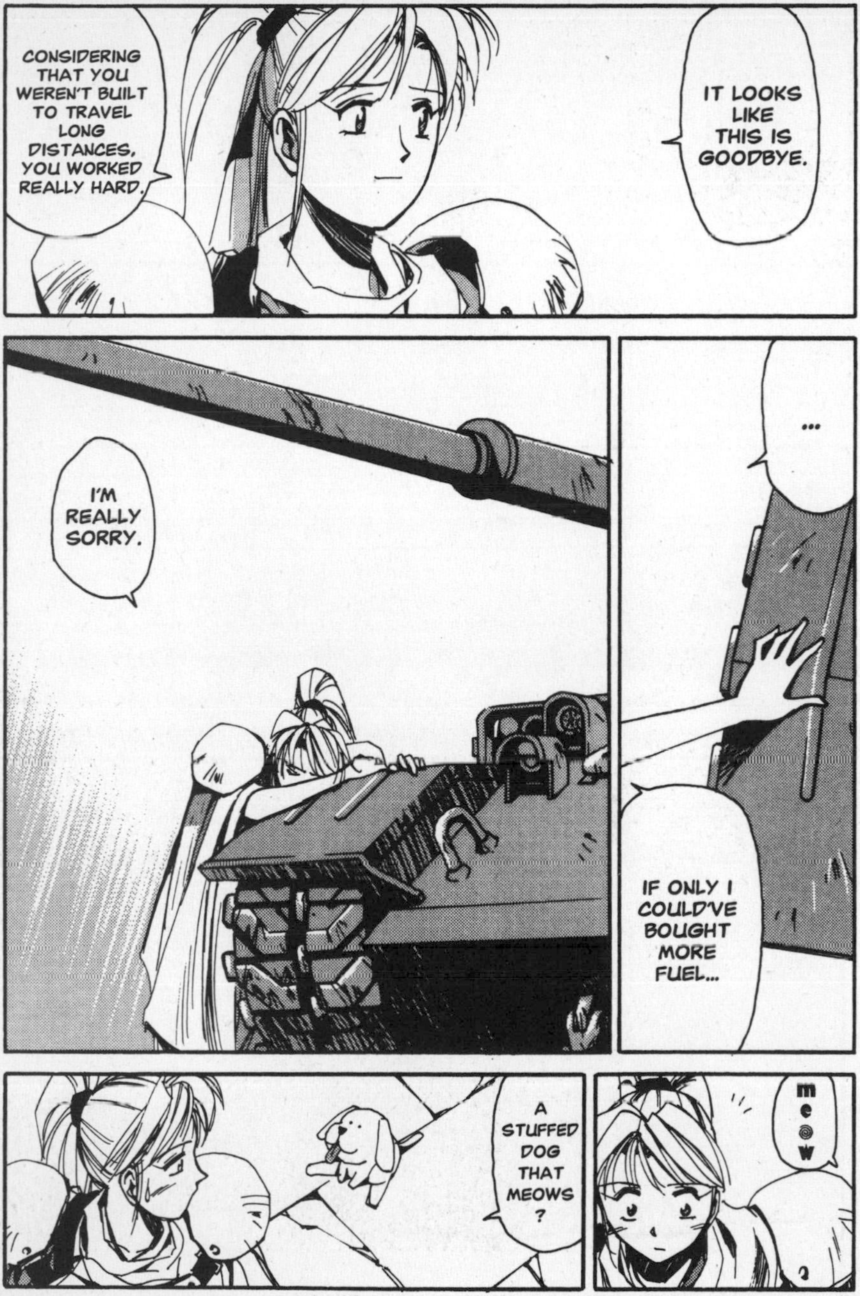
IT LOOKS LIKE THIS IS GOODBYE.
CONSIDERING THAT YOU WEREN'T BUILT TO TRAVEL LONG DISTANCES, YOU WORKED REALLY HARD.
...
IF ONLY I COULD'VE BOUGHT MORE FUEL...
I'M REALLY SORRY.
meow
A STUFFED DOG THAT MEOWS?

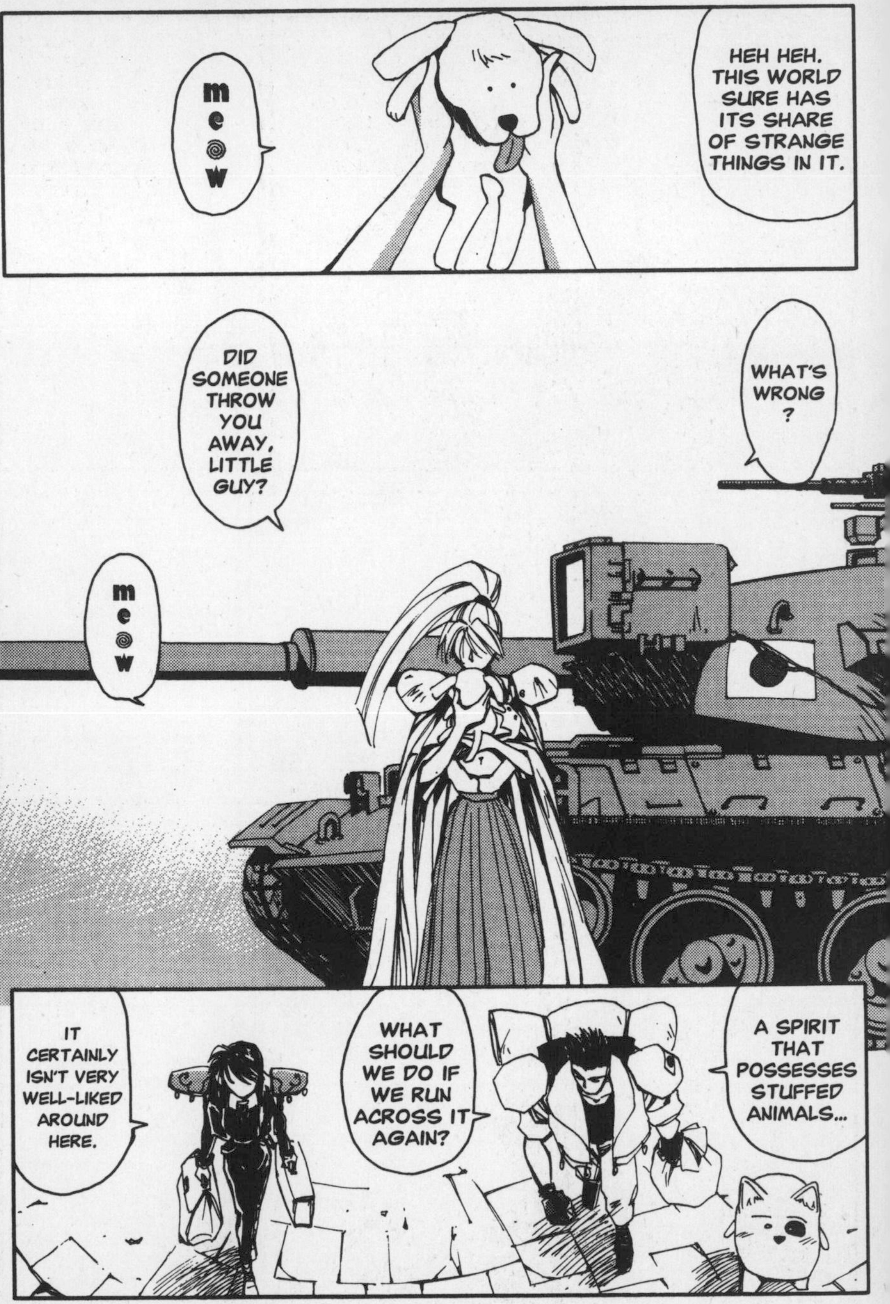
HEH HEH. THIS WORLD SURE HAS ITS SHARE OF STRANGE THINGS IN IT.
meow
WHAT'S WRONG?
DID SOMEONE THROW YOU AWAY, LITTLE GUY?
meow
A SPIRIT THAT POSSESSES STUFFED ANIMALS...
WHAT SHOULD WE DO IF WE RUN ACROSS IT AGAIN?
IT CERTAINLY ISN'T VERY WELL-LIKED AROUND HERE.

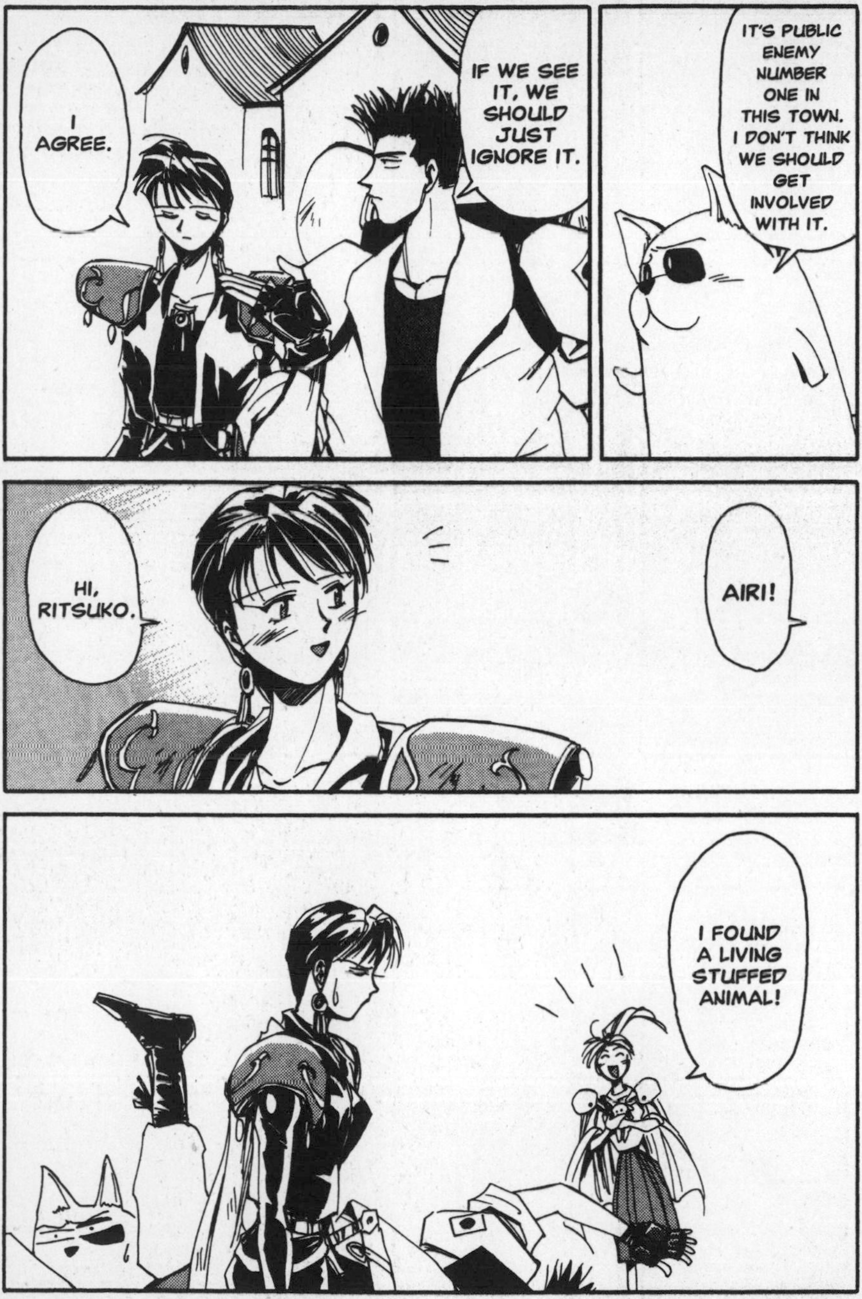
IT'S PUBLIC ENEMY NUMBER ONE IN THIS TOWN. I DON'T THINK WE SHOULD GET INVOLVED WITH IT.
IF WE SEE IT, WE SHOULD JUST IGNORE IT.
I AGREE.
AIRI!
HI, RITSUKO.
I FOUND A LIVING STUFFED ANIMAL!

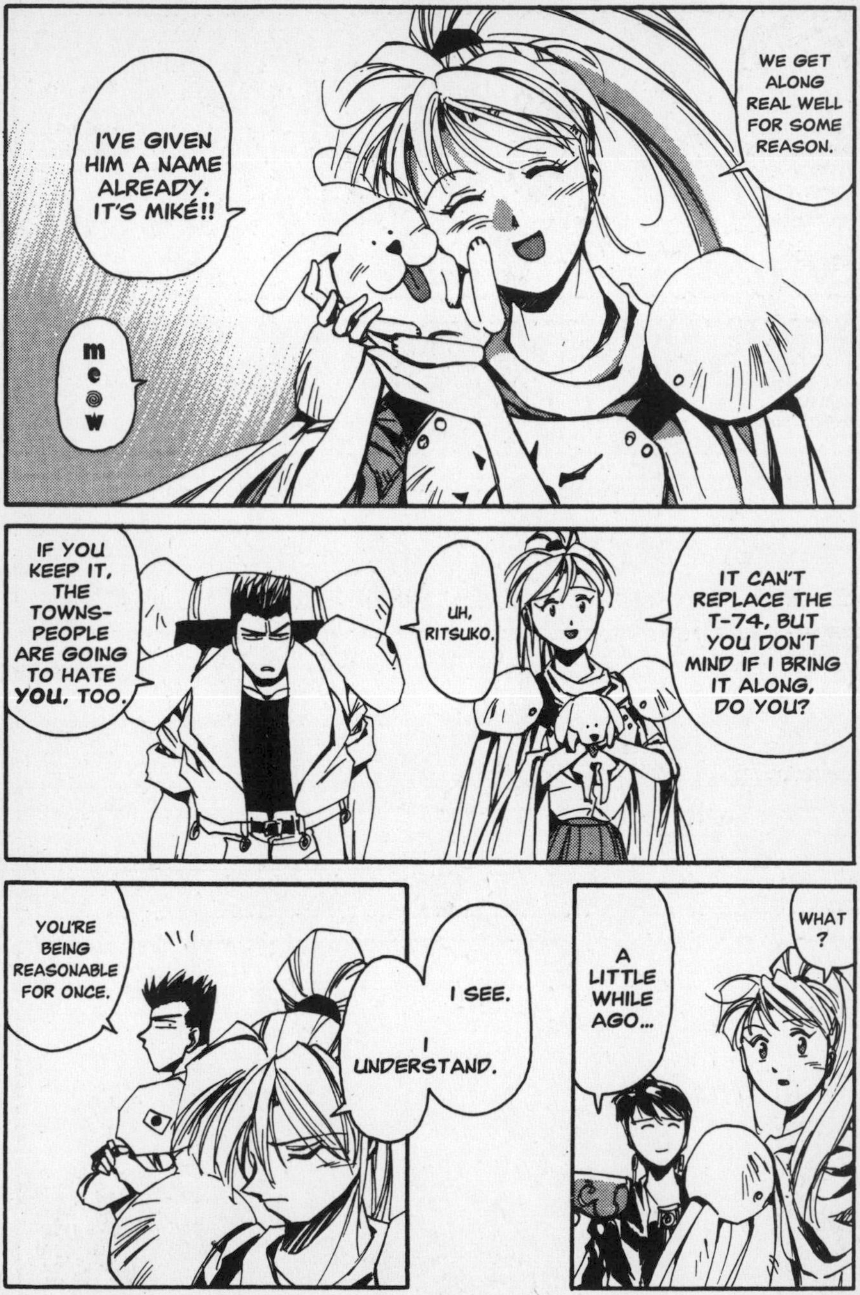
WE GET ALONG REAL WELL FOR SOME REASON.
I'VE GIVEN HIM A NAME ALREADY. IT'S MIKÉ!!
meow
IT CAN'T REPLACE THE T-74, BUT YOU DON'T MIND IF I BRING IT ALONG, DO YOU?
UH, RITSUKO.
IF YOU KEEP IT, THE TOWNS-PEOPLE ARE GOING TO HATE YOU, TOO.
WHAT?
A LITTLE WHILE AGO...
I SEE.
I UNDERSTAND.
YOU'RE BEING REASONABLE FOR ONCE.

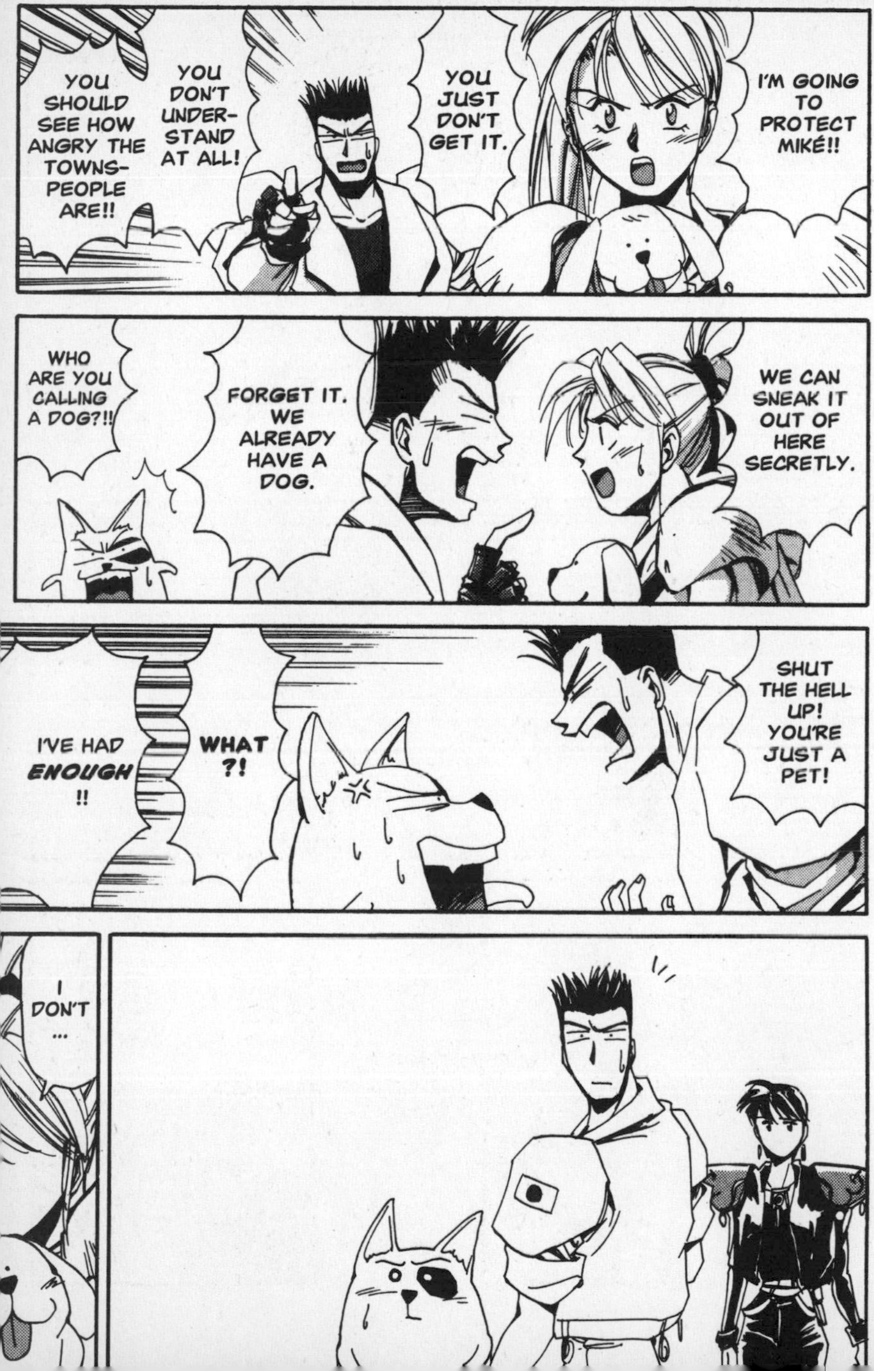
I'M GOING TO PROTECT MIKÉ!!
YOU JUST DON'T GET IT.
YOU DON'T UNDER-STAND AT ALL!
YOU SHOULD SEE HOW ANGRY THE TOWNS-PEOPLE ARE!!
WE CAN SNEAK IT OUT OF HERE SECRETLY.
FORGET IT. WE ALREADY HAVE A DOG.
WHO ARE YOU CALLING A DOG?!!
SHUT THE HELL UP! YOU'RE JUST A PET!
WHAT ?!
I'VE HAD ENOUGH !!
I DON'T ...

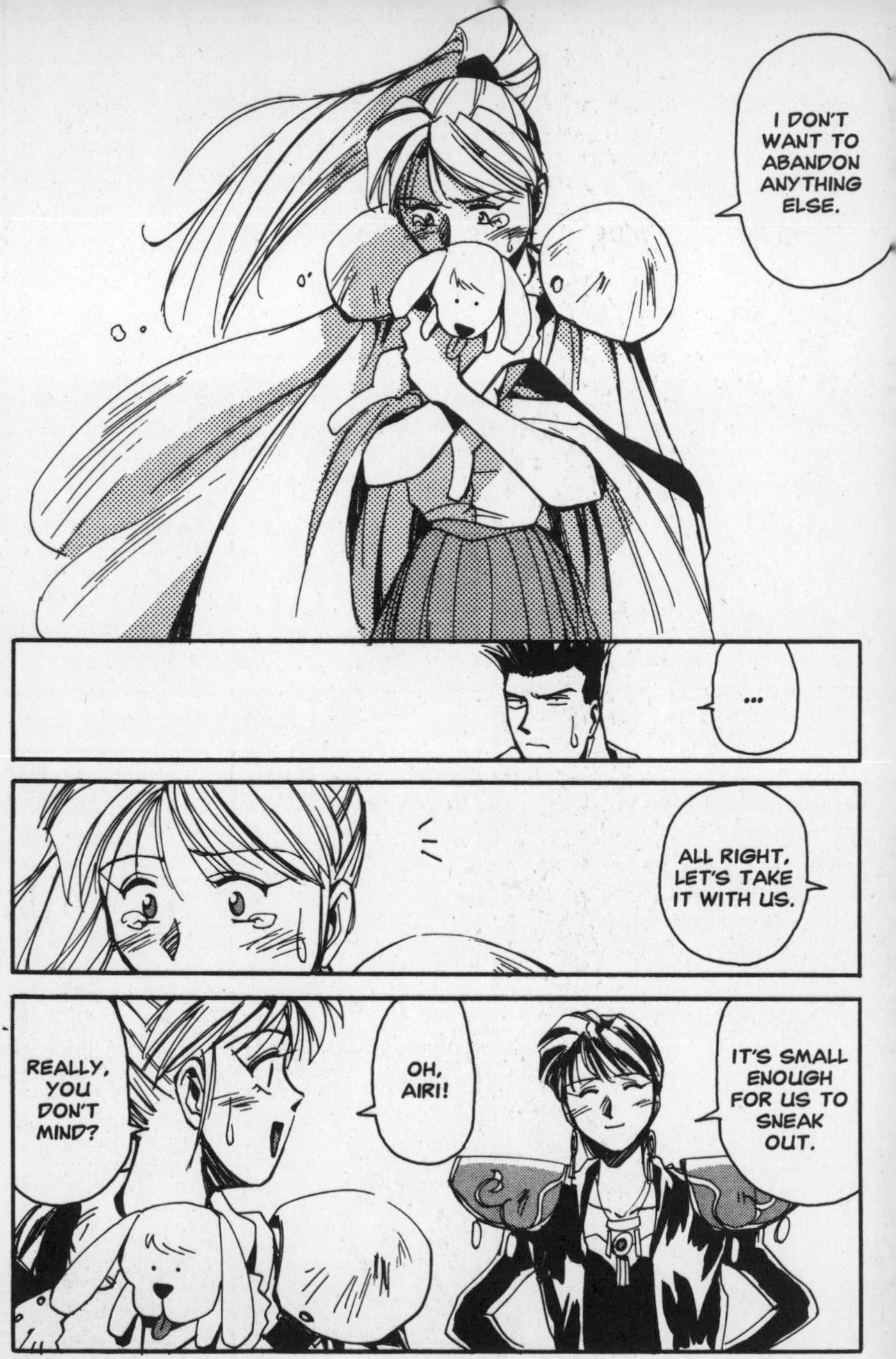
I DON'T WANT TO ABANDON ANYTHING ELSE.
...
ALL RIGHT, LET'S TAKE IT WITH US.
IT'S SMALL ENOUGH FOR US TO SNEAK OUT.
OH, AIRI!
REALLY, YOU DON'T MIND?

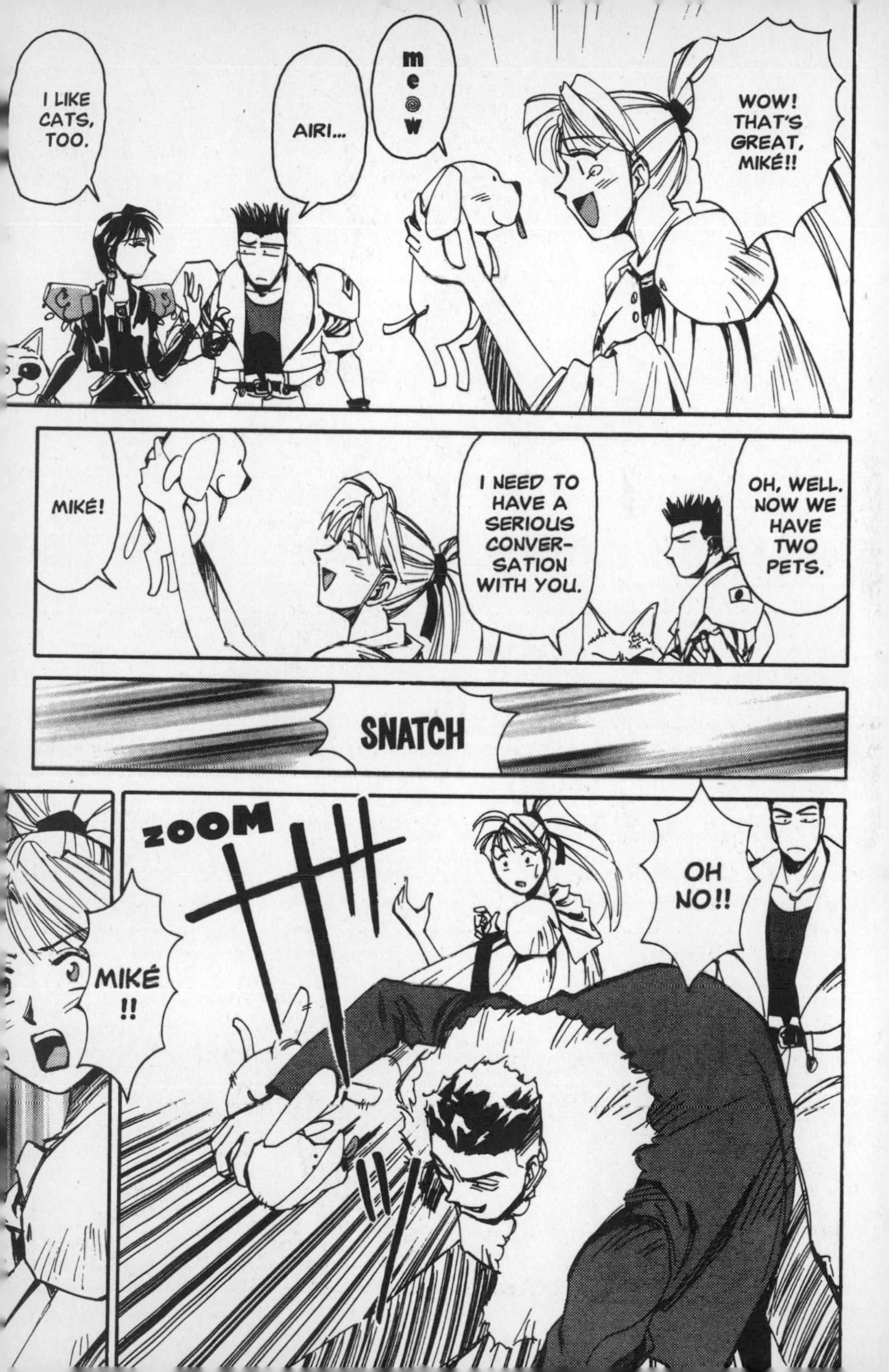
WOW! THAT'S GREAT, MIKÉ!!
meow
AIRI...
I LIKE CATS, TOO.
OH, WELL. NOW WE HAVE TWO PETS.
I NEED TO HAVE A SERIOUS CONVER-SATION WITH YOU.
MIKÉ!
SNATCH
OH NO!!
ZOOM
MIKÉ !!

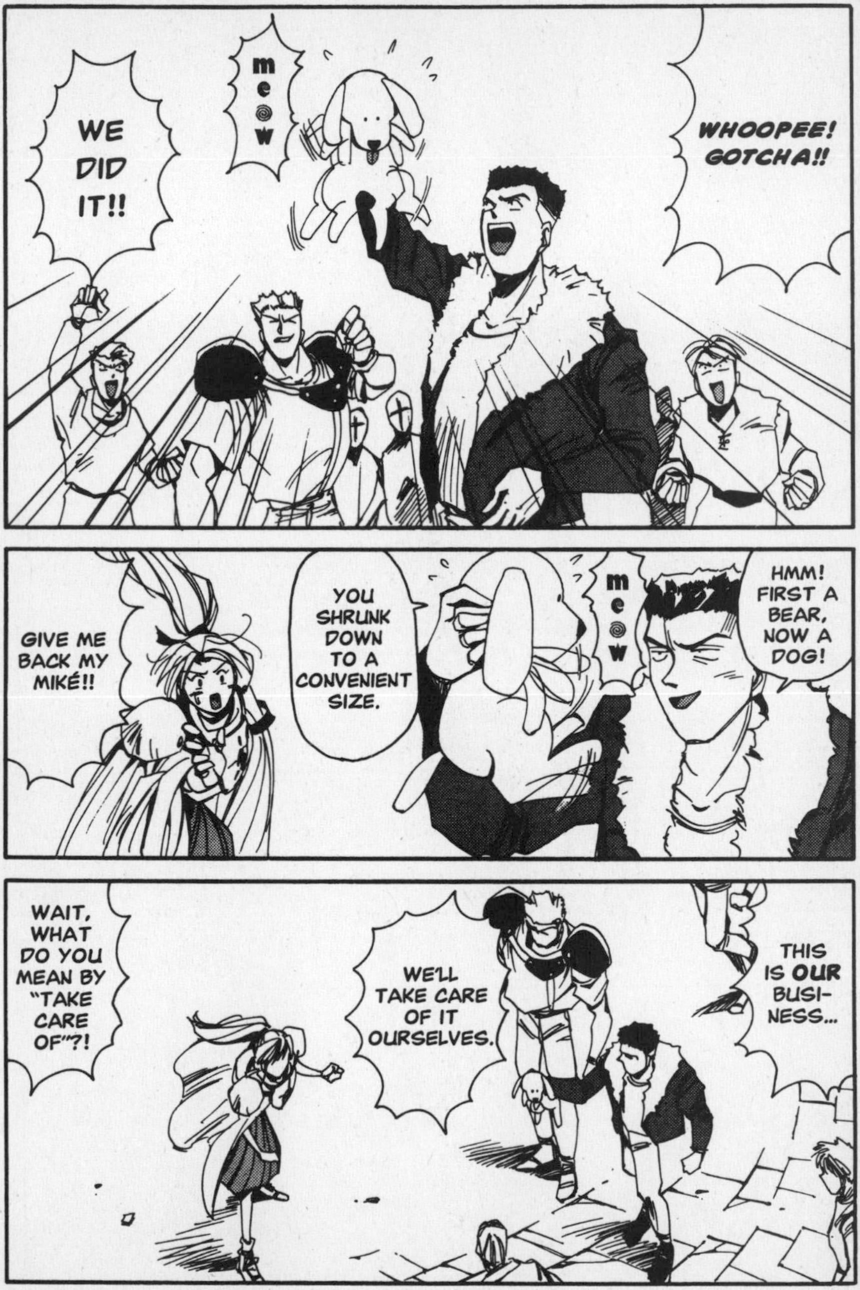
WE DID IT!!
meow
WHOOPEE! GOTCHA!!
GIVE ME BACK MY MIKÉ!!
YOU SHRUNK DOWN TO A CONVENIENT SIZE.
meow
HMM! FIRST A BEAR, NOW A DOG!
WAIT, WHAT DO YOU MEAN BY "TAKE CARE OF"?!
WE'LL TAKE CARE OF IT OURSELVES.
THIS IS **OUR** BUSINESS...

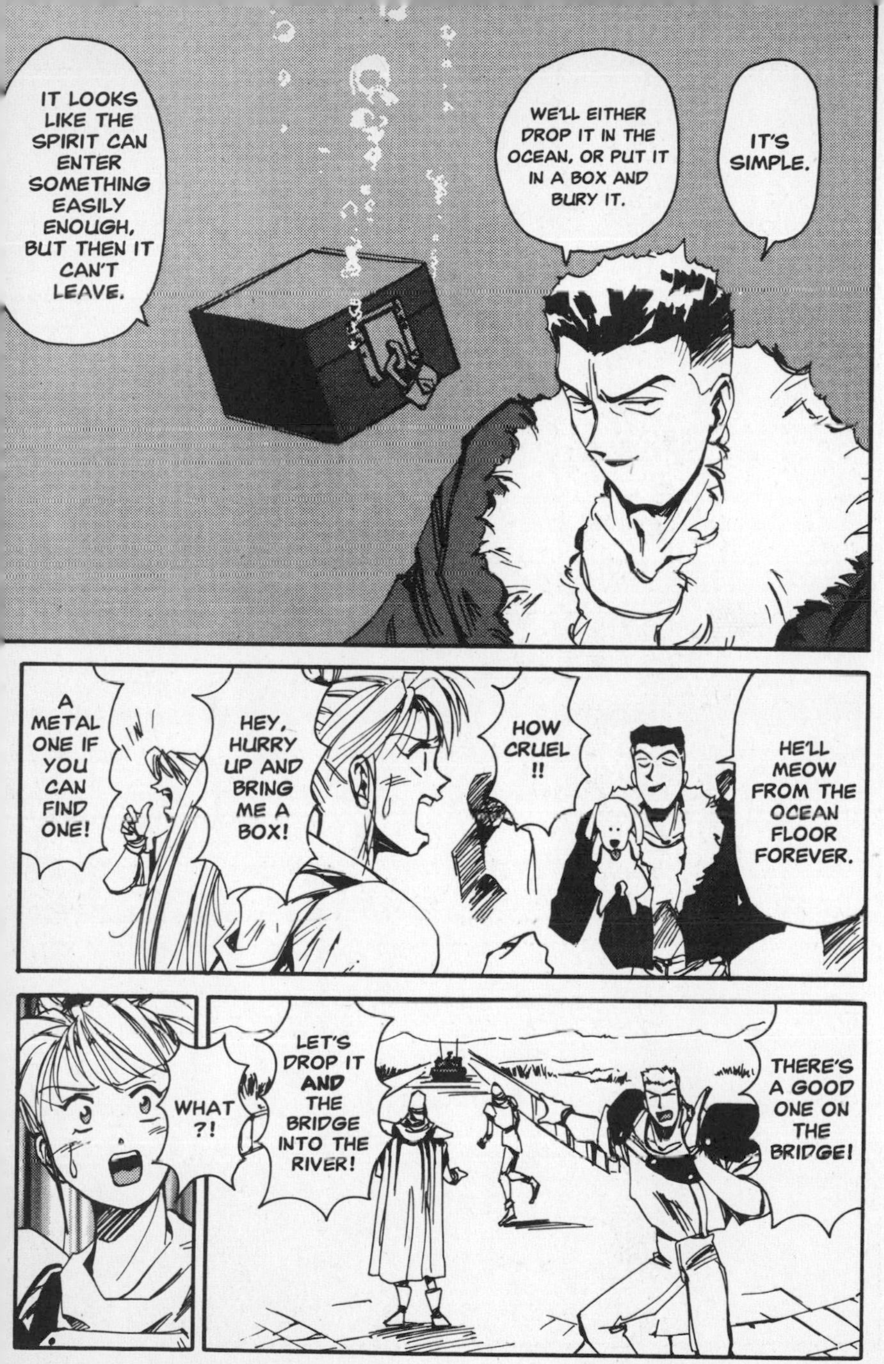
IT'S SIMPLE.
WE'LL EITHER DROP IT IN THE OCEAN, OR PUT IT IN A BOX AND BURY IT.
IT LOOKS LIKE THE SPIRIT CAN ENTER SOMETHING EASILY ENOUGH, BUT THEN IT CAN'T LEAVE.
HE'LL MEOW FROM THE OCEAN FLOOR FOREVER.
HOW CRUEL !!
HEY, HURRY UP AND BRING ME A BOX!
A METAL ONE IF YOU CAN FIND ONE!
THERE'S A GOOD ONE ON THE BRIDGE!
LET'S DROP IT **AND** THE BRIDGE INTO THE RIVER!
WHAT ?!

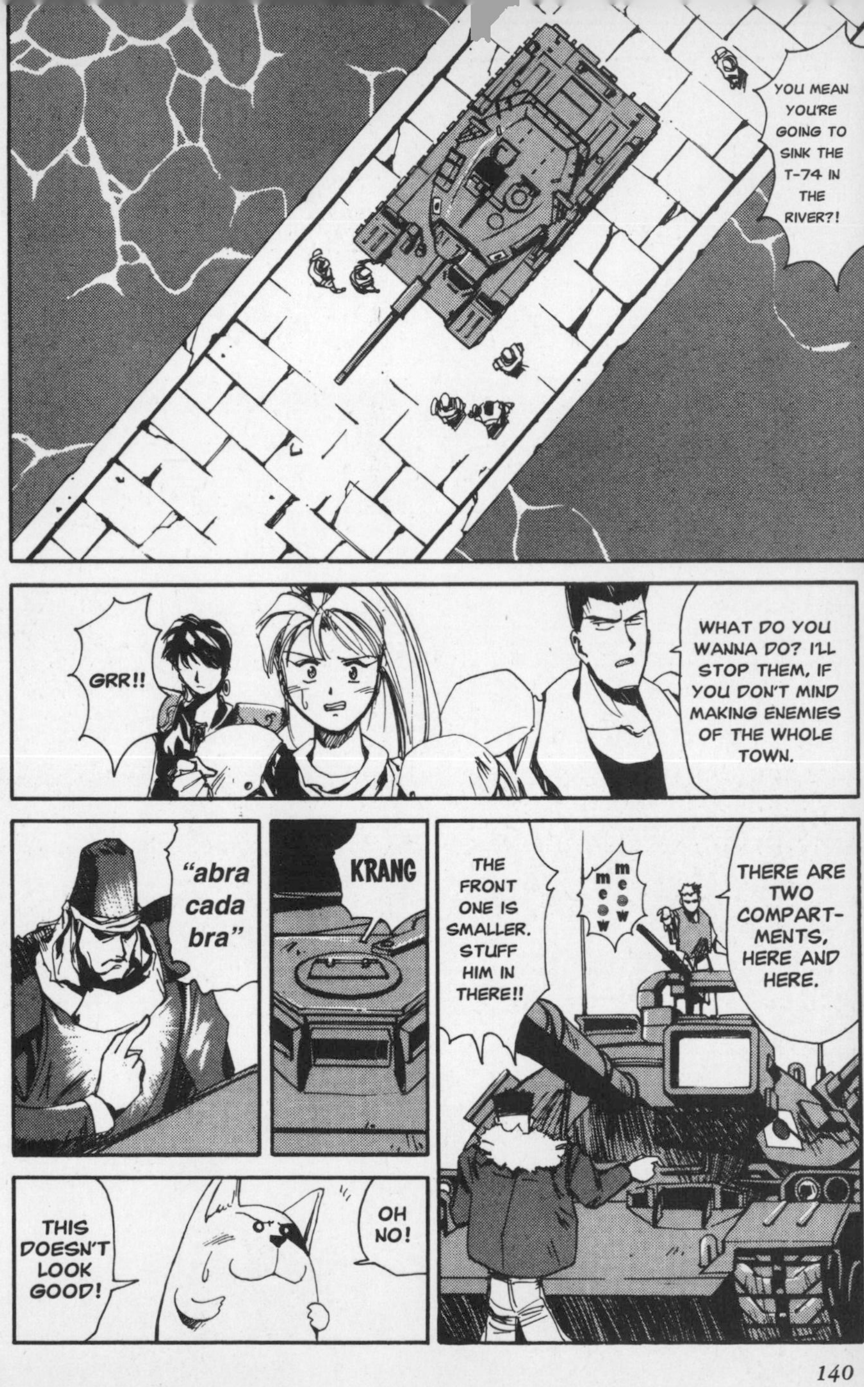
YOU MEAN YOU'RE GOING TO SINK THE T-74 IN THE RIVER?!
WHAT DO YOU WANNA DO? I'LL STOP THEM, IF YOU DON'T MIND MAKING ENEMIES OF THE WHOLE TOWN.
GRR!!
THERE ARE TWO COMPART- MENTS, HERE AND HERE.
meow
meow
THE FRONT ONE IS SMALLER. STUFF HIM IN THERE!!
KRANG
"abra cada bra"
OH NO!
THIS DOESN'T LOOK GOOD!

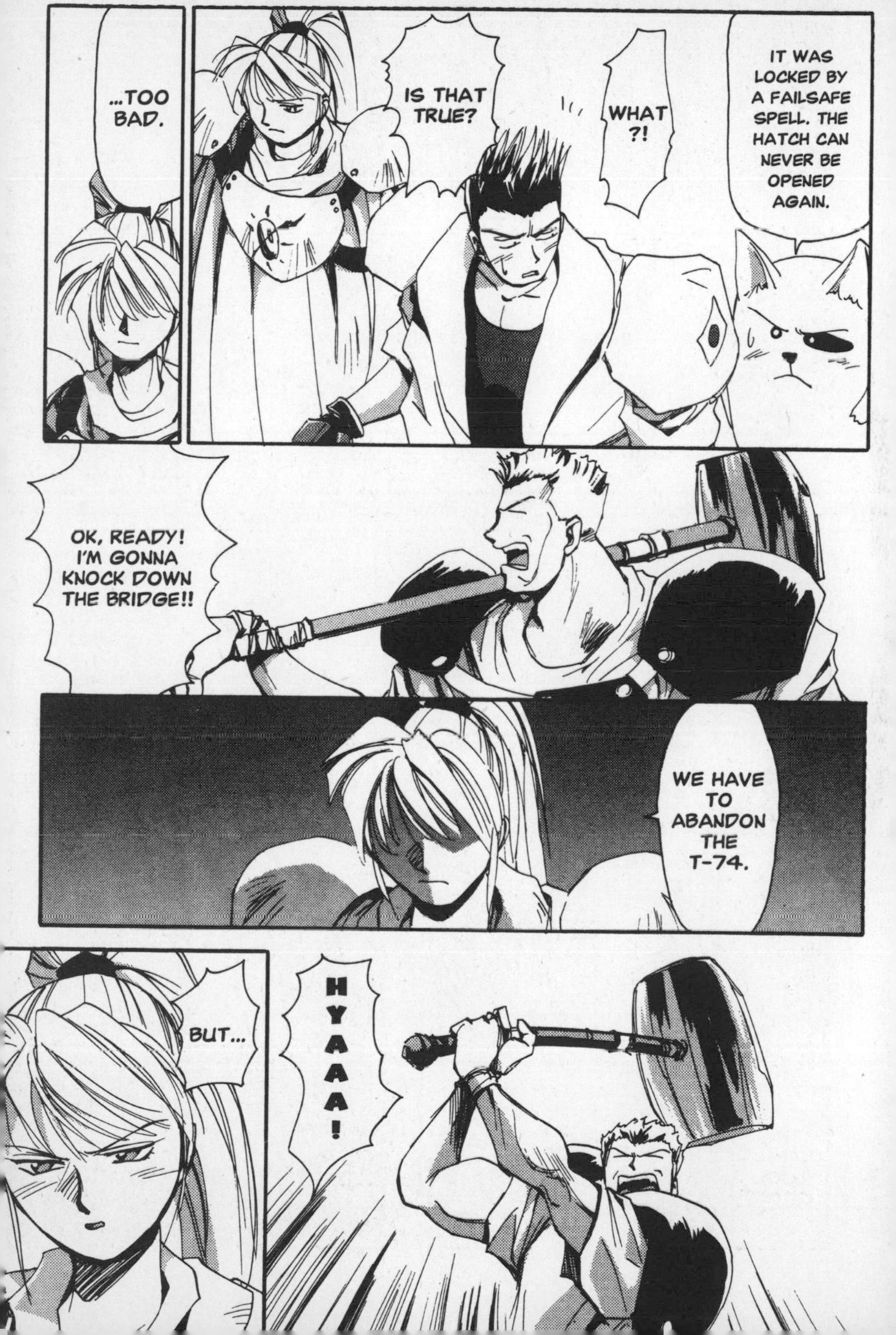
IT WAS LOCKED BY A FAILSAFE SPELL. THE HATCH CAN NEVER BE OPENED AGAIN.
WHAT?!
IS THAT TRUE?
...TOO BAD.
OK, READY! I'M GONNA KNOCK DOWN THE BRIDGE!!
WE HAVE TO ABANDON THE T-74.
BUT...
HYAAAA!

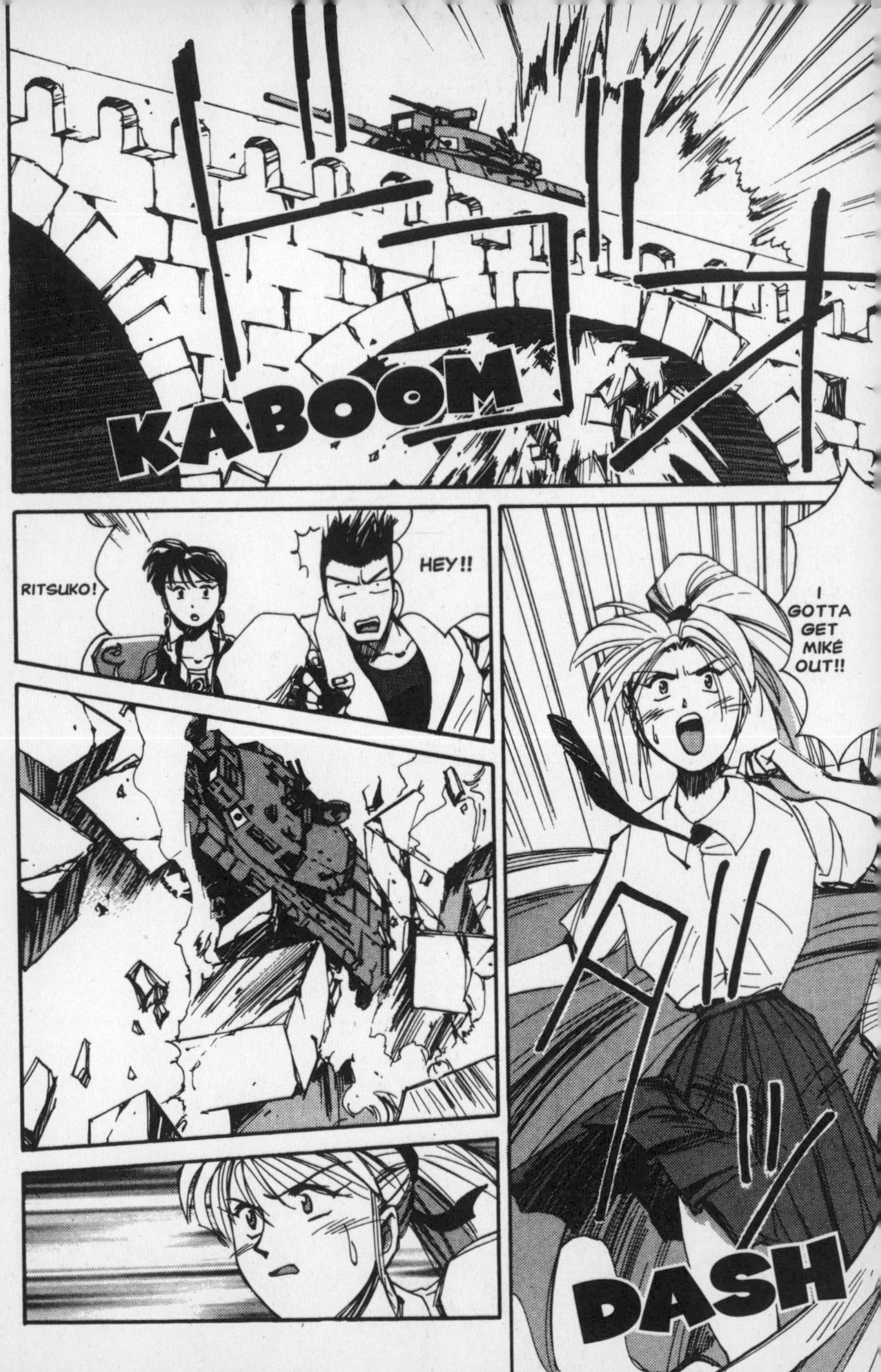
KABOOM
I GOTTA GET MIKÉ OUT!!
HEY!!
RITSUKO!
DASH

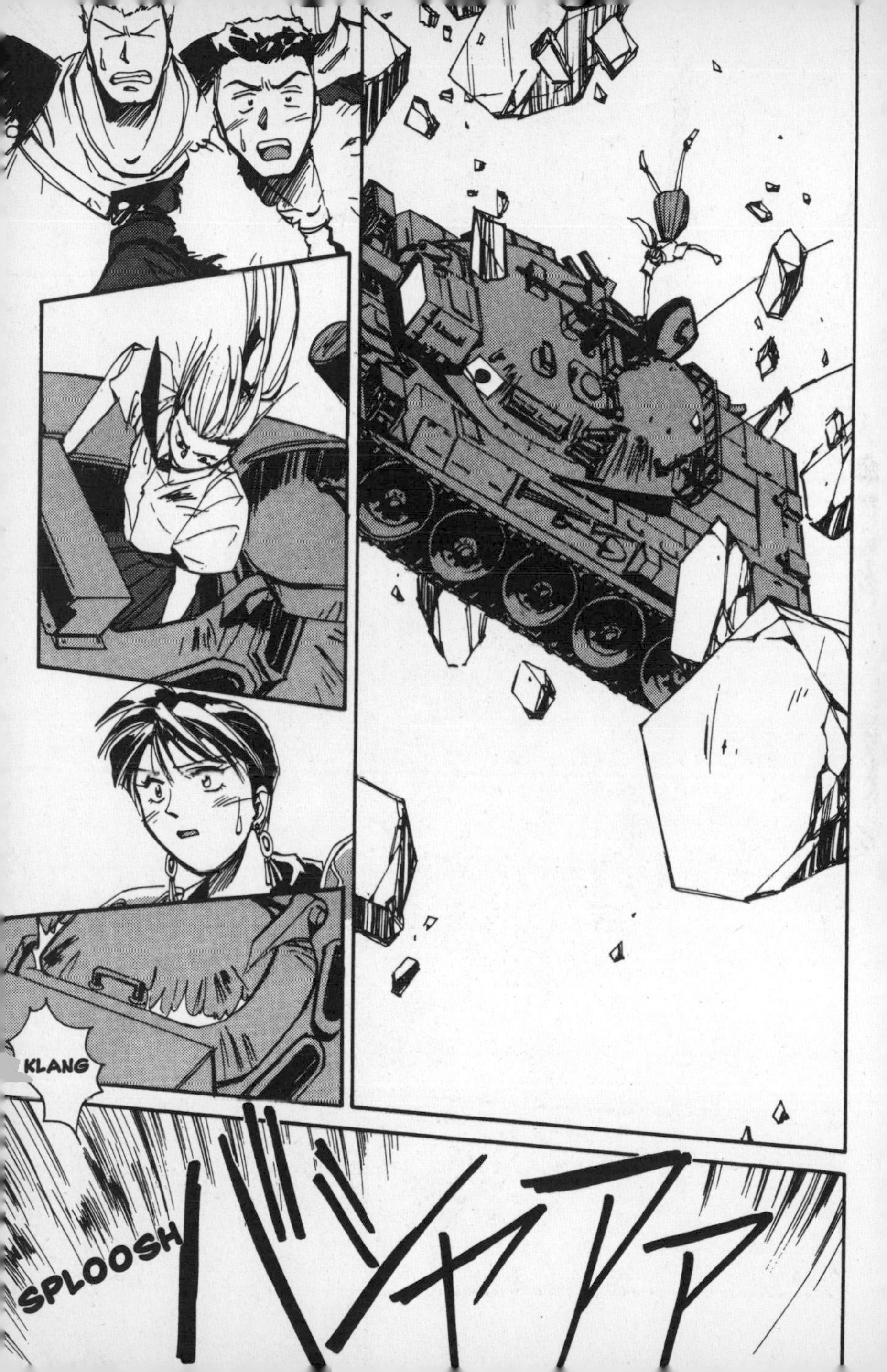
KLANG
SPLOOSH
バシャアア

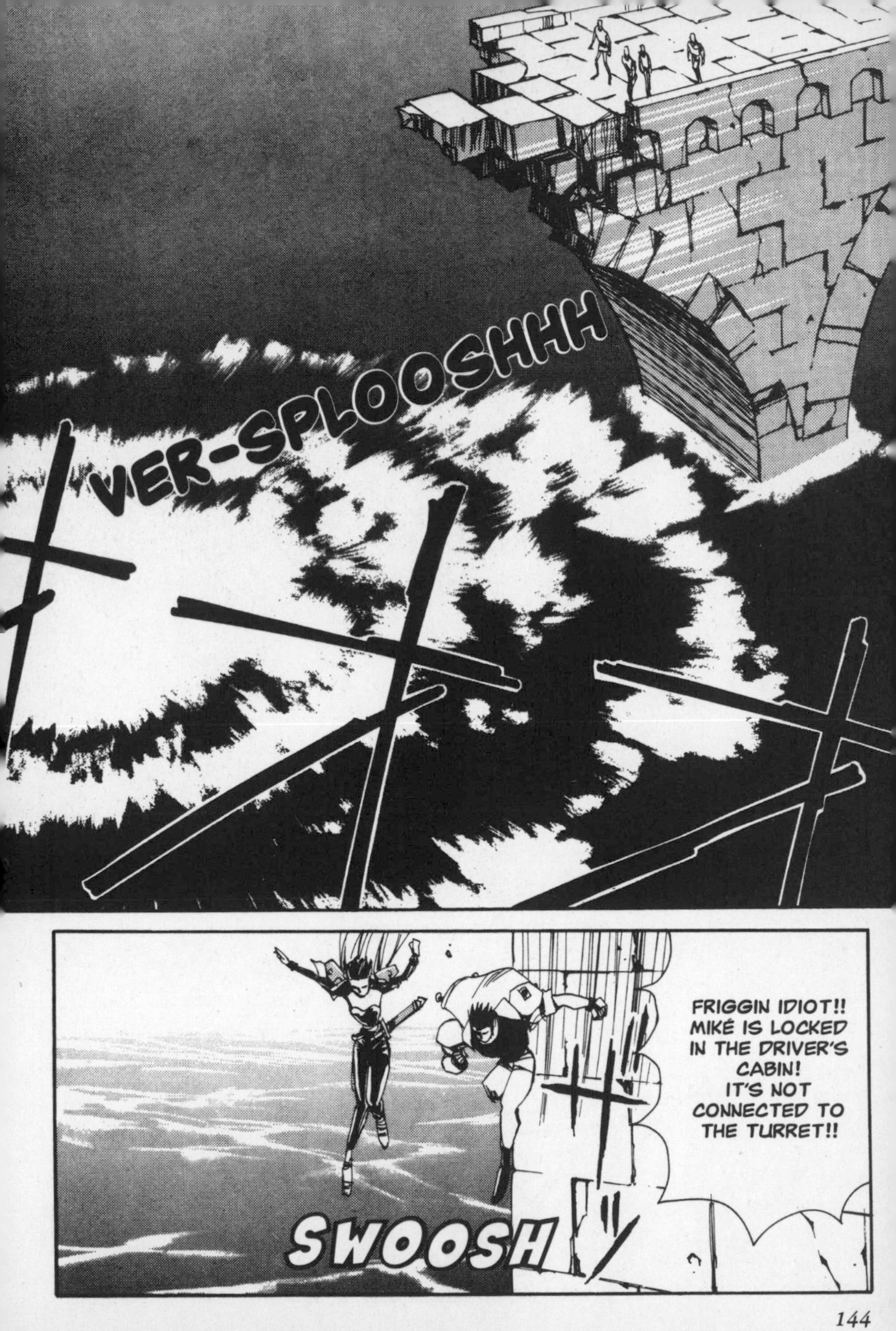
VER-SPLOOSHHH
FRIGGIN IDIOT!! MIKÉ IS LOCKED IN THE DRIVER'S CABIN! IT'S NOT CONNECTED TO THE TURRET!!
SWOOSH

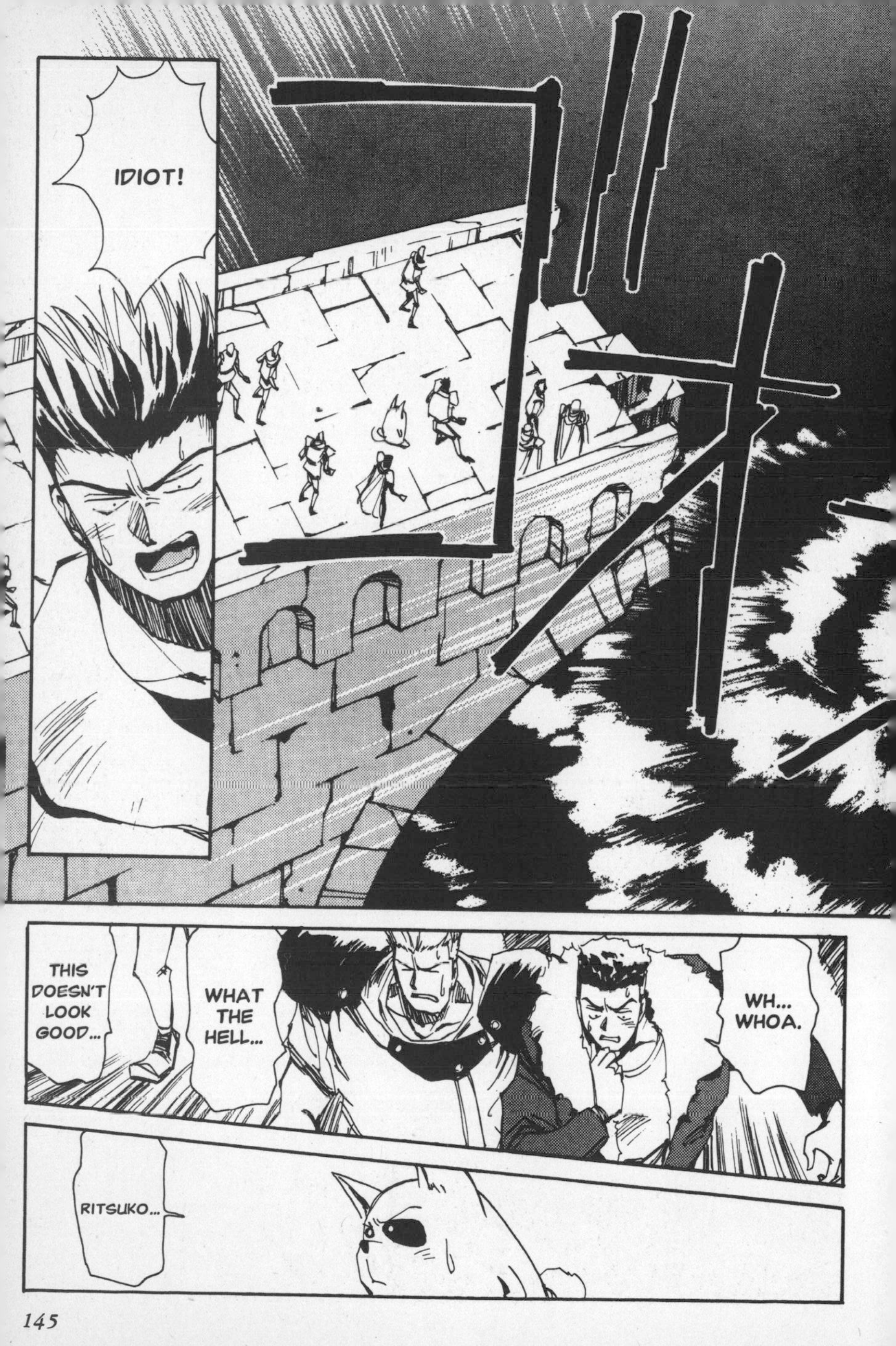
IDIOT!
WH... WHOA.
WHAT THE HELL...
THIS DOESN'T LOOK GOOD...
RITSUKO...

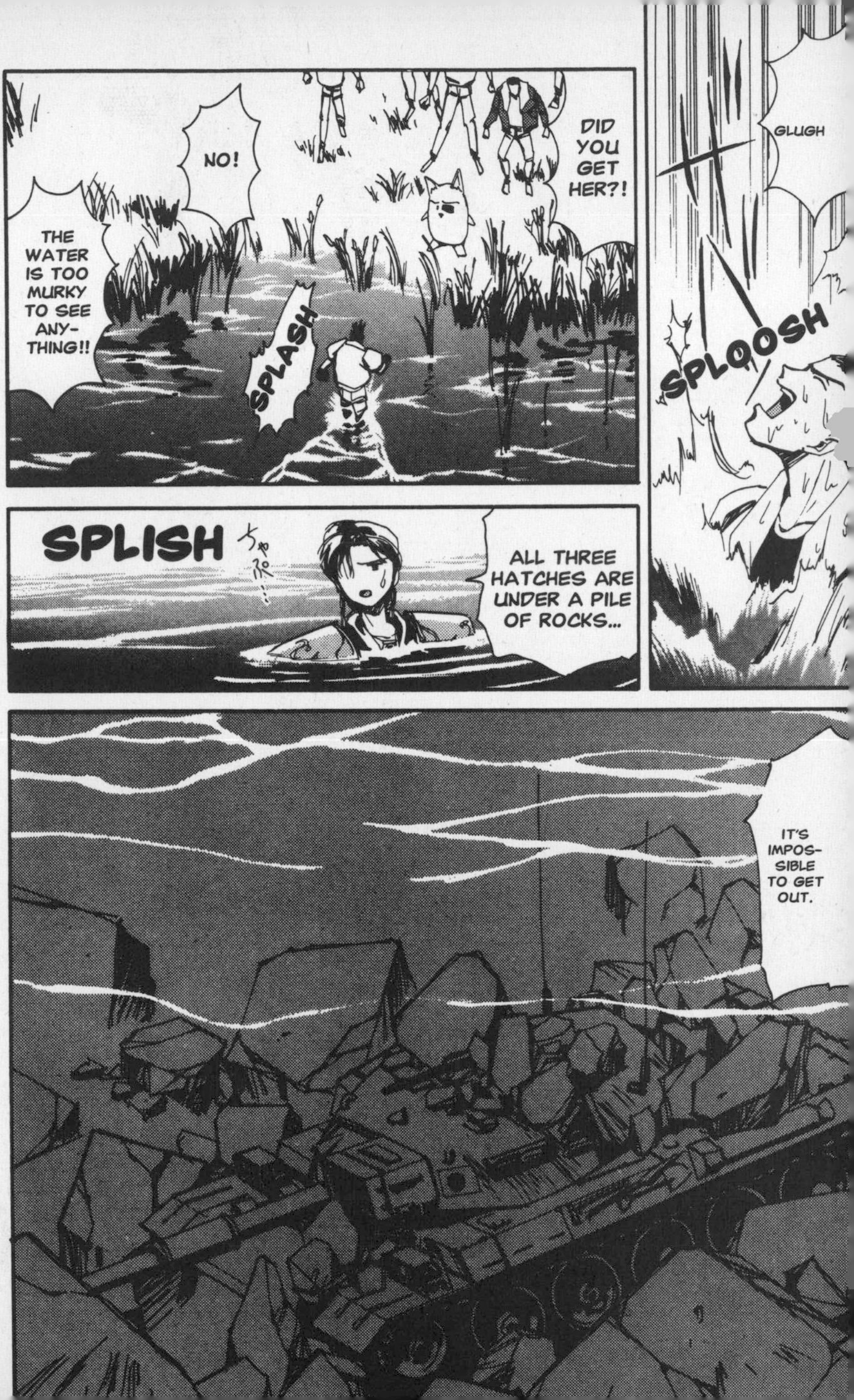
GLUGH
SPLOOSH
DID YOU GET HER?!
NO!
THE WATER IS TOO MURKY TO SEE ANY-THING!!
SPLASH
ALL THREE HATCHES ARE UNDER A PILE OF ROCKS...
SPLISH
ちゃぷ…
IT'S IMPOS-SIBLE TO GET OUT.

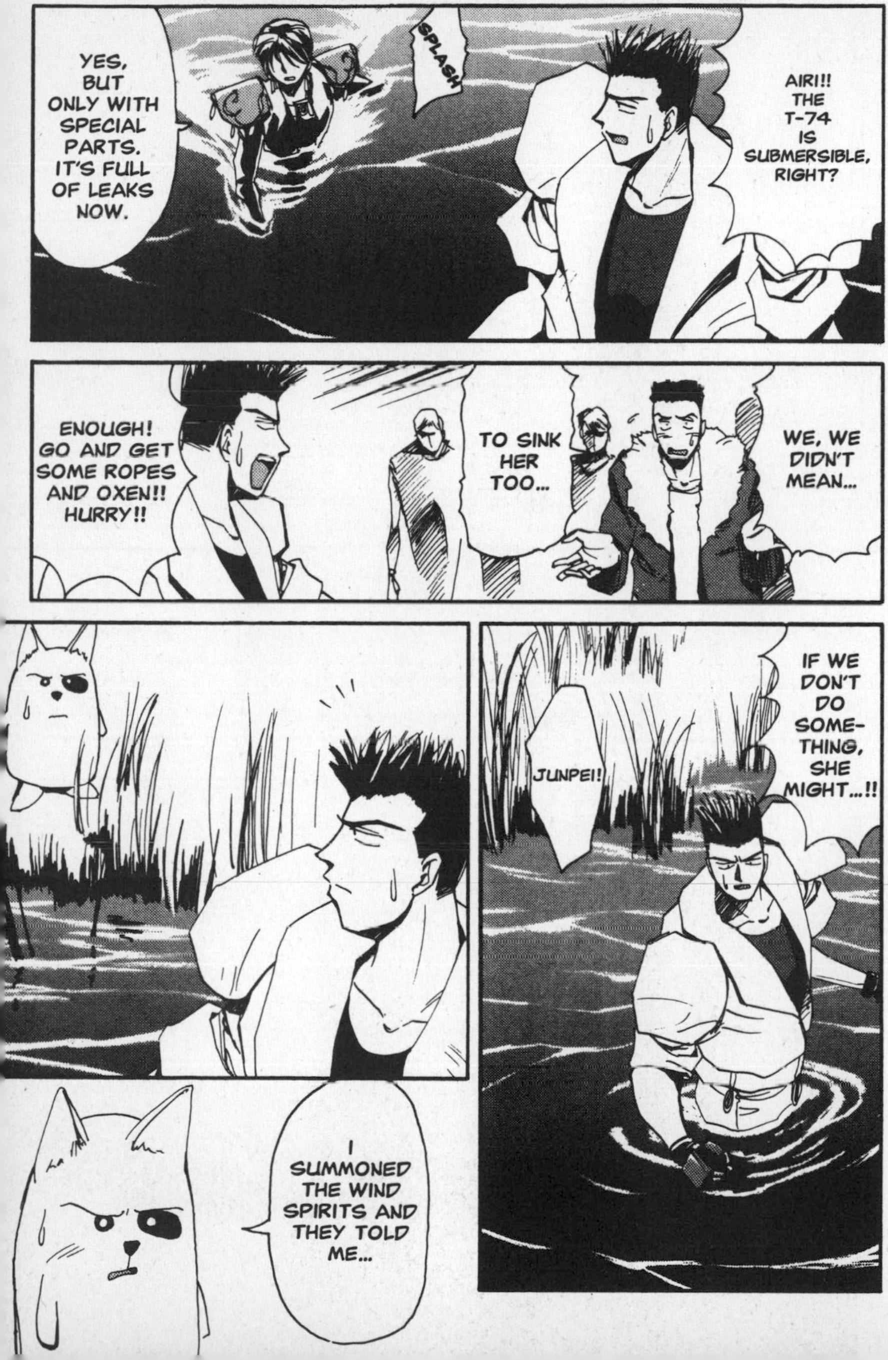
AIRI!! THE T-74 IS SUBMERSIBLE, RIGHT?
SPLASH
YES, BUT ONLY WITH SPECIAL PARTS. IT'S FULL OF LEAKS NOW.
WE, WE DIDN'T MEAN...
TO SINK HER TOO...
ENOUGH! GO AND GET SOME ROPES AND OXEN!! HURRY!!
IF WE DON'T DO SOME-THING, SHE MIGHT...!!
JUNPEI!
I SUMMONED THE WIND SPIRITS AND THEY TOLD ME...

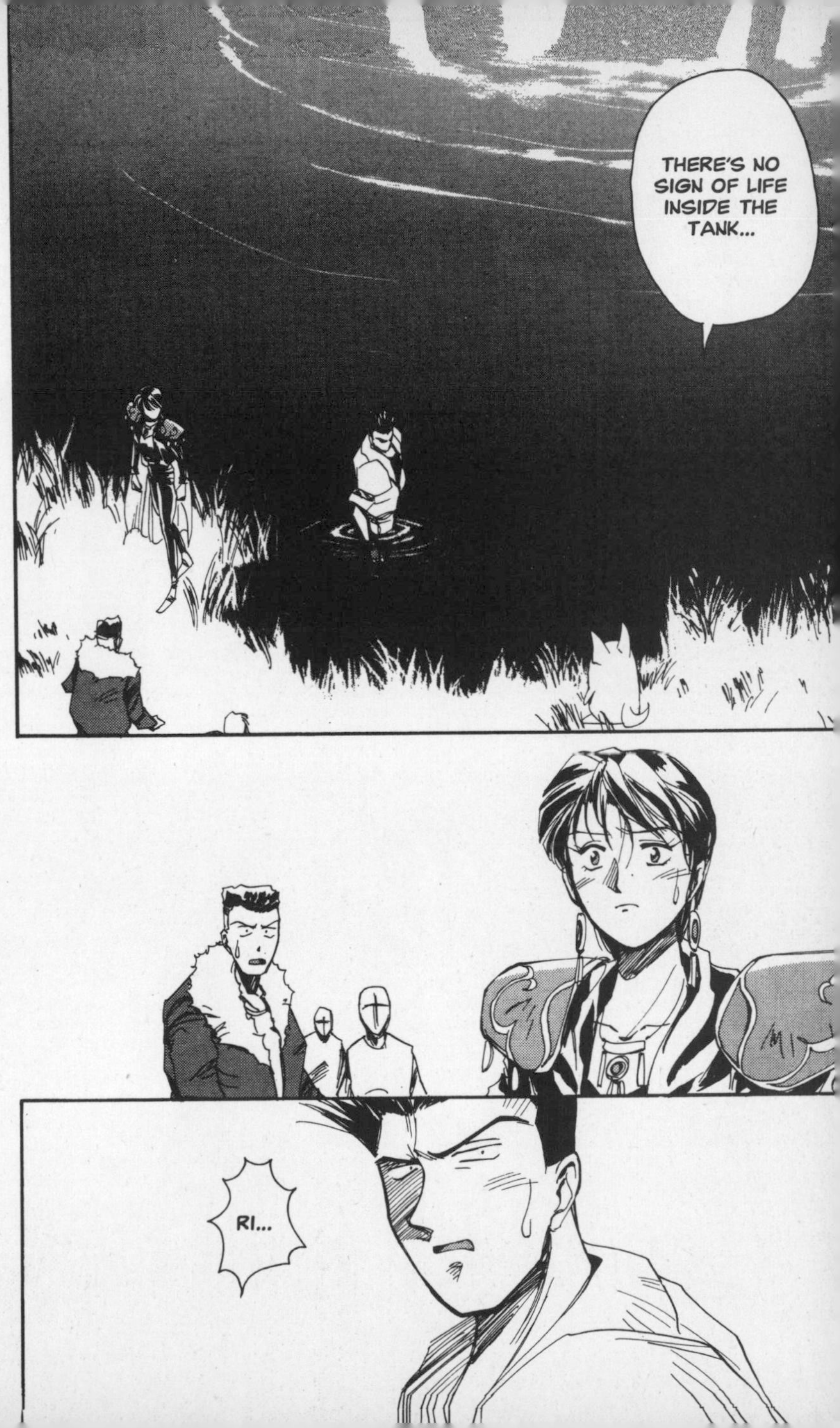
THERE'S NO SIGN OF LIFE INSIDE THE TANK...
RI...

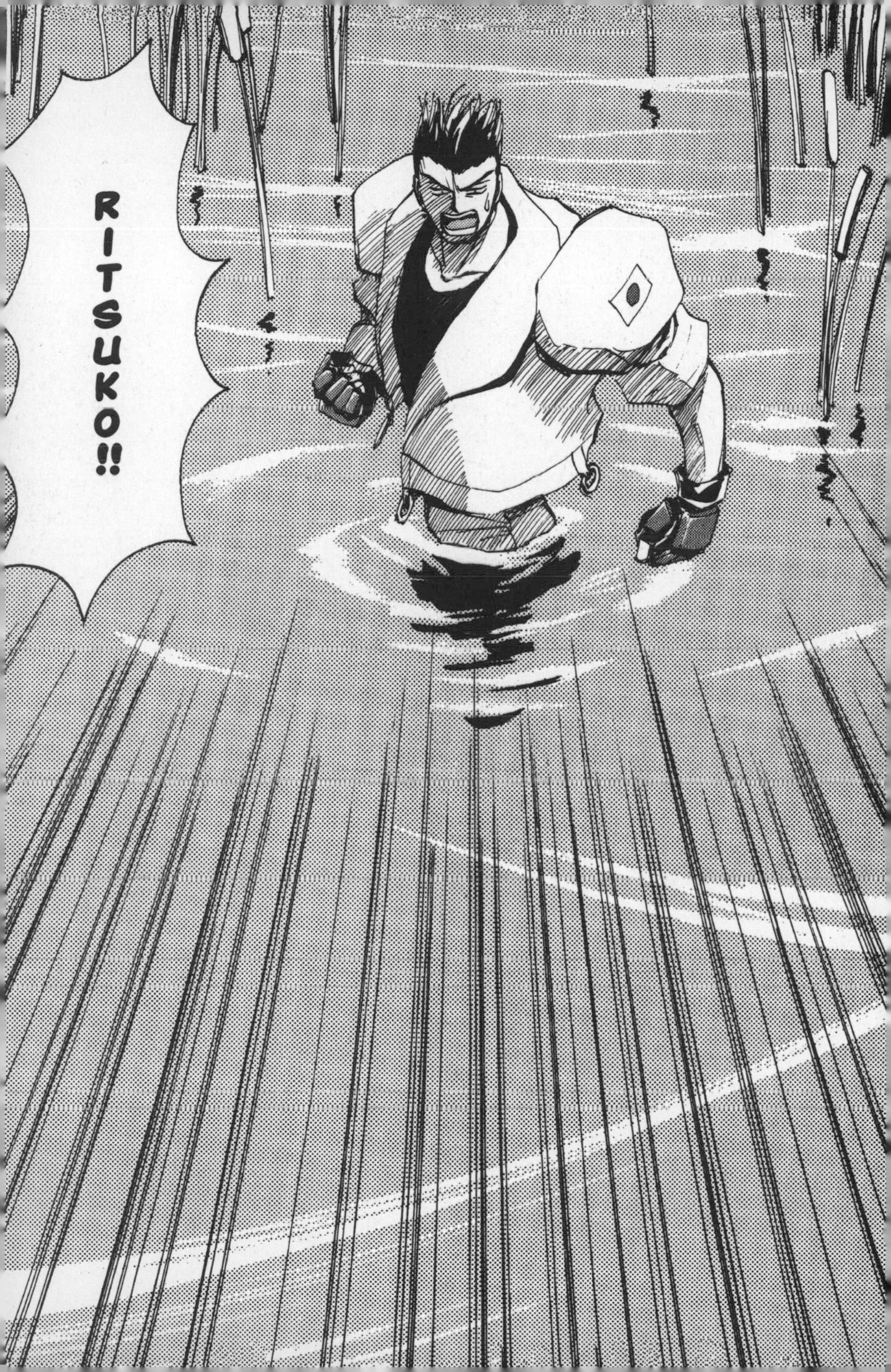
RITSUKO!!

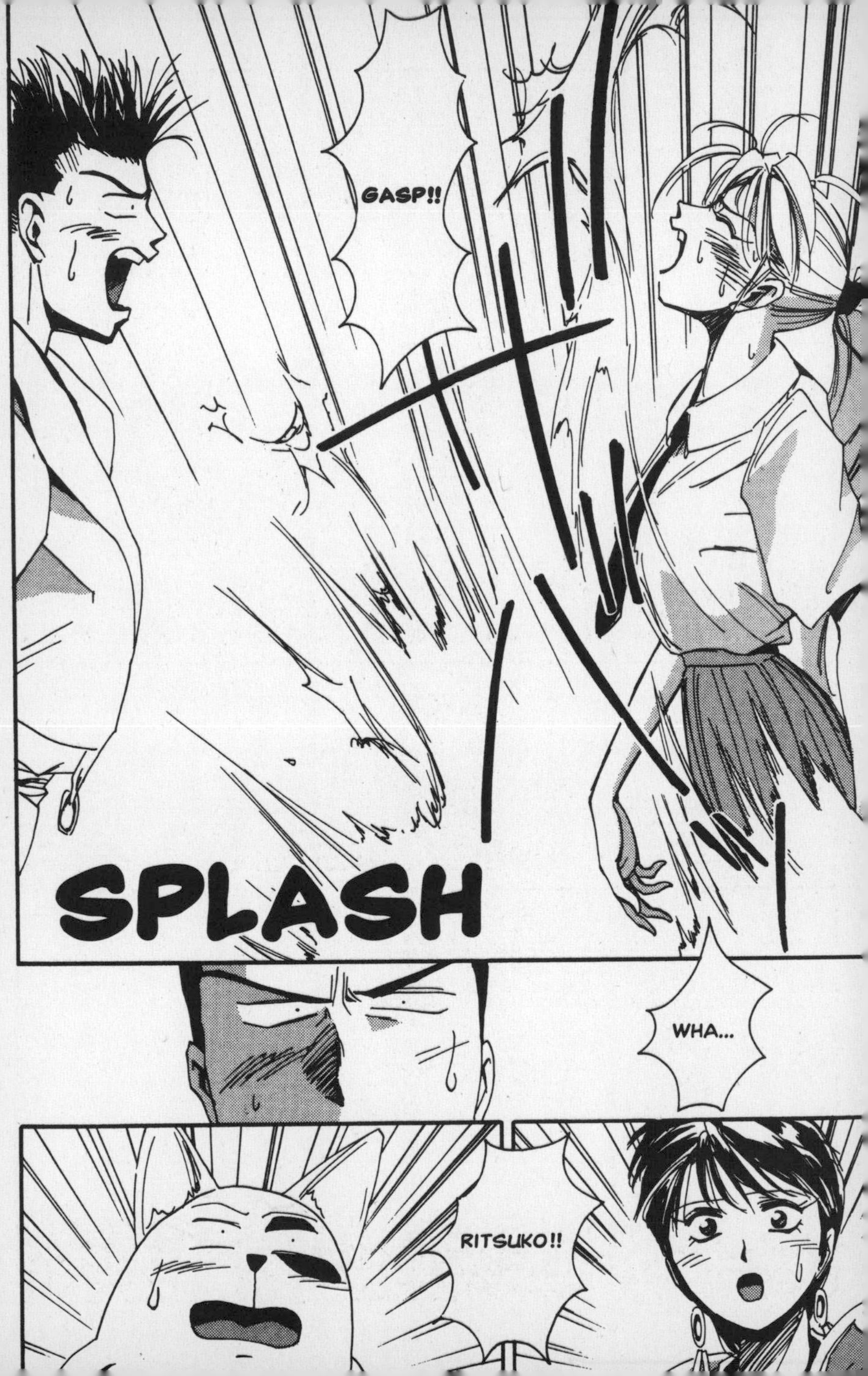
GASP!!
SPLASH
WHA...
RITSUKO!!

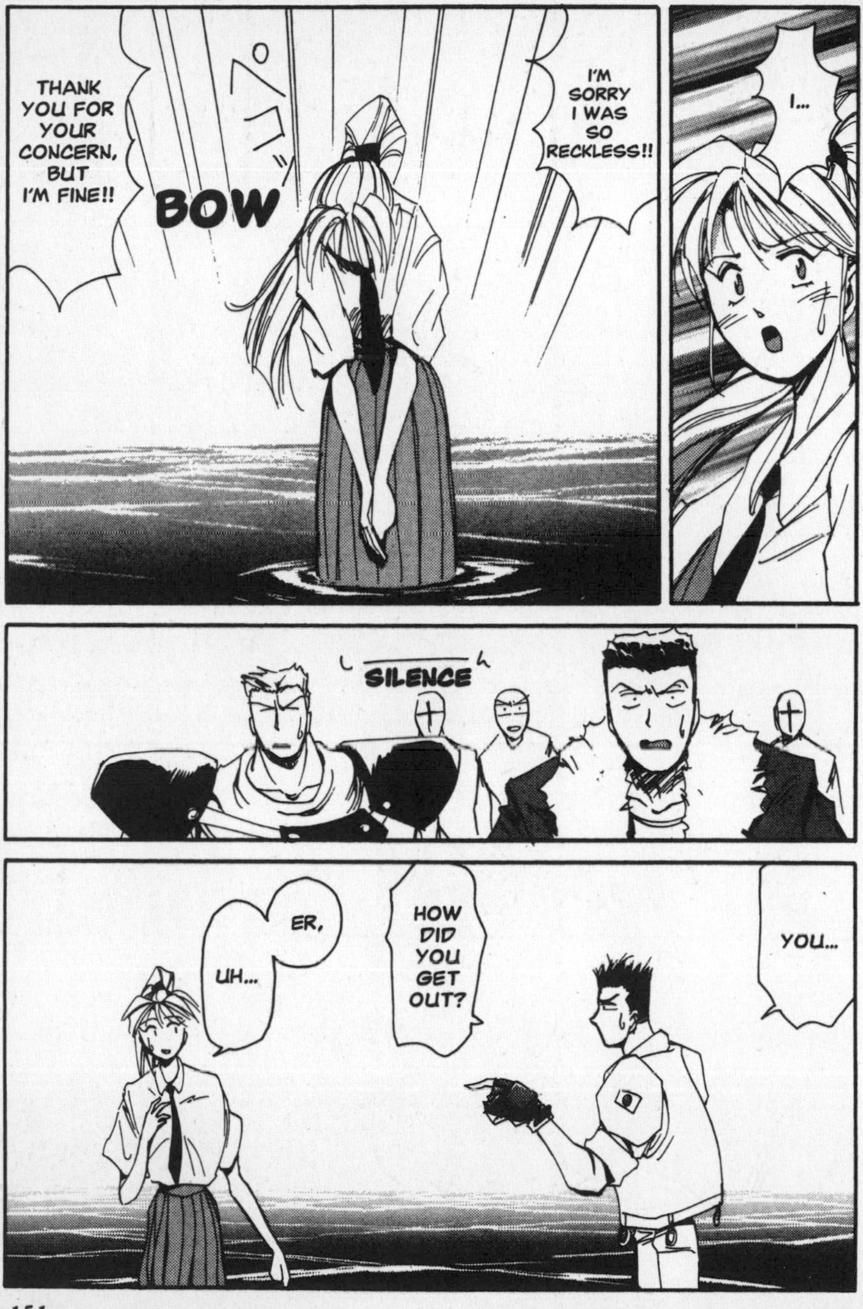
I...
I'M SORRY I WAS SO RECKLESS!!
BOW
THANK YOU FOR YOUR CONCERN, BUT I'M FINE!!
SILENCE
YOU...
HOW DID YOU GET OUT?
ER,
UH...

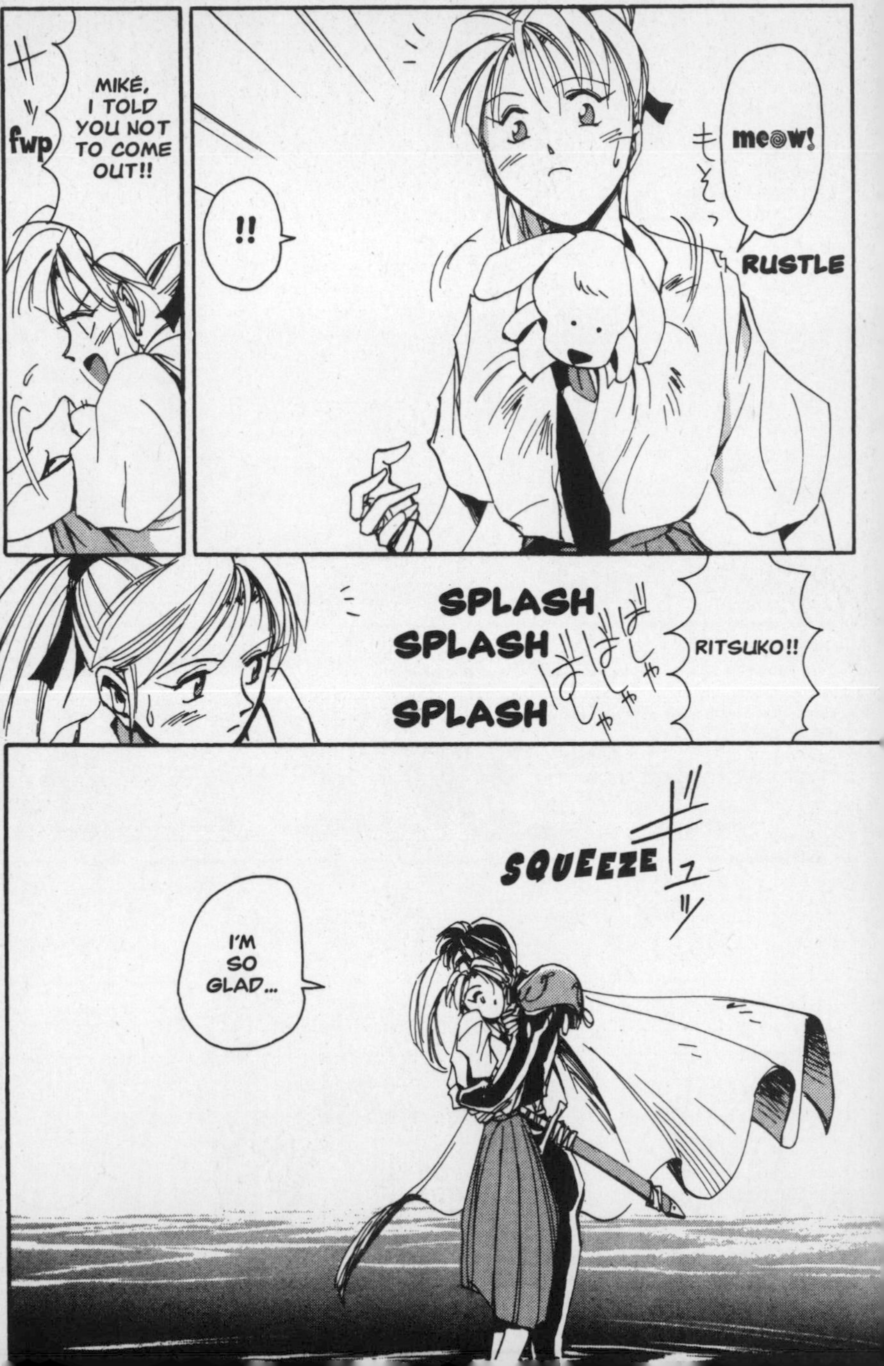
meow!
もそっ
RUSTLE
!!
fwp
MIKÉ, I TOLD YOU NOT TO COME OUT!!
RITSUKO!!
SPLASH
SPLASH
SPLASH
SQUEEZE
I'M SO GLAD...

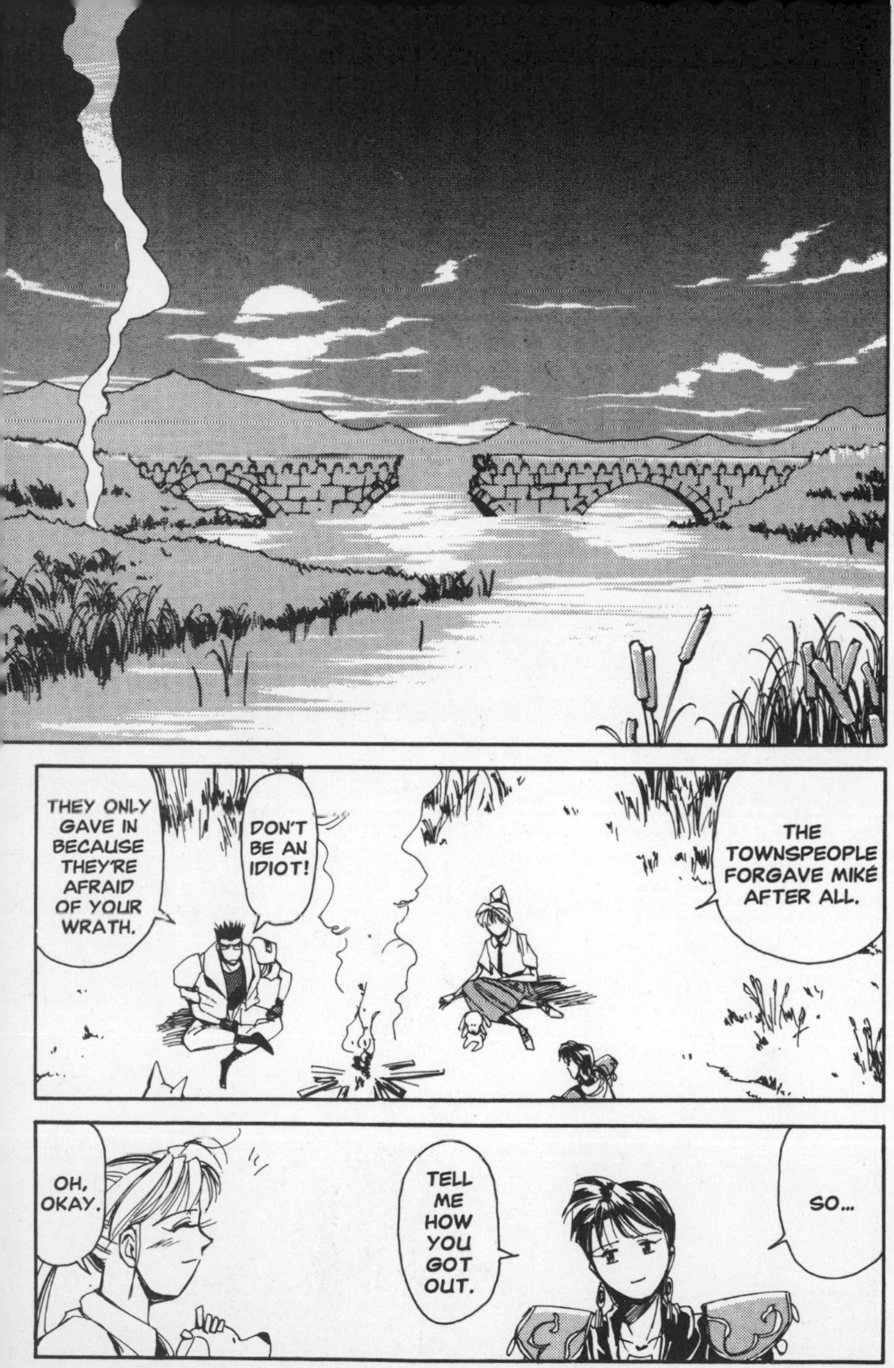
THE TOWNSPEOPLE FORGAVE MIKÉ AFTER ALL.
DON'T BE AN IDIOT!
THEY ONLY GAVE IN BECAUSE THEY'RE AFRAID OF YOUR WRATH.
SO...
TELL ME HOW YOU GOT OUT.
OH, OKAY.

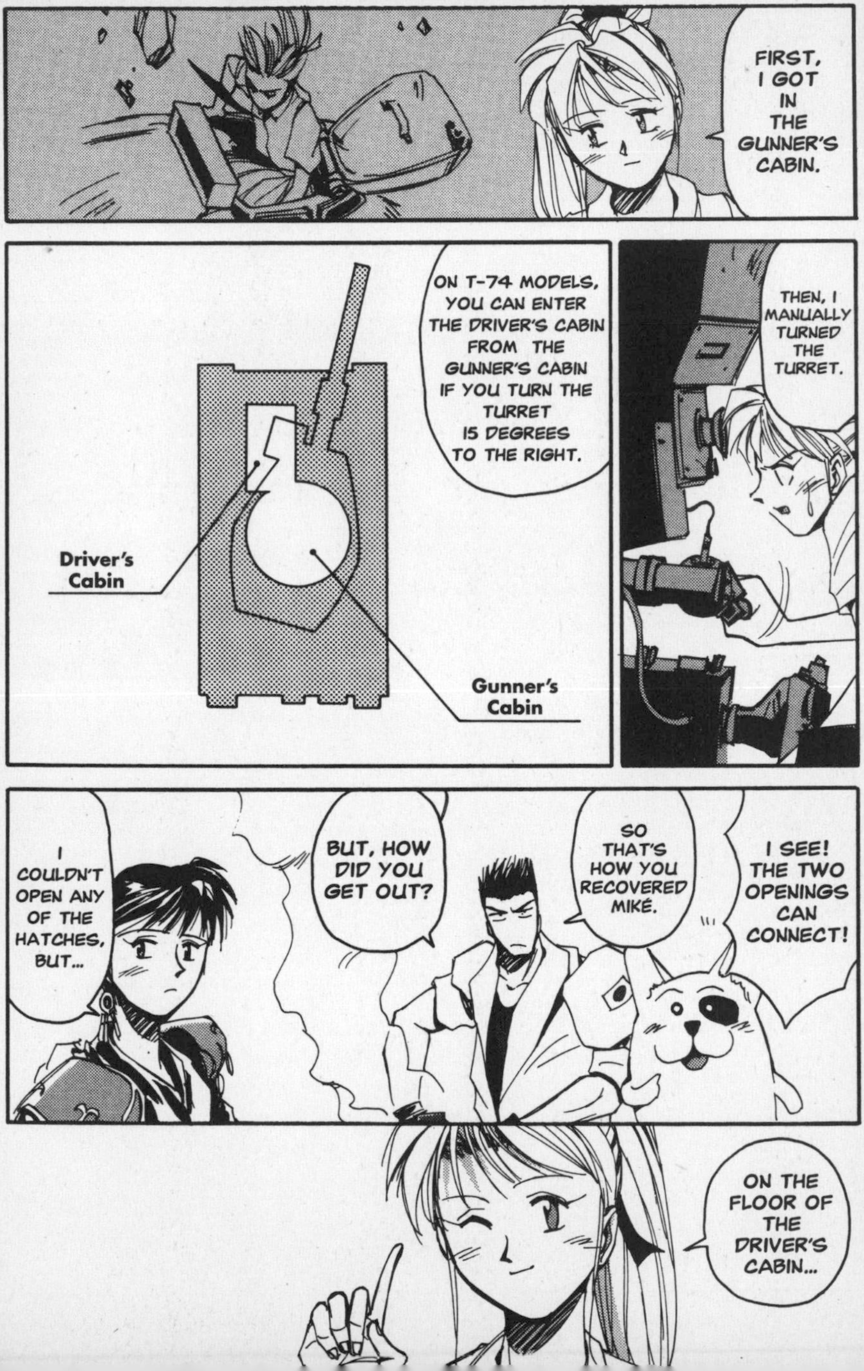
FIRST, I GOT IN THE GUNNER'S CABIN.
THEN, I MANUALLY TURNED THE TURRET.
ON T-74 MODELS, YOU CAN ENTER THE DRIVER'S CABIN FROM THE GUNNER'S CABIN IF YOU TURN THE TURRET 15 DEGREES TO THE RIGHT.
Driver's Cabin
Gunner's Cabin
I SEE! THE TWO OPENINGS CAN CONNECT!
SO THAT'S HOW YOU RECOVERED MIKE.
BUT, HOW DID YOU GET OUT?
I COULDN'T OPEN ANY OF THE HATCHES, BUT...
ON THE FLOOR OF THE DRIVER'S CABIN...

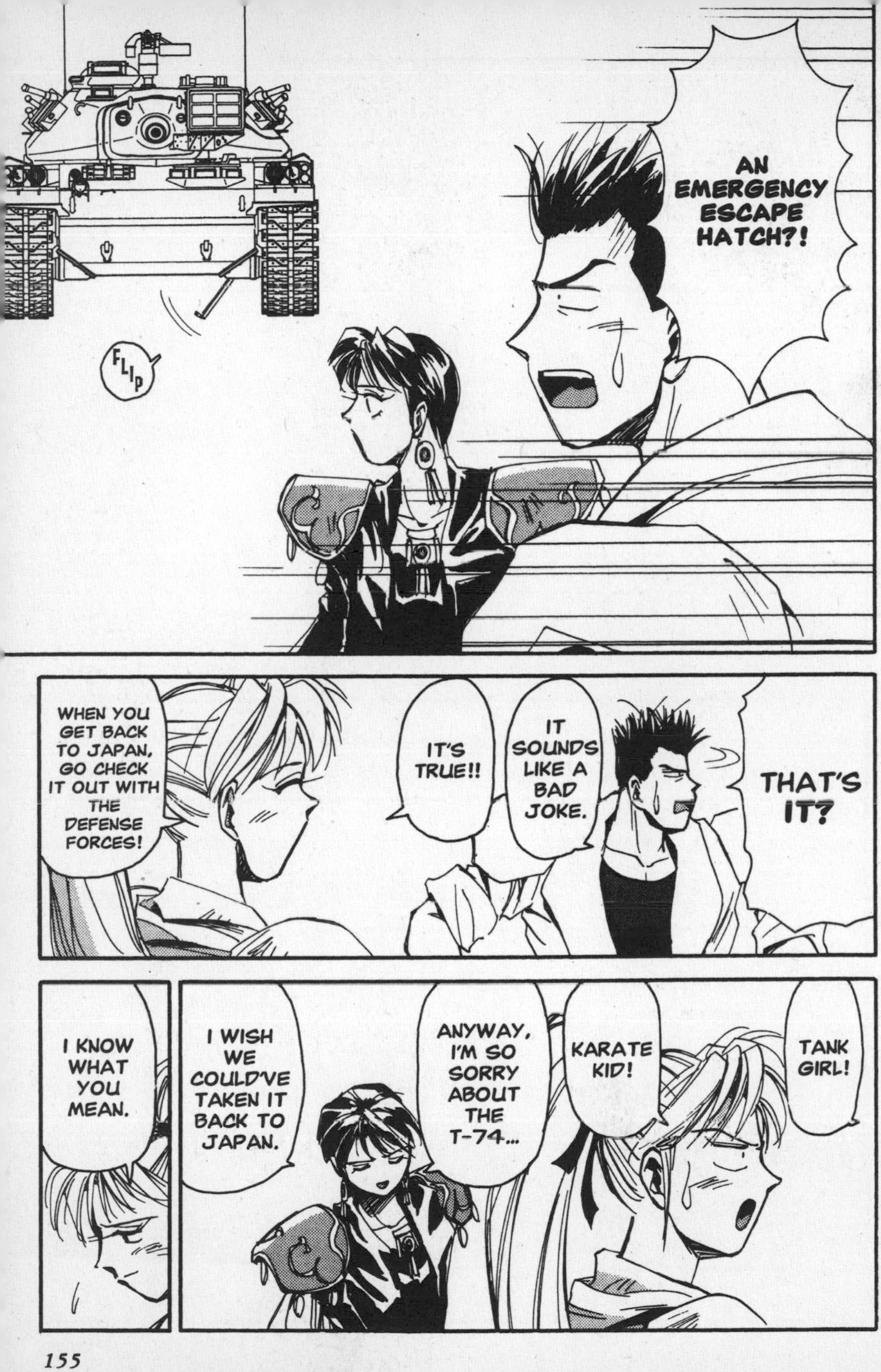
AN EMERGENCY ESCAPE HATCH?!
FLIP
THAT'S IT?
IT SOUNDS LIKE A BAD JOKE.
IT'S TRUE!!
WHEN YOU GET BACK TO JAPAN, GO CHECK IT OUT WITH THE DEFENSE FORCES!
TANK GIRL!
KARATE KID!
ANYWAY, I'M SO SORRY ABOUT THE T-74...
I WISH WE COULD'VE TAKEN IT BACK TO JAPAN.
I KNOW WHAT YOU MEAN.

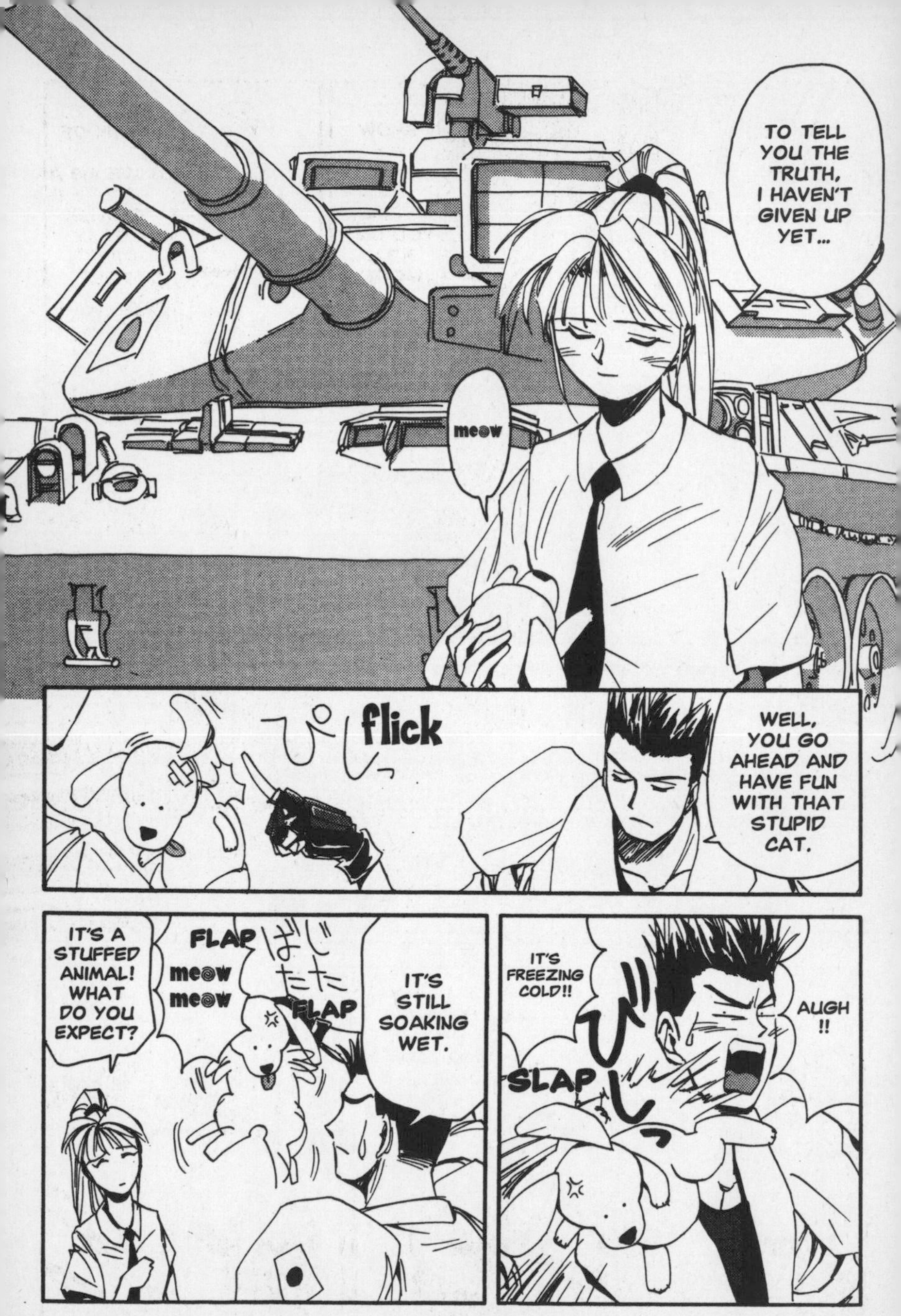
TO TELL YOU THE TRUTH, I HAVEN'T GIVEN UP YET...
meow
flick
ぴしっ
WELL, YOU GO AHEAD AND HAVE FUN WITH THAT STUPID CAT.
FLAP
ばたた
FLAP
meow meow
IT'S STILL SOAKING WET.
IT'S A STUFFED ANIMAL! WHAT DO YOU EXPECT?
SLAP
びしっ
IT'S FREEZING COLD!!
AUGH !!

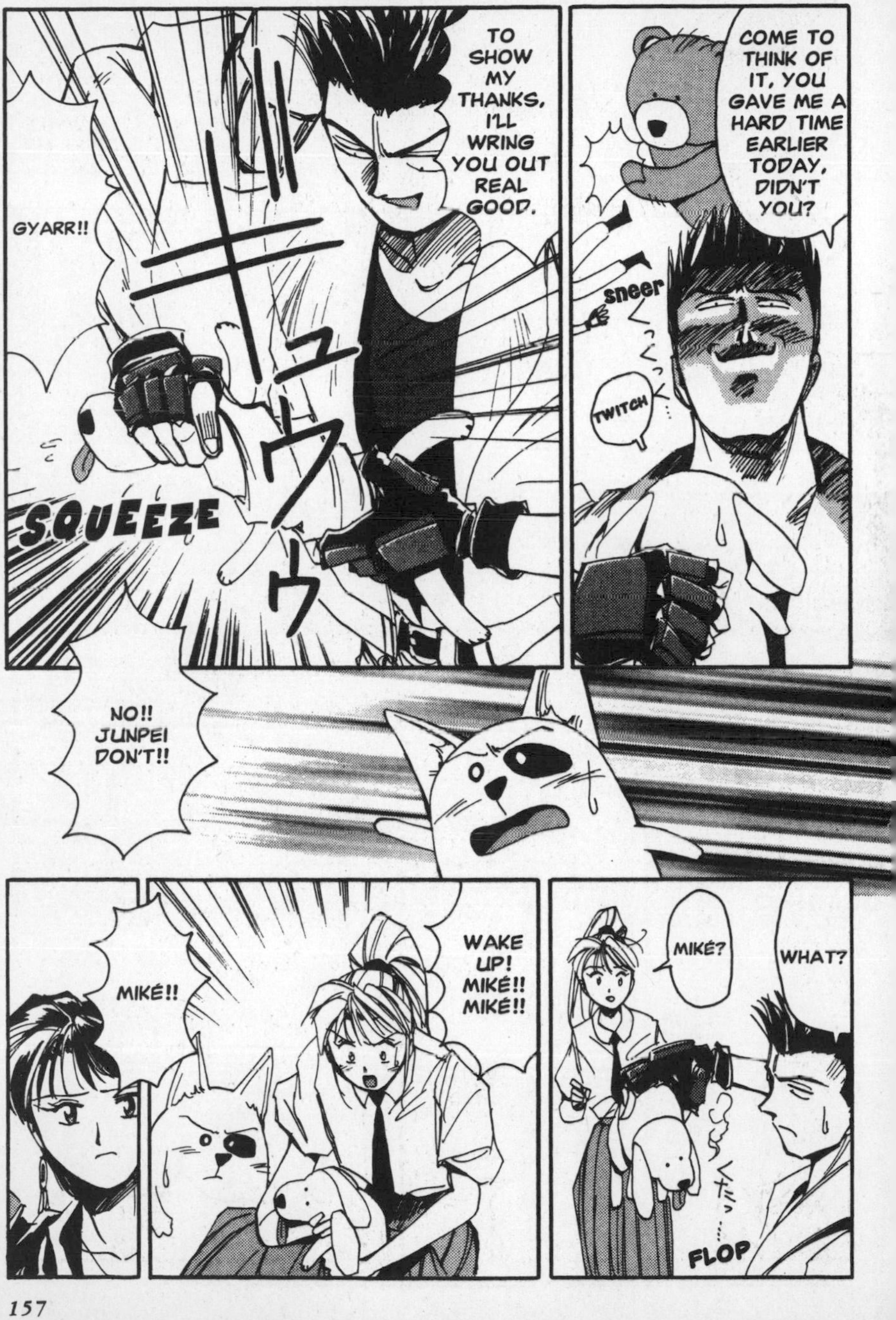
COME TO THINK OF IT, YOU GAVE ME A HARD TIME EARLIER TODAY, DIDN'T YOU?
sneer
TWITCH
TO SHOW MY THANKS, I'LL WRING YOU OUT REAL GOOD.
GYARR!!
キュウウ
SQUEEZE
NO!! JUNPEI DON'T!!
WHAT?
MIKÉ?
FLOP
WAKE UP! MIKÉ!! MIKÉ!!
MIKÉ!!

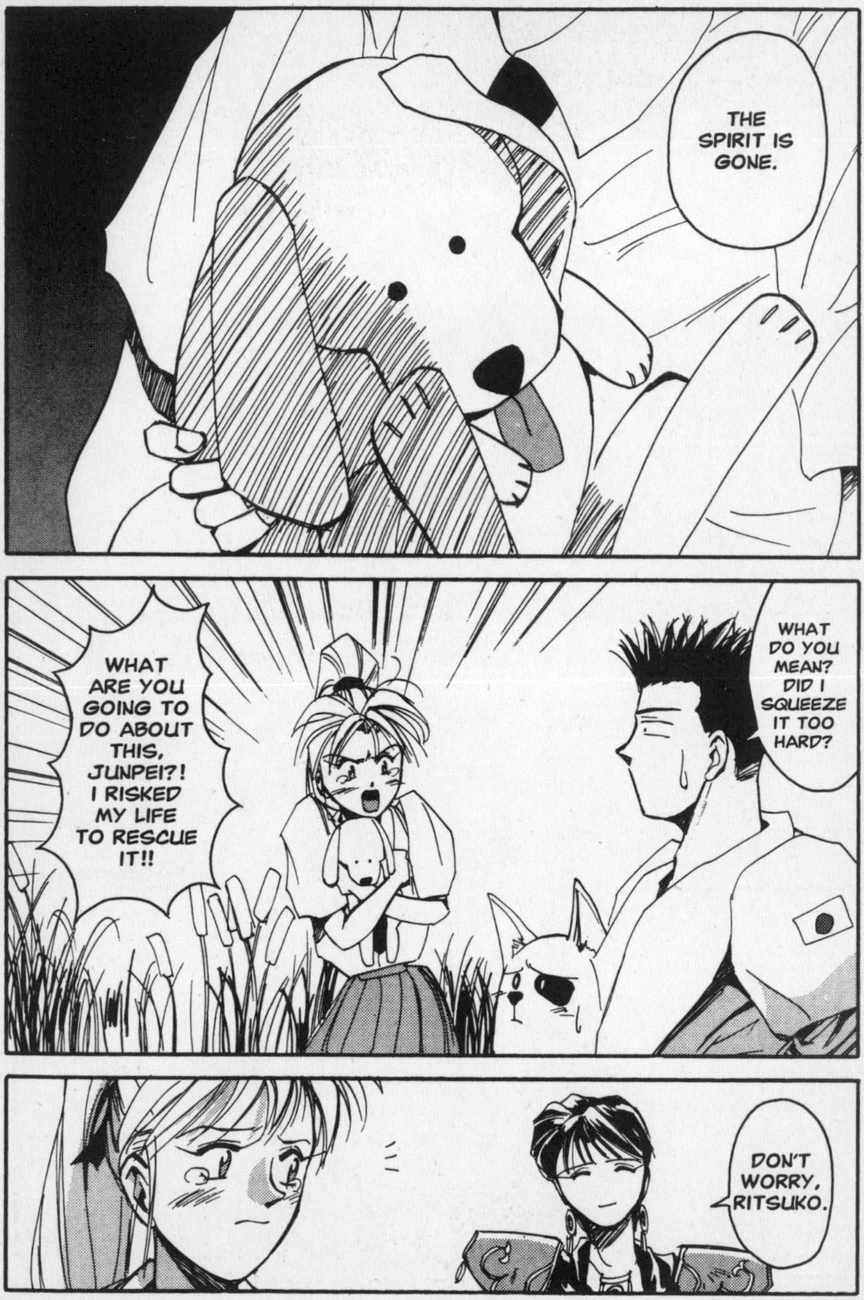
THE SPIRIT IS GONE.
WHAT DO YOU MEAN? DID I SQUEEZE IT TOO HARD?
WHAT ARE YOU GOING TO DO ABOUT THIS, JUNPEI?! I RISKED MY LIFE TO RESCUE IT!!
DON'T WORRY, RITSUKO.

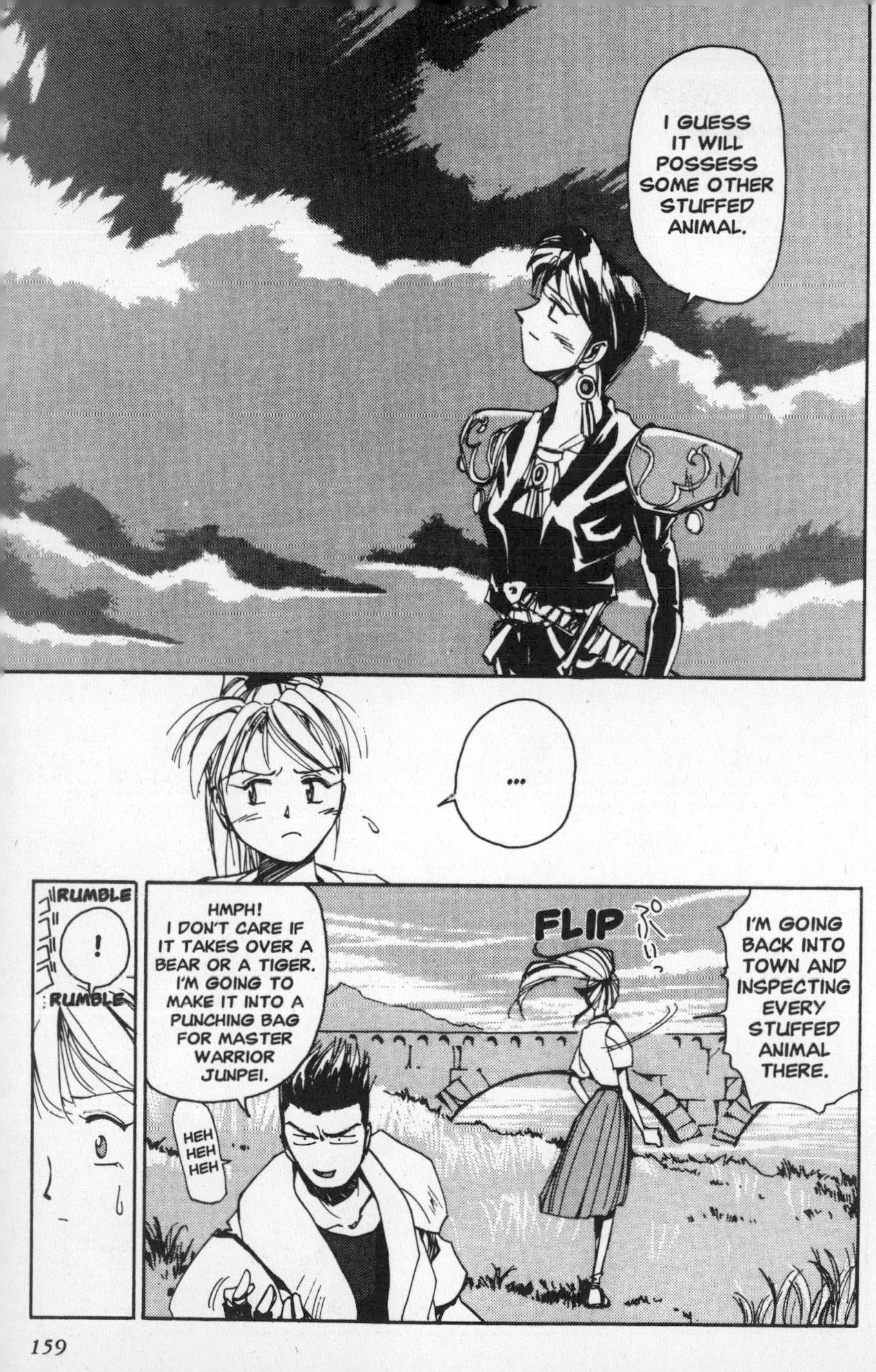
I GUESS IT WILL POSSESS SOME OTHER STUFFED ANIMAL.
...
FLIP
I'M GOING BACK INTO TOWN AND INSPECTING EVERY STUFFED ANIMAL THERE.
HMPH! I DON'T CARE IF IT TAKES OVER A BEAR OR A TIGER. I'M GOING TO MAKE IT INTO A PUNCHING BAG FOR MASTER WARRIOR JUNPEI.
HEH HEH HEH
RUMBLE
!
RUMBLE

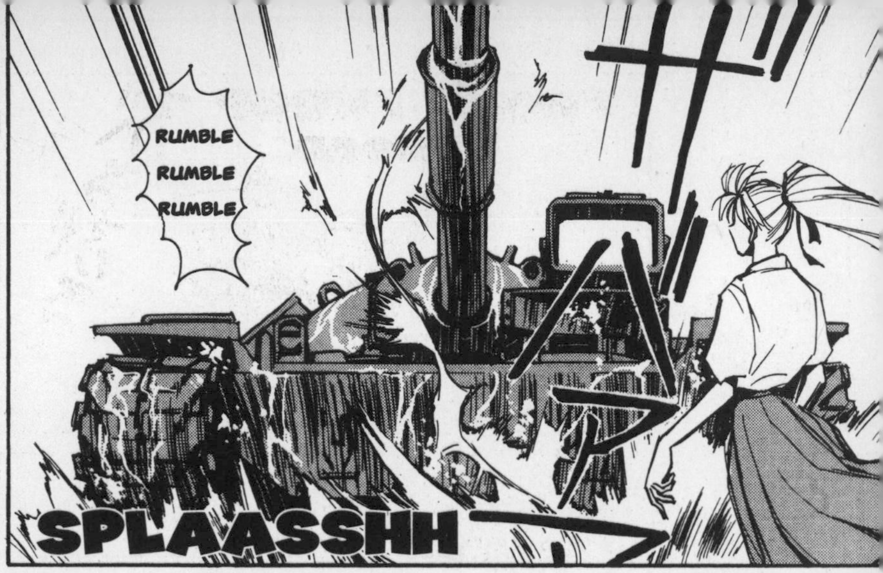
RUMBLE
RUMBLE
RUMBLE
SPLAASSHH

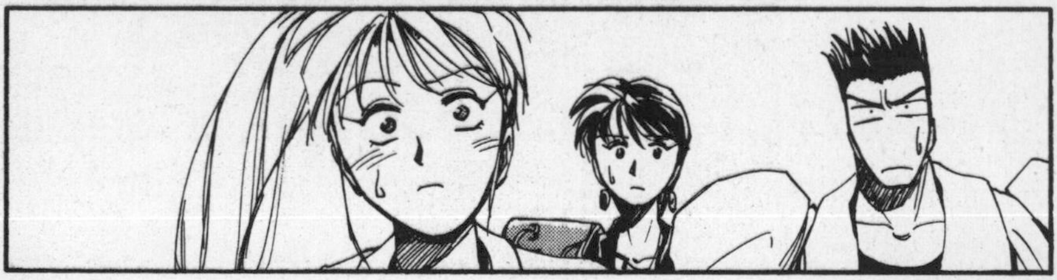

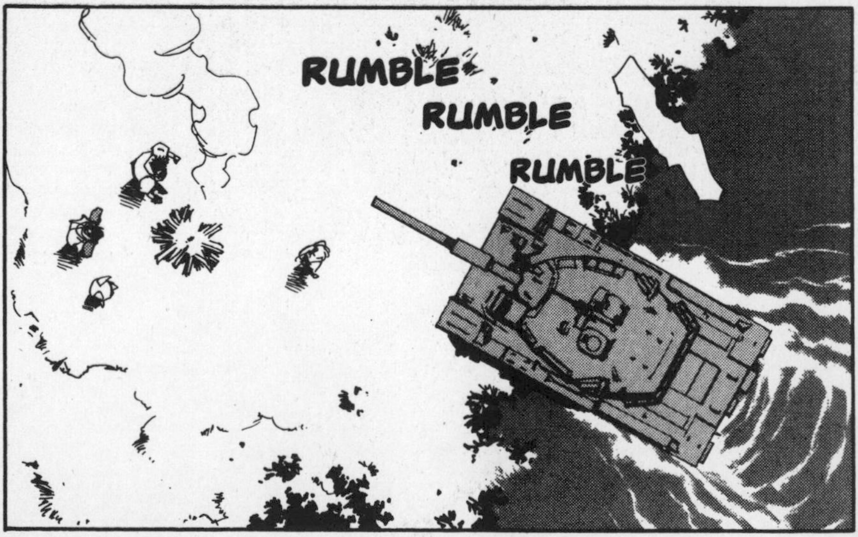
RUMBLE
RUMBLE
RUMBLE

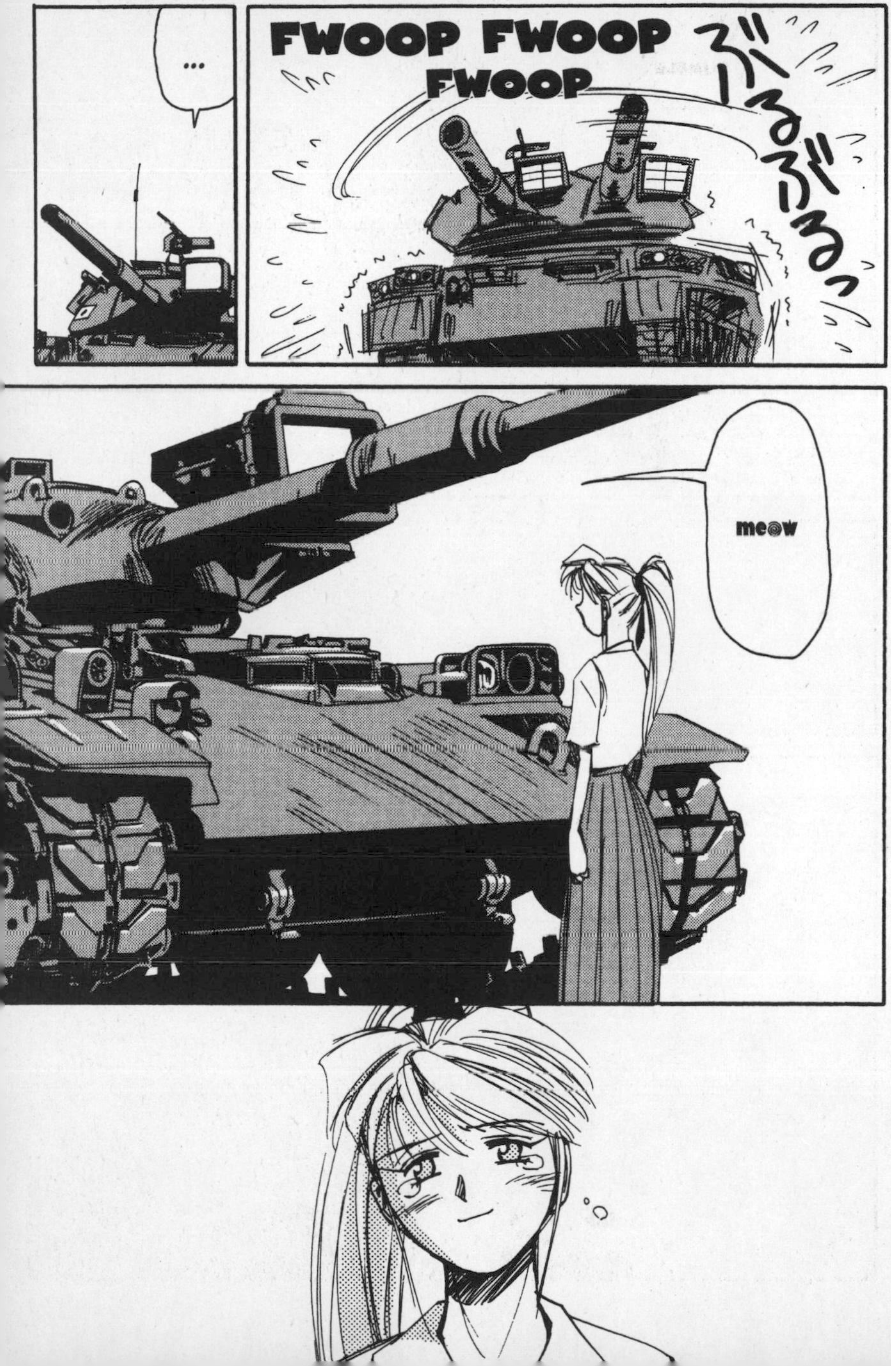
FWOOP FWOOP FWOOP
ぶるぶるっ
...
meow

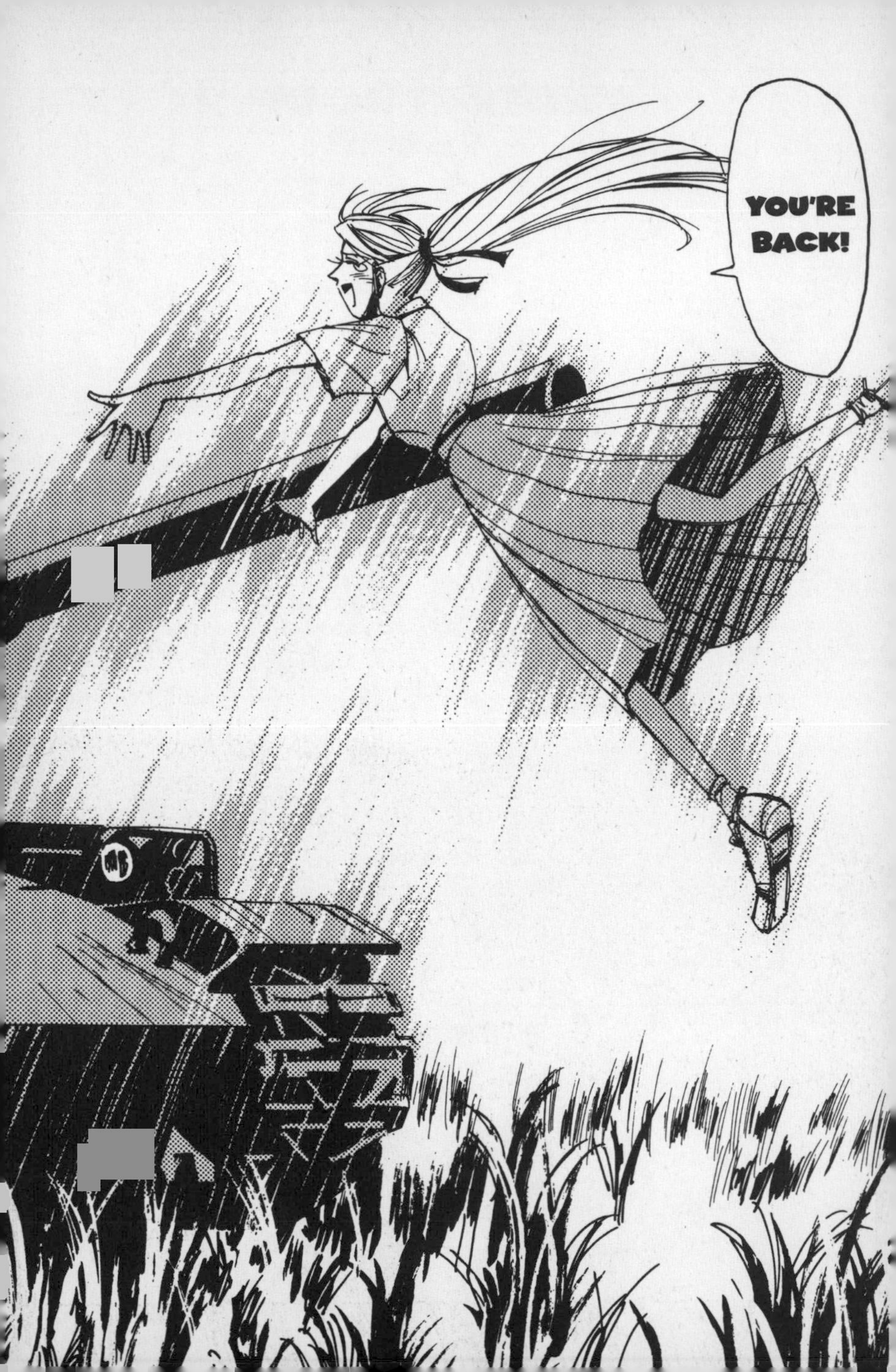
YOU'RE BACK!

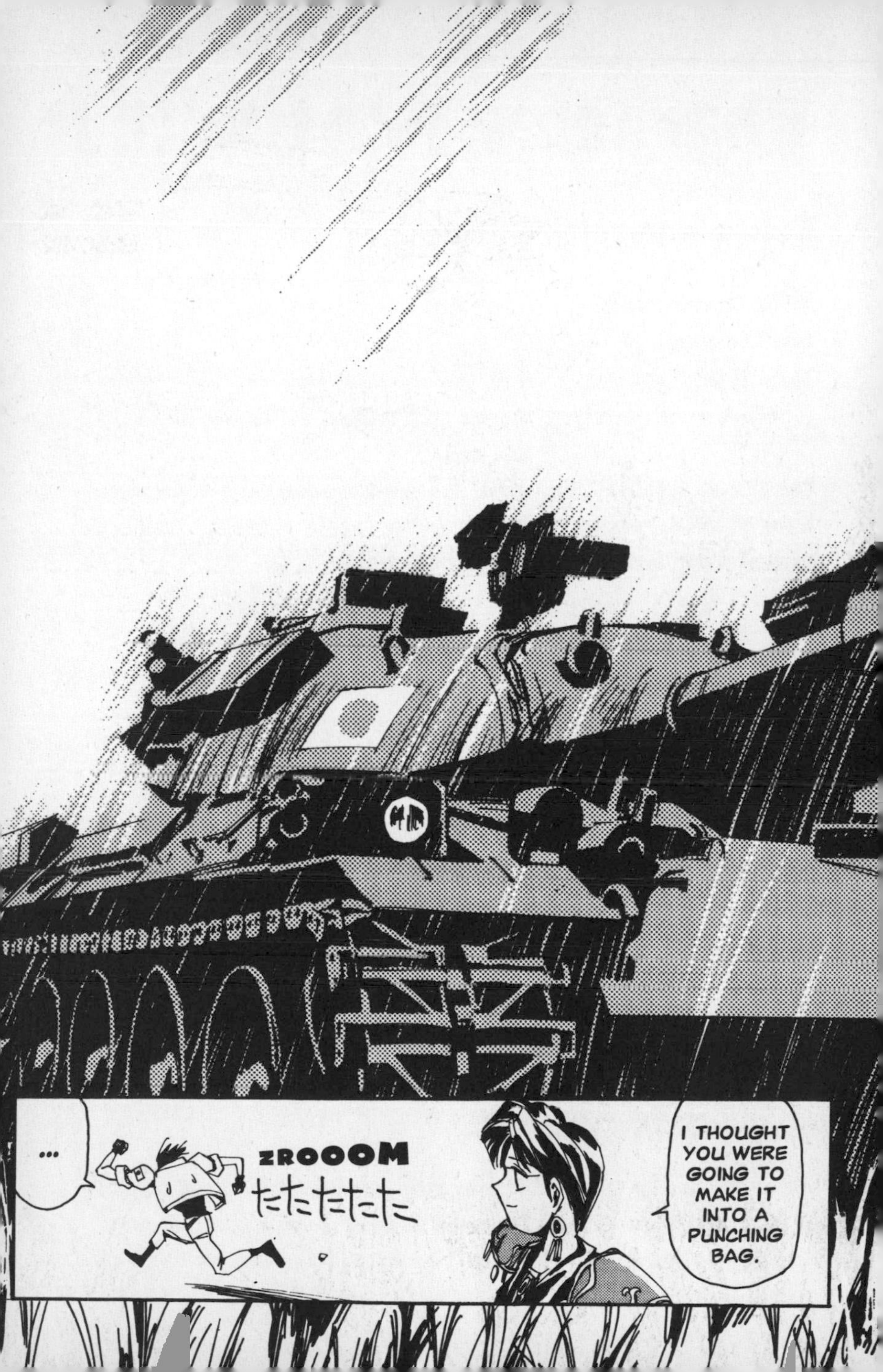
I THOUGHT YOU WERE GOING TO MAKE IT INTO A PUNCHING BAG.
ZROOOM
たたたたたた
...

Character Profile (4)

Celcia Marieclaire (Spot)

Tribe: Common Elves
Age: Unknown
Blood Type: Unknown
Sign: Crescent Moon (yup, there's such a thing in this world)

Celcia is an excellent sorceress, and one-time head of the Common Elves of the Carmagan region. Currently, however, she is stuck in the form of a dog and can't return to her original form.
Junpei calls her "Spot"

Model T-74 Tank (Miké)

The T-74 (now known as Miké) has been taken over by a cat spirit. As a result, it's become quite an unsual tank that's skittish of dogs and doesn't require fuel. It's fighting capabilities have yet to be seen.

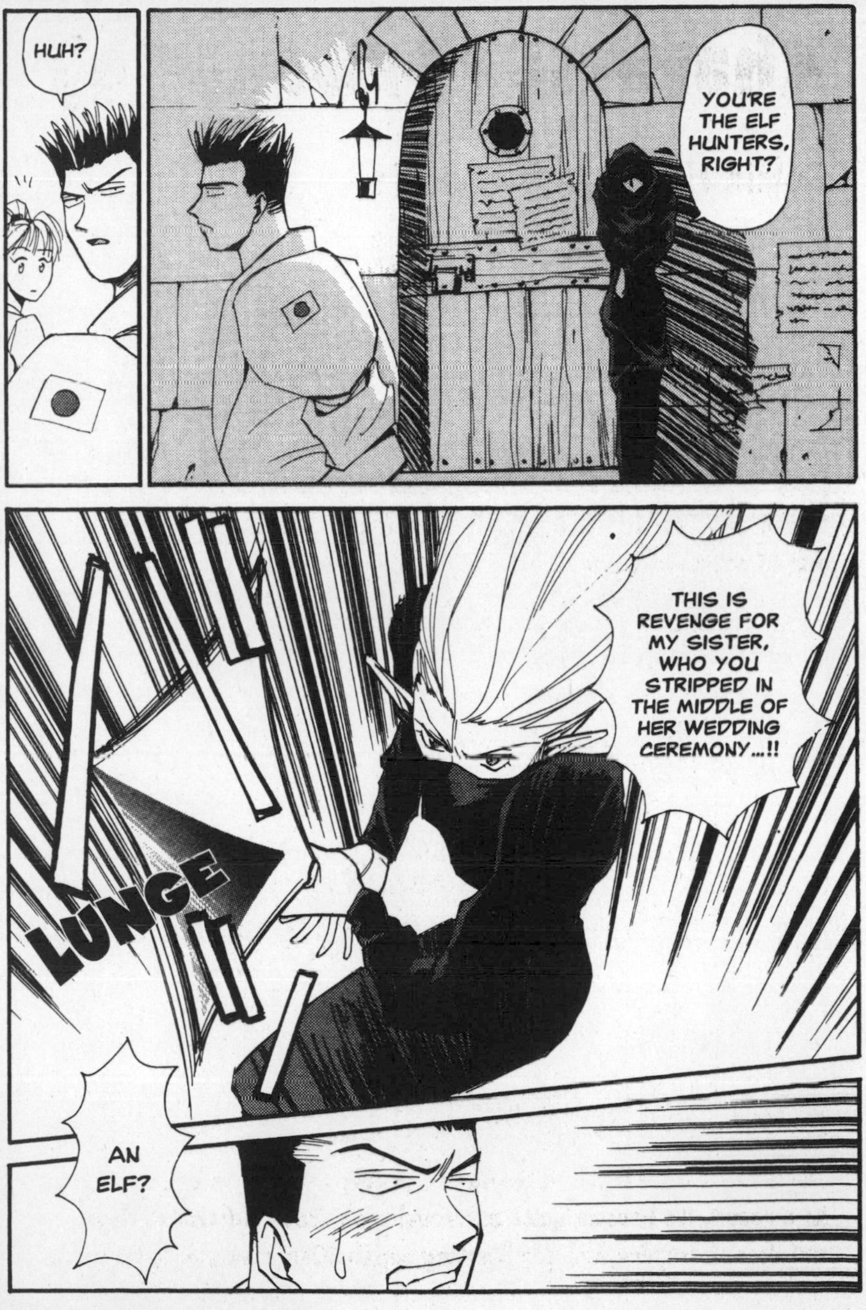
YOU'RE THE ELF HUNTERS, RIGHT?
HUH?
THIS IS REVENGE FOR MY SISTER, WHO YOU STRIPPED IN THE MIDDLE OF HER WEDDING CEREMONY...!!
LUNGE
AN ELF?

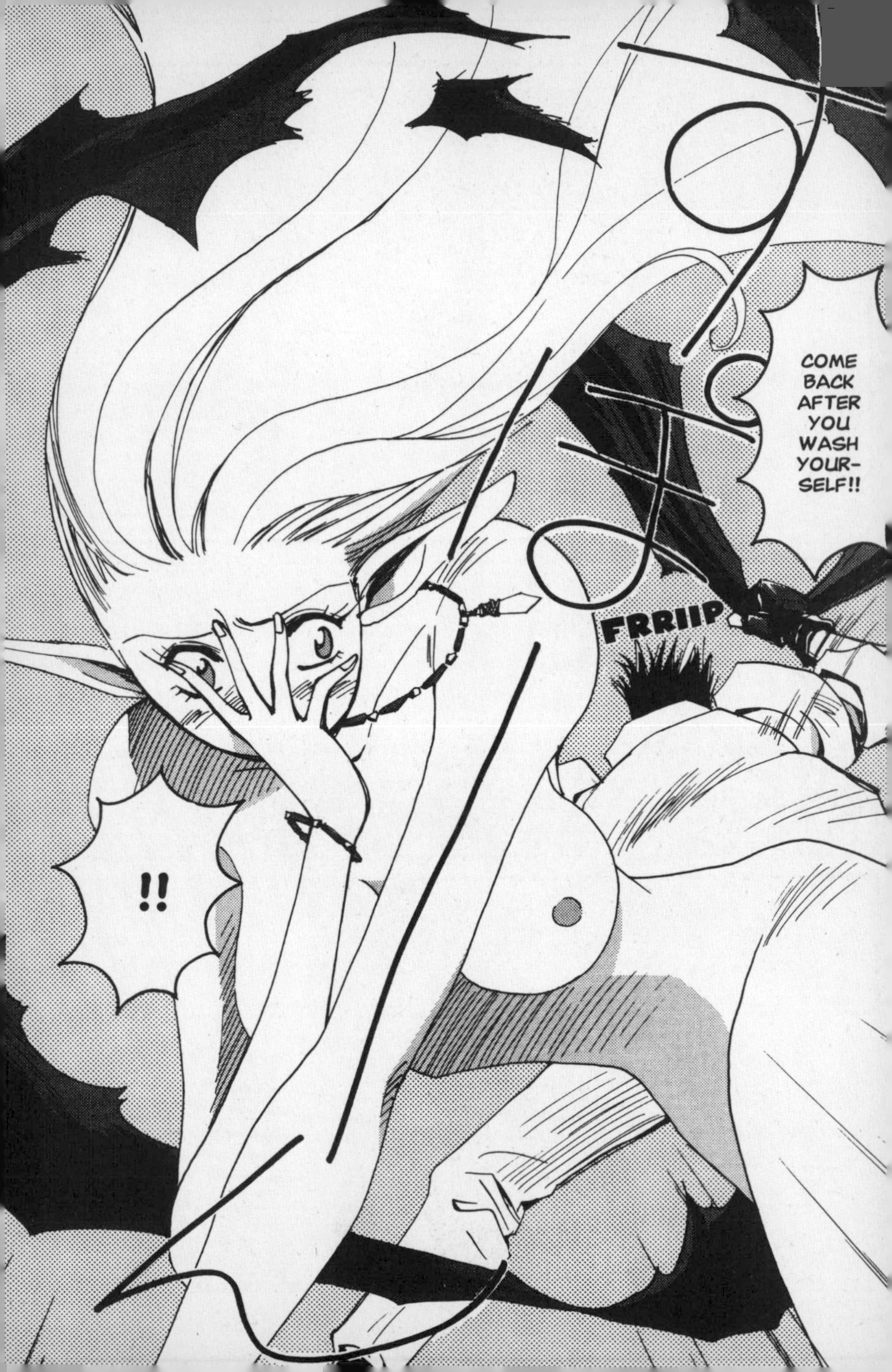
COME BACK AFTER YOU WASH YOURSELF!!
FRRIIP
!!

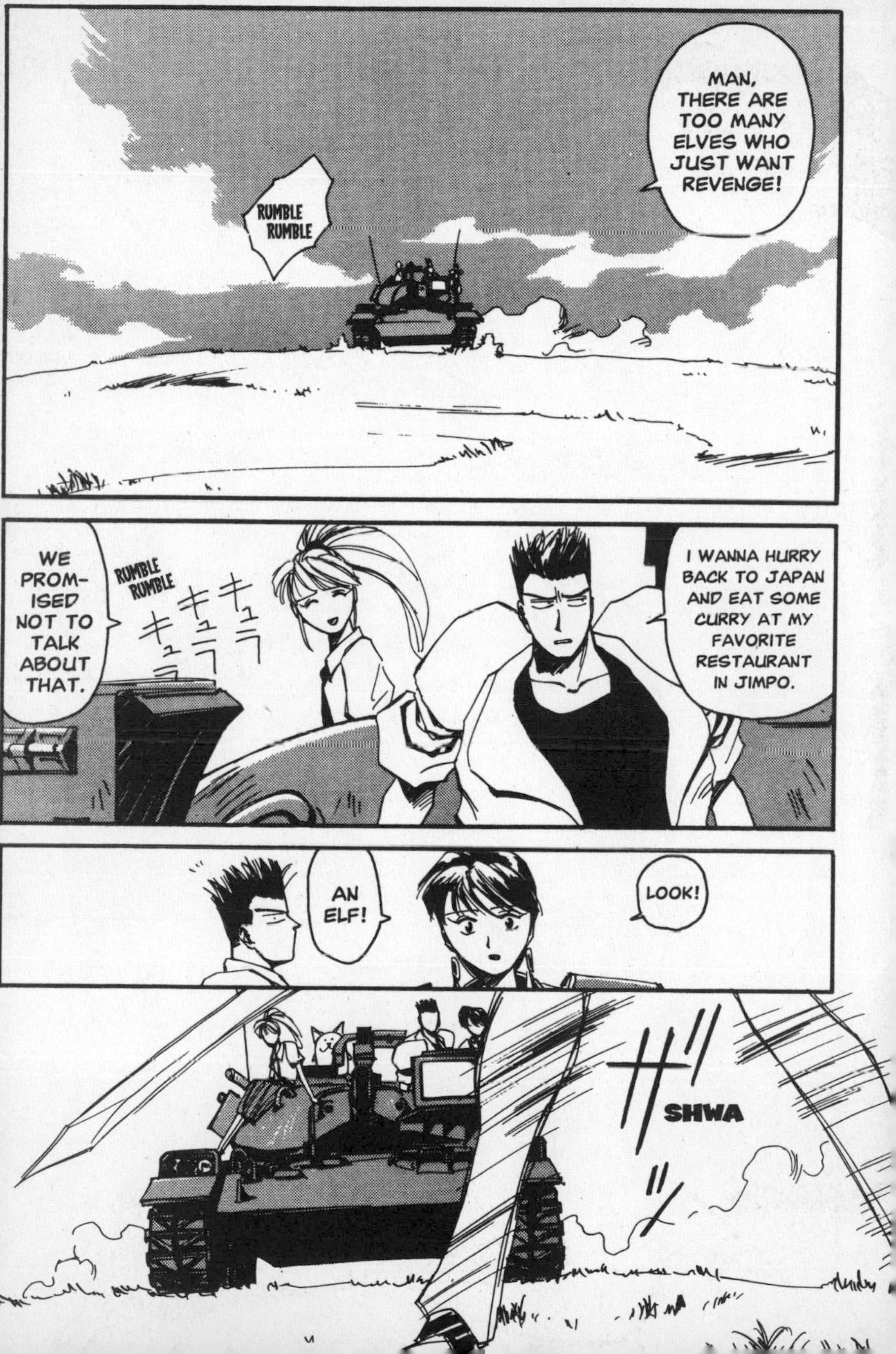
MAN, THERE ARE TOO MANY ELVES WHO JUST WANT REVENGE!
RUMBLE RUMBLE
I WANNA HURRY BACK TO JAPAN AND EAT SOME CURRY AT MY FAVORITE RESTAURANT IN JIMPO.
キュラ キュラ キュラ
RUMBLE RUMBLE
WE PROMISED NOT TO TALK ABOUT THAT.
LOOK!
AN ELF!
ザッ
SHWA

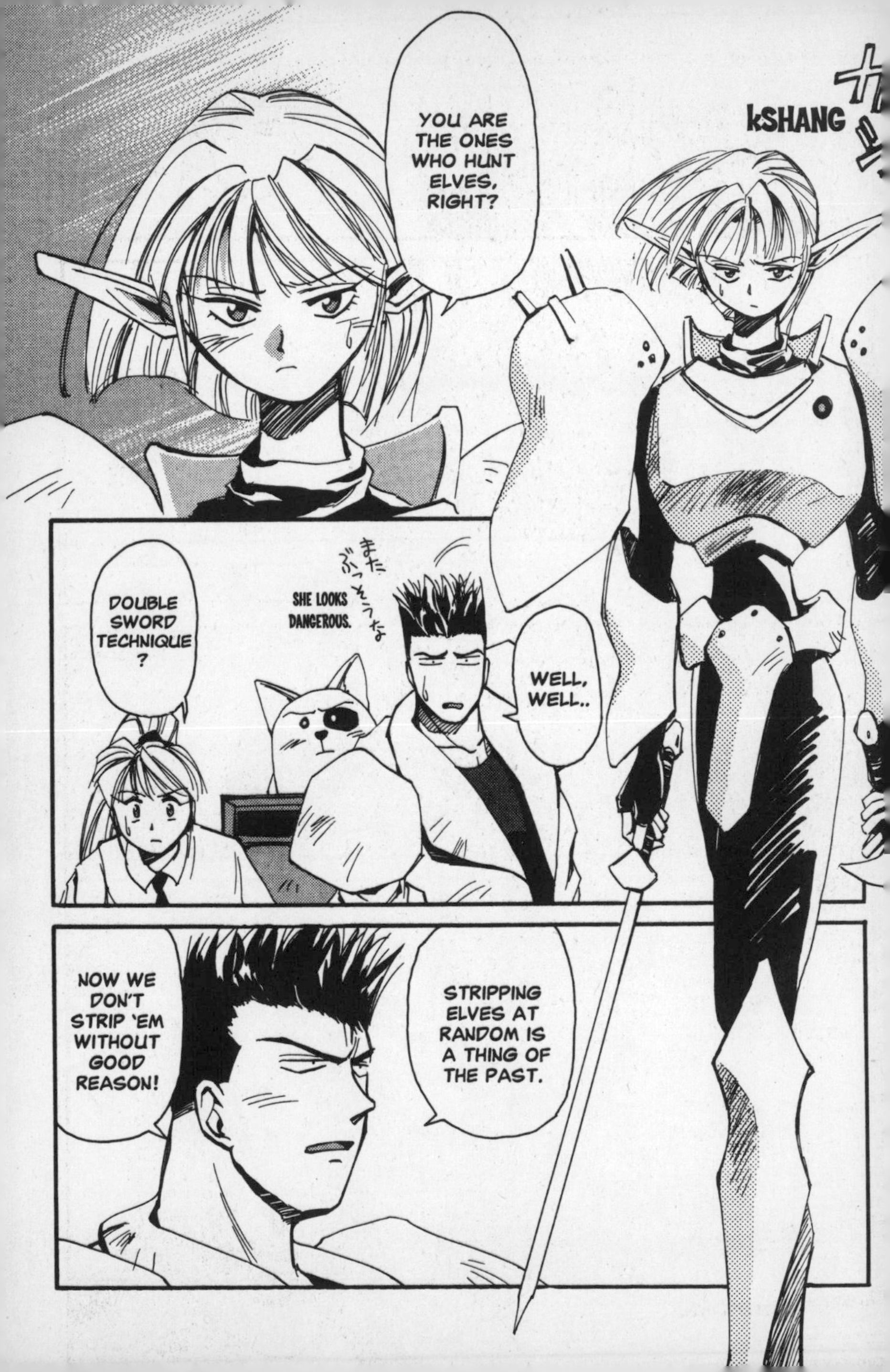
kSHANG
YOU ARE THE ONES WHO HUNT ELVES, RIGHT?
WELL, WELL..
SHE LOOKS DANGEROUS.
またぶっそうだな
DOUBLE SWORD TECHNIQUE ?
STRIPPING ELVES AT RANDOM IS A THING OF THE PAST.
NOW WE DON'T STRIP 'EM WITHOUT GOOD REASON!

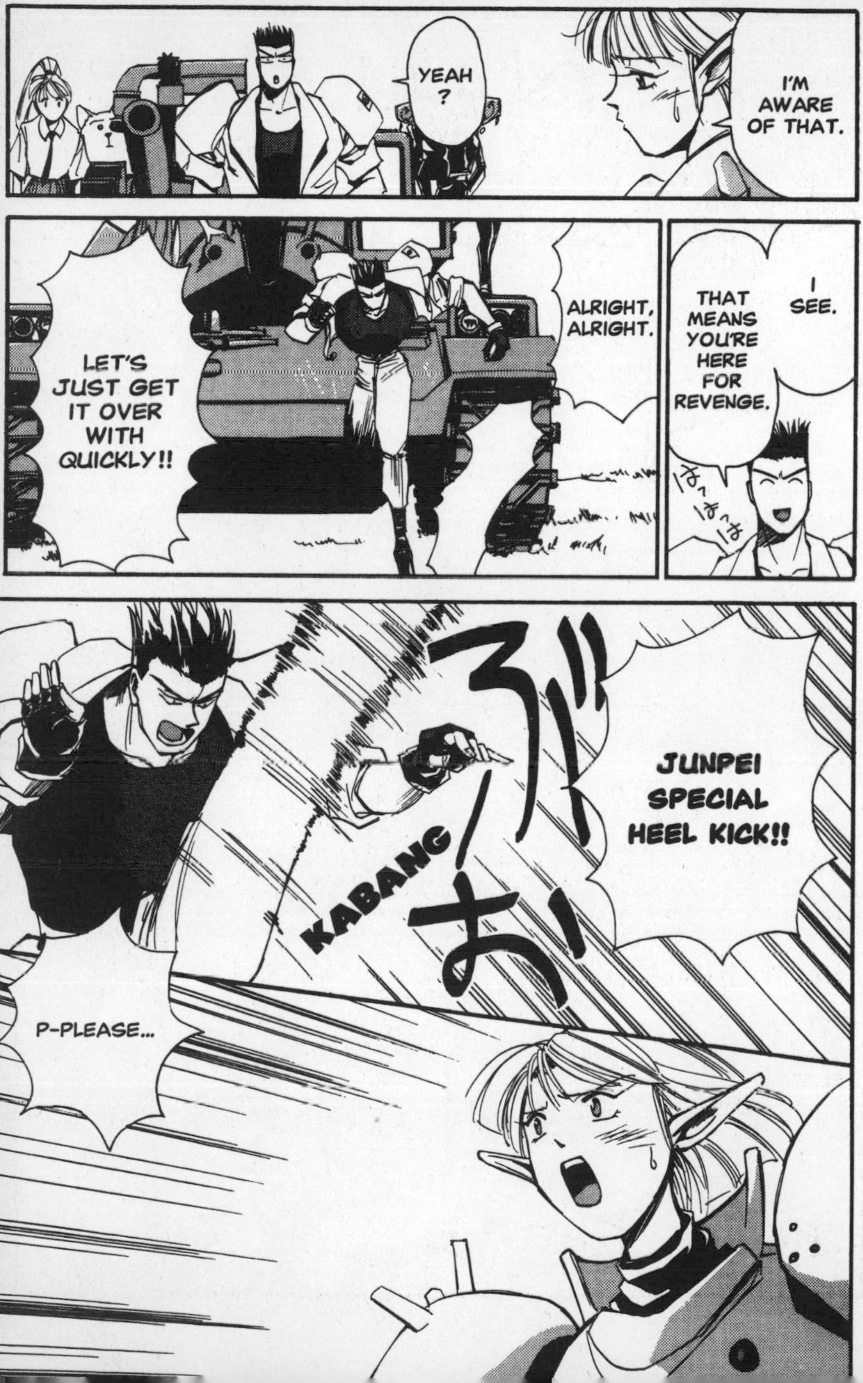
I'M AWARE OF THAT.
YEAH?
I SEE.
THAT MEANS YOU'RE HERE FOR REVENGE.
はっはっは
ALRIGHT, ALRIGHT.
LET'S JUST GET IT OVER WITH QUICKLY!!
JUNPEI SPECIAL HEEL KICK!!
KABANG
P-PLEASE...

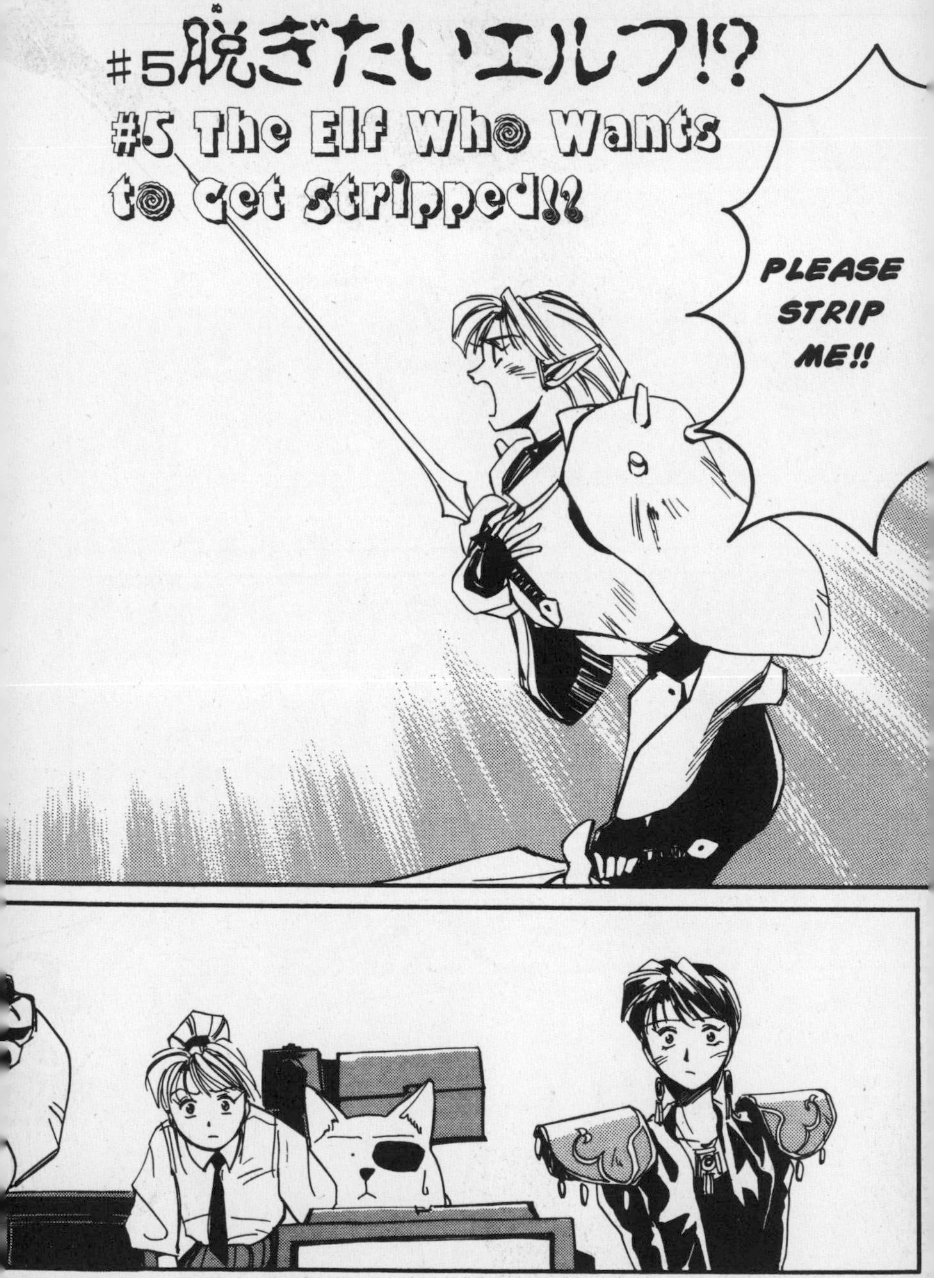
#5 脱ぎたいエルフ!?
#5 The Elf Who Wants to Get Stripped!?
PLEASE STRIP ME!!

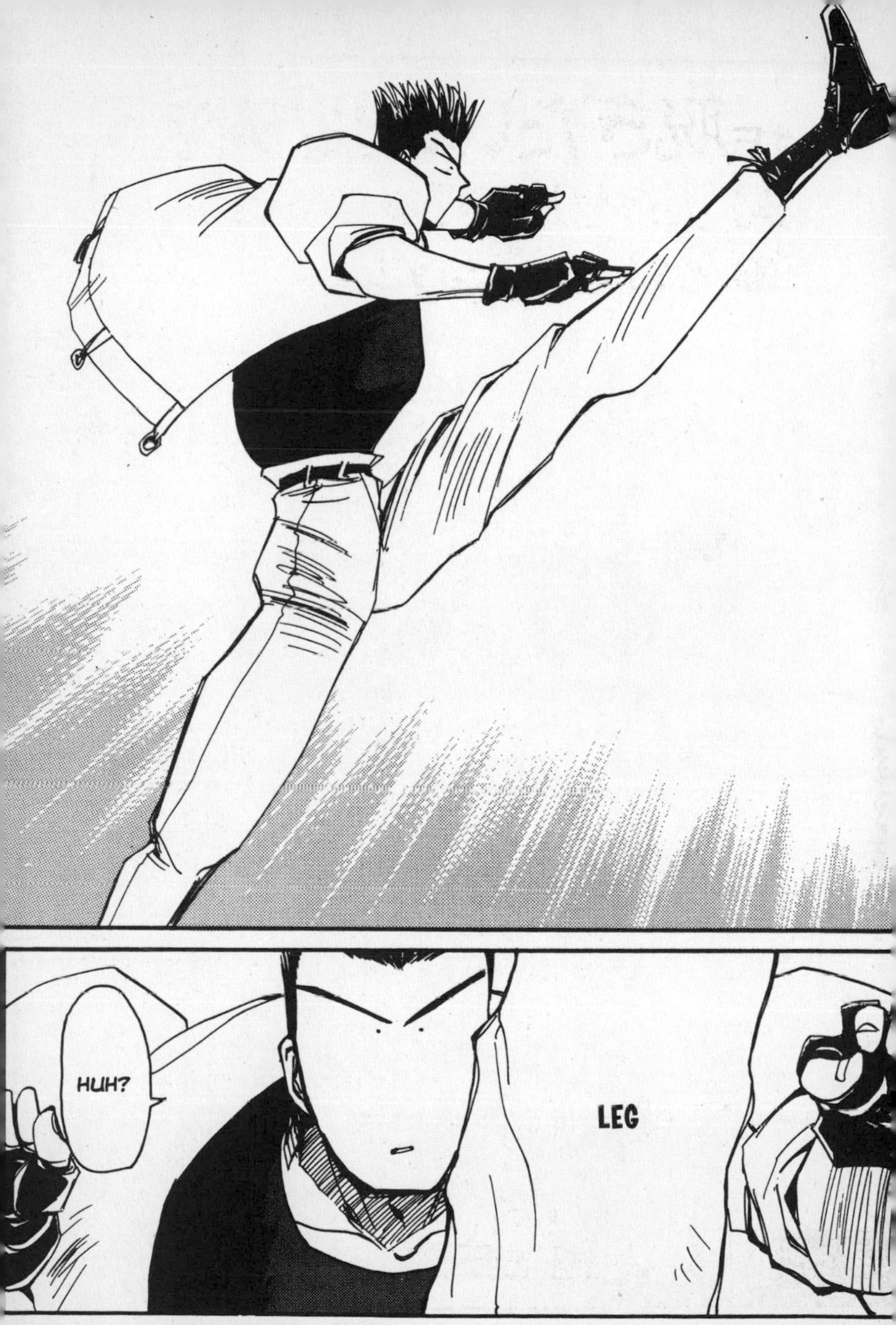
HUH?
LEG

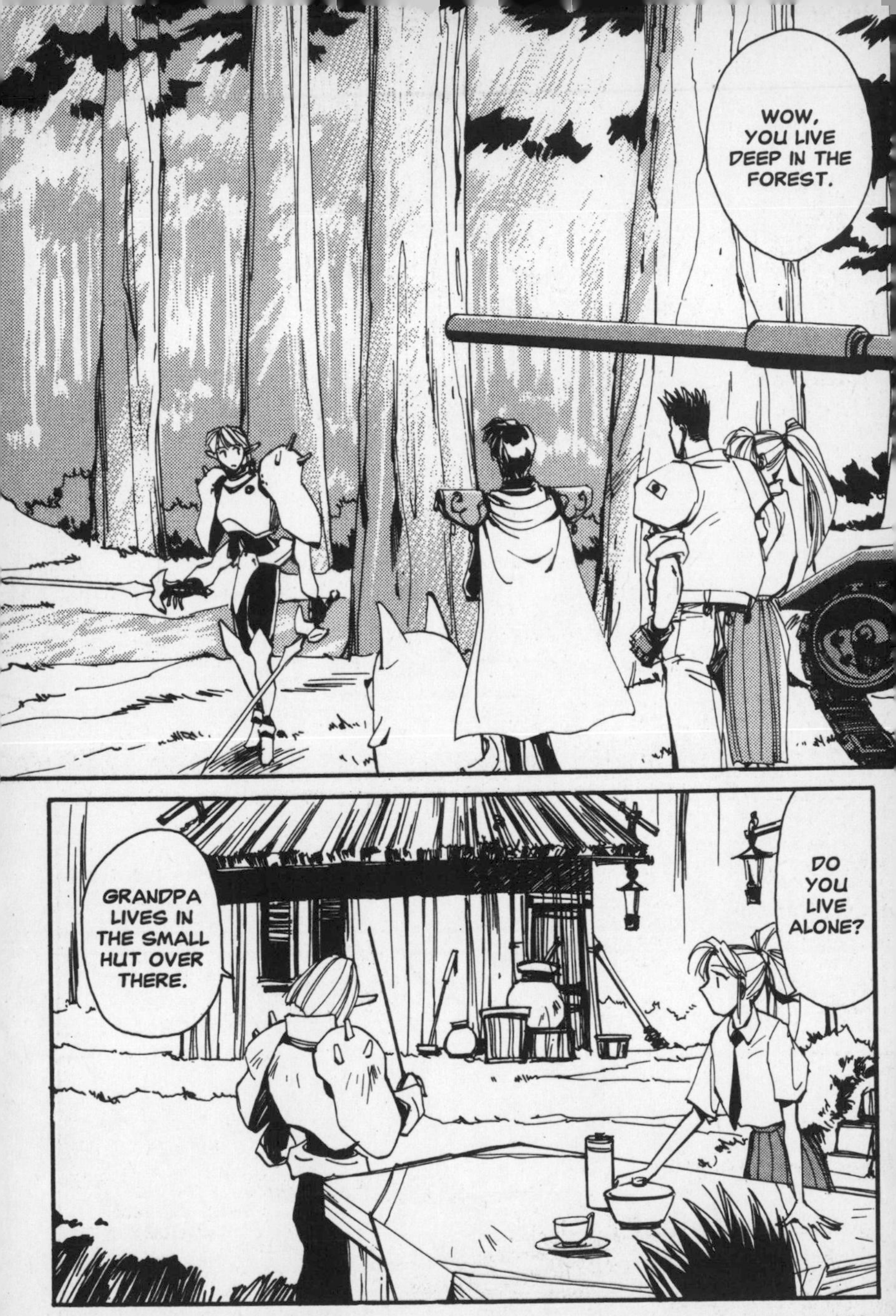
WOW, YOU LIVE DEEP IN THE FOREST.
DO YOU LIVE ALONE?
GRANDPA LIVES IN THE SMALL HUT OVER THERE.

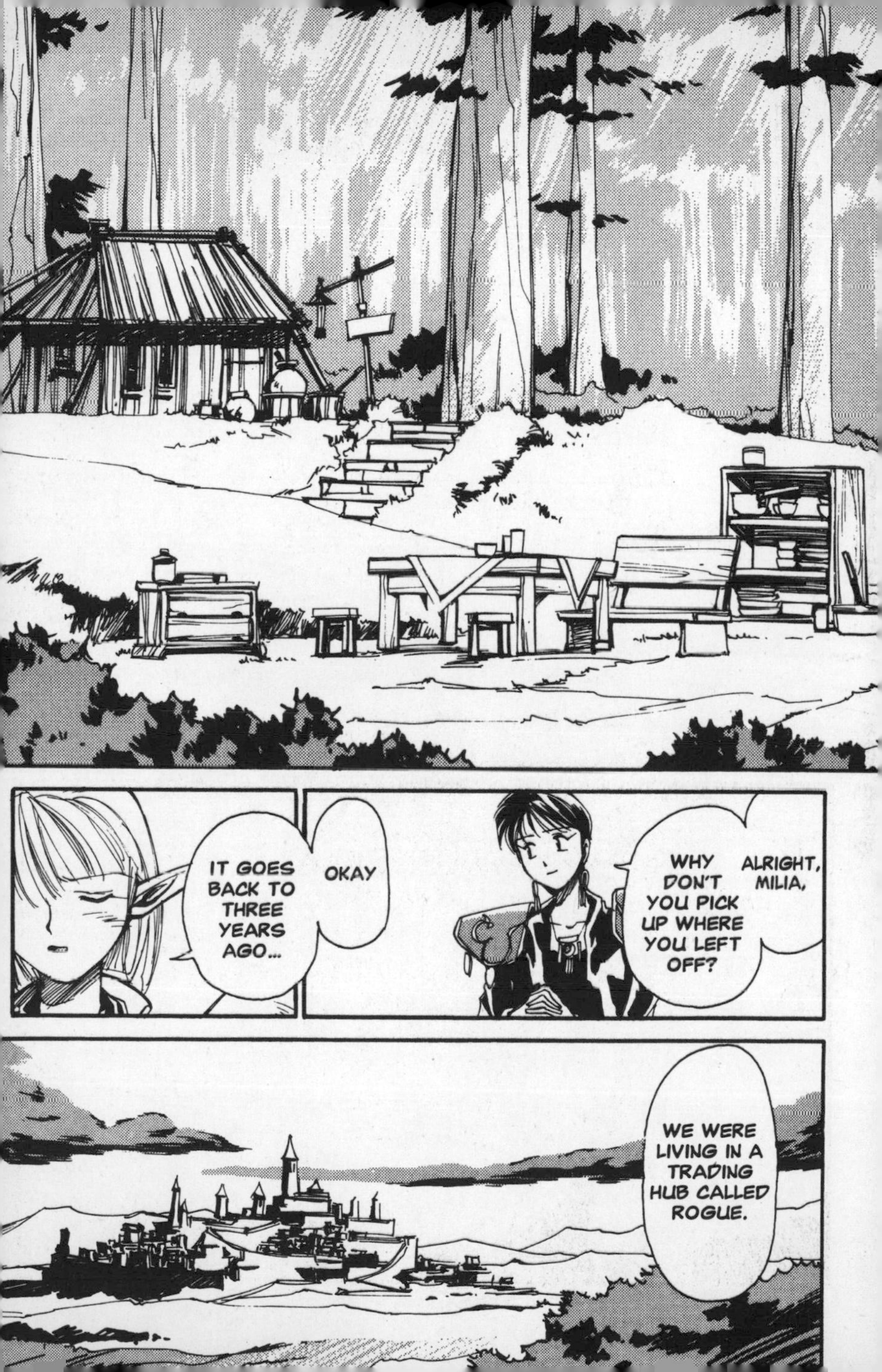
ALRIGHT, MILIA,
WHY DON'T YOU PICK UP WHERE YOU LEFT OFF?
OKAY
IT GOES BACK TO THREE YEARS AGO...
WE WERE LIVING IN A TRADING HUB CALLED ROGUE.

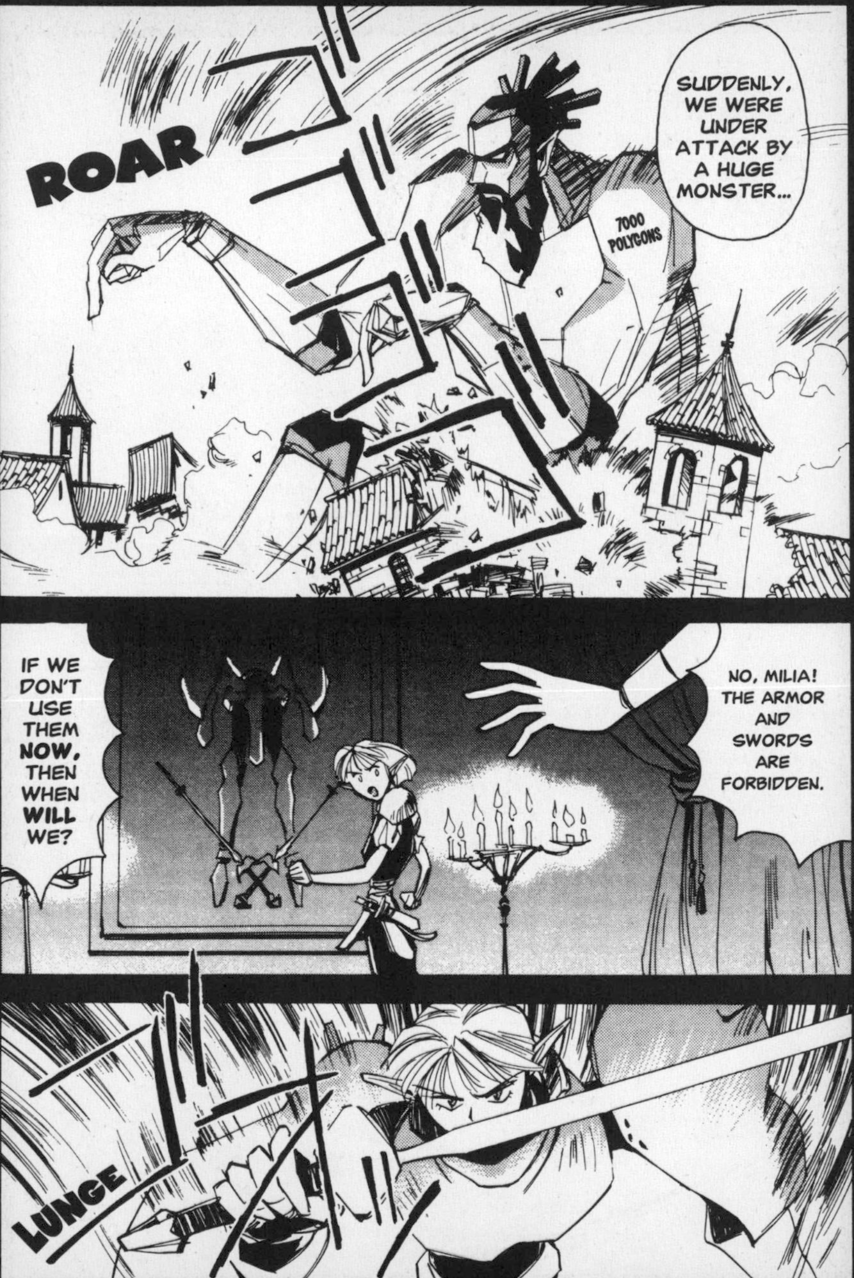
ROAR
SUDDENLY, WE WERE UNDER ATTACK BY A HUGE MONSTER...
7000 POLYGONS
NO, MILIA! THE ARMOR AND SWORDS ARE FORBIDDEN.
IF WE DON'T USE THEM NOW, THEN WHEN WILL WE?
LUNGE

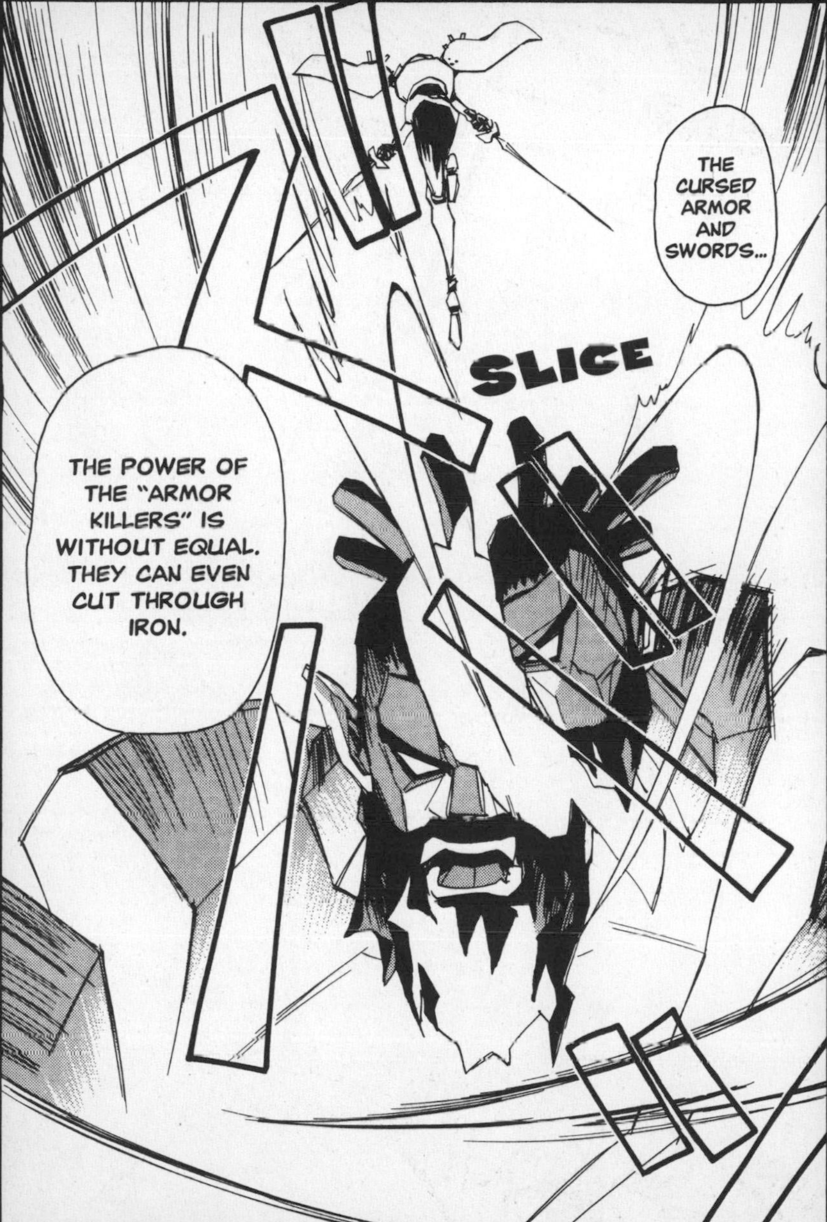
THE CURSED ARMOR AND SWORDS...
SLICE
THE POWER OF THE "ARMOR KILLERS" IS WITHOUT EQUAL. THEY CAN EVEN CUT THROUGH IRON.

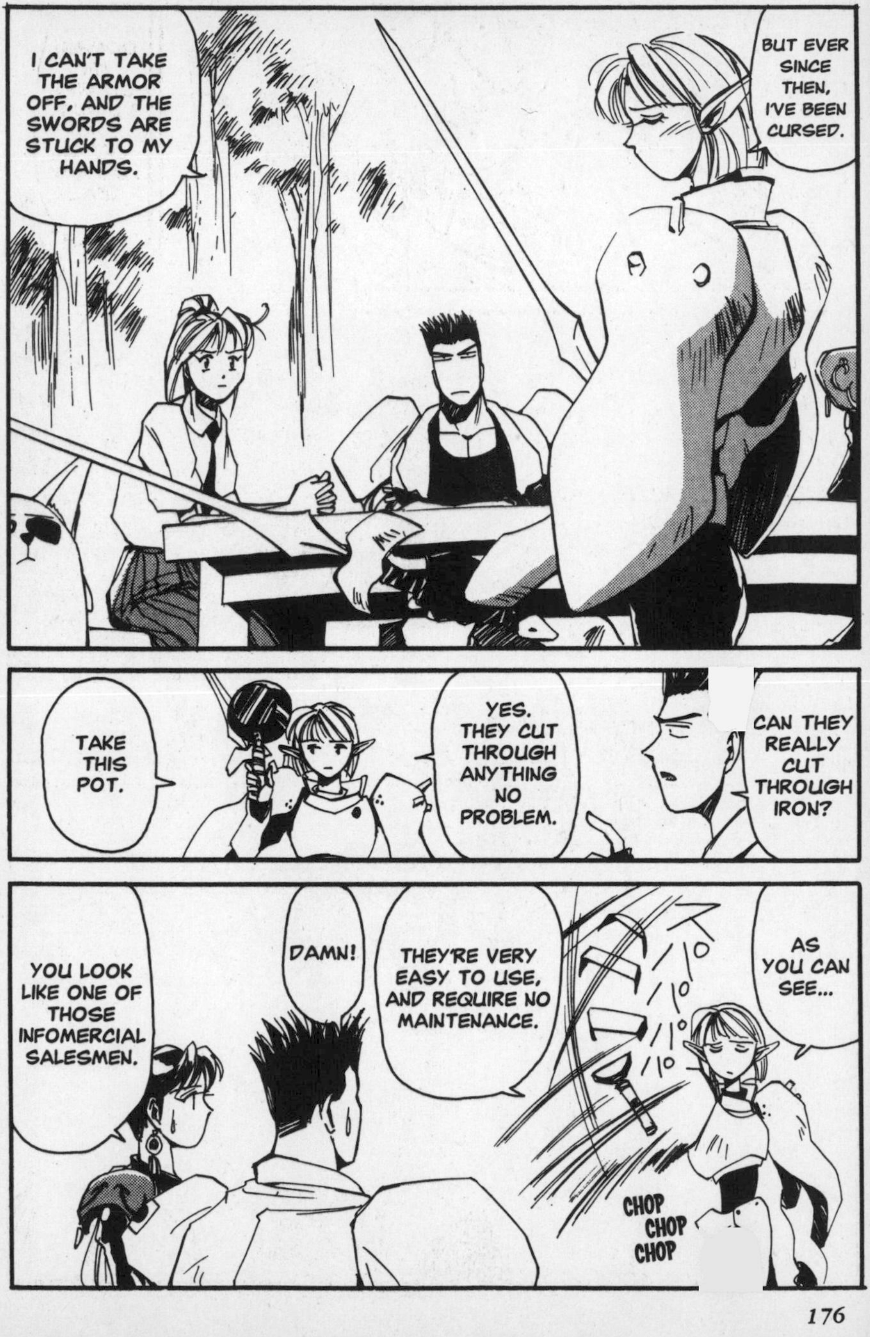
BUT EVER SINCE THEN, I'VE BEEN CURSED.
I CAN'T TAKE THE ARMOR OFF, AND THE SWORDS ARE STUCK TO MY HANDS.
CAN THEY REALLY CUT THROUGH IRON?
YES. THEY CUT THROUGH ANYTHING NO PROBLEM.
TAKE THIS POT.
AS YOU CAN SEE...
CHOP
CHOP
CHOP
THEY'RE VERY EASY TO USE, AND REQUIRE NO MAINTENANCE.
DAMN!
YOU LOOK LIKE ONE OF THOSE INFOMERCIAL SALESMEN.

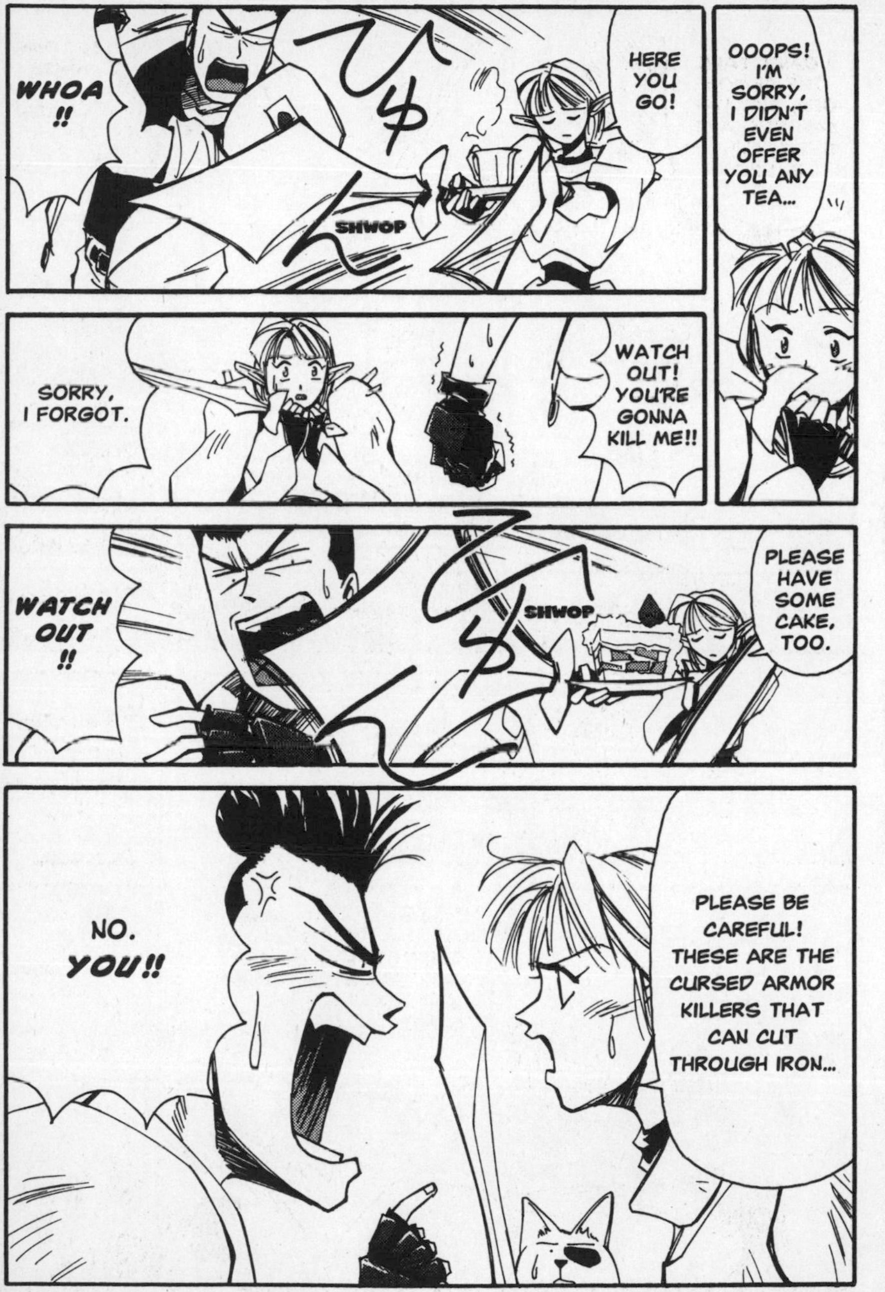
OOOPS! I'M SORRY, I DIDN'T EVEN OFFER YOU ANY TEA...
HERE YOU GO!
SHWOP
WHOA !!
WATCH OUT! YOU'RE GONNA KILL ME!!
SORRY, I FORGOT.
PLEASE HAVE SOME CAKE, TOO.
SHWOP
WATCH OUT !!
PLEASE BE CAREFUL! THESE ARE THE CURSED ARMOR KILLERS THAT CAN CUT THROUGH IRON...
NO. YOU!!

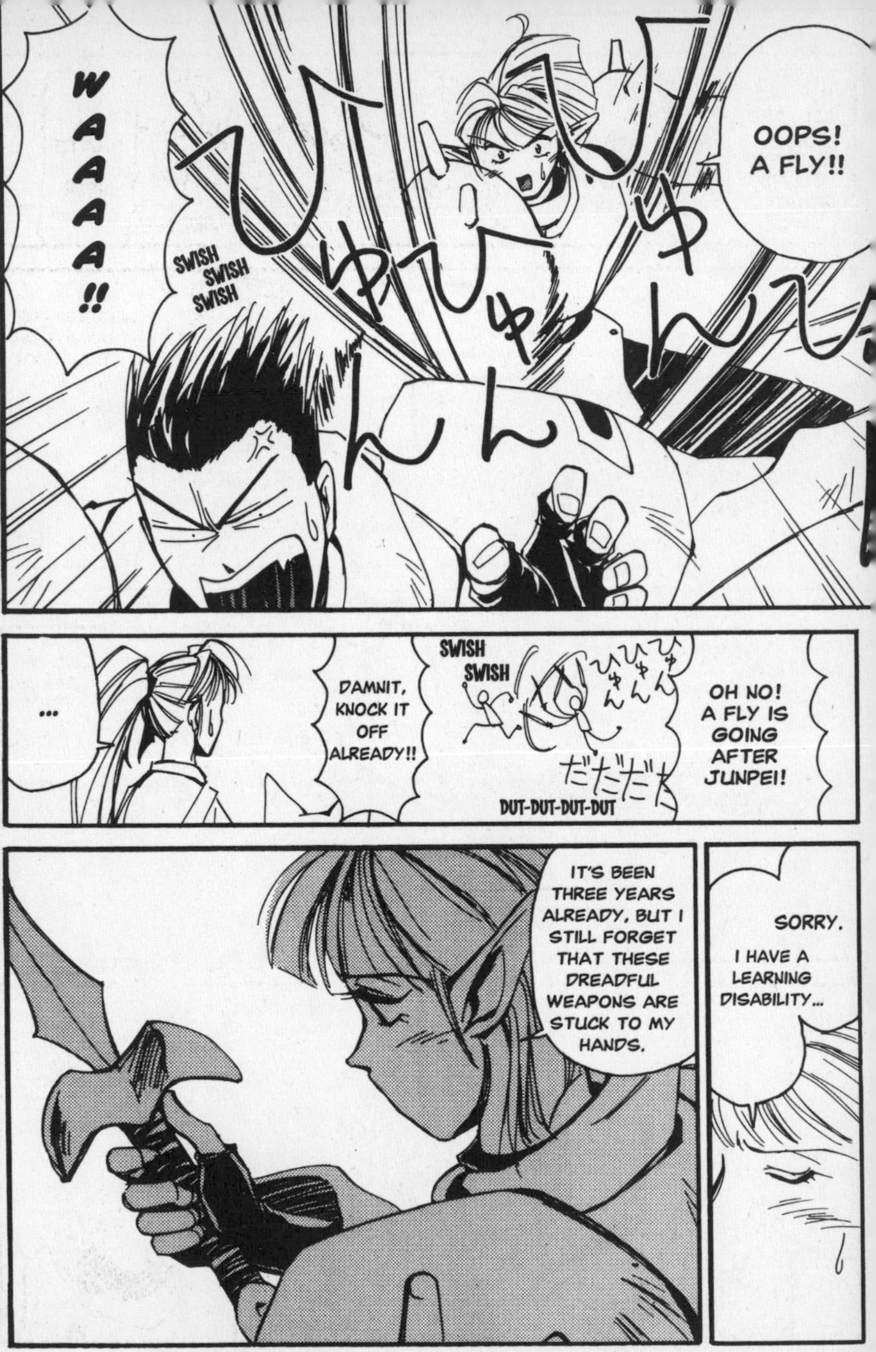

OOPS! A FLY!!
SWISH SWISH SWISH
WAAAAA!!
OH NO! A FLY IS GOING AFTER JUNPEI!
SWISH SWISH
DUT-DUT-DUT-DUT
DAMNIT, KNOCK IT OFF ALREADY!!
...
SORRY. I HAVE A LEARNING DISABILITY...
IT'S BEEN THREE YEARS ALREADY, BUT I STILL FORGET THAT THESE DREADFUL WEAPONS ARE STUCK TO MY HANDS.

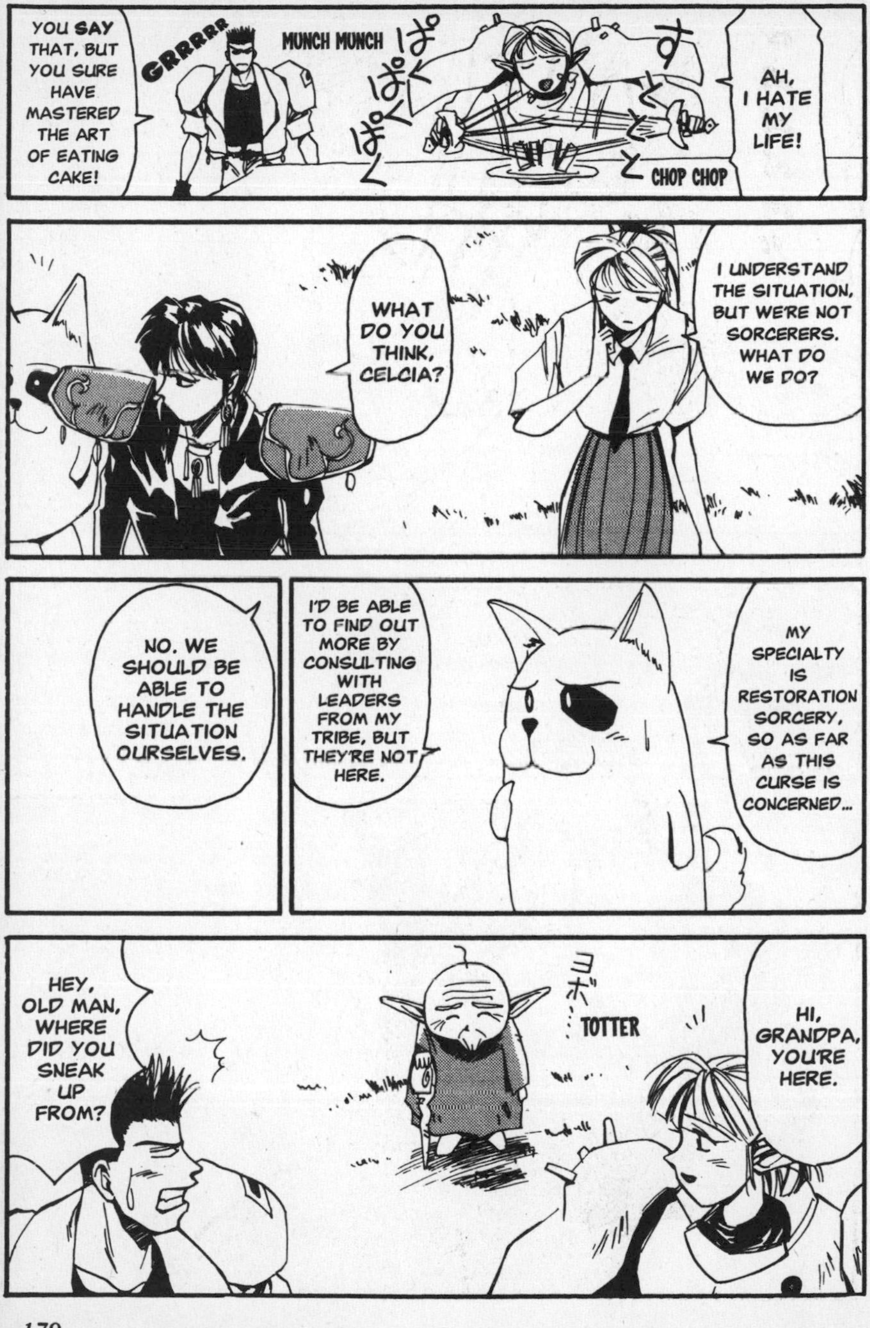
AH, I HATE MY LIFE!
CHOP CHOP
MUNCH MUNCH
GRRRRRR
YOU SAY THAT, BUT YOU SURE HAVE MASTERED THE ART OF EATING CAKE!
WHAT DO YOU THINK, CELCIA?
I UNDERSTAND THE SITUATION, BUT WE'RE NOT SORCERERS. WHAT DO WE DO?
MY SPECIALTY IS RESTORATION SORCERY, SO AS FAR AS THIS CURSE IS CONCERNED...
I'D BE ABLE TO FIND OUT MORE BY CONSULTING WITH LEADERS FROM MY TRIBE, BUT THEY'RE NOT HERE.
NO. WE SHOULD BE ABLE TO HANDLE THE SITUATION OURSELVES.
HI, GRANDPA, YOU'RE HERE.
ヨボ…
TOTTER
HEY, OLD MAN, WHERE DID YOU SNEAK UP FROM?

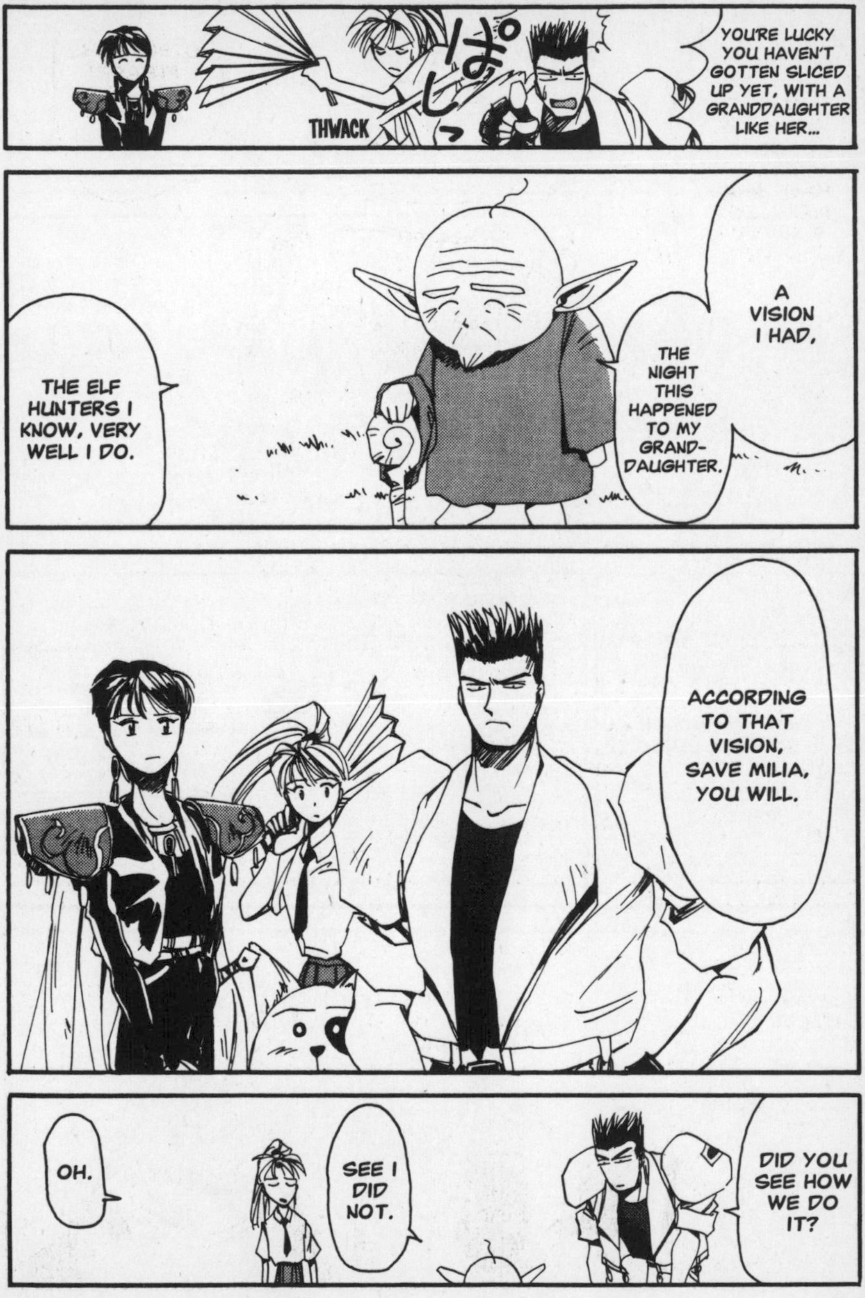
YOU'RE LUCKY YOU HAVEN'T GOTTEN SLICED UP YET, WITH A GRANDDAUGHTER LIKE HER...
ぱしっ
THWACK
A VISION I HAD,
THE NIGHT THIS HAPPENED TO MY GRAND-DAUGHTER.
THE ELF HUNTERS I KNOW, VERY WELL I DO.
ACCORDING TO THAT VISION, SAVE MILIA, YOU WILL.
DID YOU SEE HOW WE DO IT?
SEE I DID NOT.
OH.

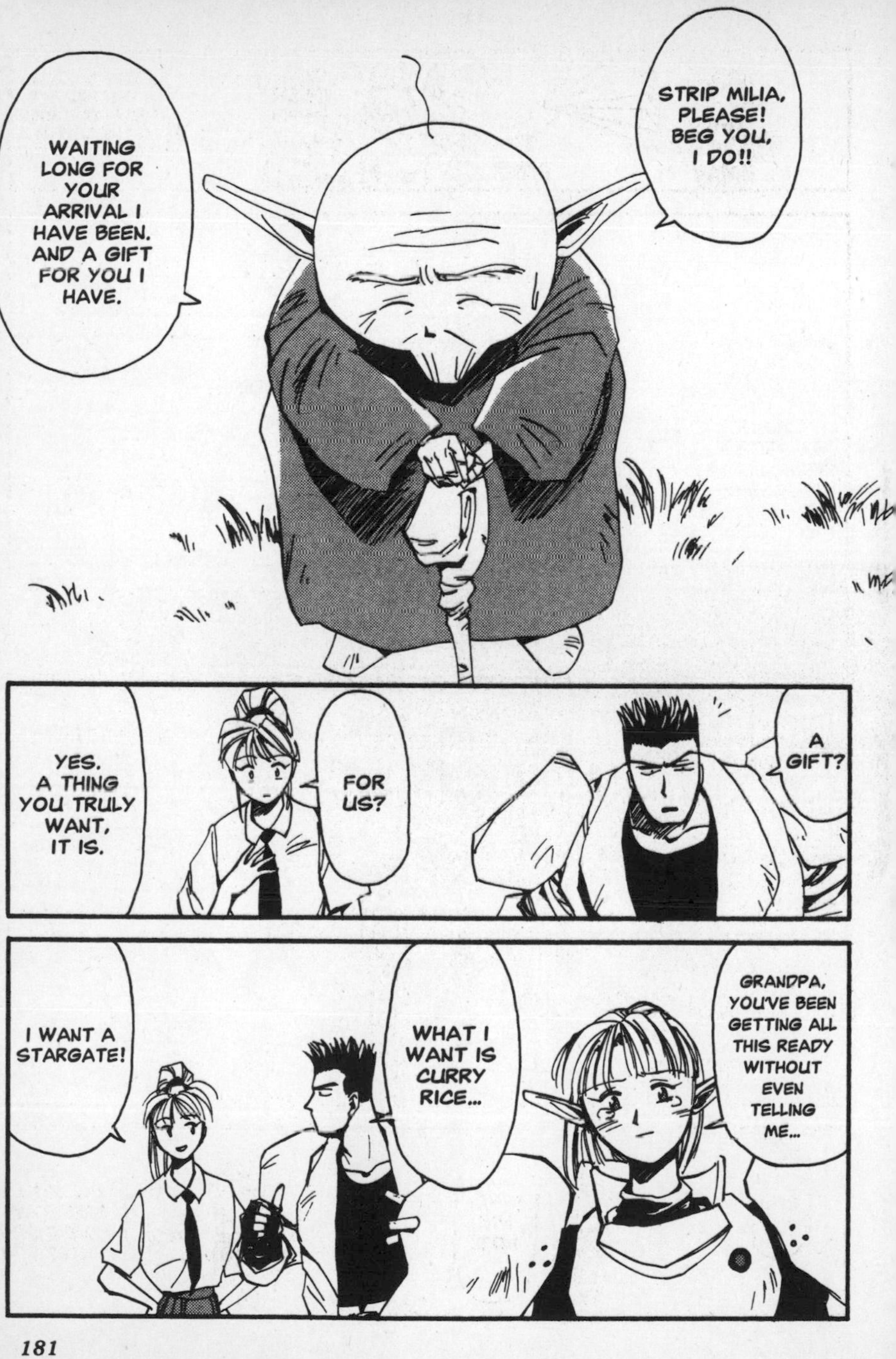
STRIP MILIA, PLEASE! BEG YOU, I DO!!
WAITING LONG FOR YOUR ARRIVAL I HAVE BEEN. AND A GIFT FOR YOU I HAVE.
A GIFT?
FOR US?
YES. A THING YOU TRULY WANT, IT IS.
GRANDPA, YOU'VE BEEN GETTING ALL THIS READY WITHOUT EVEN TELLING ME...
WHAT I WANT IS CURRY RICE...
I WANT A STARGATE!

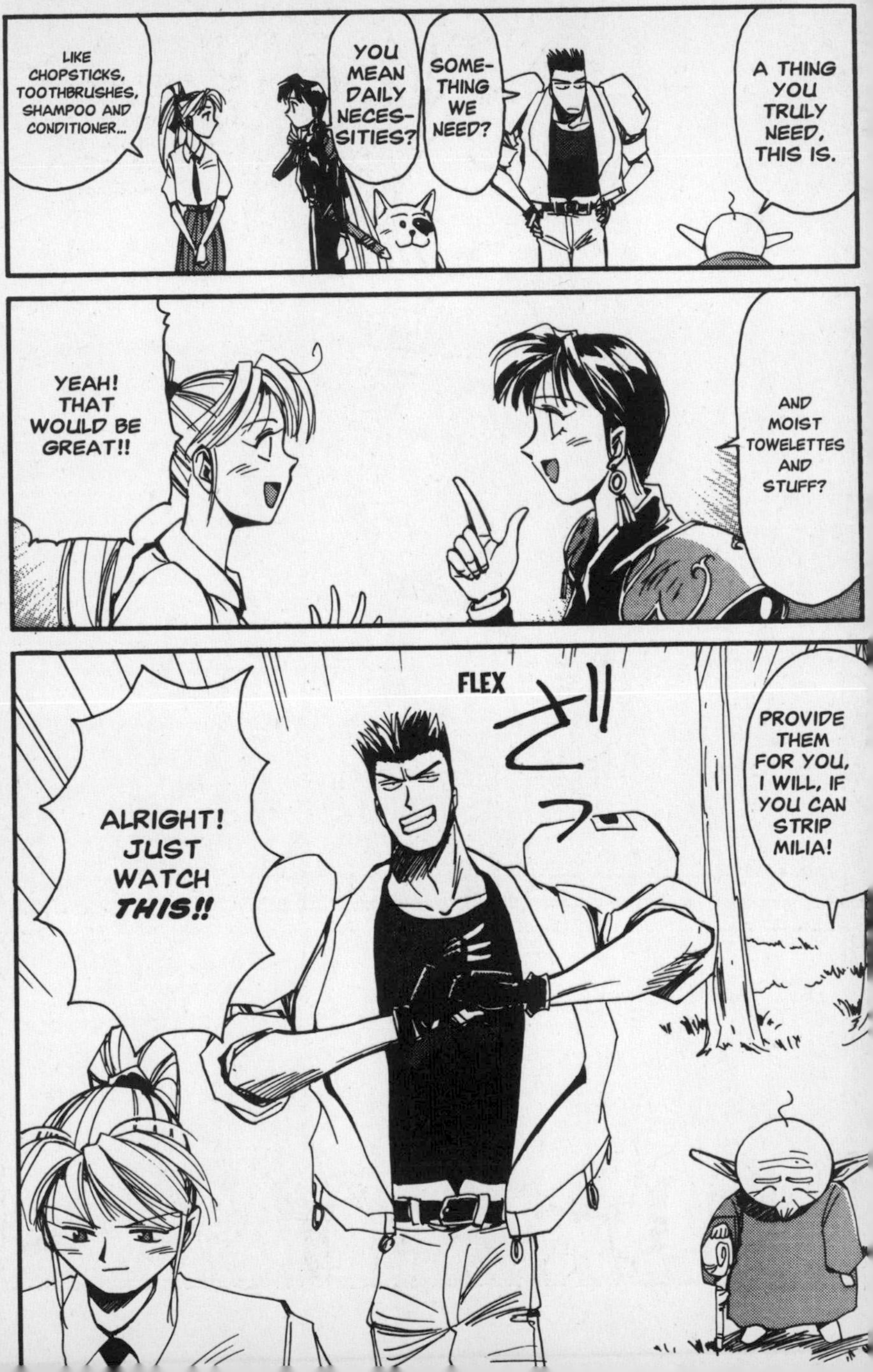
A THING YOU TRULY NEED, THIS IS.
SOME-THING WE NEED?
YOU MEAN DAILY NECES-SITIES?
LIKE CHOPSTICKS, TOOTHBRUSHES, SHAMPOO AND CONDITIONER...
AND MOIST TOWELETTES AND STUFF?
YEAH! THAT WOULD BE GREAT!!
PROVIDE THEM FOR YOU, I WILL, IF YOU CAN STRIP MILIA!
FLEX
ALRIGHT! JUST WATCH THIS!!

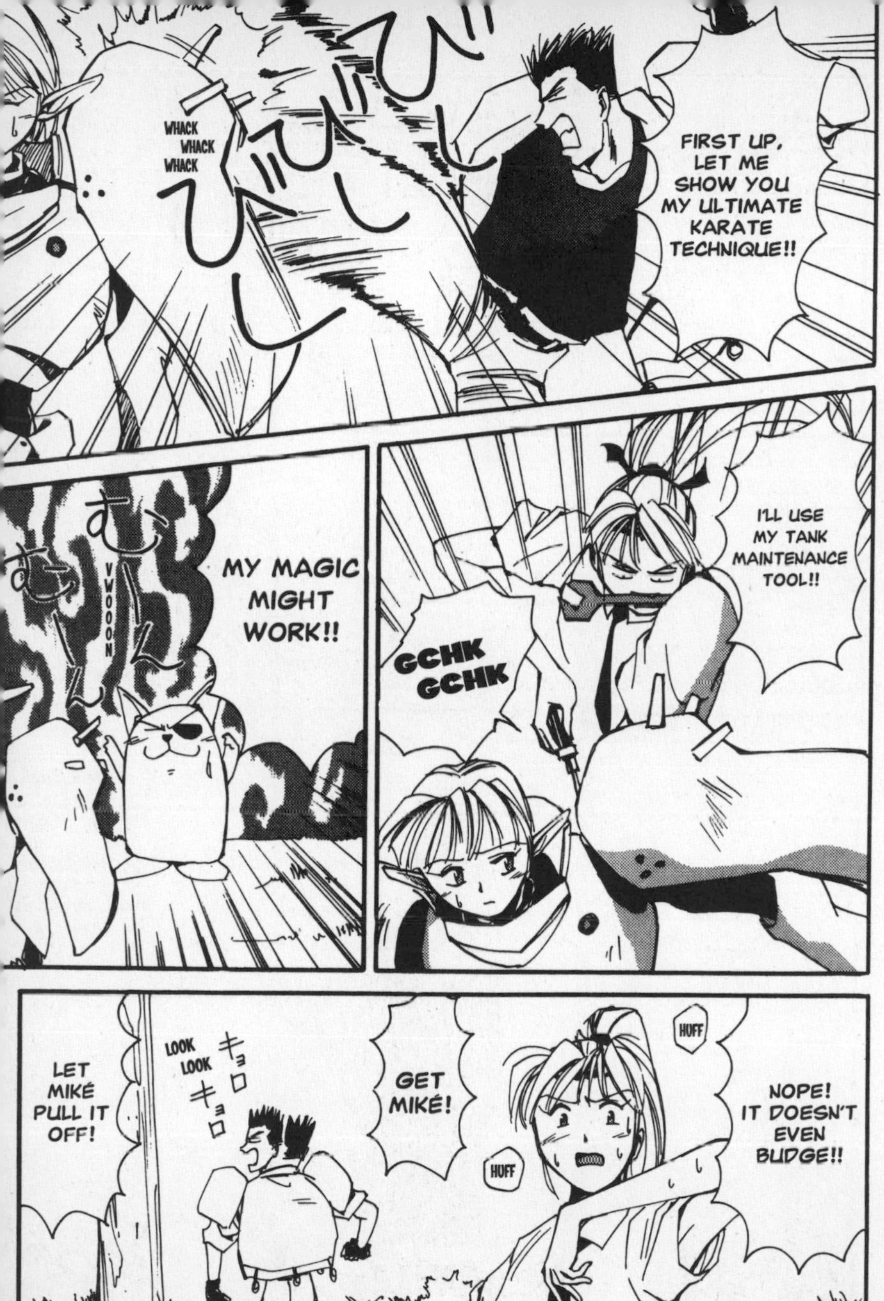
FIRST UP, LET ME SHOW YOU MY ULTIMATE KARATE TECHNIQUE!!
WHACK WHACK WHACK
I'LL USE MY TANK MAINTENANCE TOOL!!
GCHK GCHK
MY MAGIC MIGHT WORK!!
VWOOON
NOPE! IT DOESN'T EVEN BUDGE!!
HUFF
HUFF
GET MIKÉ!
LOOK LOOK
キョロ キョロ
LET MIKÉ PULL IT OFF!

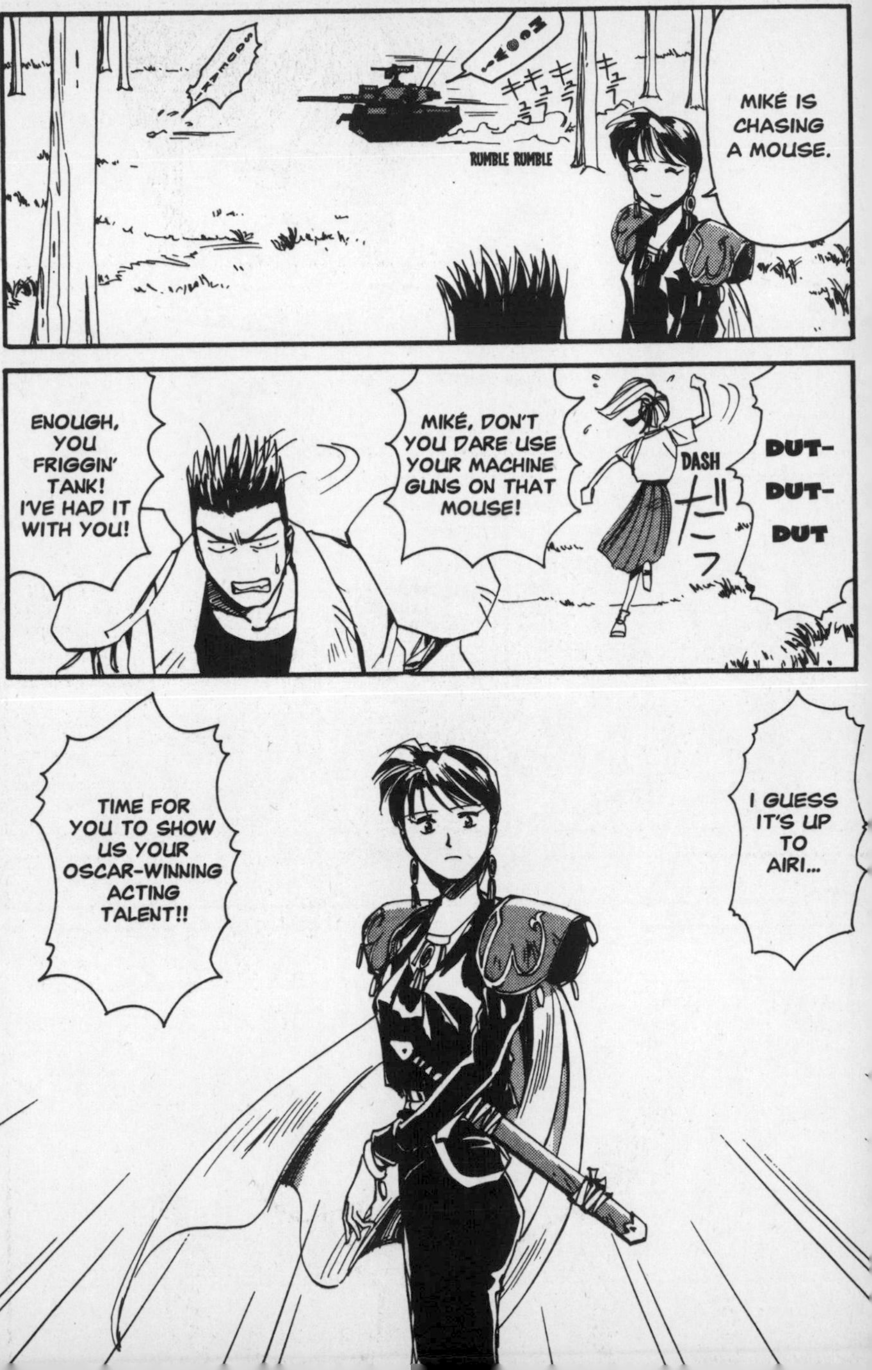
MIKÉ IS CHASING A MOUSE.
RUMBLE RUMBLE
DUT-DUT-DUT
DASH
MIKÉ, DON'T YOU DARE USE YOUR MACHINE GUNS ON THAT MOUSE!
ENOUGH, YOU FRIGGIN' TANK! I'VE HAD IT WITH YOU!
I GUESS IT'S UP TO AIRI...
TIME FOR YOU TO SHOW US YOUR OSCAR-WINNING ACTING TALENT!!

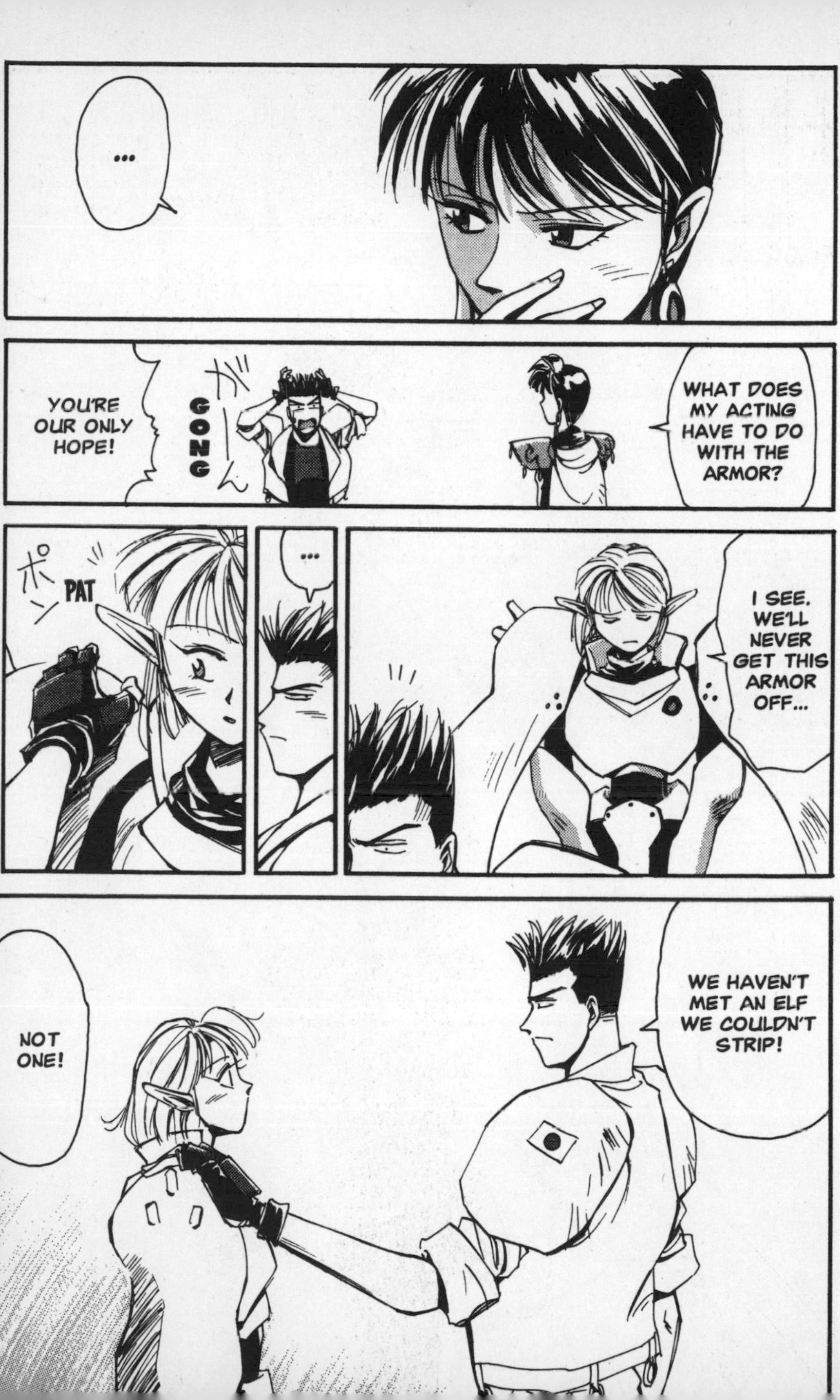
...
WHAT DOES MY ACTING HAVE TO DO WITH THE ARMOR?
GONG
YOU'RE OUR ONLY HOPE!
I SEE. WE'LL NEVER GET THIS ARMOR OFF...
...
PAT
WE HAVEN'T MET AN ELF WE COULDN'T STRIP!
NOT ONE!

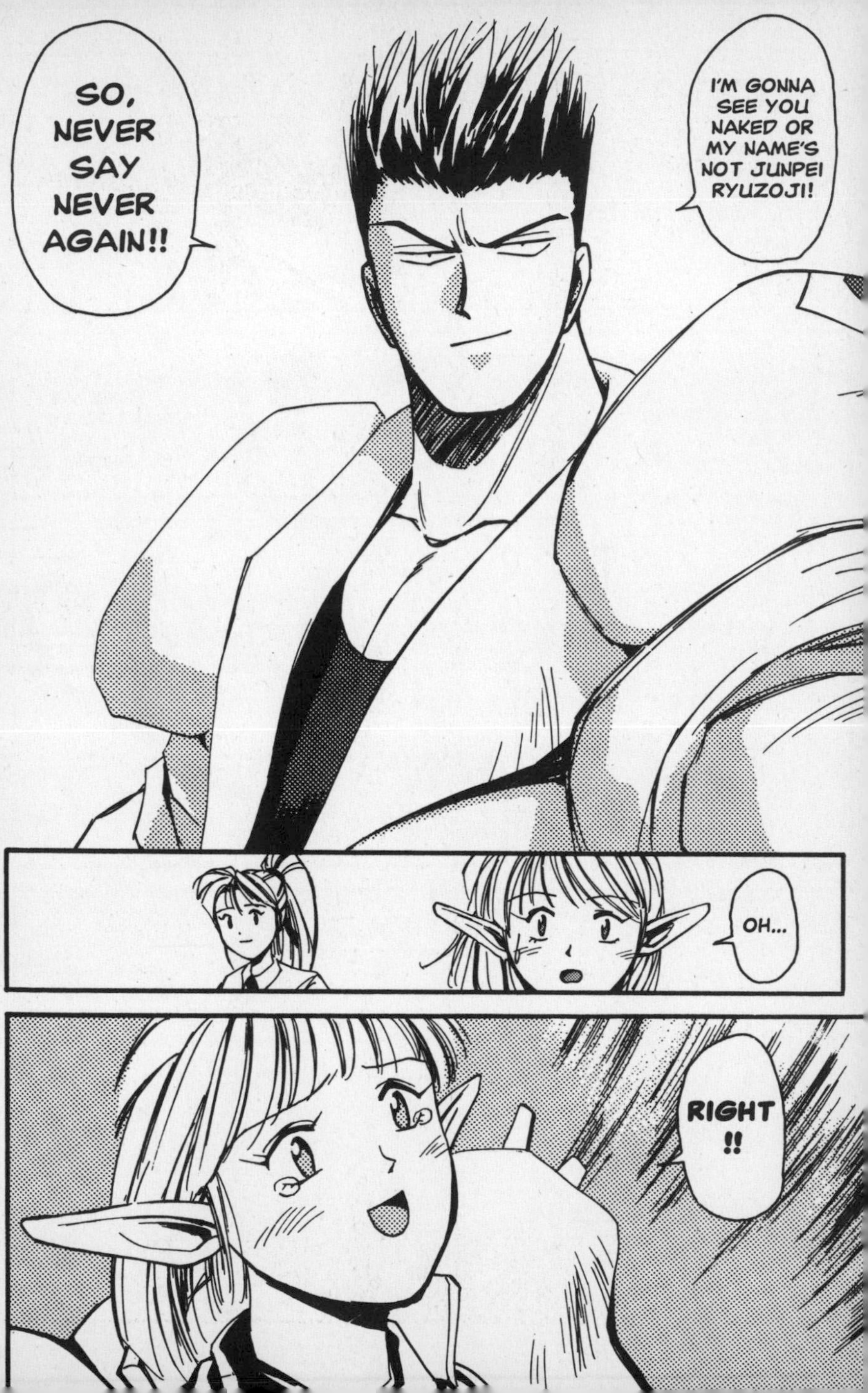
I'M GONNA SEE YOU NAKED OR MY NAME'S NOT JUNPEI RYUZOJI!
SO, NEVER SAY NEVER AGAIN!!
OH...
RIGHT !!

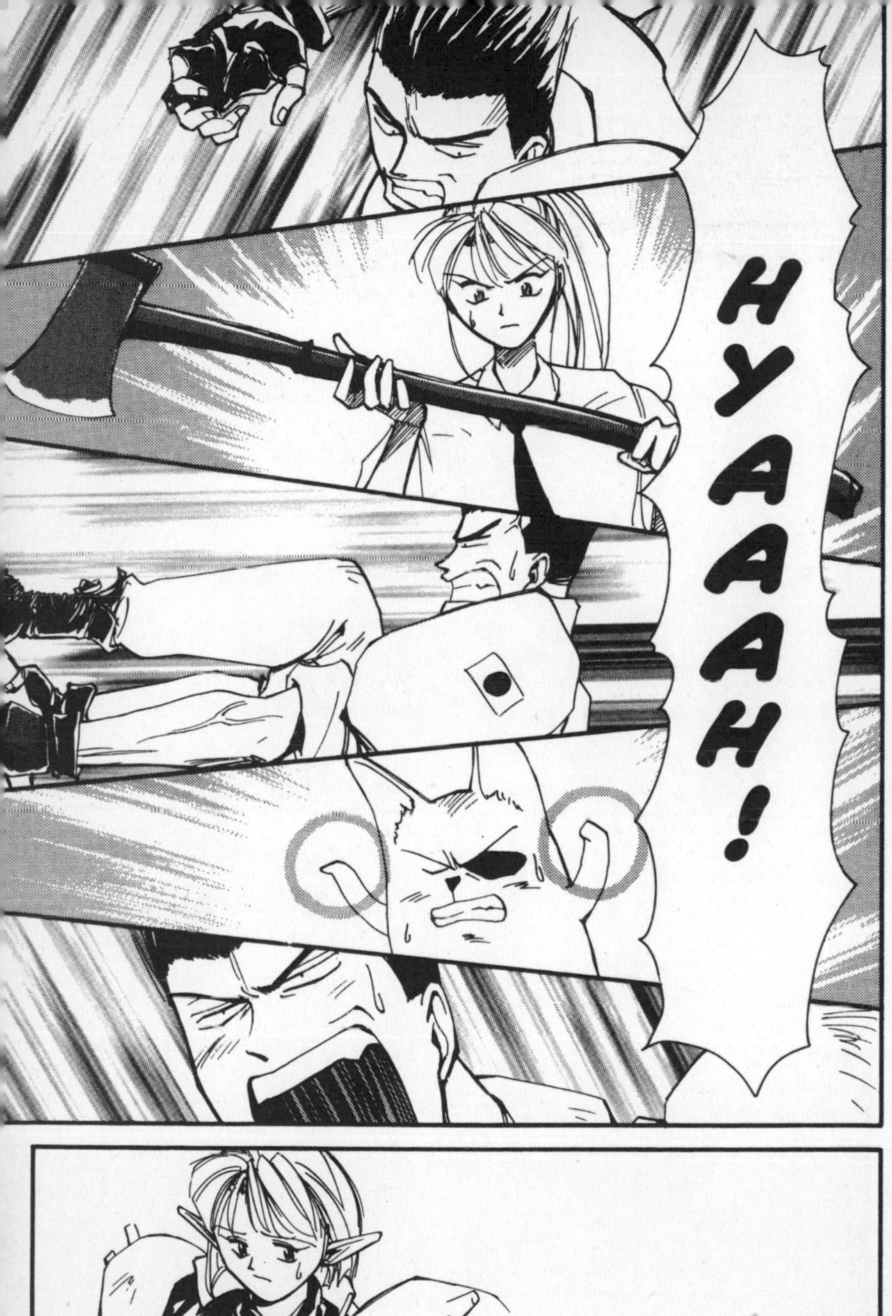
HYAAAAH!

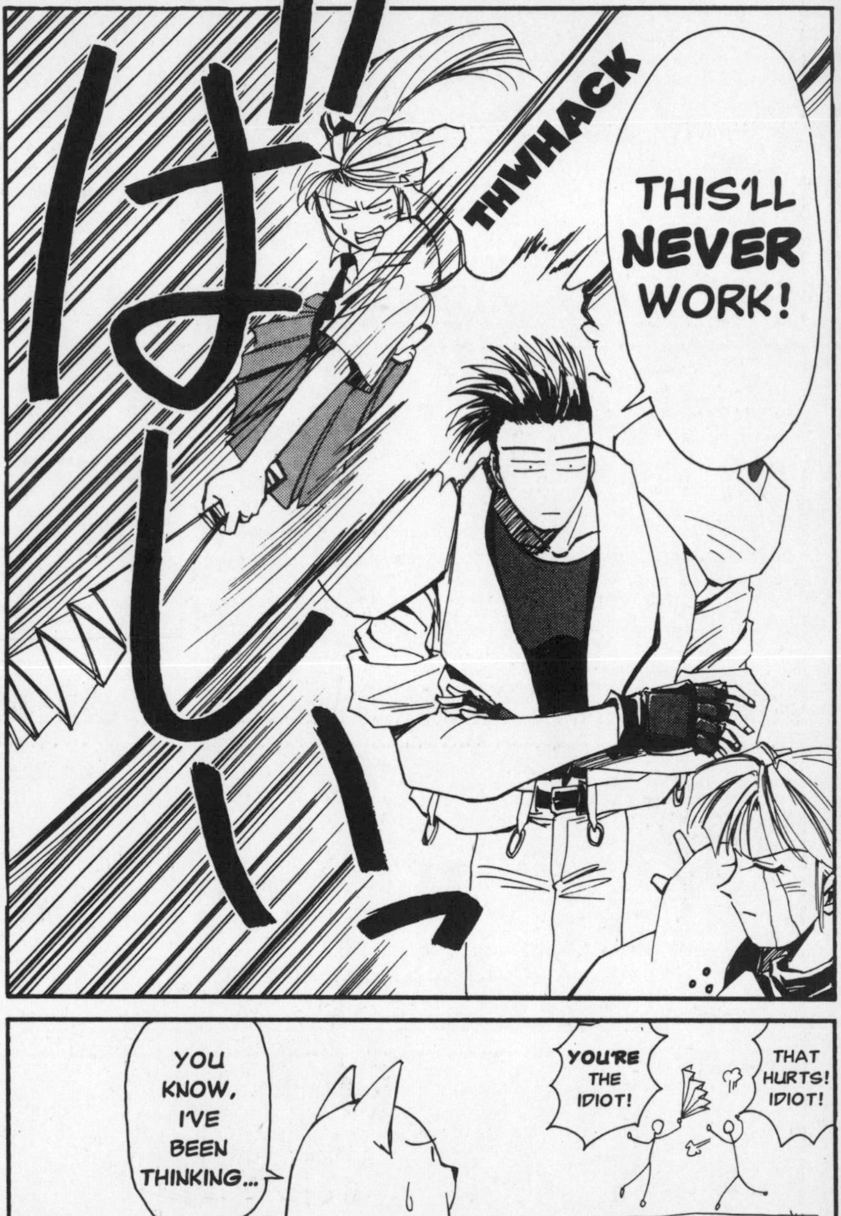
THIS'LL NEVER WORK!
THWHACK
THAT HURTS! IDIOT!
YOU'RE THE IDIOT!
YOU KNOW, I'VE BEEN THINKING...

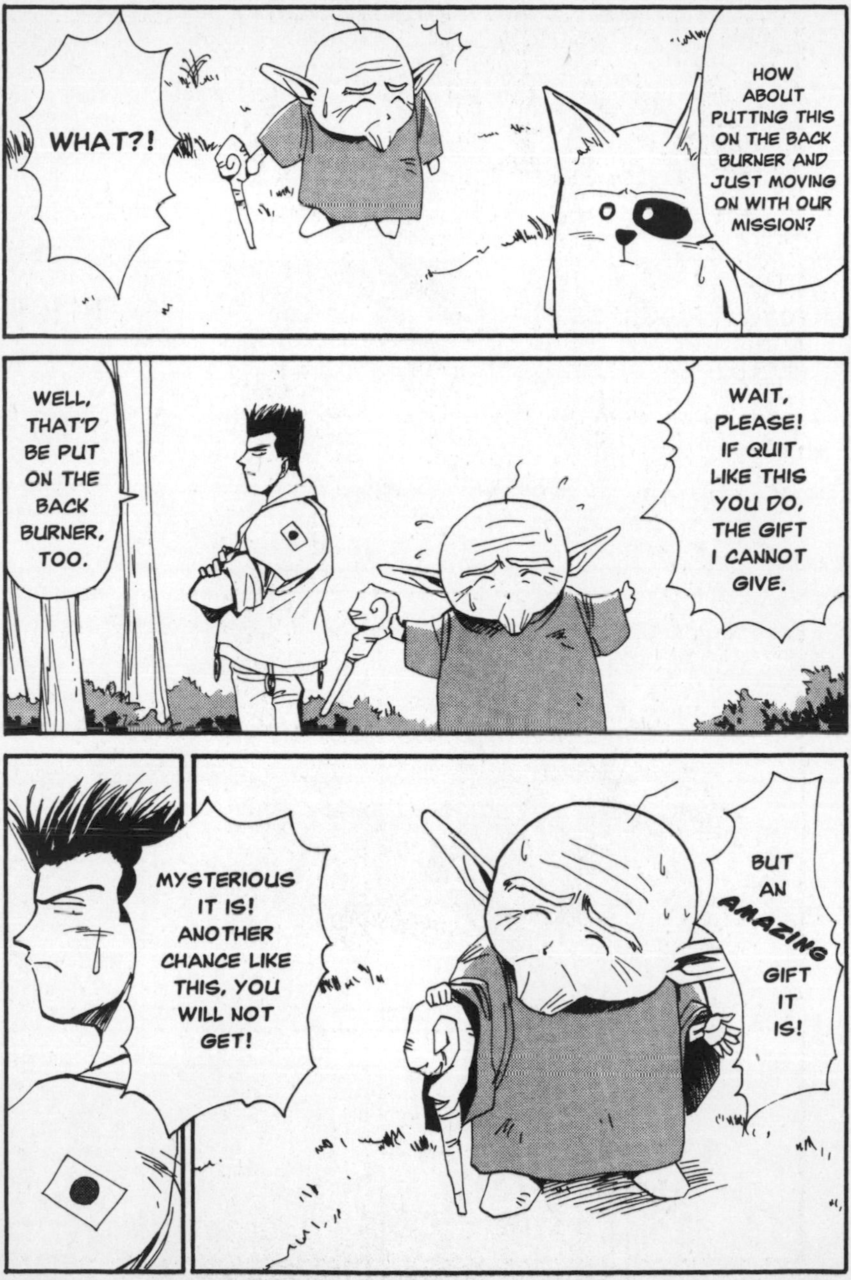
HOW ABOUT PUTTING THIS ON THE BACK BURNER AND JUST MOVING ON WITH OUR MISSION?
WHAT?!
WAIT, PLEASE! IF QUIT LIKE THIS YOU DO, THE GIFT I CANNOT GIVE.
WELL, THAT'D BE PUT ON THE BACK BURNER, TOO.
BUT AN AMAZING GIFT IT IS!
MYSTERIOUS IT IS! ANOTHER CHANCE LIKE THIS, YOU WILL NOT GET!

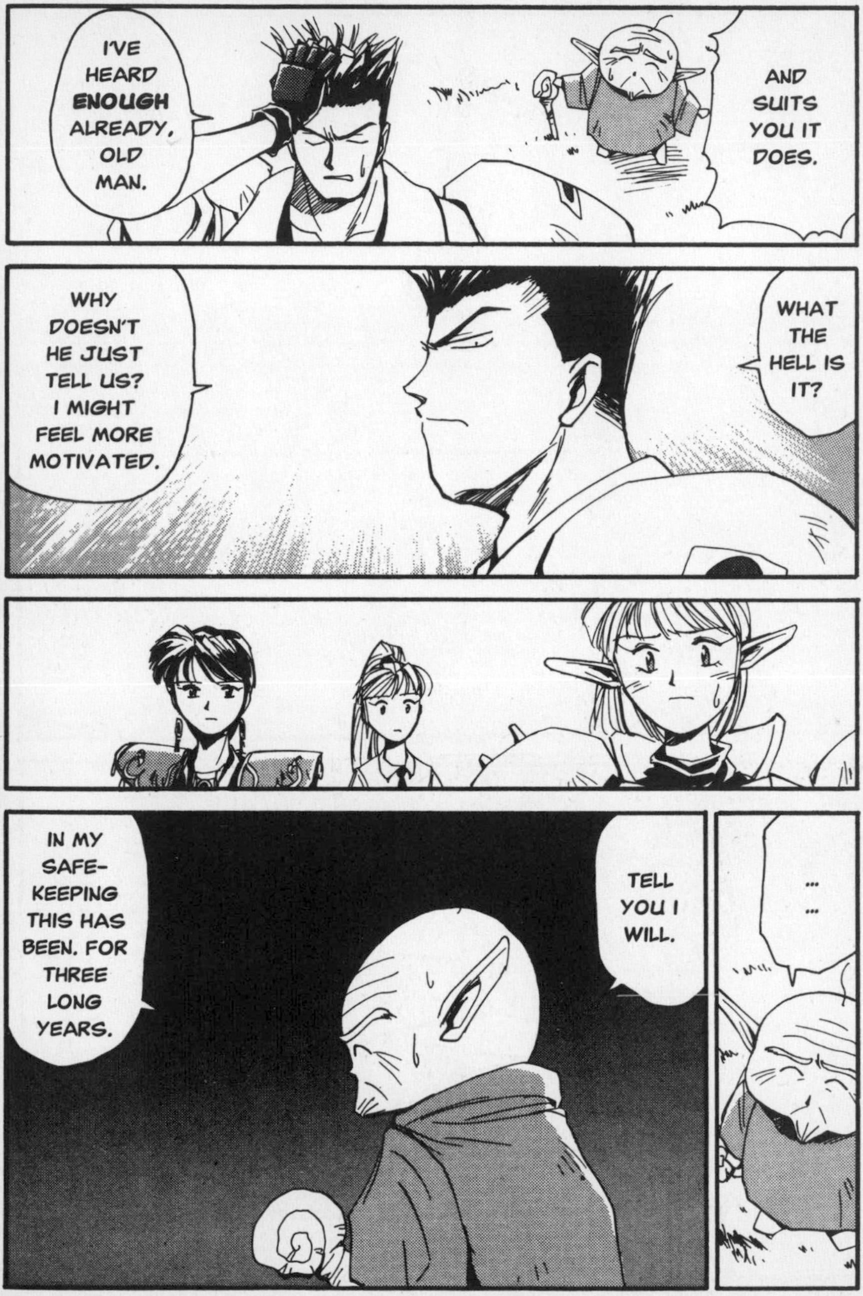
I'VE HEARD ENOUGH ALREADY, OLD MAN.
AND SUITS YOU IT DOES.
WHY DOESN'T HE JUST TELL US? I MIGHT FEEL MORE MOTIVATED.
WHAT THE HELL IS IT?
IN MY SAFE-KEEPING THIS HAS BEEN. FOR THREE LONG YEARS.
TELL YOU I WILL.
...
...

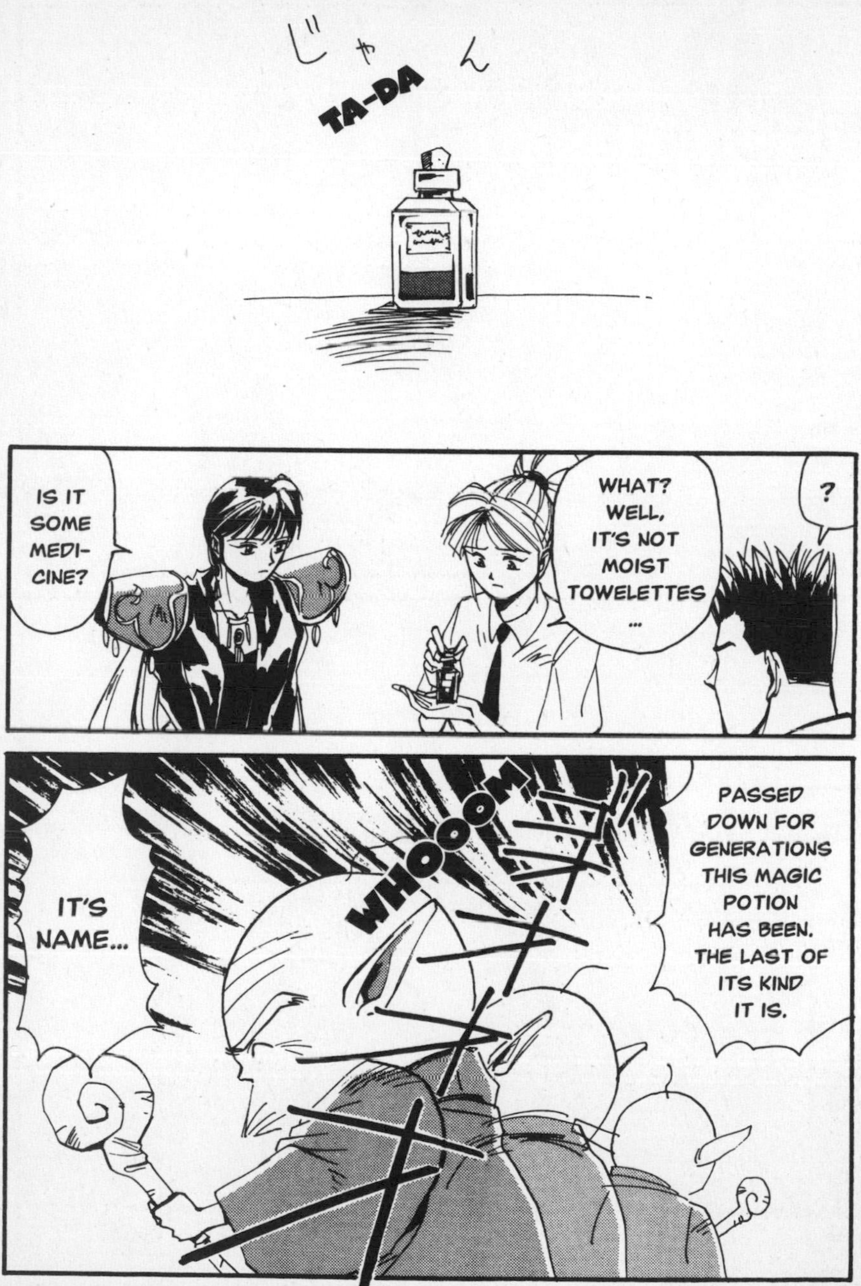
じゃん
TA-DA
?
WHAT? WELL, IT'S NOT MOIST TOWELETTES ...
IS IT SOME MEDI-CINE?
PASSED DOWN FOR GENERATIONS THIS MAGIC POTION HAS BEEN. THE LAST OF ITS KIND IT IS.
WHOOOM
IT'S NAME...

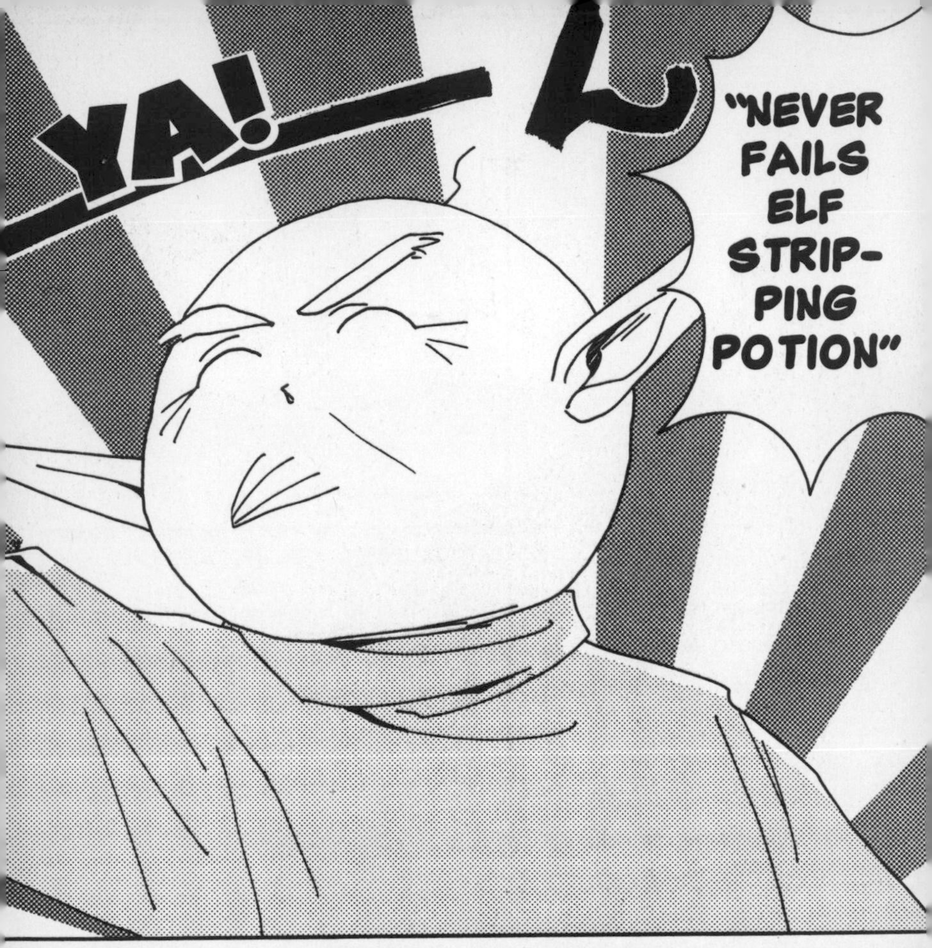
YA!
"NEVER FAILS ELF STRIP-PING POTION"

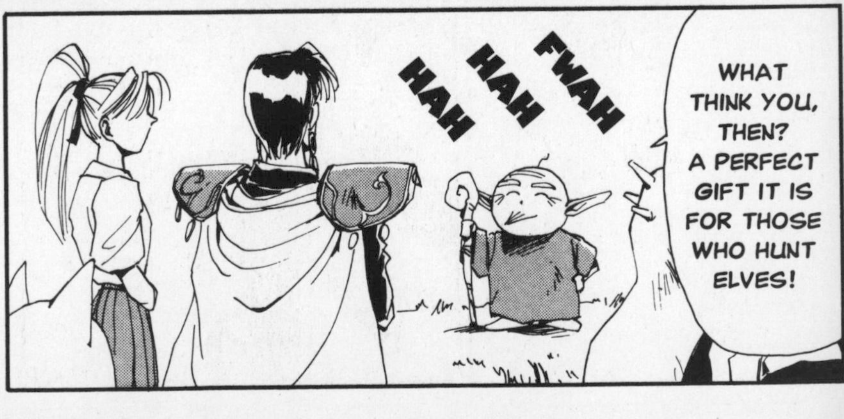
WHAT THINK YOU, THEN? A PERFECT GIFT IT IS FOR THOSE WHO HUNT ELVES!
FWAH HAH HAH

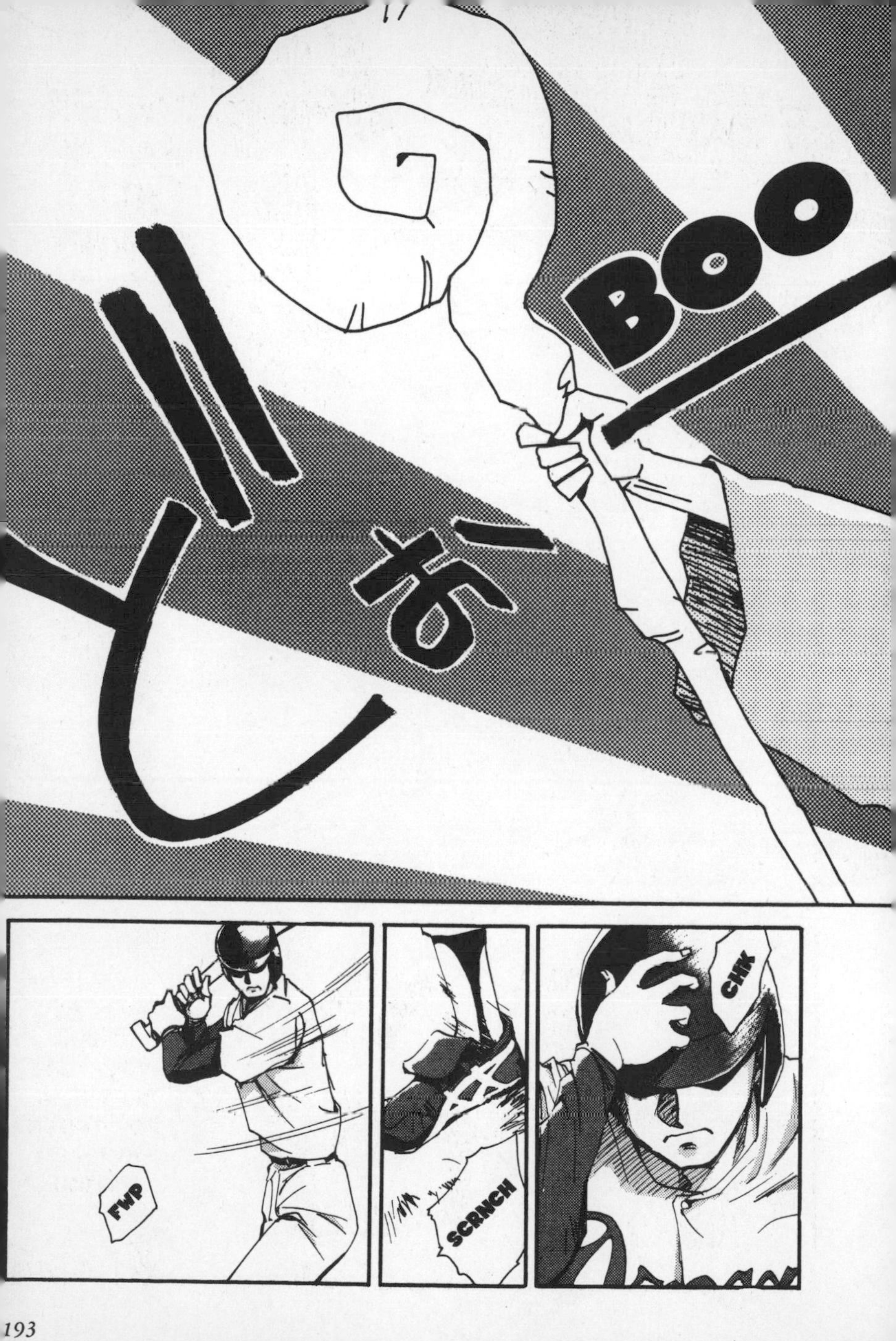
BOO
CHK
SCRNCH
FWP

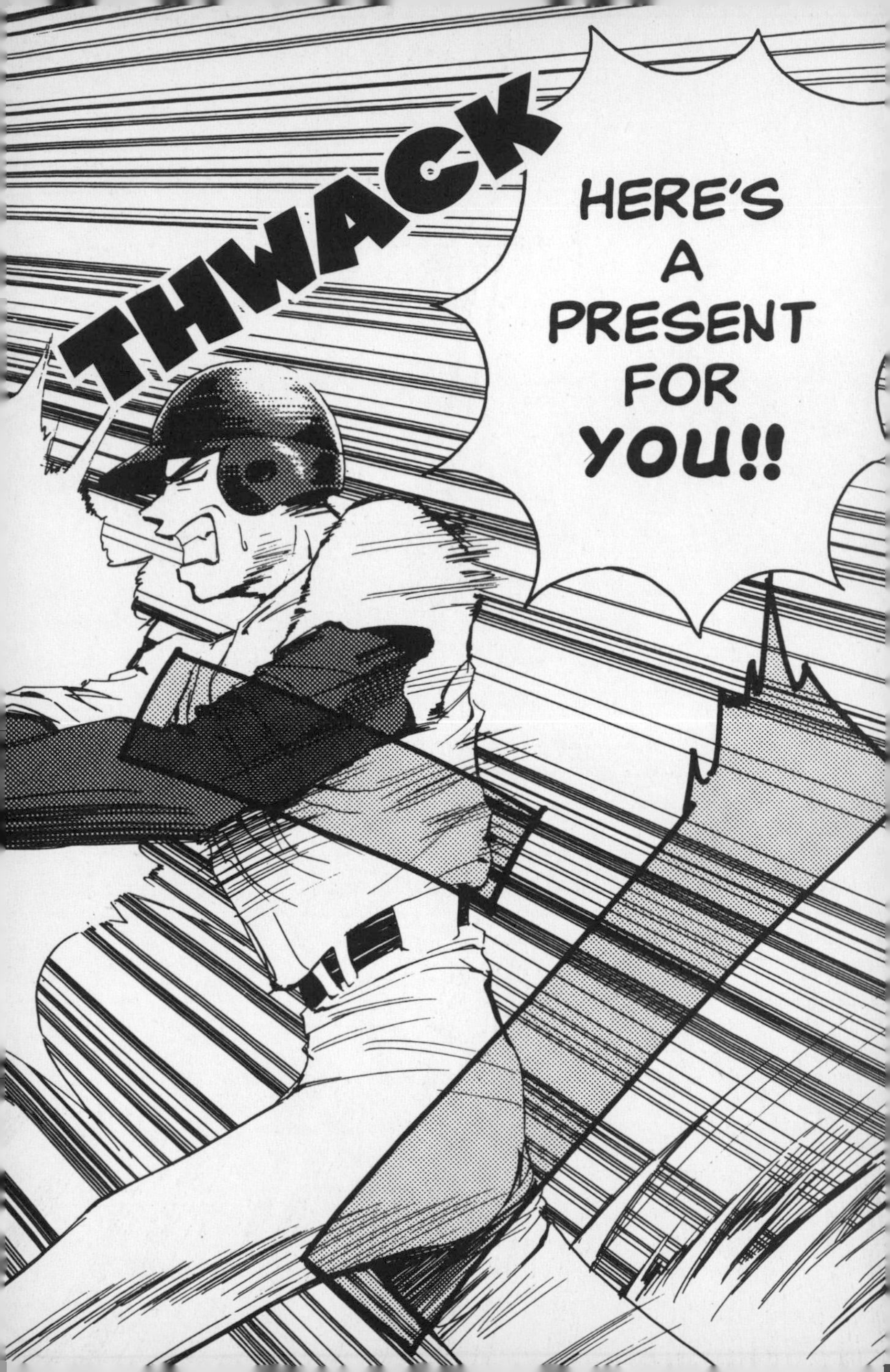
THWACK
HERE'S A PRESENT FOR YOU!!

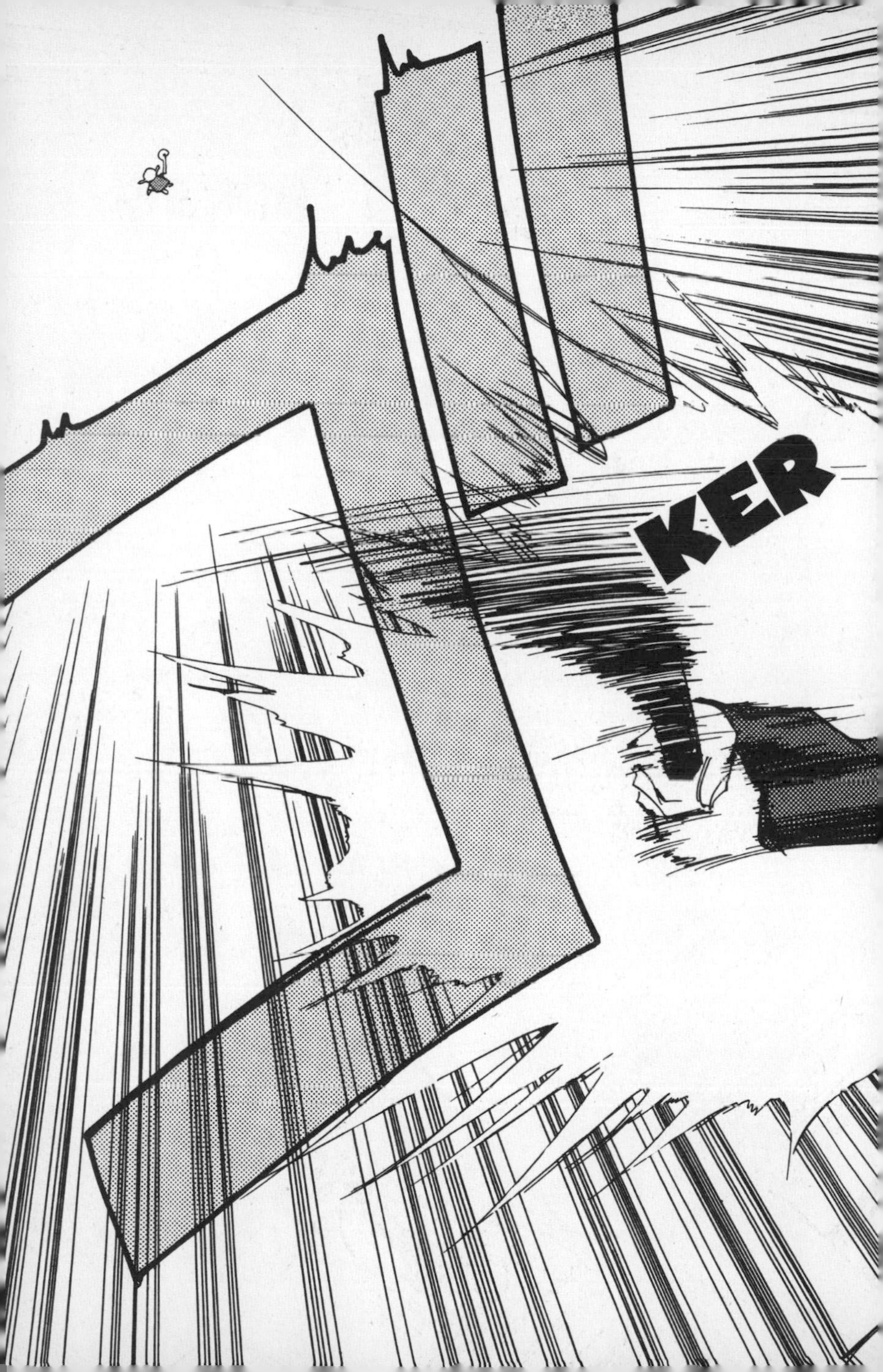
KER

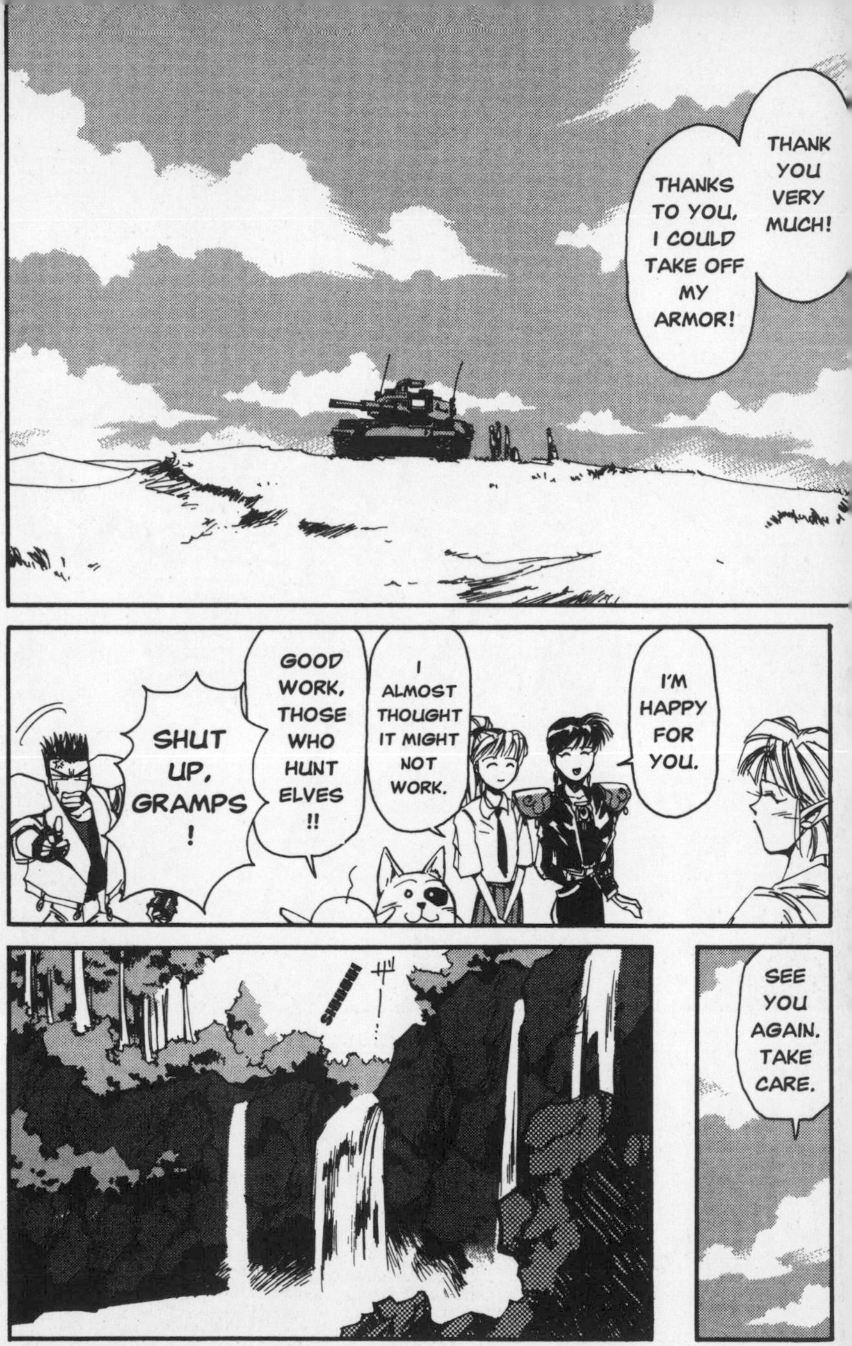
THANK YOU VERY MUCH!
THANKS TO YOU, I COULD TAKE OFF MY ARMOR!
I'M HAPPY FOR YOU.
I ALMOST THOUGHT IT MIGHT NOT WORK.
GOOD WORK, THOSE WHO HUNT ELVES !!
SHUT UP, GRAMPS !
SEE YOU AGAIN. TAKE CARE.
ザー…
SHHHHH

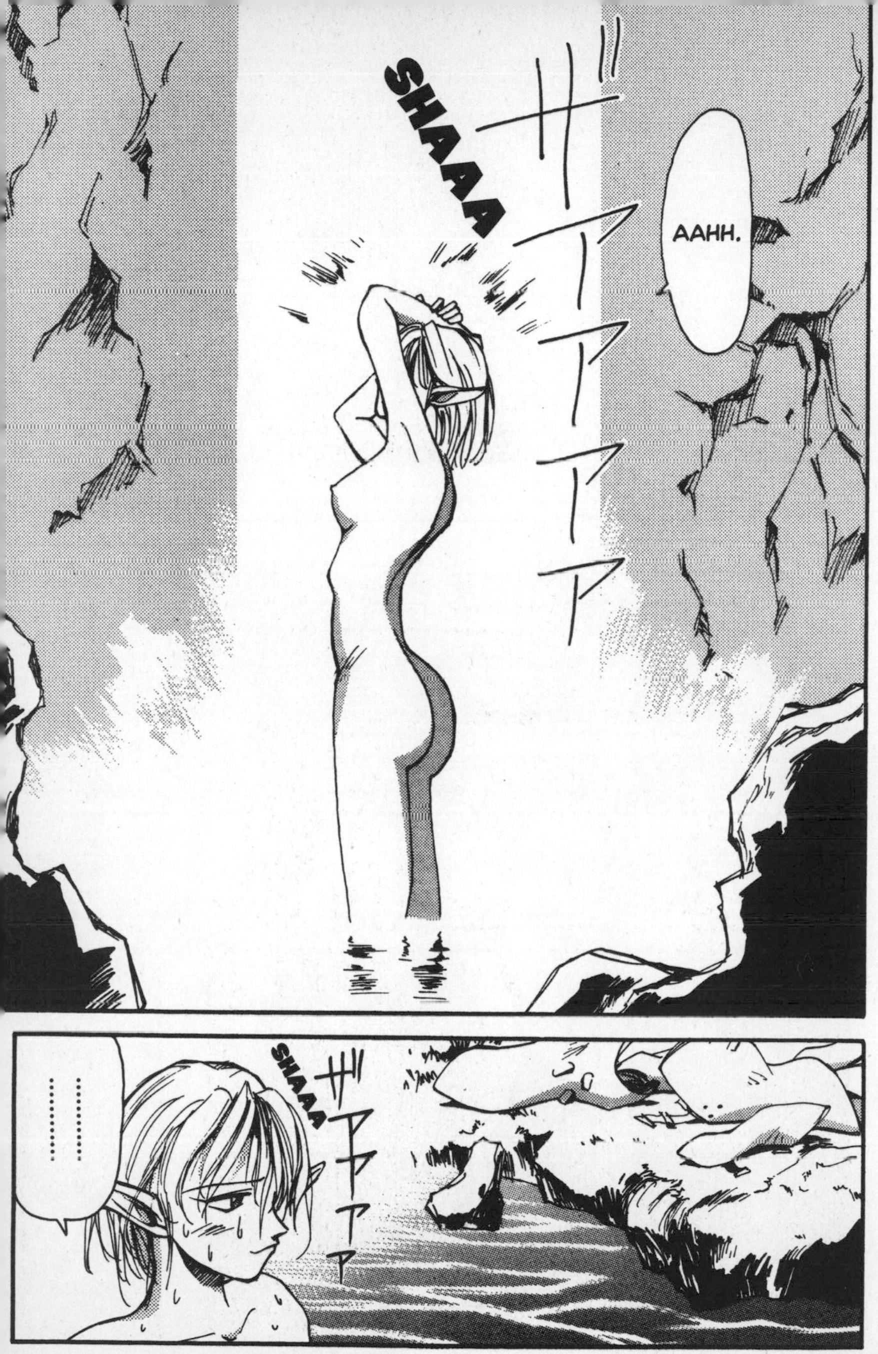
AAHH.
SHAAA
SHAAA
......

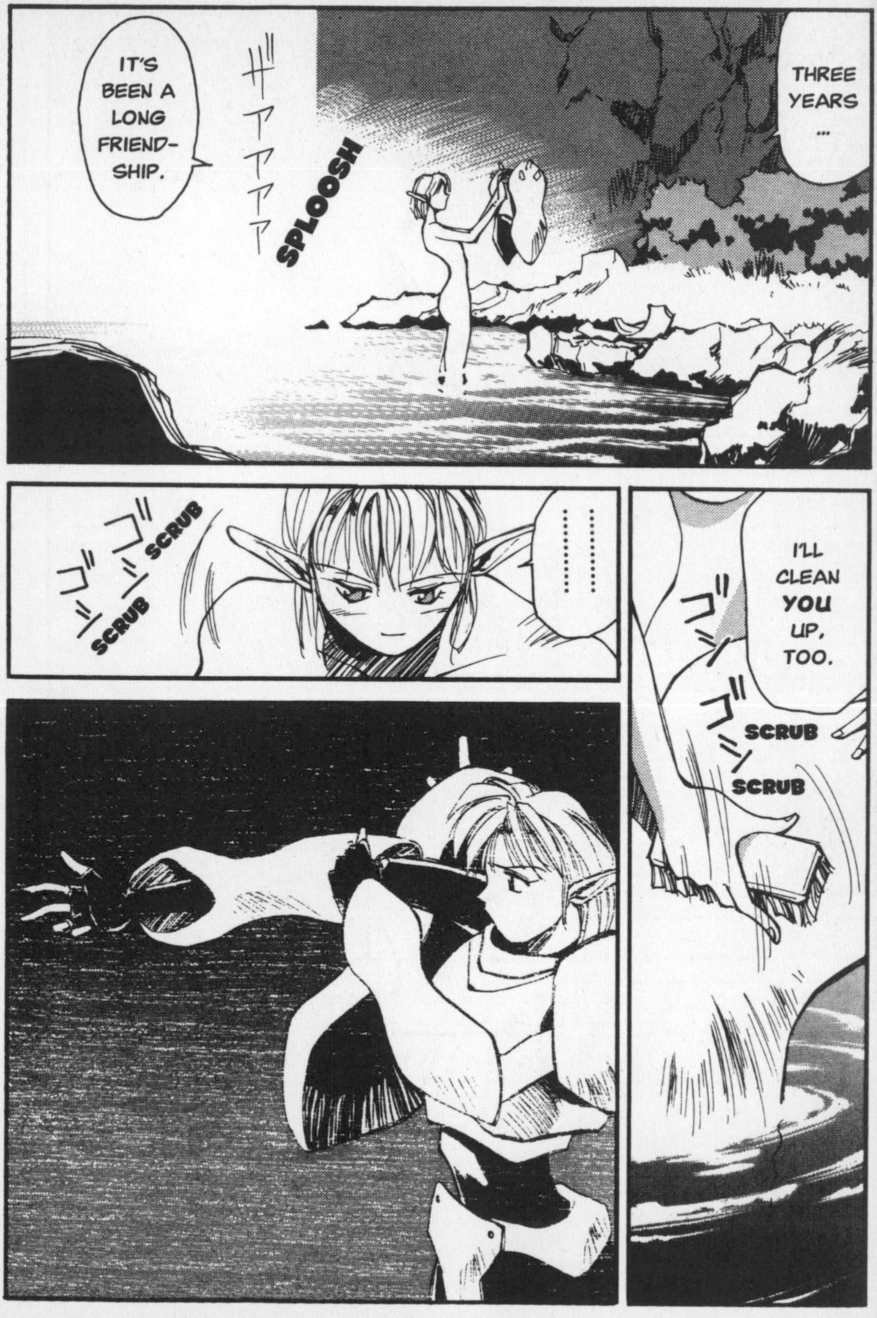
THREE YEARS ...
IT'S BEEN A LONG FRIEND-SHIP.
ザァァァァ
SPLOOSH
......
ゴシ ゴシ
SCRUB SCRUB
I'LL CLEAN **YOU** UP, TOO.
ゴシ ゴシ
SCRUB SCRUB

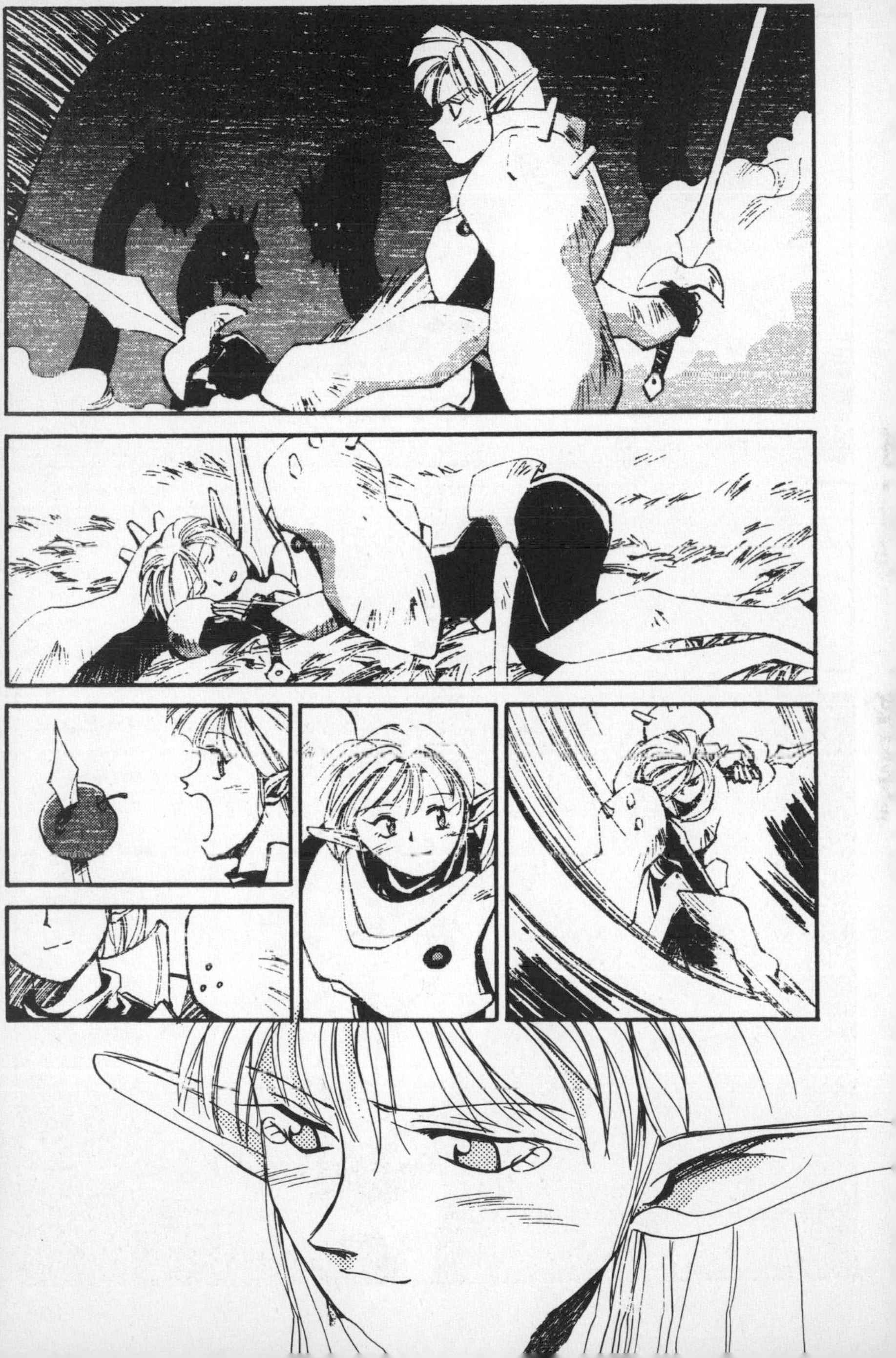

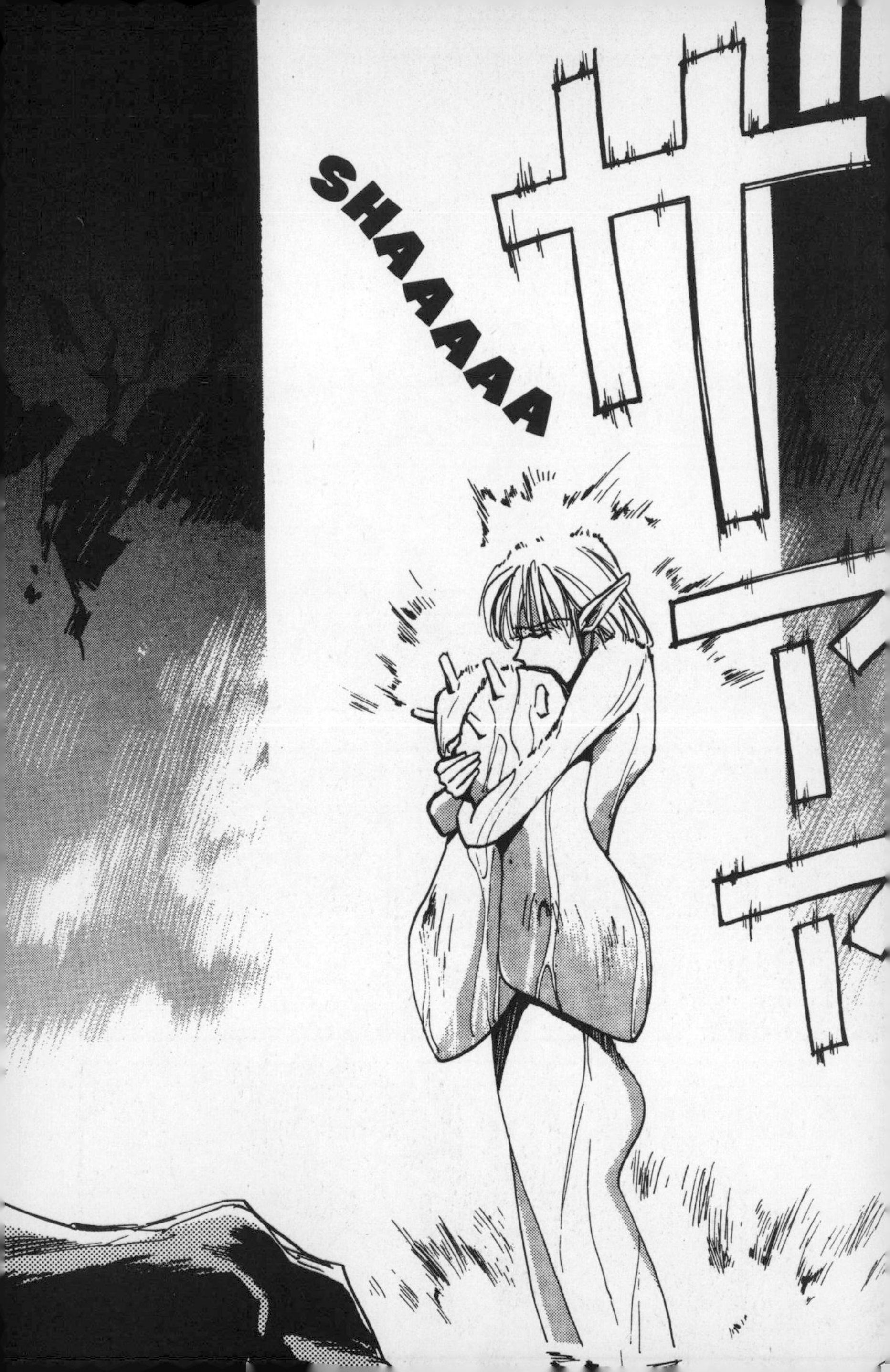
SHAAAAA

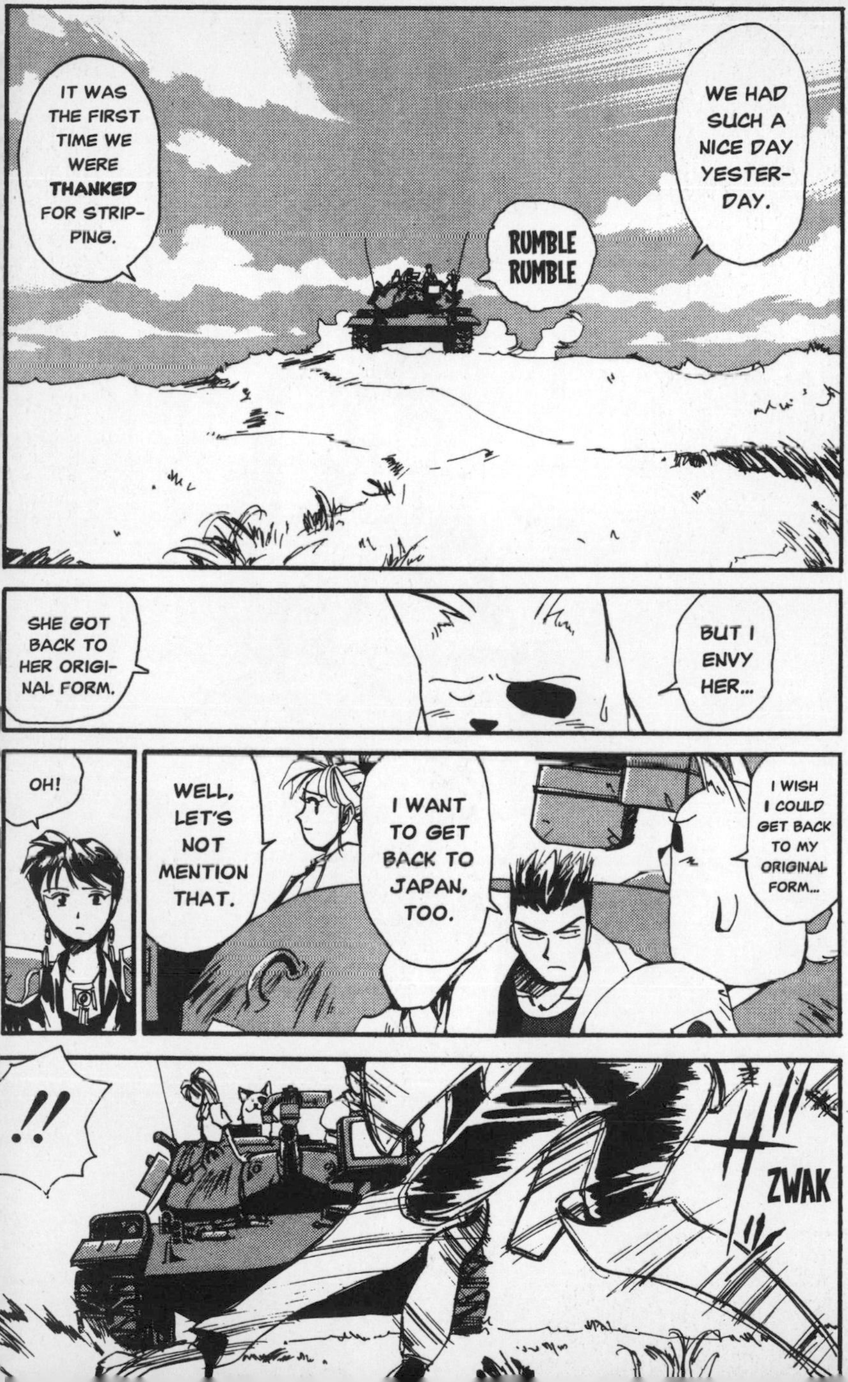
WE HAD SUCH A NICE DAY YESTER-DAY.
RUMBLE RUMBLE
IT WAS THE FIRST TIME WE WERE THANKED FOR STRIP-PING.
BUT I ENVY HER...
SHE GOT BACK TO HER ORIGI-NAL FORM.
I WISH I COULD GET BACK TO MY ORIGINAL FORM...
I WANT TO GET BACK TO JAPAN, TOO.
WELL, LET'S NOT MENTION THAT.
OH!
ZWAK
!!

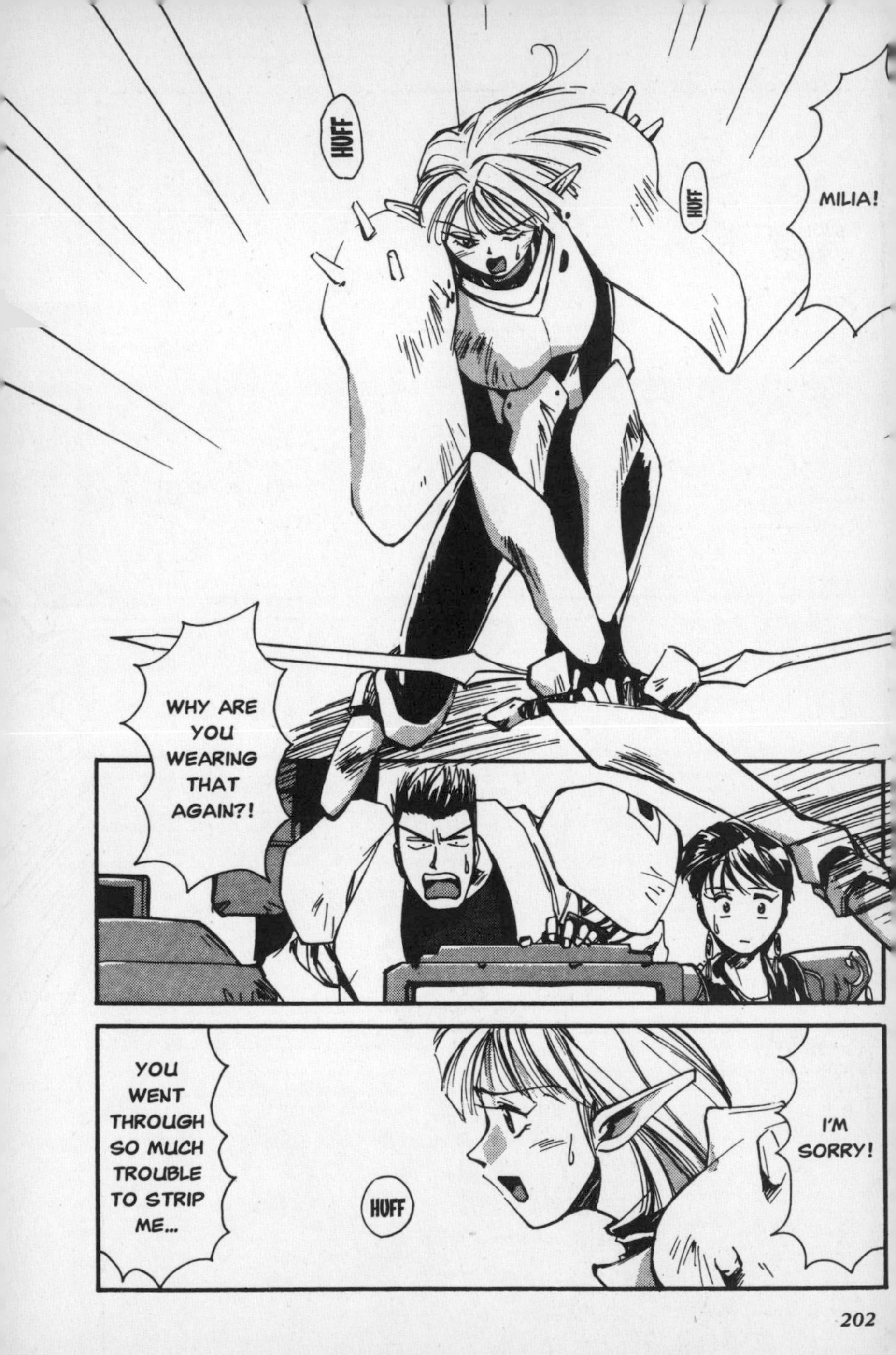
MILIA!
HUFF
HUFF
WHY ARE YOU WEARING THAT AGAIN?!
I'M SORRY!
HUFF
YOU WENT THROUGH SO MUCH TROUBLE TO STRIP ME...

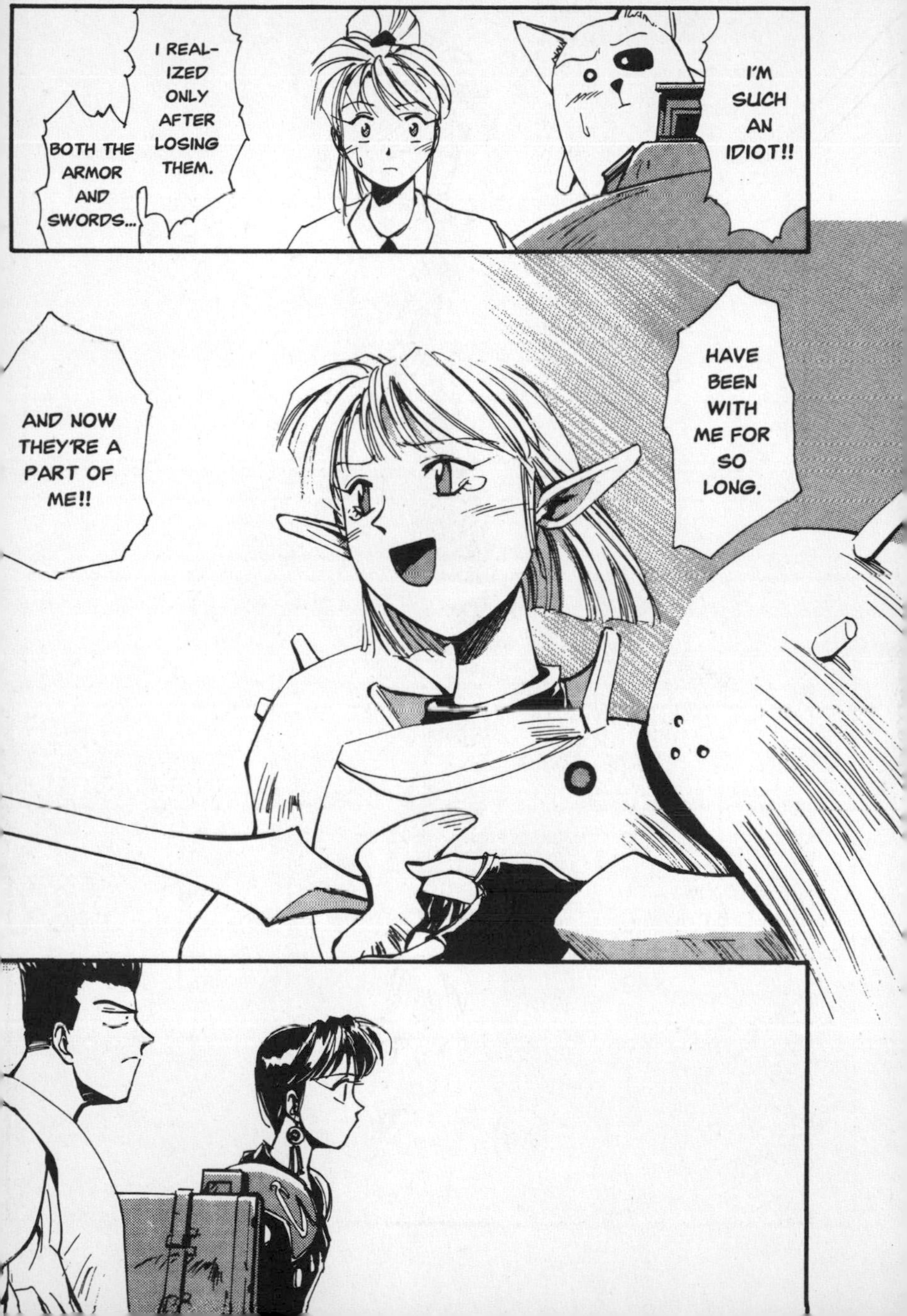
I'M SUCH AN IDIOT!!
I REAL-IZED ONLY AFTER LOSING THEM.
BOTH THE ARMOR AND SWORDS...
HAVE BEEN WITH ME FOR SO LONG.
AND NOW THEY'RE A PART OF ME!!

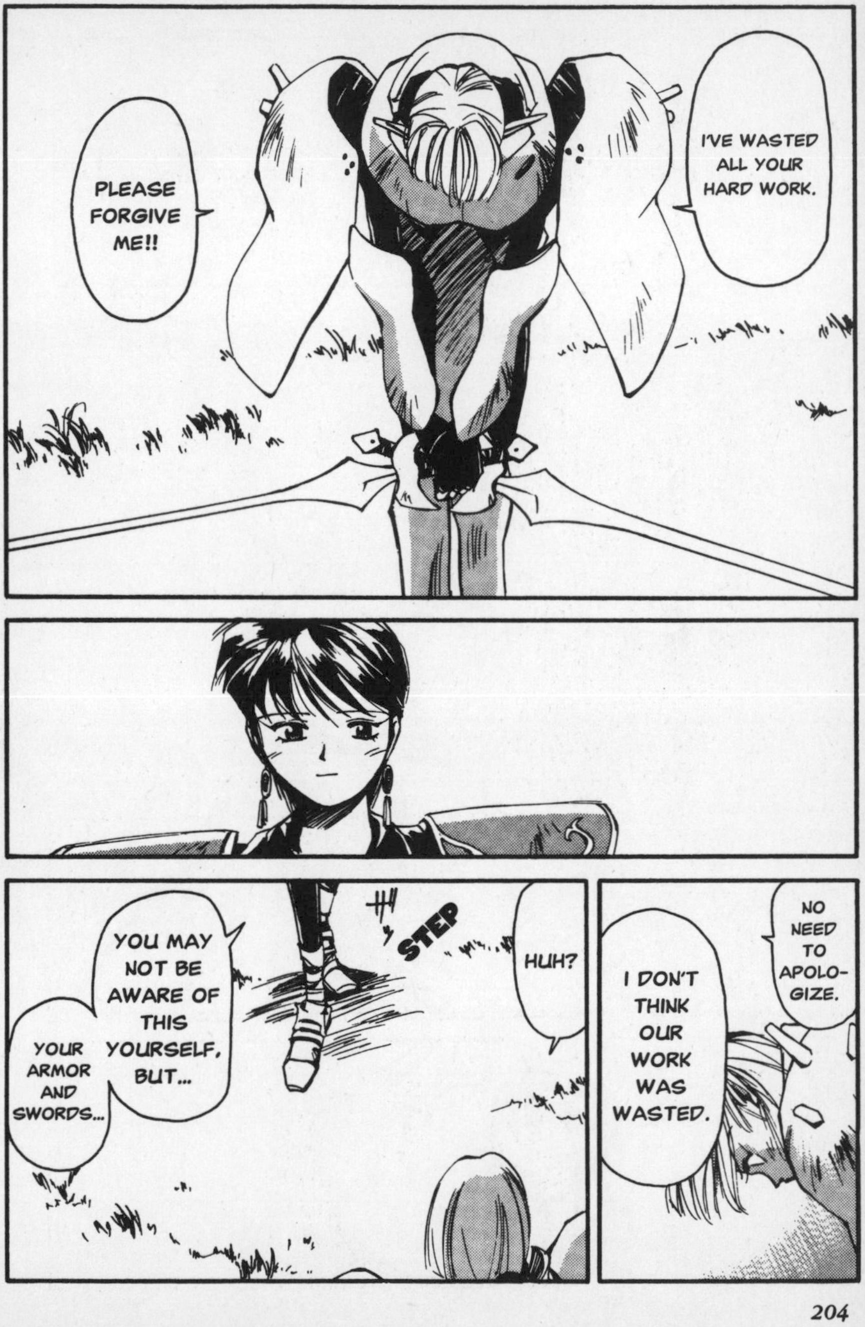

PLEASE FORGIVE ME!!
I'VE WASTED ALL YOUR HARD WORK.
NO NEED TO APOLOGIZE.
I DON'T THINK OUR WORK WAS WASTED.
HUH?
STEP
YOU MAY NOT BE AWARE OF THIS YOURSELF, BUT...
YOUR ARMOR AND SWORDS...

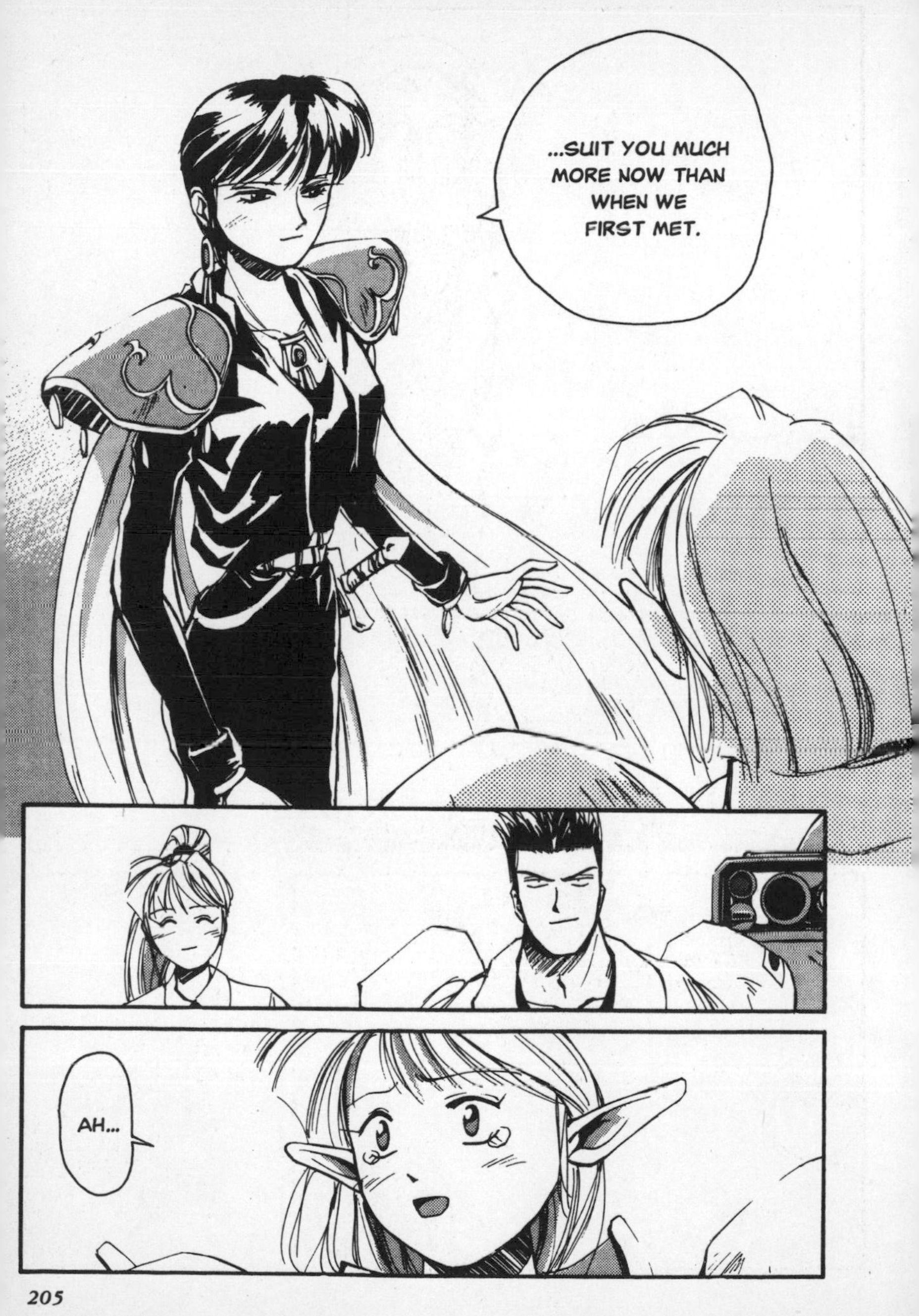
...SUIT YOU MUCH MORE NOW THAN WHEN WE FIRST MET.
AH...

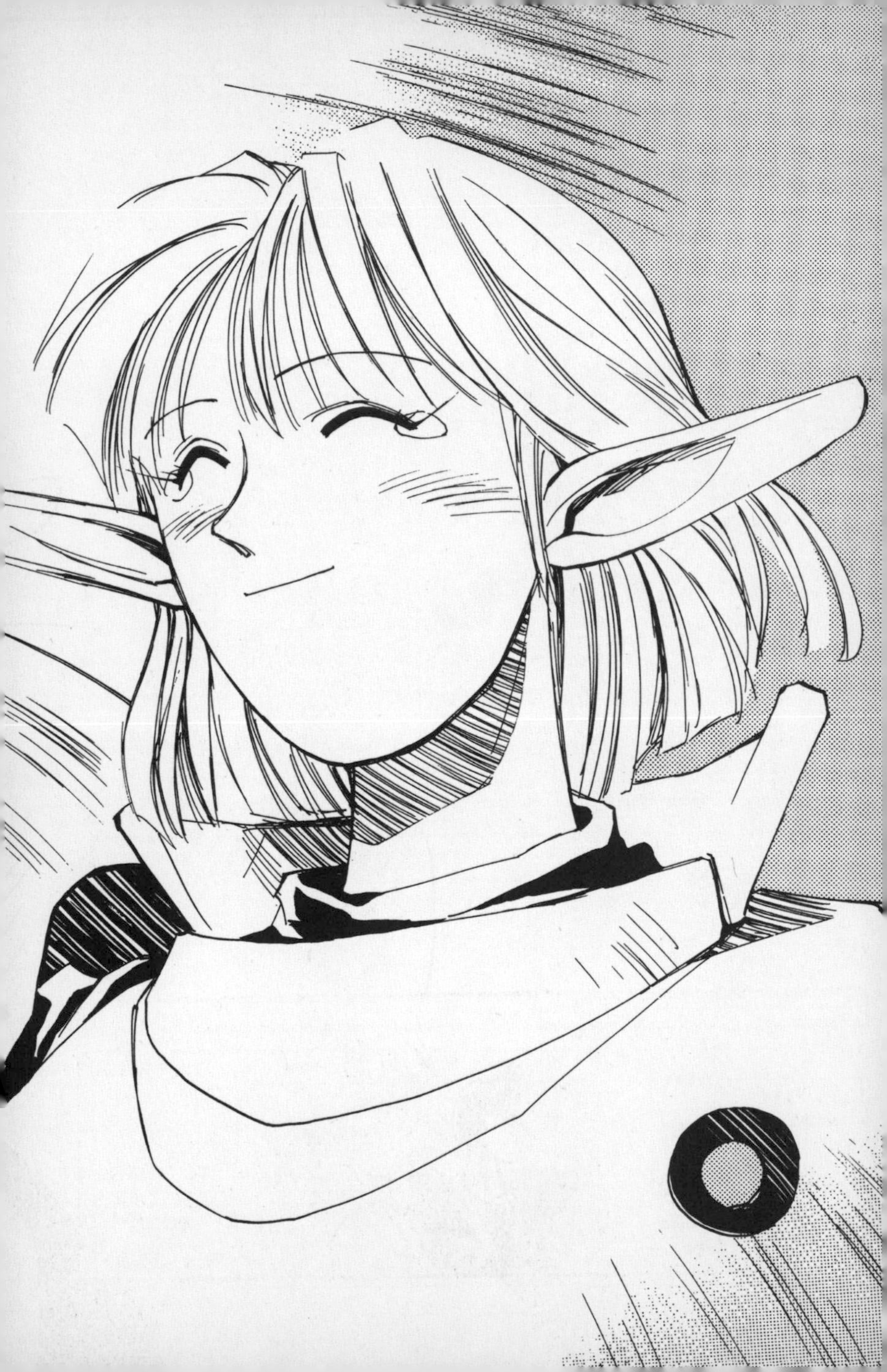

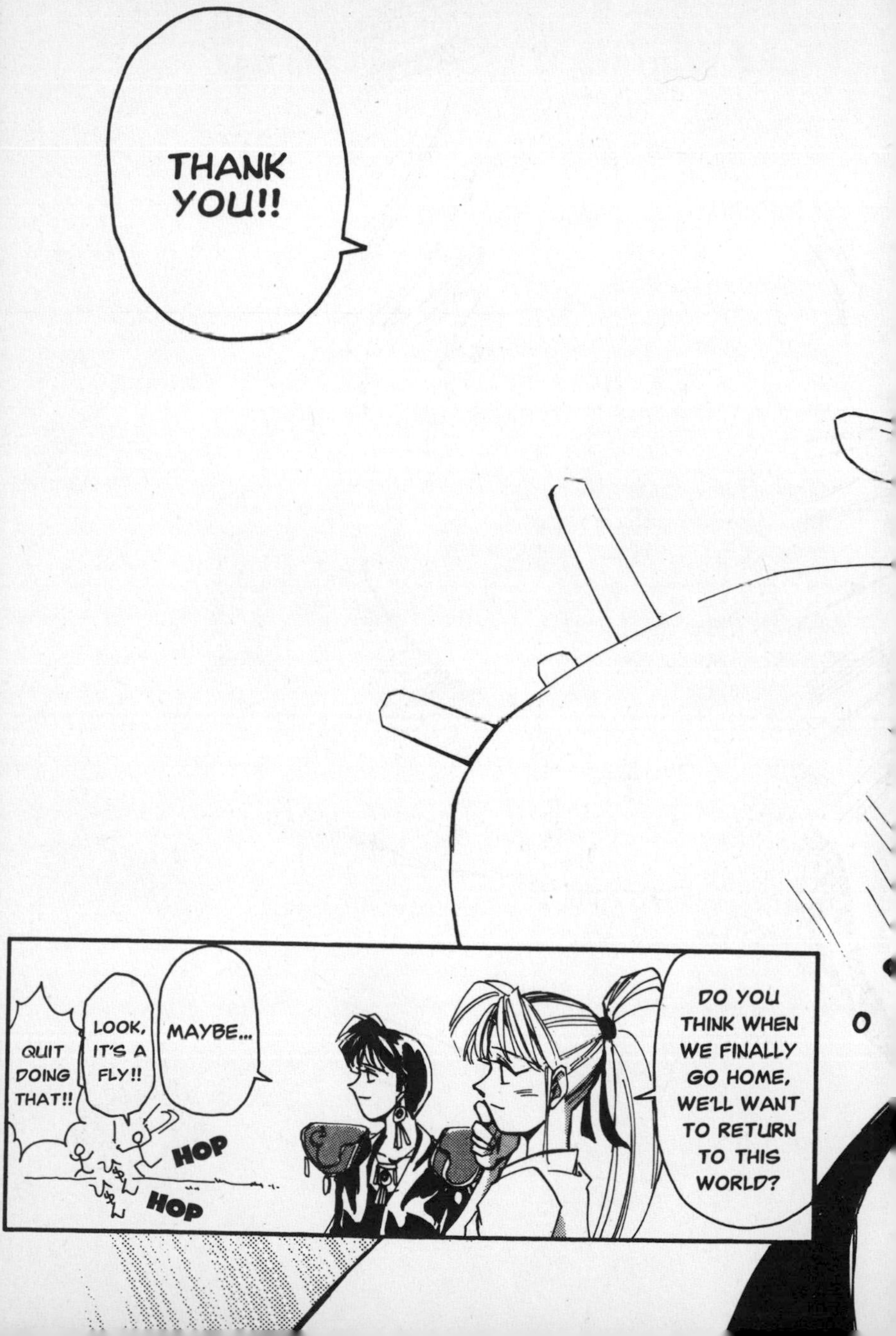
THANK YOU!!
DO YOU THINK WHEN WE FINALLY GO HOME, WE'LL WANT TO RETURN TO THIS WORLD?
MAYBE...
LOOK, IT'S A FLY!!
QUIT DOING THAT!!
HOP
HOP

Those Who Hunt Elves *Volume One*

© YU YAGAMI 1995
First published in 1995 by Media Works Inc., Tokyo, Japan.

English translation rights arranged with Media Works Inc.

Translator **EIKO MCGREGOR**
ADV Manga Translation Staff **JAVIER LOPEZ, KAY BERTRAND, AMY FORSYTH, BRENDAN FRAYNE**
Print Production/Art Studio Manager **LISA PUCKETT**
Graphic Artists **JORGE ALVARADO, KRISTINA MILESKI, RYAN MASON, SHANNON RASBERRY**
International Coordinators **TORU IWAKAMI, ATSUSHI KANBAYASHI**

Publishing Editor **SUSAN ITIN**
Editorial Assistant **MARGARET SCHAROLD**
President, C.E.O. & Publisher **JOHN LEDFORD**

Email: editor@adv-manga.com
www.adv-manga.com
www.advfilms.com

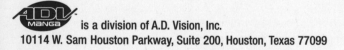 is a division of A.D. Vision, Inc.
10114 W. Sam Houston Parkway, Suite 200, Houston, Texas 77099

English text ©2003 by A.D. Vision, Inc. under exclusive license.
ADV MANGA is a trademark of A.D. Vision, Inc.

ISBN: 1-4139-0014-3

First printing, December 2003
10 9 8 7 6 5 4 3 2 1
Printed in Canada

LETTER FROM THE ADV MANGA TRANSLATION STAFF

Dear Reader,

On behalf of the ADV Manga translation team, thank you for purchasing an ADV book. We are enthusiastic and committed to our work, and strive to carry our enthusiasm over into the book you hold in your hands.

Our goal is to retain the true spirit of the original Japanese book. While great care has been taken to render a true and accurate translation, some cultural or readability issues may require a line to be adapted for greater accessibility to our readers. At times, manga titles that include culturally-specific concepts will feature a "Translator's Notes" section, which explains noteworthy references to the original text.

We hope our commitment to a faithful translation is evident in every ADV book you purchase.

Sincerely,

Javier Lopez,
Lead Translator

Eiko McGregor

Kay Bertrand

Brendan Frayne

Amy Forsyth

The Mission
doesn't end
with the Anime!

AT BOOKSTORES EVERYWHERE!

The acclaimed FULL METAL PANIC! manga
is available NOW from ADV Manga!

KYOYA'S NOT DONE YET... NOT BY A LONG SHOT!

THE SWORD ASHURA SLASHES THROUGH
TWO OTHER EXCITING SERIES FROM ADV MANGA!

[A PALACE APPEARS IN THE SKY OVER TOKYO, AND KYOYA'S INVITED ABOARD—FOR SINISTER REASONS!]

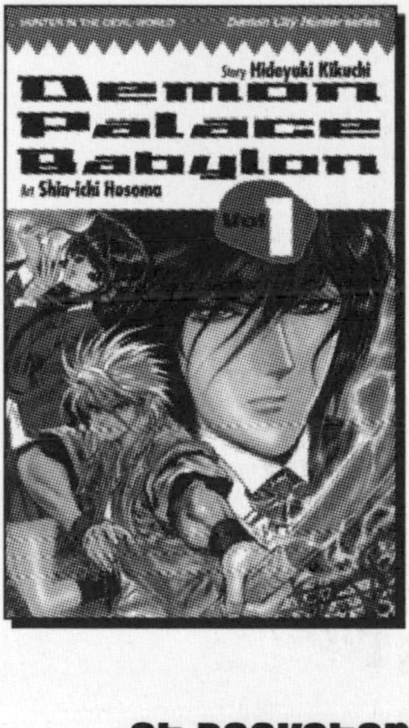
Story Hideyuki Kikuchi
Demon Palace Babylon
Art Shin-ichi Hosoma
vol 1

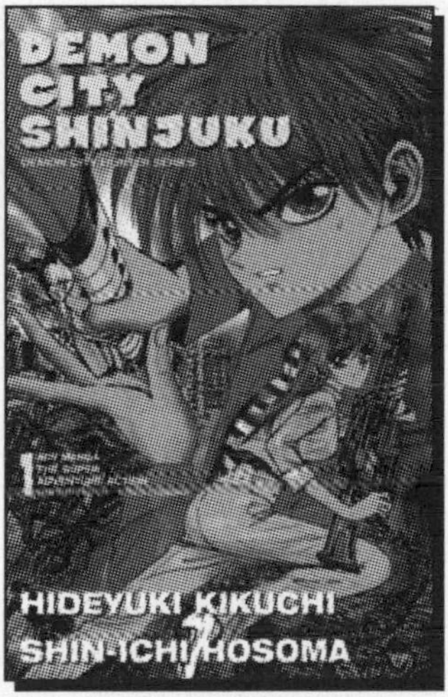
DEMON CITY SHINJUKU
HIDEYUKI KIKUCHI
SHIN-ICHI HOSOMA

[THE PRESIDENT OF EARTH'S RULING FEDERATION IS DYING FROM A DEMONIC CURSE, AND ONLY KYOYA CAN SAVE HIM!]

AT BOOKSTORES EVERYWHERE, EXCLUSIVELY FROM ADV MANGA!

ADV Manga

www.adv-manga.com

DEMAND YOUR ANIME
ANIME NETWORK NOW AVAILABLE IN SELECT CITIES
LOG ON TO WWW.THEANIMENETWORK.COM
AND DEMAND THE NATION'S ONLY 24 HOUR ANIME CHANNEL.
[THEN WATCH FOR NEON GENESIS EVANGELION!]
ANIME NETWORK
01

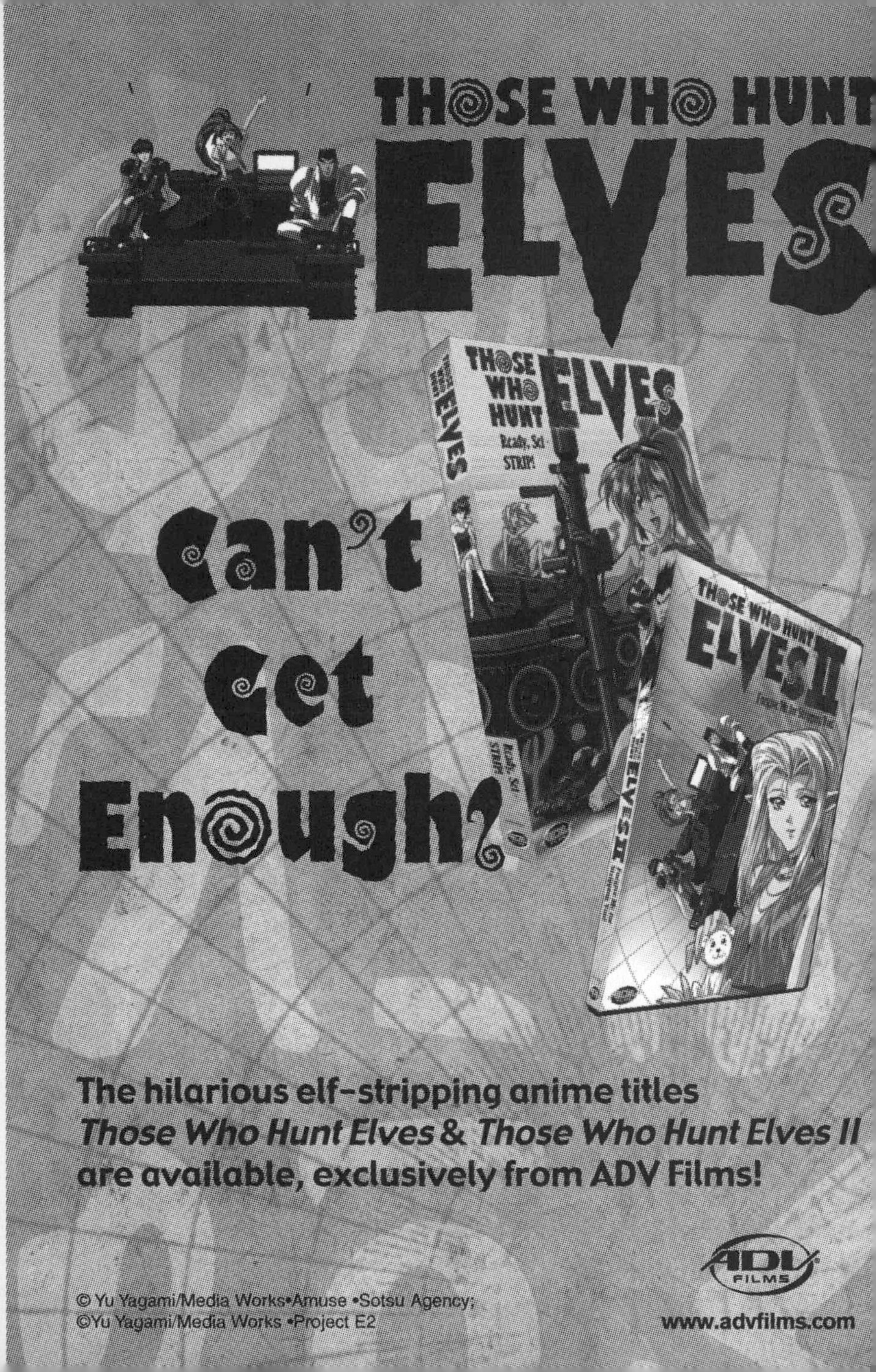
THOSE WHO HUNT ELVES
THOSE WHO HUNT ELVES Ready, Set STRIP!
THOSE WHO HUNT ELVES II
Can't Get Enough?
The hilarious elf-stripping anime titles
Those Who Hunt Elves & *Those Who Hunt Elves II*
are available, exclusively from ADV Films!
ADV FILMS
© Yu Yagami/Media Works•Amuse •Sotsu Agency;
©Yu Yagami/Media Works •Project E2
www.advfilms.com

4. Would you subscribe to digital cable if you could get a 24 hour/7 day a week anime channel (like the Anime Network)?
- ☐ Yes
- ☐ No

5. Would you like to see the Anime Network in your area?
- ☐ Yes
- ☐ No

6. Would you pay $6.99/month for the Anime Network?
- ☐ Yes
- ☐ No

7. What genre of manga and anime would you like to see from ADV?
(*Check all that apply*)
- ☐ adventure
- ☐ romance
- ☐ detective
- ☐ fighting
- ☐ horror
- ☐ sci-fi/fantasy
- ☐ sports

8. How many manga titles have you purchased in the last year?
- ☐ none
- ☐ 1-4
- ☐ 5-10
- ☐ 11+

9. Where do you make your manga purchases? (*Check all that apply*)
- ☐ comic store
- ☐ bookstore
- ☐ newsstand
- ☐ online
- ☐ other: _____
- ☐ department store
- ☐ grocery store
- ☐ video store
- ☐ video game store

10. What's your favorite anime-related website?
- ☐ advfilms.com
- ☐ anipike.com
- ☐ rightstuf.com
- ☐ animenewsservice.com
- ☐ animenewsnetwork.com
- ☐ animeondvd.com
- ☐ animenation.com
- ☐ animeonline.net
- ☐ planetanime.com
- ☐ other: _____

All information provided will be used for internal purposes only. We promise not to sell or otherwise divulge your information.

ANIME SURVEY

PLEASE MAIL THE COMPLETED FORM TO: EDITOR – ADV MANGA
℅ A.D. Vision, Inc. 10114 W. Sam Houston Pkwy., Suite 200 Houston, TX 77099

Name:

Address:

City: State: Zip:

E-Mail:

Male ☐   Female ☐   Age:

Cable Provider:

☐ **CHECK HERE IF YOU WOULD LIKE TO RECEIVE OTHER INFORMATION OR FUTURE OFFERS FROM ADV.**

1. Annual Household Income (*Check only one*)
- ☐ Under $25,000
- ☐ $25,000 to $50,000
- ☐ $50,000 to $75,000
- ☐ Over $75,000

2. How do you hear about new Anime releases? (*Check all that apply*)
- ☐ Browsing in Store
- ☐ Internet Reviews
- ☐ Anime News Websites
- ☐ Direct Email Campaigns
- ☐ Magazine Ad
- ☐ Online Advertising
- ☐ Conventions
- ☐ TV Advertising
- ☐ Online forums (message boards and chat rooms)
- ☐ Carrier pigeon
- ☐ Other:_____

3. Which magazines do you read? (*Check all that apply*)
- ☐ Wizard
- ☐ SPIN
- ☐ Animerica
- ☐ Rolling Stone
- ☐ Maxim
- ☐ DC Comics
- ☐ URB
- ☐ Polygon
- ☐ Original Play Station Magazine
- ☐ Entertainment Weekly
- ☐ YRB
- ☐ EGM
- ☐ Newtype USA
- ☐ SciFi
- ☐ Starlog
- ☐ Wired
- ☐ Vice
- ☐ BPM
- ☐ I hate reading
- ☐ Other:

But Wait! There's More!

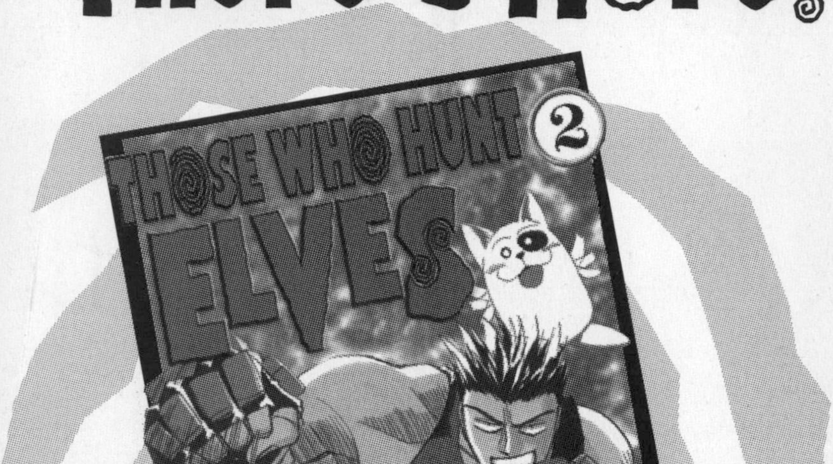
THOSE WHO HUNT ELVES
2
Yu Yagami

More elf stripping adventures coming soon, exclusively from ADV Manga!

ADV MANGA

www.adv-manga.com